Dear Rosalind
Happy Camping. *Malcolm*
x

Camping &
Caravanning

Great Britain & Ireland 1997

GW00418159

RAC

Published by RAC Publishing, RAC House,
Bartlett Street, South Croydon, CR2 6XW

© RAC Motoring Services Limited 1996

A CIP catalogue record for this book is available from
the British Library.

ISBN 0-86211-361-X

Produced for RAC Publishing by:
West One Publishing Ltd, Portland House,
4 Great Portland Street, London, W1N 5AA
Tel: 0171-580 6886

Design: Cooling Brown, London

Origination & reprographics:
Facsimile Graphics, Coggeshall, Essex

Cartography: RAC Publishing

Printed and bound in Spain by Grafo, S.A. Bilbao

Advertising Managers: West One Publishing

Contents

Directory of Sites

Chipping Norton Club Site

A WELCOME SITE FOR NON-MEMBERS TOO.

If you think Camping and Caravanning Club sites are among the most inviting in Britain, you're right. But if you think only Club members can enjoy them, then you're in for a pleasant surprise.

The vast majority of our 84 sites are open to non-members, which means everyone can take advantage of some of the best camping spots in Britain.

You'll find our Club sites on the coast, in the mountains, near famous cities and even on a Royal estate. Each one is an ideal place to relax or use as a base for exploring and sightseeing.

Our sites are each run to the same high standard by friendly wardens who can provide a

wealth of local information. Site fees are great value - in the low season all children accompanied by an adult camp free, and that's just one of our special family deals offered throughout the year.

So come and enjoy some of the best sites in Britain. You're guaranteed a friendly welcome all over the country with the Camping and Caravanning Club.

Call our Sites Department or complete the coupon below for our free Mini Sites Guide.

TELEPHONE
01203 856 798

Please quote Ref: 8421

The Camping and Caravanning Club

The friendly Club

Please send me a free Mini Sites Guide listing all Club sites open to non-members.

Name .... Address ....

....

Postcode .... Telephone ....

Post to: The Camping and Caravanning Club, Sites Department, **FREEPOST 8421**, Coventry CV4 8BR.

How to use the guide

For easy reference, the guide is arranged in alphabetical order by town. Explanations of all the symbols used in the directory are provided on the inside front flap of the cover. Alongside the opening dates are shown symbols to indicate if the site accepts touring tents, caravans or motorhomes.

Size

The total area of the site is given in acres; not all this area may be used for touring pitches. We give the number of pitches for touring visitors in caravans, motor caravans and tents, and how many of these pitches are level, and how many have electric hook-ups. We also give the number of static caravans on the site. Please note that these are not necessarily for hire. Where caravans and chalets are available for hire, it is shown under rental. We next list the number of hot showers, WCs and chemical waste disposal points (CWPs) on the site.

ᵫ Disabled facilities

Sites shown with this symbol have some facilities for the disabled, but it is essential to ask the site in advance whether they cater for your personal requirements.

↑ Dogs

Most sites accept dogs, but owners are expected to keep their pets under control (often on a lead while on the site) and to exercise them with consideration for other campers. Some sites will permit only one dog per camping unit, while others will not accommodate certain breeds – it is advisable to check when booking.

Prices

The prices are those quoted to us by the site management and show the price for two people plus car/caravan, car tent or motorhome.

It is always advisable to confirm charges before your arrival at a site.

A typical entry from the guide.

| COCKERMOUTH Cumbria | 10A1 |

Wyndham Hall Caravan Park
Old Keswick Road, Cockermouth CA13 9SF
☎ **01900-822571**
Open 1 March-15 November 🚐 🚍

A family site. Short walk into the market town (Cockermouth), and quarter of an hour drive to Keswick.

Size 12½ acres, 42 touring pitches, 24 with electric hookup, 42 level pitches, 105 static caravans, 9 ⚲, 21 WCs, 2 CWPs
⚑ ✗ 🍴 ⛽ 🅿 GR 🔍 ⚠ 🎣 🔌 Calor Gaz WS
➡ Off the A66 on the Old Keswick Road.

Credit cards

Where a site accepts credit cards, the cards accepted are shown after the price information.

Description and directions

The short description of the site gives an idea of what sort of site it is, what amenities it has and what the surroundings are like. The directions should enable you to locate the site from the nearest main road.

Caravan Storage

'WS' shows a site which has winter storage for caravans. Please contact the site direct (not the RAC) if you wish to store a caravan.

Caravan Security

The fact that over 5,000 caravans are stolen every year, with an estimated value of £12m, is not generally known. In fact, nobody knows exactly how much crime is committed because every caravan theft is a recent phenomenon and records are sketchy. But, we do know that very few caravans which are stolen are returned to their original owners. Some disappear into an illegal network of buyers and sellers; others cannot be traced when they are found by the police because all identifying marks have been removed. The police frequently have to return the suspect caravan to the thieves because they cannot prove it belongs to someone else.

The only way to beat the thieves and avoid becoming an insurance statistic is to introduce top security measures. But, be warned many thieves are well equipped with caravan door-keys, jemmies, grappling devices and low-loader trailers. To prevent crime, owners need to be one step ahead all the time.

Records show that thieves are most likely to strike:

1) At Easter, in June, July and August. Thefts of caravans drop in November, December, January and February - when demand for caravan holidays is lowest.

2) Directly from storage compounds (private drives are the second most popular target area).

3) By towing the caravans away on trailers.

4) By breaking or forcing caravan doors or windows

So the storage of a caravan must be high on the list of priorities if it is to be kept securely. It is often beneficial to pay for a higher security compound. However, as well as storage, it is vital to ensure proper security devices and locks.

Caravan Watch

Early in 1995 the Essex Police launched a crime prevention initiative called Caravan Watch with a view to raising public awareness of caravan theft in the Essex area. The aim of the scheme is to encourage owners to make their caravans as secure as possible, more identifiable and therefore less attractive to a thief.

The scheme has generated wide interest already and has spread to other areas of the country such as Lincolnshire, Yorkshire, Cheshire, and Sussex. For a small fee of £2, you can register all the details of your caravan with the scheme. The more details a caravanner can supply, the better the chance of recovering a stolen vehicle. The fee is for life - there is no annual fee and if you change your vehicle the Essex police will supply a new sticker for free.

A sticker displayed on the caravan identifies the make and registration number of the usual towing vehicle. With the sticker displayed, a thief either risks towing a caravan with an unmatched tow vehicle, or risks breaking into the caravan to try and remove the sticker.

For more information on Essex Police Caravan Watch Scheme, please contact Wickford police station tel: 01268 561312.

We are grateful to The Caravan Club for their help in compiling this feature.

Security devices and locks
Many caravan security devices are available on the market, from hitchlocks to steady locks, from alarms to wheelclamps. Prices vary from £30 to over £100, and it is difficult to decide which would be the most effective. Here is some advice to follow when choosing a security system.

FROM ONLY
£5.50
PER PITCH
PER NIGHT

LOOK OUT FOR THE NUMBER 1, LET THE NUMBER 1 LOOK AFTER YOU.

Your No. 1 choice for Tenting and Touring Holidays.
26 scenic locations for 1997, in England and Wales.
From only £5.50 per pitch per night, it's great value for money. Many special offers, including 7 nights for the price of 6 and special ferry prices to the Isle of Wight.
Now _more_ Main Service Pitches, _more_ Disabled and Family Suites and _more_ Electrical Hook-ups.
FREE family daytime activities with fun pools and the Tiger Club for 5-11 year olds. **FREE** sparkling evening entertainment.
Plus excellent touring facilities, including showers, shaver and hairdryer points, disposal points and washing-up sinks.

Call 0990 233 444 for your free 1997 Touring brochure, quoting TMA03. Or complete the coupon.

Please complete the coupon below and send to Haven Touring, FREEPOST Dept 1HH, Newcastle Upon Tyne X, NE85 2BR.

Mr/Mrs/Ms_____Initial_____

Surname_____

Address_____

_____

Postcode_____

Tel_____

SMILE, YOU'RE IN
Haven Touring

A company within The Rank Organisation Plc.   TMA03

Hitchlocks

These products should envelop the hitch-head and completely cover the securing bolts. Hitchlocks which leave the bolt exposed are virtually worthless - a thief will unbolt it and fit one he has bought with him. Providing you lock the car and caravan together, a good hitchlock should deter an opportunist thief and will offer a reasonable degree of protection on site, at roadside stops and service stations. However, when a caravan is in storage or at home, a hitchlock is not enough.

Wheelclamps

The wide variety of wheelclamps on the market gives plenty of choice. Look for one which appears robust and has a lock which cannot readily be attacked by hacksaw or drill. Any products with thin radiating arms, or exposed locks, are likely to prove vulnerable.

Other security measures include posts which are cemented into the ground so that the caravan can be secured to it by a hitchlock. High security door locks with cylindrical keys are more effective than the standard variety, but if the caravan door has a window in it, the thief will simply remove the window and operate the door handle from inside. As an added disincentive, it is advisable to replace the road wheels for long-term storage. These must be locked securely in position - otherwise the thief can bring his own wheels and swap them over.

Alarms

Another way of protecting your caravan is by investing in a good alarm system. There are several effective alarms on the market at the moment - here is a brief summary of some of them.

Passive Infra Red Detector (PIR)

PIRs are sensitive to moving heat sources. They find subjects moving across their field of view easier to detect than those moving directly towards them, so you have to be careful when positioning a PIR. Because most surfaces radiate heat to a certain extent, it is possible that other stimuli (even a spider or a moth) will trigger off a false alarm.

More and more sophisticated alarms are coming onto the market. Soon they will be able to differentiate between false and genuine signals.

Pressure Mat
These pressure-sensitive mats are concealed under the carpet and should give an instant reaction from the siren when stepped on. Do not put the mat by the door where a thief may expect it, and so step over it. The siren should be instant as even a short delay could enable the thief to remove items of value from the caravan.

Contacts
Magnetic contacts are aligned so they sit next to each other on adjacent edges of a closed door, window or locker. As soon as the door is open, contact between them is broken and the siren is triggered.

Tilt sensors
A tilt sensor is inactive when level, but will give a signal if tipped forwards, backwards and/or from side to side. Most tilt sensors can be adjusted for sensitivity so they will ignore gentle wind rocking but will react to significant movement

Corner steady protection
This device can detect movement of a corner steady (as it is difficult to move a caravan without raising the steadies). The device is fitted inside the caravan on the floor above the steady, where it can detect high frequency vibration caused, for example, when metal contacts metal.

12N/12S Plug connection
This is a control unit capable of monitoring the alarm circuit of the caravan and the tow car. Any change in the voltage of this circuit (light of an open car door, brake lights or a moving car) will trigger the siren.

Power consumption
Be careful to check how much your chosen alarm system will drain the battery. Some place a higher drain than others.

Caravan checklist

Don't neglect the servicing of your caravan. An on-the-spot caravan check at the M5 service area in Exeter, reported in Practical Caravan, revealed more faults than the Devon and Cornwall Police expected. Out of 118 caravans inspected, only 33 were in a satisfactory condition. The message to all caravanners is to make thoroughly sure that their vans are in good repair and working order before setting out on a journey. The check list should cover:

● The tyres (32 tyres in the spot check were perished and two caravans had had blow-outs during the journey so far).

● The brakes (many of the caravans had neglected brakes).

● The lights (15 had defective lighting).

● The weight distribution when loading the caravan (37 vans had too much downward pressure exerted on the towbar - in some cases by more than 100 per cent above the factory recommendations - and most vans had at least 80 kg on the hitch).

● Also make sure the van has registration plates on the back.

● Make sure the jockey wheel braces are not worn.

The ideal alarm system will have:

● A sensor to detect interference with one or more corner steadies.

● PIR or pressure mat to detect intruders by activating a siren after a very short delay.

● Internal battery or anti-tamper circuit in case the thief has cut wires.

THE PERLE

First choice for family caravanning and great value for money!

This is the ideal family caravan, for long-haul annual holidays, club rallies or short week-end trips. A Perle caravan means those extra breaks are a reality. From its striking glacier-white exterior, to the spacious interior with its warm cherry-oak effect furniture, the Perle will turn heads and attract admiring glances wherever you go!

- Glacier-white bodywork with strong and attractive GRP panels to front and rear
- Centre-sited gas locker to store 2x7kg cylinders, vastly improves towing characteristics
- Convenient-to-use cassette toilet unit
- Fully-fitted shower room
- Exterior side-access storage locker
- Internal under-floor spare-wheel storage well (except on Argos)
- Single-key security locking system

Anti-theft action

1. Register your caravan's details with the Caravan Club's Theftcheck Scheme (tel: 01342 327433).

2. Immobilise your caravan at all times, even when stopping briefly.

3. Invest in a reliable alarm - the initial outlay is worth the security and peace of mind.

4. Remove all personal belongings and contents from the caravan whenever it is not in use. Leave curtains open, so potential thieves can see nothing of value inside.

5. Take a photograph of the caravan and keep it at home, along with any registration documents. Make a note of any identifying scratches, marks or bumps.

6. Mark the serial or chassis number in several places inside the caravan using an ultraviolet pen. Make a note of mark locations.

7. Ensure the chassis (VIN) number is etched on all windows and the caravan roof.

8. Don't choose a storage place on price alone - consider security.

In the event of a caravan theft, notify the police and insurance company. Give the police a full description, including chassis number and any identifying marks.

Theftcheck

Theftcheck is the largest computerised caravan register in the country and it is free to members of The Caravan Club. The individual chassis number of your caravan is logged into the Club's computer along with the owner's name and address. The Club recommends that members also etch their caravan windows with the caravan chassis number. A window etching kit is available from the Club at nominal cost.

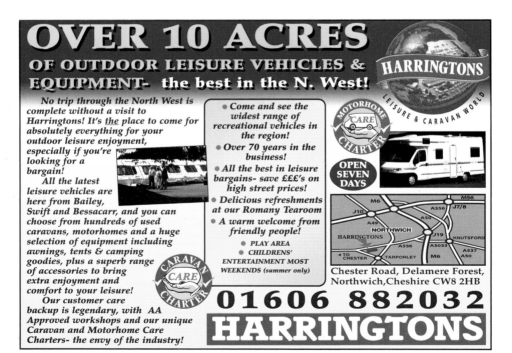

AMERICAN DREAM

Experience the

Where
quality is
our first
priority

Just a taste of what's available from the largest
American Motorhome display in the U.K.

★ No.1 in customer care & satisfaction. Full service workshops
with factory trained technicians.

★ Competitive finance rates.

★ Full main dealer warranty program

★ Westcroft offers 3 years/36,000 mile warranty on 1995
Chevrolet chassis.

★ Disabled conversions.

★ L.P.G. fill up station.

★ Friendly advice.

★ Always a good selection of new & pre-owned units in stock.

★ Overnight customer hook up parking facilities.

WESTCROFT
AMERICAN
MOTORHOMES

CANNOCK RD., WOLVERHAMPTON WV10 8QU
TEL: 01902 731324 FAX: 01902 724494

Caravans, trailers and the Law

This summary refers only to the more important motoring laws relating to trailers and caravans. It is believed to be correct at the time of going to press.

AVOIDANCE OF DANGER

A motor vehicle, every trailer drawn thereby and all parts and accessories of such vehicles and trailers shall at all times be in such condition that no danger is caused or likely to be caused to any person in or on the vehicle or trailer on a road. This includes passengers and/or load, and is endorsable with three Penalty Points.

LIGHTING

Number plate
Must be of similar dimensions to that of the towing vehicle and bearing the same mark and numbers. It must be illuminated at night.

Front lamps
If a trailer exceeds 1600mm in overall width or 2300 mm in overall length, and was manufactured after 1 October 1985, it must be fitted with two white front lamps.

Rear lamps and reflectors
Two red rear lamps and two red rear reflex reflectors must be fitted to a trailer. The reflectors must be of the triangular type, marked BS.AU 40L 111 or L11A, or bear an approved mark incorporating 111 or 111A.

Stop lamps
Two red stop lamps must be fitted to most trailers, but where the stop lamps at the rear of the towing vehicle can be seen by an observer standing centrally six metres behind the trailer, no stop lamps are required provided the trailer was manufactured before 1 October 1990.

Direction indicators
Direction indicators must be fitted to most trailers, but where the direction indicator on each side of the towing vehicle can be seen by an observer standing centrally six metres behind the trailer no direction indicators are required, provided the trailer was manufactured before 1 October 1990.

Rear fog lamps
At least one rear fog lamp must be fitted to a trailer manufactured after 1 April 1980 that exceeds 1300mm in overall width. A trailer that is being drawn by a vehicle that is not required to be fitted with a rear fog lamp is not itself required to be fitted with a rear fog lamp.

Side reflex reflectors
A trailer that exceeds five metres in overall length, excluding its drawbar, is required to be fitted with amber side reflex reflectors bearing an approval mark including the Roman numeral I.

Parking without lights
The provisions permitting certain types of motor vehicles to park without lights on roads subject to a speed limit of 30mph or less do not apply when a trailer is attached to the vehicle.

BRAKES

Unbraked trailers
Existing and new trailers do not require brakes if:
a) the sum of their maximum design axle weights does not exceed 750kg, and
b) their laden weight on the road does not exceed half the **towing vehicle's** kerbside weight.

Trailers that can be **towed by motorcycles do** not require brakes. **Unbraked trailers must** have at least one whe**el prevented from** turning by means of bl**ocks, chain, etc., when** disconnected from the **towing vehicle.**

BRAKED TRAILERS

All trailers required to have brakes must also be fitted with a parking brake.

Trailers first used before 1 April 1983 must comply with the Road Vehicles (Construction and Use) Regulations. These permit brakes to apply automatically if a trailer overruns, i.e. overrun (inertia) brakes. These brakes must be efficient but no specific performance is set.

Trailers first used after 1 April 1983 must comply with the latest EU Braking Directives of the Europe Braking Regulations (ECE). These also permit overrun brakes. However, in order to comply with international standards, it is usually necessary for the design to undergo a type approval test. The trailer's braking efficiency must be at least 45% and the parking brake capable of holding the laden trailer on a 16% gradient.

A modern braked trailer must be fitted with an emergency device which will automatically apply the trailer's brakes if it becomes uncoupled from the towing vehicle; except that this does not apply to a single axle trailer up to 1,500kg maximum gross axle weight, provided that it is fitted with a chain which will prevent the coupling head from touching the road if the trailer becomes detached.

MOTORWAY LANES

No motor vehicle drawing a trailer shall be driven in the right-hand lane of a motorway with three or more lanes which are open for use, except where this lane has to be used to pass a vehicle carrying or drawing a load of exceptional width.

PASSENGERS

No passenger may be carried in a moving caravan with less than four wheels or two close-coupled wheels on each side.

INSURANCE

A driver intending to use his vehicle for towing must make sure that his insurance policy for the towing vehicle covers such use. If he is taking a trailer abroad he must ensure his green card mentions the trailer.

SPEED LIMITS

When towing a trailer the towing vehicle is restricted to 60mph on motorways and dual carriageways, and 50mph on all other roads except where a lower speed limit is in force.

TYRES

Tyres fitted for use with the old maximum speed of 50mph may not be suited to the current maximum of 60mph. Trailers first used after 1 April 1987, must be fitted with tyres suitable for 62mph (100kph) at the maximum design axle weight. From 1 January 1992, the maximum tyre depth is 1.6mm.

MIRRORS

The driver of a towing vehicle must have an adequate view to the rear. Any rear view mirror must not project more than 200mm outside the width of the caravan when being towed or the width of the towing vehicle when being driven solo.

Dornafield Caravan Park, Newton Abbot

Thames Bridge House Caravan Site
Clifton, Abingdon OX14 3EH
☎ 01885-407725
Open April-October ▲ ⚑ ⇲
Size 12 touring pitches, 12 with electric hookup, 6 static caravans, 3 ☍, 6 WCs, 1 CWP
£ car/tent £5-£8, car/caravan £8-£10
Rental ⚑ £95-£135
⚖¼ ✗¼ 🚽¼ ⊡ 🗲 ▨ Calor Gaz ➤
Last arrival time: 9:00
➡ Off the A415, signposted to the site. Four miles N from Abingdon and four miles from Wallingford.

Reedham Ferry Camping & Caravan Park
Ferry Road, Reedham, Acle NR13 3HA
☎ 01493-700429 Fax 01493-700999
Open March-end October ▲ ⚑ ⇲
Size 4 acres, 20 touring pitches, 20 with electric hookup, 20 level pitches, 4 ☍, 4 WCs
£ car/tent £6.50-£14, car/caravan £6.50-£14, motorhome £6.50-£14
⒞ Visa
✗ 🚽 ▨ ♿ ➤
Last arrival time: 10:00
➡ Seven miles S of Acle on B1140, situated on the N bank of the River Yare.

Camping & Caravanning Club Site
Dunstan Hill, Dunstan, Alnwick
☎ 01665-576310
Open end March-start November ▲ ⚑ ⇲
Size 12 acres, 150 touring pitches, 66 with electric hookup, 12 ☍, 19 WCs, 1 CWP
£ car/tent £9.20-£12.05, car/caravan £9.20-£12.05, motorhome £9.20-£12.05, motorbike/tent £9.20, children £1.40
⒞ MasterCard Visa
⊡ 🗲 ♿ ➤
Last arrival time: 11:00

➡ Travelling N on A1 turn right for Seahouses on B1340. Site is ¾ mile S of Embleton, follow signs for Craster.

Proctors Steads Caravan & Camping Park
Procters Steads, Craster, Alnwick NE66 3TF
☎ 01665-576613
Open March-October ▲ ⚑ ⇲

A good sheltered, level site covering 3½ acres one mile from the sea, Dunstanburgh Castle and Craster. Excellent for beaches, golf courses and coastal walks.

Size 3½ acres, 70 touring pitches, 40 with electric hookup, 70 level pitches, 20 static caravans, 8 ☍, 10 WCs, 1 CWP
£ car/tent £7-£8, car/caravan £7-£8, motorhome £7-£8, motorbike/tent £7, children £1
Rental ⚑ Chalet.
⚖ ✗ 🚽 ⊡ 🗲 ⊡ Calor Gaz ♿ ➤ WS
Last arrival time: 10:00
➡ From A1 take B1340 for 2 miles. Follow signs.

Clennell Hall
Alwinton NE65 7BG
☎ 01669-650341
Open all year ▲ ⚑ ⇲

A caravan site situated in the Border country of the Cheviot Hills and set in the grounds of Clennel Hall, a 16th century, Grade II Listed building. The caravan site provides an ideal base for many outdoor pursuits, which are available within a short distance, such as: fishing, bird watching, orienteering, mountain biking, walking, trail riding, golf and pony trekking.

Size 13½ acres, 50 touring pitches, 40 with electric hookup, 50 level pitches, 15 static caravans, 8 🚿, 10 WCs, 1 CWP
£ car/tent £6-£7.50, car/caravan £7.50, motorhome £7.50, motorbike/tent £6
🛒 ✕ 🍴 🗑 📞 🖨 GR 🛝 🎣 ♿ 🎯 WS
➜ From Rothbury follow the B6341 for 4 miles, turn right signed Harbottle and Alwinton. Go through Harbottle village and follow the sign for Alwinton, continue for 2 miles and after second bridge turn right signed Clennel Hall. From Otterburn take the B6341. Turn left 5 miles beyond Elsdon and turn left again ½ mile beyond Holystone, onto road to Harbottle.

Situated within Grizedale Forest, this site is not permitted to accepted caravans. Ideal for walkers, it is located halfway between Lake Windermere and Coniston Water.

Size 2 acres, 60 touring pitches, 11 with electric hookup, 2 🚿, 5 WCs, 1 CWP
£ car/tent £8.20-£10.40, car/caravan £8.20-£10.40, motorhome £8.20-£10.40, motorbike/tent £8.20, children £1.30
CC MasterCard Visa
🗑 📞 GR 🎣
Last arrival time: 11:00
➜ From A5092 take road signed Colton, Oxen Park for 5 miles to site on right.

ANDOVER Hampshire	4B3

Wyke Down Caravan & Camping Park
Picket Piece, Andover SP11 6LX
📞 **01264-352048 Fax 01264-324661**
Open all year 🏕 🚐 🏕

A family-owned park with country pub and golf driving range. Ample space for caravans and tents. A relaxing, peaceful setting with scenic views.

Size 7 acres, 150 touring pitches, 31 with electric hookup, 150 level pitches, 4 🚿, 14 WCs, 1 CWP
£ car/tent £8, car/caravan £8, motorhome £8, motorbike/tent £7, children £1   ➜

AMBLESIDE Cumbria	10B2

Camping & Caravanning Club Site
Grizedale Hall, Grizedale, Ambleside LA22 0GL
📞 **01229-860257**
Open end March-end September 🏕 🚐 🏕

← **Wyke Down**

🦶 🎛 📞 🎛 🎛 📺 🔲 🔲 🆔 🎛 Gaz ♿
➜ Follow International Camping signs from A303, Andover Ring Road, then through village. Picket Piece signposted approximately two miles ahead.

Wild Rose Park
Ormside, Appleby-in-Westmorland CA16 6EY
📞 **017683-51077** Fax **017683-52551**
Open all year 🏕 🚐 🚏

Beautifully landscaped park in quiet countryside, with superb views across the

Eden Valley to the Pennines. Level or gently sloping hardstanding and grass pitches.

Size 40 acres, 240 touring pitches, 200 with electric hookup, 150 level pitches, 180 static caravans, 20 🚿, 60 WCs, 3 CWPs
£ car/tent £7.10-£11.10, car/caravan £7.10-£11.10, motorhome £7.10-£11.10, motorbike/tent £2.75, children £1.30
CC MasterCard Visa
🦶 ✖ 🍴 🎛 📞 🎛 🎛 🔲 📺 🔲 🔲 Calor Gaz ♿ 🐕 WS
Last arrival time: 10:30
➜ From B6260 take road marked to Ormside and Souloy at village of Burrells. After 1½ miles take left turn to Ormside. Take first right and right again into park.

Camping & Caravanning Club Site
Slindon Park, Slindon, Arundel BN18 0RG
📞 **01243-814387**
Open late March-late September 🏕 🚐 🚏
Size 2 acres, 46 touring pitches, 12 with electric hookup, 1 CWP

£ car/tent £6.70-£8.30, car/caravan £6.70-£8.30, motorhome £6.70-£8.30, motorbike/tent £6.70, children £0.90
CC MasterCard Visa
🔋 🛏
Last arrival time: 11:00
➜ From A27 turn towards Eartham, then towards Slindon. Site on right.

Maynard's Caravan & Camping Park
Crossbush, Arundel BN18 9PQ
🔋 **01903-882075**
Open all year 🅰 🚐 🚐
Size 2½ acres, 70 touring pitches, 62 with electric hookup, 70 level pitches, 4 ℞, 9 WCs, 1 CWP
£ car/tent £7.50, car/caravan £7.50, motorhome £7.50, motorbike/tent £7.50, children £0.50-£1
🔋 ✖ 🕊 🔋 🗇 🅰 🖽 🔌 Calor Gaz ♿ 🛏 WS
➜ From Arundel ¾ mile on A27 to Worthing. Turn left into car park for Howards Hotel.

Sandybrook Hall Holiday Centre
Buxton Road, Ashbourne DE6 2AQ
🔋 **01335-342679**
Open 1 April-1 November 🅰 🚐 🚐
Size 20 acres, 70 touring pitches, 28 with electric hookup, 15 level pitches, 20 static caravans, 9 ℞, 13 WCs, 1 CWP
🔋 ✖ 🕊 🗇 🔋 🗇 🔲 🖽 🆖 📺 🅰 🖽 🔌 Calor Gaz ♿ 🛏
➜ 1 mile N of Ashbourne on A515. Opposite Dovedale turn-off.

Ashburton Caravan Park
Waterleat, Ashburton TQ13 7HU
🔋 **01364-652552**
Open Easter-September 🅰 🚐

Secluded, south-facing wooded river valley within Dartmoor National Park. A haven of peace, centrally located for easy access to the moors, coast or the historic cities of Exeter and Plymouth.

Size 4 acres, 35 touring pitches, 4 with electric hookup, 35 level pitches, 9 static caravans, 6 ℞, 7 WCs, 1 CWP
£ car/tent £7-£9, motorhome £7-£9, motorbike/tent £7, children £1.50-£2.25
Rental 🚐 £100-£280
🔋 🗇 🔋 🗇 Calor Gaz ♿ 🛏
Last arrival time: 10:30

Churchill Farm
Buckfastleigh, Ashburton TQ11 0EZ
☎ 01364-642844
Open Easter-November ▲ 🚐 🚍
Size 2 acres, 25 touring pitches, 8 with
electric hookup, 20 level pitches, 2 🚿, 4
WCs, 1 CWP
£ car/tent £5-£8, car/caravan £5-£8,
motorhome £5-£8, motorbike/tent £5,
children £0.50-£1.50
🛒¼ ✕¼ 🍴¼ 📞 🚻 🐾
Last arrival time: 10:00
➔ From the A38 exit at Dart Bridge, junction
for Buckfastleigh/Totnes, head towards
Buckfast Abbey. At mini-roundabout, drive
up the hill towards Holne. Turn left at the
junction (into no-through road) towards
Holy Trinity Church ½ mile. The farm
entrance is opposite the church.

Parkers Farm Holiday Park
Ashburton TQ13 7LJ
☎ 01364-652598 Fax 01364-654004
Open Easter-October ▲ 🚐 🚍

*A large working farm with beautifully
terraced marked pitches overlooking
Dartmoor. 12 miles from Torbay. Family
run, very clean and friendly. Free showers.
Children's and pets paradise. 1996 prices.
Also cottages and caravans.*

Size 10 acres, 80 touring pitches, 80 with
electric hookup, 80 level pitches, 25 static
caravans, 8 🚿, 12 WCs, 3 CWPs
£ car/tent £4.50-£8.50, car/caravan £4.50-
£8.50, motorhome £4.50-£8.50,
motorbike/tent £4.50, children £1
Rental 🚐 Chalet. £90-£400
㏄ MasterCard Visa
🛒 🍴 📞 🚻 💱 GR 🛍 🏧 🎮 🍴 Calor Gaz ♿ 🐾
WS

➔ Take the main A38 Exeter to Plymouth.
When you see the sign 26 miles to
Plymouth, take the second left at Alston
Cross, marked Woodland and Denburt. 400
yards down the road.

River Dart Country Park
Holne Park, Ashburton TQ13 7NP
☎ 01364-652511 Fax 01364-652511
Open 1 April-30 September ▲ 🚐 🚍

*Magnificent 90 acre park once part of a
Victorian country estate. The camping area
is set along the fringes of woodland in gently
sloping parkland. An ideal site for exploring
Dartmoor and the South Devon coast.* ➔

← River Dart

Size 90 acres, 120 touring pitches, 120 level pitches, 12 🚿, 16 WCs, 1 CWP
£ car/tent £8-£10.80, car/caravan £8-£10.80, motorhome £8-£10.80, motorbike/tent £8, children £3.25-£4.20
CC MasterCard Visa
🛒 ✕ 📻 🔲 🔌 🔲 🔳 🔲 🔲 🔲 📺 ⚠ 🔲 🔲 Calor Gaz ⚐ 🐕
Last arrival time: 10:00
➡ M5 Motorway at Exeter, take A38 Expressway towards Plymouth. Exit at Peartree Cross junction. Follow brown signs.

Broad Hembury Farm Caravan & Camping
Steeds Lane, Kingsnorth, Ashford TN26 1NQ
📞 01233-620859 Fax 01233-620859
🅰 ⚐ 🚐
Size 5 acres, 60 touring pitches, 48 with electric hookup, 60 level pitches, 25 static caravans, 6 🚿, 16 WCs, 1 CWP
£ car/tent £9-£11, car/caravan £9-£11, motorhome £9-£11, motorbike/tent £9, children £1.50
Rental ⚐
CC MasterCard Visa
🛒 ✕¼ 📻¼ 🔲 🔌 🔲 GR 🔲 📺 ⚠ 🔲 Calor Gaz 🐕
➡ From J10 on M20 take A2070 for 2 miles, then continue on A2042 following signs for Kingsnorth. Left at second cross roads in village.

Wansbeck Riverside Park
Green Lane, Ashington NE63 8TX
📞 01670-814444
Open all year 🅰 ⚐ 🚐
Size 75 touring pitches, 25 with electric hookup, 10 level pitches, 8 🚿, 10 WCs, 1 CWP
£ car/tent £6.70-£7.75, car/caravan £7.35-£10, motorhome £7.35-£10, motorbike/tent £6.70
🛒 📻 🔲 🔌 🔲 🔲 Calor Gaz ⚐ 🐕
Last arrival time: 10:00

➜ Just off A1068 between Guideport and Ashington. Only 4 miles from Morpeth and the A1.

ASTON CANTLOW Warwickshire　　8A4

Island Meadow Caravan Park
The Mill House, Aston Cantlow B95 6JP
📞 **01789-488273 Fax 01789-488273**
Open 1 March-31 October 🛆 🚐 🚏

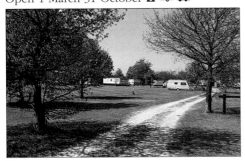

Quiet, peaceful, secluded riverside park beside picturesque and historic village. Ideal centre for Shakespeare's country, only six miles from Stratford-upon-Avon. English Tourist Board grading four ticks.

Size 7 acres, 24 touring pitches, 24 with electric hookup, 24 level pitches, 56 static caravans, 4 🕭, 11 WCs, 1 CWP
£ car/tent £6, car/caravan £8, motorhome £8, motorbike/tent £6, children £0.75
Rental 🚐 £152 (low season)-£258 (high season)
🛉 ✕¼ 🗑 📞 🗍 🖉 Calor Gaz 🕭 🛏
Last arrival time: 9:00
➜ From A46 Stratford to Alcester, or from A3400 Stratford to Henley-in-Arden, follow signs for Aston Cantlow Village.

AXMINSTER Devon　　3E3

Andrewshayes Caravan Park
Dalwood, Axminster EX13 7DY
📞 **01404-831225 Fax 01404-831225**
Open 1 April-31 October 🛆 🚐 🚏
Size 12 acres, 90 touring pitches, 80 with electric hookup, 40 level pitches, 80 static caravans, 12 🕭, 18 WCs, 2 CWPs
£ car/tent £8, car/caravan £8-£9.50, motorhome £8-£9.50, motorbike/tent £5, children £1

Rental 🚐 £85-£360
⊂⊂ MasterCard Visa
🛉 ✕ ✕¼ 🖤 🖤¼ 🗑 📞 🗍 GR ⚠ 🖾 Calor Gaz
🕭 🛏 WS
Last arrival time: 10:00
➜ Turn N at Taunton Cross on A35, 3 miles from Axminster, 6 miles from Honiton, signposted to Dalwood and Stockland.

AYSGARTH North Yorkshire　　10C2

Street Head Caravan Park
Newbiggin, Leyburn DL8 3TE
📞 **01969-663472**
Open 1 March-end October 🛆 🚐 🚏
Size 4 acres, 30 touring pitches, 24 with electric hookup
£ car/tent £6.50-£9.25, car/caravan £7.50-£11, motorhome £6.50-£9.25
🛉 ✕¼ 🖤¼ 🗑 🗍 Calor Gaz 🛏 WS
➜ Turn W off A684 onto B6160. Site is 2½ miles on right adjacent to Street Head Inn.

Westholme Caravan Park
Aysgarth DL8 3SP
📞 **01969-663268**
Open 1 March-31 October 🛆 🚐 🚏

Set in the Yorkshire Dales National Park, enjoying striking views amidst splendid walking and touring country.

Size 22 acres, 69 touring pitches, 44 with electric hookup, 69 level pitches, 42 static caravans, 8 🕭, 16 WCs, 2 CWPs
🛉 ✕ 🖤 🗑 📞 🗍 🖉 GR TV ⚠ 🖾 🗍 Calor Gaz
🛏
➜ 7 miles W of Leyburn turn left off A684, ¾ mile after junction with B6160. 1 mile E of Aysgarth.

Camping & Caravanning Club Site

Hopping Farm, Youlgreave, Bakewell DE45 1NA

☎ 01629-636555

Open end March-end September ▲ ⊕ 🚐
Size 11.9 acres, 100 touring pitches, 54 with electric hookup, 1 CWP
£ car/tent £6.70-£8.30, car/caravan £6.70-£8.30, motorhome £6.70-£8.30, motorbike/tent £6.70, children £0.90
㏄ MasterCard Visa
🔌 🗚 🗺 🛉
Last arrival time: 11:00
➜ Take A515 from Buxton (not A6), signposted 'Monyask Youlgreave Arbor Low' , turn left, head for Youlgreave then turn right down lane by church wall. Over bridge, then turn right up farm track for ½ mile.

Greenhills Caravan Park

Crow Hill Lane, Nr Ashford-in-the-Water, Bakewell DE4 1PX

☎ 01629-813467 Fax 01629-815131

Open all year ▲ ⊕ 🚐
Size 8 acres, 100 touring pitches, 35 with electric hookup, 50 level pitches, 65 static caravans, 8 🚿, 17 WCs, 1 CWP
£ car/tent £8-£10, car/caravan £8-£10, motorhome £8-£10, motorbike/tent £8, children £1
🛒 🗑 🔌 🗚 🗺 🔌 Calor Gas 🛉
Last arrival time: 10:00
➜ One mile NW of Bakewell on A6, turn S signed Over Haddon to site on right.

Waren Caravan Park

Waren Mill, Bamburgh NE70 7EE

☎ 01668-214366 Fax 01668-214224

Open 27 March-31 October ⊕ 🚐

Beautiful park amidst stunning Northumbrian scenery. Shop, restaurant, solarium, games room, heated outdoor pool, laundry.

Size 99 acres, 200 touring pitches, 57 with electric hookup, 140 level pitches, 345 static caravans, 32 🚿, 16 WCs, 2 CWPs
🛒
➜ At ¼ mile S of Belford on A1 turn E on B1342. Site in 2½ miles.

Barnstones Caravan & Camping Site

Great Bourton, Banbury OX7 2BB.

☎ 01295-750289

Open all year ▲ ⊕ 🚐

Beautiful award winning park situated on the edge of a pretty village close to the Cotswolds. Delightfully landscaped with trees and flower beds. Immaculate toilet block, free showers, laundry room and children's play area.

Size 2½ acres, 49 touring pitches, 49 with electric hookup, 49 level pitches, 3 🚿, 5 WCs, 1 CWP

£ car/tent £4.50, car/caravan £4.50, motorhome £4.50, motorbike/tent £4.50, children £0.50

🔳¼ ✖¼ 🗇¼ 🔳 🗇 ⚠ 🏧 Calor Gaz ♿
➡ From junction 11 of the M40 (Chipping Norton) continue to the the third roundabout and take the A423 to Southam. After 2 miles turn right to Great Bourton. Site is 100 yards on the right.

Mollington Touring Caravan Park
The Yews, Mollington, Banbury OX17 1AZ
📞 **01295-750731**
Open March-November ⚊ 🚐 🚛

Located on the edge of a lovely village within easy reach of many National Trust properties, the Cotswolds, Stratford-upon-Avon, Warwick, Oxford and more.

Size 2 acres, 24 touring pitches, 24 with electric hookup, 20 level pitches, 4 🚿, 4 WCs, 1 CWP
£ car/tent £4-£5, car/caravan £5-£6, motorhome £5-£6, motorbike/tent £4
🔳¼ ✖¼ 🔳 🗇 🐕
Last arrival time: 11:00
➡ Site is directly off A423 Banbury to Southam road, 200 yards past Mollington, turn left from Banbury direction. Signposted close to site.

Farm Meadow Caravan & Camping Park
The Grove, Banham Zoo, Banham NR16 2HB
📞 **01953-888370** Fax **01953-887445**
Open all year ⚊ 🚐 🚛
Size 13 acres, 67 touring pitches, 60 with electric hookup, 67 level pitches, 6 🚿, 12 WCs, 1 CWP

£ car/tent £5-£7, car/caravan £6.50-£9, motorhome £6.50-£9, motorbike/tent £5
CC MasterCard Visa

🔳 ✖ 🗇 🔳 ⚠ 🏧 🗇 Calor ♿ 🐕 WS
➡ Banham is situated on the B1113 Norwich to Bury St Edmunds road, halfway between Attleborough and Diss.

Camping & Caravanning Club Site
Dockenflatts Lane, Lartington, Barnard Castle
📞 **01833-630228**
Open March-November ⚊ 🚐 🚛
Size 90 touring pitches, 37 with electric hookup, 90 level pitches, 8 🚿, 13 WCs, 1 CWP
£ car/tent £8.75-£11.55, car/caravan £8.75-£11.55, motorhome £8.75-£11.55, motorbike/tent £8.75, children £1.40
CC MasterCard Visa
🗇 🔳 ⚠ 🏧 ♿ 🐕
Last arrival time: 11:00 ➡

← Camping & Caravanning Club Site

➜ Take A66 from Scotch Corner, then B6277 for Barnard Castle, cross A67 and head for Lartington, turn left at site sign before reaching Lartington.

West Roods Working Farm
Boldron, Barnard Castle DL12 9SW
📞 01833-690116
Open April-October **A** 🚐 🚏
Size 1 acre, 16 touring pitches, 4 with electric hookup, 2 level pitches, 1 ℞, 1 WC, 1 CWP
£ car/tent £6, car/caravan £6, motorhome £6, motorbike/tent £6, children £0.50
📞 🔲 ⚠ 🔀 🐕
Last arrival time: 10:00
➜ Site entrance from N side of A66, 2½ miles E of Bowes, ½ mile W of road to Boldron village.

Midland Caravan Park
Braunton Road, Barnstaple EX31 4AU
📞 01271-43691 Fax 01271-43691
Open April-30 September **A** 🚐 🚏

Level, well protected grass park overlooking the River Taw Estuary. Ideally situated to enjoy all of North Devon's beaches and attractions, and Exmoor.

Size 8½ acres, 35 touring pitches, 35 with electric hookup, 35 level pitches, 62 static caravans, 8 ℞, 24 WCs, 1 CWP
£ car/tent £5-£7, car/caravan £7-£9, motorhome £7-£9, motorbike/tent £5, children £1.50
Rental 🚐

✕ 🔲 📞 🔲 📺 ⚠ 🔀 🔌 Calor Gaz 🐕
Last arrival time: 9:00
➜ Take A361 through Barnstaple and follow Braunton and Ilfracombe signs. Park is 2 miles W of Barnstaple on right of dual carriageway.

Bath Marina & Caravan Park
Brassmill Lane, Bath BA1 3JT
📞 01225-428778 Fax 01225-428778
Open all year 🚐 🚏
Size 4 acres, 88 touring pitches, 88 with electric hookup, 88 level pitches, 9 ℞, 23 WCs, 2 CWPs
£ car/caravan £10.50-£13.50, motorhome £10.50-£13.50, children £0.75
CC MasterCard Visa
🔋 ✕¼ 🔲 📞 ⚠ 🔀 Calor Gaz ♿ 🐕
Last arrival time: 12:00
➜ Two miles W of Bath on A4 at Newbridge.

Brakes Coppice Farm
Telham Lane, Battle TN33 0SJ
☎ 01424-830347 Fax 01424-830347
Open 1 March-30 October

Small secluded woodland site with coarse fishing lake in 13½ acres. Five miles from the coast.

Whydown Farm Tourist Caravan Park
Crazy Lane, Sedlescombe, Battle TN33 0QT
☎ 01424-870147
Open 1 March-31 October ▲ 🚐 🚍

Small quiet secluded family site situated in a suntrap valley in the heart of 1066 countryside within easy reach of beach and all historical sites. Just off the A21.

Size 26 touring pitches, 26 with electric hookup, 20 level pitches, 3 🚿, 5 WCs, 2 CWPs
£ car/tent £6.50-£8, car/caravan £6.70-£8, motorhome £6.70-£8, motorbike/tent £6.50
🛒¼ ✗¼ ●¼ 🔥 🔥 🔥 Calor 👤 🐕 WS

➡ Travelling south on A21, turn left 100 yards past junction B2244 opposite Blackbrooks Garden Centre, into Crazy Lane. Site 70 yards on right.

Highclere Farm Country Touring Park
Newbarn Lane, Seer Green, Beaconsfield HP9 2QZ
☎ 01494-874505 Fax 01494-875238
Open 1 March-31 January ▲ 🚐

A quiet meadowland site, one mile from the railway station. Cheap travel cards for London. Legoland 11 miles. Pub food ¼ mile, swimming 1½ miles.

Size 2 acres, 45 touring pitches, 45 with electric hookup, 45 level pitches, 6 🚿, 8 WCs, 2 CWPs
£ car/tent £8-£8.50, car/caravan £8-£9, motorhome £8-£9, motorbike/tent £8
Rental Chalet.
℃ MasterCard Visa
🛒 ✗¼ ●¼ 🔥 🔥 🔥 🔥 Calor Gaz 👤 🐕
Last arrival time: 10:00
➡ Leave the M40 at junction 2 onto the A40 to Gerrards Cross. Turn left after ¼ mile to Seer Green and follow the tourist signs.

Camping & Caravanning Club Site
Anstead, Beadnell NE67 5BX
☎ 01665-720586
Open end March-end September ▲ 🚐 🚍
Size 12 acres, 150 touring pitches, 150 level pitches, 6 🚿, 17 WCs, 1 CWP ➡

← **Camping & Caravanning Club Site**

£ car/tent £8.75-£11.55, car/caravan £8.75-£11.55, motorhome £8.75-£11.55, motorbike/tent £8.75, children £1.30
CC MasterCard Visa
🔋 📞 🐕 ⛺
Last arrival time: 11:00
➡ From A1 to Alnwick take a right fork (B1340). This takes you to Beadnell itself, the site is on coastal front on left, after a left hand bend.

Family-run site in area of outstanding natural beauty with direct access to wood and heathland. Ideal base for walking and touring Dorset.

Size 8½ acres, 71 touring pitches, 40 with electric hookup, 40 level pitches, 10 ⛴, 10 WCs, 1 CWP
£ car/tent £5.60-£8.60, car/caravan £5.60-£8.60, motorhome £5.60-£8.60, motorbike/tent £5.60, children £0.90
🛒 🔋 📞 🔲 GR 🔍 🛆 🚻 Calor Gaz 🐕 WS
Last arrival time: 9:30
➡ At Bere Regis turn S off A35 onto Wool/Bovington Tank Museum Road. At top of Rye Hill turn right. Park is 200 yards ahead.

BELLINGHAM Northumberland   13E3

Brown Rigg Caravan & Camping Park
Bellingham NE48 2JY
📞 **01434-220175**
Open Easter-31 October A 🚐 🚏
A family run site within the Northumberland National Park. ½ mile south of Bellingham on B6320. Walking, golf, fishing nearby. Hadrian's Wall and Kielder Water 9 miles.

Size 6 acres, 60 touring pitches, 24 with electric hookup, 60 level pitches, 6 ⛴, 10 WCs, 1 CWP
£ car/tent £5, car/caravan £6.50, motorhome £6.50, motorbike/tent £2, children £0.75
🛒 🛒¼ ✗¼ 🍴¼ 🔋 📞 🔲 GR 🔍 🛆 🚻 Calor Gaz
♿ 🐕
Last arrival time: 8:30
➡ From A69 ½ mile W of Hexham to Chollerford/Bellingham. At Chollerford take B6318, left over N Tyne River to roundabout signposted B6329 Bellingham.

BERE REGIS Dorset   4A4

Rowlands Wait Touring Park
Rye Hill, Bere Regis BH20 7LP
📞 **01929-471958**
Open 16 March-31 October A 🚐 🚏

BERKELEY Gloucestershire   7E4

Hogsdown Farm
Lower Wick, Dursley GL11 6DS
📞 **01453-810224**
Open all year A 🚐 🚏
Size 4 acres, 40 touring pitches, 25 with electric hookup, 40 level pitches, 2 ⛴, 7 WCs, 2 CWPs
£ car/tent £5.50, car/caravan £7, motorhome £7, motorbike/tent £6, children £0.50
Rental 🚐
🛒 🛒¼ 🔋 📞 🔲 🔳 🛆 🚻 Calor 🐕 WS
Last arrival time: 10:30
➡ Between junctions 13 and 14 on A38. One mile off A38 opposite Berkeley turning.

BERROW Worcestershire   7E4

Three Counties Caravan Park
Sledge Green, Berrow WR13 6JW
📞 **01684-833439** Fax **01684-833439**
Open Easter-end October A 🚐 🚏

A peaceful and quiet site with an open, gently sloping field, offering fine views of the Malvern Hills. A good touring centre for many local activities.

Size 2 acres, 50 touring pitches, 20 with electric hookup, 50 level pitches, 4 ℞, 10 WCs, 1 CWP
£ car/tent £6.50, car/caravan £6.50, motorhome £6.50, motorbike/tent £6.50
CC MasterCard Visa
📞 🗗 ⚠ 🖾 Calor & 🐾 WS
Last arrival time: 9:00

➜ On A438 Tewkesbury to Ledbury road. 1 mile on left after passing under M50 motorway.

BERWICK-UPON-TWEED Northumberland   13F2

Berwick Holiday Centre
Magdalene Fields, Berwick-upon-Tweed TD15 1NE
📞 01289-232459 Fax 01289-232459
Open March-October 🚐 🚎

A family holiday park close to excellent beaches and with indoor and outdoor heated pools, leisure facilities, kids clubs, live entertainment, bars and food. A 'British Holidays Park'.

Size 58 acres, 35 touring pitches, 35 level pitches, 120 static caravans, 1 CWP
CC Visa
🛒 ✕ 🍽 🗗 🗐 🗒 🍴 🐾
➜ Signposted on A1 from both N and S, signs directing you to Berwick Holiday Centre in town.

Haggerston Castle Caravan Park
Boal, Berwick-upon-Tweed TD15 2RA
📞 01289-381333
Open 9 March-9 January 🚐 🚎

➜

← Haggerston Castle Caravan Park

A beautiful rural setting with lakes and swans. Easy access to Northumbrian countryside, castles and beaches. On-site facilities include bowling green, tennis, entertainment and boats.

Size 220 acres, 159 touring pitches, 159 with electric hookup, 159 level pitches, 800 static caravans, 16 showers, 16 WCs, 2 CWPs
£ car/caravan £6.50-£17.50, motorhome £6.50-£17.50

Rental
CC MasterCard Visa
GR TV
Calor WS
➡ 7½ miles S of Berwick on A1.

Ord House Caravan Park

East Ord, Berwick-upon-Tweed TD15 2NS
01289-305288 Fax 01289-330832
Open 1 March-9 January

40 acre tree-lined estate dominated by an 18th century mansion containing a licensed club. Luxury toilet and shower facilities. Recreation and play area. Practise golf.

Size 41 acres, 70 touring pitches, 60 with electric hookup, 34 level pitches, 220 static caravans, 8 ⬛, 16 WCs, 2 CWPs
£ car/tent £5-£10, car/caravan £7-£11.50, motorhome £7-£11.50
CC MasterCard Visa
⬛ ⬛¼ ✕ ⬛ ⬛ ⬛ ⬛ ⬛ ⬛ ⬛ Calor ⬛ ⬛
Last arrival time: 11:00
➡ On A1 Berwick bypass. Turn off at second roundabout at East Ord and follow caravan symbol.

Heyford Leys Farm

Camp Road, Upper Heyford, Bicester OX6 3LU
⬛ **01869-232048 Fax 01869-232048**
Open 1 April-31 October ⬛ ⬛ ⬛
Size 10 acres, 22 touring pitches, 10 with electric hookup, 22 level pitches, 47 static caravans, 2 ⬛, 4 WCs,, 1 CWP
£ car/tent £5-£9, car/caravan £6.50-£8.50, motorhome £6.50-£8.50, motorbike/tent £5
CC MasterCard Visa
⬛ ⬛ ⬛ ⬛ ⬛ ⬛ ⬛ Calor ⬛ ⬛

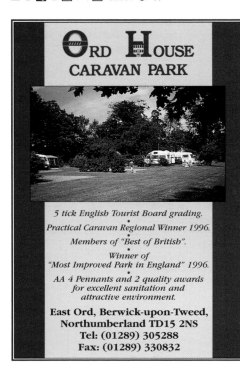

➡ From junction 10 M40 follow B430 for 1½ miles.

Steart Farm Touring Park

Bideford EX39 5DW
⬛ **01237-431836**
Open Easter-30 October ⬛ ⬛ ⬛
Size 10 acres, 60 touring pitches, 18 with electric hookup, 25 level pitches, 4 ⬛, 6 WCs, 1 CWP
£ car/tent £7, car/caravan £7, motorhome £7, motorbike/tent £4
CC MasterCard Visa
⬛¼ ✕¼ ⬛¼ ⬛ ⬛ ⬛ ⬛ Calor Gaz ⬛ WS
Last arrival time: 11:00
➡ Follow A39 from Bideford through Fairy Cross and Horns Cross. Site is 2 miles past Horns Cross. From Bude, take A39 past Clovelly Cross and Bucks Cross. Site is ½ mile past Bucks Cross on left.

Quex Caravan Park

Birchington
⬛ **01843-841273**
Open 1 March-31 October ⬛ ⬛

Ideally situated for exploring East Kent, an attractive three acre touring area approximately two miles from sandy beaches. Channel ferries and the Channel Tunnel are close by.

Size 60 touring pitches, 38 with electric hookup, 108 static caravans, 8 ⬛, 9 WCs, 1 CWP
CC Visa
⬛ Calor Gaz WS   ➡

← Quex Caravan Park

➡ Follow signs to Margate on A299. Turn left at roundabout on A28 (to Margate). Turn right at 'T' junction in Birchington and follow Tourist Board signs.

Two Chimneys Caravan Park
Five Acres, Shottendane Road, Birchington CT7 0HD
☎ 01843-841068 Fax 01843-848099
Open Easter-end October ⚊ 🚐 🚏

A lovely country site near sandy beaches and close to the city of Canterbury.

Size 10 acres, 90 touring pitches, 60 with electric hookup, 140 level pitches, 50 static caravans, 13 🚿, 22 WCs, 1 CWP
£ car/tent £6.50-£14, car/caravan £6.50-£14, motorhome £6.50-£14, motorbike/tent £6.50
Rental 🚐 Chalet. £140-£390
CC MasterCard Visa
🛒 ✗¼ 🛍 🗑 🛒 🗄 🔲 📶🔍 🐟 GR 🐟 🛍 ⚠ 🔲 🍴
Calor Gas ♿ 🐕 WS
Last arrival time: 10:00
➡ From the A299 follow A28 to Birchington Square, turn right at the church into Park Lane (B2048). Left at Manston Road (B2050), first left into Shottendane Road. Site is 300 yards on the right.

Green Caravan Park
Wentnor, Bishop's Castle SY9 5EF
☎ 01588-650605
Open Easter-October ⚊ 🚐 🚏
Size 15 acres, 140 touring pitches, 30 with electric hookup, 140 level pitches, 20 static caravans, 10 🚿, 19 WCs, 1 CWP

£ car/tent £6, car/caravan £6, motorhome £6, motorbike/tent £6, children £1
🛒 🗑 🛍 🗄 ⚠ 🔲 Calor Gas 🐕 WS
Last arrival time: 9:00
➡ Take Longden road off A5 Shrewsbury bypass. Site 15 miles on right.

Kneps Farm Holiday Park
River Road, Thornton Cleveleys, Blackpool FY5 5LR
☎ 01253-823632 Fax 01253-863967
Open 1 March-31 October ⚊ 🚐 🚏

Situated in the Wyre Estuary Country Park with easy access to the premier resorts of Blackpool, Wyre and Fylde, the Trough of Bowland, the Yorkshire Dales, the English Lake District and many more places of interest.

Size 10 acres, 72 touring pitches, 62 with electric hookup, 72 level pitches, 88 static caravans, 11 🚿, 17 WCs, 1 CWP
£ car/tent £7.75-£10.25, car/caravan £7.75-£10.25, motorhome £7.75-£10.25, motorbike/tent £7.75, children £1-£1.50
CC MasterCard Visa
🛒 ✗ 🛍 🗑 🛍 🗄 ⚠ 🔲 Calor Gas ♿ 🐕
Last arrival time: 8:00
➡ Leave M55 at junction 3 and follow A585 for Fleetwood. At the first roundabout turn right onto B5412. After 1 mile, turn right after the school into Stanah Road, which leads to River Road.

Maaruig Caravan Park
71 Pilling Lane, Preesall, Blackpool FY6 0HB
☎ 01253-810404

Open 1 March-4 January ▲ ⏏ ⇶
Size 1 acre, 28 touring pitches, 28 with electric hookup, 28 level pitches, 4 ⛾, 6 WCs, 1 CWP
£ car/caravan £7.50, motorhome £7.50, children £0.50
⛽¼ ⊡ 🐾
Last arrival time: 9:30
➜ M6 (jn 32) join M55 (jn 3) exit onto A585 for Fleetwood. At third set of traffic lights turn right onto A588 for Lancaster. 5 miles to Ford garage on left. Follow signs for Knott-End onto B5377 up to T-junction. Turn left then first right onto Pilling Lane. Round the corner, second caravan park on left.

Mariclough And Hampsfield Camp Site
Preston New Road, Peel, Blackpool FY4 5JR
📞 **01253-761034**
Open Easter-November ▲ ⏏ ⇶
Size 2 acres, 50 touring pitches, 30 with electric hookup, 30 level pitches, 3 ⛾, 6 WCs, 1 CWP
£ car/tent £4, car/caravan £6, motorhome £4, motorbike/tent £4, children £1
⛽ ⊡ 📞 Calor Gaz ♿ 🐾
Last arrival time: 10:00
➜ From M55 junction 4 turn left at roundabout. Proceed straight through the traffic lights. Site is just on the left.

Marton Mere Holiday Park
Mythope Road, Blackpool FY4 4XN
📞 **01253-767544 Fax 01253-791252**
Open March-October ▲ ⏏ ⇶

A family holiday park set in 93 acres just three miles from Blackpool. Heated indoor pool, kids clubs, tennis and bowling included in the wide range of leisure

facilities, restaurants and bars, excellent cabaret entertainment. A 'British Holidays Park'.

Size 93 acres, 420 touring pitches, 420 with electric hookup, 420 level pitches, 900 static caravans, 26 ⛾, 40 WCs, 20 CWPs
£ car/tent £9-£12, car/caravan £14-£16, motorhome £14-£16, motorbike/tent £9
Rental ⏏ £90-£454
㏄ MasterCard Visa
⛽ ✗ ⛽ ⊡ 📞 ⊡ ▣ ▦◪ 🔲 ◪ GR ◪ TV 🅿 🎠 ⊡
Calor Gaz ♿ 🐾 WS
Last arrival time: 10:00
➜ Take junction 4 off M55 (A583) towards Blackpool. At second set of traffic lights turn right into Mythop Road. Site is 100 yards on left.

Stanah House Caravan Park
River Road, Thornton, Blackpool FY5 5LR
📞 **01253-824000 Fax 01253-863060**
Open March-October ▲ ⏏ ⇶

A small select touring site, overlooking the River Wyre with good views of the Fells and Lake District mountains. Close access to a slipway for sailing and water-skiing.

Size 6 acres, 55 touring pitches, 50 with electric hookup, 55 level pitches, 4 ⛾, 6 WCs, 1 CWP
£ car/tent £8.50, car/caravan £8.50, motorhome £8.50, motorbike/tent £8.50
㏄ MasterCard Visa
⛽ ⛽¼ ✗¼ ⛽¼ ⊡ 📞 🅿 🎠 Calor Gaz ♿ 🐾 WS
➜ Leave M55 junction 3 onto A585. After 6 miles at roundabout by River Wyre Hotel, turn right onto B5415 signposted Little Thornton and Stanah picnic area. Follow picnic area signs and continue to very end of River Road, turn right into Caravan Site nearest river.

Willowgrove Caravan Park
Sandy Lane, Preesall, Blackpool FY6 0EJ
📞 01253-811306 Fax 01253-812627
🚐 🚏

The park is peaceful and quiet with ducks and swans to feed and coarse fishing. The area is flat for bicycles and wheelchairs.

Size 27 acres, 60 touring pitches, 52 with electric hookup, 60 level pitches, 100 static caravans, 10 ⏃, 16 WCs, 2 CWPs
👌

➡ From M55 take junction 3 to Fleetwood, turn right following Fleetwood sign. 3 miles, turn left at traffic lights. 1 mile at traffic lights bear right, keeping Shell garage on the right. 1 mile at traffic lights turn right to Preesall. Continue over Shard roundabout and take first left for 4 miles. Continue on ignoring right bend towards Lancaster. 1¼ miles to 'T' junction, turn right onto Sandy Lane and park is 300 yards on left.

Inside Park Caravan & Camping
Blandford Forum DT11 0HG
📞 01258-453719 Fax 01258-454026
Open Easter- 31 October 🏕 🚐 🚏

Set in parkland in the heart of our family run farm, we offer all modern comfortable facilities and plenty of space in which to unwind. Open Easter to 31 October.

Size 13 acres, 100 touring pitches, 90 with electric hookup, 60 level pitches, 12 ⏃, 14 WCs, 1 CWP
£ car/tent £7-£12, car/caravan £7-£12, motorhome £7-£12, motorbike/tent £7
CC MasterCard Visa
🔧 🔲 🍴 🔲 📻 🔲 ⛰ 🎣 Calor Gaz 👌 🐾 WS
Last arrival time: 8:30
➡ From the junction of the A354 and A350, take the Blandford St Mary exit and follow the signs to the park.

Camping & Caravanning Club Site
Old Callywith Road, Bodmin PL31 2DZ
📞 01208-73834
Open March-November 🏕 🚐 🚏

Size 10½ acres, 175 touring pitches, 53 with electric hookup, 6 🞾, 18 WCs, 1 CWP
£ car/tent £8.20-£10.40, car/caravan £8.20-£10.40, motorhome £8.20-£10.40, motorbike/tent £8.20, children £1.30
CC MasterCard Visa
🖃 🔌 Gaz 🕇
Last arrival time: 11:00
➡ From A389 follow signs for site.

Glenmorris Park

Longstone Road, St Mabyn, Bodmin PL30 3BY
📞 **01208-841677** Fax **01208-841677**
Open April-October 🛆 ⛴ 🚐
Size 11 acres, 100 touring pitches, 50 with electric hookup, 100 level pitches, 6 static caravans, 12 🞾, 21 WCs, 2 CWPs
£ car/tent £5-£7, car/caravan £5-£7, motorhome £5-£7, motorbike/tent £5
Rental ⛴ Chalet. £65-£250.
CC MasterCard Visa
🛒 🛒¼ 🖃 🔌 🍴 ▣ GR ▣ 🜂 🗙 Calor Gaz 🕇 WS
Last arrival time: 10:30
➡ ½ mile SW of Camelford on A39 fork left on B3266 for 6½ miles. Turn right (signposted St Mabyn), ¼ mile to site, 5½ miles from Bodmin.

Camping & Caravanning Club Site

Bar Lane, Roecliffe, Boroughbridge YO5 9LS
📞 **01423-322683**
🛆 ⛴ 🚐
Size 6½ acres, 100 touring pitches, 39 with electric hookup, 6 🞾, 14 WCs, 1 CWP
£ car/tent £8.75-£11.55, car/caravan £8.75-£11.55, motorhome £8.75-£11.55, motorbike/tent £8.75, children £1.40
CC MasterCard Visa
🛒 🖃 GR 🜂 🗙 🕇
Last arrival time: 11:00
➡ Leave A1 signposted Boroughbridge, turn W off main street signposted Roecliffe. Site is on right.

White Cat Park

Shaw Lane, Old Leake PE22 9LQ
📞 **01205-870121**
Open March-November 🛆 ⛴ 🚐
Size 2½ acres, 40 touring pitches, 36 with electric hookup, 40 level pitches, 5 static caravans, 2 🞾, 6 WCs, 1 CWP
£ car/tent £4.50-£5.50, car/caravan £4.50-£5.50, motorhome £4.50-£5.50, motorbike/tent £4.50
Rental ⛴ caravans £78-£92
🛒 🛒¼ 🗙¼ 🚐¼ 🔌 🖃 🗙 Calor Gaz 🕇 WS
Last arrival time: 10:00
➡ Take A52 Skegness Road as far as the Old Leake Road. Turn right opposite B1184 Sibsey Road. The site is 300 yards on the left.

Cara Touring Park

Old Bridge Road, Iford, Bournemouth BH6 5RQ
📞 **01202-482121** Fax **01734-452063**
Open all year ⛴ 🚐
Size 3 acres, 36 touring pitches, 36 with electric hookup, 36 level pitches, 1 static caravans, 6 🞾, 6 WCs,
£ car/caravan £7.30-£9.95, motorhome £6.60-£8.60
Rental ⛴ £90-£270
🛒 🗙¼ 🚐¼ 🖃 🔌 Calor
➡ A35 between Christchurch and Boscombe. One mile from Christchurch and 1½ miles from Boscombe.

Chesildene Touring Caravan Site

2 Chesildene Avenue, Bournemouth BH5 0DS
📞 **01202-513238**
Open 1 April-31 October ⛴ 🚐
Size 3 acres, 75 touring pitches, 75 with electric hookup, 75 level pitches, 6 🞾, 16 WCs, 1 CWP
£ car/caravan £6.50-£9, motorhome £6.50-£9, children £0.50
🛒 🛒¼ 🖃 🔌 🍴 GR ▣ 🜂 🗙 Calor Gaz ♿ WS

➡

← Chesildene Touring Caravan Site

➜ From A338 to Bournemouth, turn right onto A3060 and follow camping signs for one mile.

St Leonards Farm Camping & Caravan Park
West Moors, Bournemouth BH22 OAQ
☎ 01202-872637
Open Easter-30 September ⚊ �' 🚐

Quiet, level site near Bournemouth, Poole, cross channel ferries and the New Forest. Easy access off A31. Electric hook-ups, modern facilities including those for disabled, launderette.

Size 8 acres, 110 touring pitches, 40 with electric hookup, 12 🚿, 2 CWPs
£ car/tent £7-£10, car/caravan £7-£10, motorhome £7-£10, motorbike/tent £7, children £1
🅿¼ ✗¼ 🅿¼ ▣ 🔌 ⊟ ⚠ 🏥 Calor Gaz ♿ ♁ WS
➜ On A31 4 miles W of Ringwood, opposite West Moors garage.

Thriftwood Camping & Caravanning Park
Plaxdale Green Road, Stansted, Brands Hatch TN15 7PB
☎ 01732-822261 Fax 01732-822261
⚊ �' 🚐
Size 22 acres, 160 touring pitches, 102 with electric hookup, 160 level pitches, 10 static caravans, 9 🚿, 18 WCs, 1 CWP

£ car/tent £8-£10.75, car/caravan £8-£10.75, motorhome £8-£10.75, motorbike/tent £6, children £1.50
Rental 🚐 £125-£320
CC MasterCard Visa
🅿 ✗¼ 🅿¼ ▣ 🔌 ⊟ ⚠ 🏥 Calor Gaz ♁ WS
Last arrival time: 10:00
➜ M26 junction 2A and M20 junction 2. Follow caravan & camping signs N on A20.

Harrow Wood Farm Caravan Park
Poplar Lane, Bransgore
☎ 01425-672487
Open 1 March-6 January 🚐 🚐

Situated in a pleasant village right on the edge of the New Forest, this six acre site offers the perfect centre from which to explore the surrounding area. Christchurch, Highcliffe and the market town of Ringwood are but a short drive away.

Size 6 acres, 60 touring pitches, 60 with electric hookup, 60 level pitches, 6 🚿, 12 WCs, 3 CWPs
£ car/caravan £8-£12, motorhome £8-£12
🅿¼ ✗¼ 🅿¼ ▣ 🔌 ⊟ 🅿 Calor WS
➜ Take Ringwood Road into Bransgore. Follow signs to site, between Three Tuns Pub and the Crown Inn.

Lobb Fields Caravan & Camping Park
Saunton Road, Braunton EX33 1EB
☎ 01271-812090 Fax 01271-812090
Open Easter October

A large, level, grassy park facing south with panoramic views across to the Taw/Torridge Estuary. One mile from Saunton Golf Club and 1½ miles from a large beach. Dishwashing facilities are available, as are hairdryer and razor points.

Size 14 acres, 100 touring pitches, 33 with electric hookup, 180 level pitches, 20 ☂, 50 WCs, 2 CWPs
£ car/caravan £5.50-£8
🅿 📞 🍴 ⚠ ☒ Calor Gaz
➡ In Braunton at traffic lights, turn W off A361 to B3231, towards Saunton and Croyde. The site is one mile on the right.

BRENTWOOD Essex   5D2

Camping & Caravanning Club Site
Warren Lane, Frog Street, Kelvedon Hatch, Brentwood CM15 0JD
📞 **01277-372773**
Open March-September ▲ 🚐 🚎
Size 12 acres, 150 touring pitches, 60 with electric hookup, 6 ☂, 15 WCs, 1 CWP
£ car/tent £8.75-£11.55, car/caravan £8.75-£11.55, motorhome £8.75-£11.55, motorbike/tent £8.75, children £1.40
℃ MasterCard Visa
📞 ⚠ ☒ ♿ 🐕 WS
Last arrival time: 11:00

BRIDGNORTH Shropshire   7E3

Park Grange
Morville, Bridgnorth WV16 4RN
📞 **01746-714285**
Open all year 🚐 🚎

Size 12 acres, 5 touring pitches, 5 level pitches, 4 static caravans
£ car/caravan £5-£6, motorhome £5-£6
Rental 🚐 caravans £95-£260
📋 ⚠ ☒ 🐕
Last arrival time: 8:00
➡ Signposted from A458.

BRIDGWATER Somerset   3E2

Fairways International Touring Caravan & Camping Site
Bath Road, Bawdrip, Bridgwater TA7 8PP
📞 **01278-685569**
Open 1 March-15 November ▲ 🚐 🚎

A purpose built caravan park set in rural Somerset, on the edge of the Polden Hills.

Size 6 acres, 200 touring pitches, 132 with electric hookup, 200 level pitches, 13 ☂, 20 WCs, 1 CWP
£ car/tent £6-£9, car/caravan £6-£9, motorhome £6-£9, motorbike/tent £6, children £0.60
℃ MasterCard Visa
📞 ✗¼ 🚐¼ 🍴 📞 🍴 📺 ⚠ ☒ Calor Gaz ♿ 🐕 WS
➡ Site situated at junction of A39 and B3141, behind BP Garage.
See advert on next page

Mill Farm Caravan & Camping Park
Fiddington, Bridgwater TA5 1JQ
📞 **01278-732286**
Open all year ▲ 🚐 🚎   ➡

← Mill Farm Caravan & Camping Park

Inland family holiday park situated in a picturesque valley between the beautiful Quantock Hills and the sea. Children's paradise, swimming pool with slides, boating, riding, large sandpit, games and TV rooms, trampolines, holiday cottage.

Size 10 acres, 125 touring pitches, 125 with electric hookup, 125 level pitches, 18 ☕, 56 WCs, 3 CWPs
£ car/tent £6-£8, car/caravan £6-£8, motorhome £6-£8, motorbike/tent £6, children £0.50
Calor Gaz WS
→ Leave M5 at Bridgwater, junction 23 or 24, take A39 west for 6 miles. Turn right to Fiddington, then follow camping signs. Camp is 1 mile from main road.

BRIDLINGTON East Yorkshire   11F3

Barmston Beach Holiday Park
Sands Lane, Barmston, Driffield, Bridlington YO25 8PJ
☎ 01262-468202
Open Easter-end September Å
Size 23 acres, 16 touring pitches, 8 with electric hookup, 16 level pitches, 300 static caravans, 20 ☕, 13 WCs
→ Take the main A165 road from Bridlington to Kingston-upon-Hull. The turning to Barmston is signposted about six miles S of Bridlington.

Shirley Caravan Park
Jewison Lane, Sewerby, Bridlington YO16 5YG
☎ 01262-676442 Fax 01388-834550

Open 1 March-30 November 🚐 🚙
Size 25 acres, 46 touring pitches, 46 with electric hookup, 46 level pitches, 410 static caravans, 12 🚿, 26 WCs
£ car/caravan £7.50-£8.50, motorhome £7.50-£8.50
Rental 🚐 £95-£275
🛒 ✗ 🛏 🖺 📞 🖥 🄶🅁 🅰 🅇 🍴 Calor ♿ 🐕
➡ At roundabout on A165 take B1255 to Flamborough for two miles. Left on to unclassified road signed Jewison Lane and Bempton. Site is ¼ mile on left.

Thorpe Hall Caravan Site
Rudston, Driffield YO25 0JE
📞 **01262-420393 Fax 01262-420588**
Open March-October 🅰 🚐 🚙

Quiet and sheltered within Thorpe Hall's kitchen garden's brick walls, in the beautiful East Riding countryside of the great Wold valley of the Gypsy race.

Size 4½ acres, 90 touring pitches, 53 with electric hookup, 6 🚿, 19 WCs, 1 CWP
£ car/tent £4.20-£8.30, car/caravan £4.70-£9.10, motorhome £4.70-£9.10
🛒 🖺 📞 🖥 🄳 🄶🅁 🅰 🅣🅥 🅇 Calor Gaz ♿ 🐕
Last arrival time: 10:00
➡ 4½ miles W of Bridlington on B1253

BRIDPORT Dorset   **3E3**

Binghams Farm Touring Caravan Park
Melplash, Bridport DT6 3TT
📞 **01308-488234**
Open all year 🅰 🚐 🚙
Size 3 acres, 60 touring pitches, 40 with electric hookup, 60 level pitches, 5 🚿, 7 WCs, 1 CWP

£ car/tent £8-£10.50, car/caravan £8-£10.50, motorhome £8-£10.50, motorbike/tent £8, children £0.50-£1
🖺 📞 🖥 🅁 🄶🅁 🅀 🅰 🅇 Calor Gaz ♿ 🐕
Last arrival time: 9:00
➡ From A35 at Bridport take A3066 to Beaminster. After 2 miles, turn left into Binghams Farm.

Eype House Caravan & Camping Park
Eype, Bridport DT6 6AL
📞 **01308-24903**
Open Easter-October 🅰 🚐 🚙

A small, quiet, family run park in an area of outstanding natural beauty, on the coastal path, with the beach only 300 yards away. Dogs welcome.

Size 4 acres, 20 touring pitches, 20 level pitches, 35 static caravans, 4 🚿, 10 WCs, 1 CWP
£ car/tent £5.50-£9.50, motorhome £5.50-£9.50, motorbike/tent £5.50
Rental 🚐 £85-£290
🛒 ✗¼ 🛏 🖺 📞 🄳 🄲 Calor Gaz 🐕
Last arrival time: 9:00
➡ A35 (1¼ miles from Bridport) signposted to Eypes Mouth.

Freshwater Beach Holiday Park
Burton Bradstock, Bridport DT6 4PT
📞 **01308-897317 Fax 01308-897336**
Open 21 March-9 November 🅰   ➡

← **Freshwater Beach**

Situated at the mouth of the River Bride with its own private beach, and nightly entertainment in the high season. A golf course adjoins the site.

Size 40 acres, 425 touring pitches, 171 with electric hookup, 425 level pitches, 250 static caravans, 34 ℞, 171 WCs, 4 CWPs
℃ MasterCard Visa
🐂 ✗ 🍴 📶 🔌 🔲 🏤 ⚠ 🔳 🔌 Calor Gaz ♿ 🐾
Last arrival time: 11:30
→ At Bridport take B3157 Weymouth road. Site entrance 1½ miles on right from Crown roundabout.

Highlands End Farm Holiday Park
Eype, Bridport DT6 6AR
📞 01308-422139 **Fax** 01308-425672
Open March-October ⛺ 🚐 🚍
Size 28 acres, 120 touring pitches, 120 with electric hookup, 120 level pitches, 160 static caravans, 15 ℞, 24 WCs, 2 CWPs
£ car/tent £7.50-£11.25, car/caravan £7.50-£11.25, motorhome £7.50-£11.25, motorbike/tent £7.50, children £1.25-£1.40
Rental 🚐
℃ MasterCard Visa
🐂 ✗ ✗¼ 🍴 🍴¼ 📶 🔌 🔲 🏤 🔳🔍 🏤 GR ⚠ 🔳 🔌 Calor Gaz ♿ 🐾
Last arrival time: 11:00
→ One mile W of Bridport on the A35. Turn S for the village of Eype at the picnic area.

West Bay Holiday Park
West Bay, Bridport DT6 4HB
📞 01308-422424 **Fax** 01308-421371
Open Easter-end October
Size 26 acres, 150 touring pitches, 39 with electric hookup, 131 level pitches, 40 static caravans, 8 ℞, 24 WCs
℃ Visa
🍴 🔌 ♿
→ Leave the main Dorchester Road (A35) heading towards Bridport. Take the first exit at the first roundabout, second exit at the second roundabout into West Bay. The park is on your right.

BRIGHTON East Sussex	5D4

Downsview Caravan Park
Bramlands Lane, Woodmancote, Henfield BN5 9TG
📞 01273-492801 **Fax** 01273-495214
Open mid March-mid November ⛺ 🚐 🚍
Size 4½ acres, 12 touring pitches, 12 with electric hookup, 12 level pitches, 24 static caravans, 4 ℞, 7 WCs, 1 CWP
Rental 🚐 Chalet.
℃ MasterCard Visa
🐂 📶 🔌 🔲 Calor Gaz 🐾 WS
Last arrival time: 9:00
→ Signed off A281 in village of Woodmancote, 2½ miles E of Henfield, 6½ miles N of Brighton.

BRISTOL	3E1

Brook Lodge Camping & Caravan Park
Cowslip Green, Redhill, Bristol BS18 7RD
📞 01934-862311
Open 1 March-31 October ⛺ 🚐 🚍
Size 3.2 acres, 29 touring pitches, 25 with electric hookup, 29 level pitches, 4 ℞, 8 WCs, 1 CWP
£ car/tent £7.50-£9.50, car/caravan £8-£9.50, motorhome £8-£9.50, motorbike/tent £7.50
Rental 🚐 Chalet.
🐂 📶 🔌 🔲 🏤 ⚠ 🔳 Calor WS
Last arrival time: 11:00

➜ From Bristol take A38 SW for 9½ miles, park signposted on left. From Bath take A4 to Bristol and turn left at Southern Ring Road onto A38. From M5 S junction 19 take A369/B3129/B3130 to A38, 3 miles S.

Salthouse Farm Caravan Site
Severn Beach, Bristol
📞 **01179-632274**
Open 1 April-end October 🅰 ⛺ 🚐

Set in a farm courtyard with level, grassy pitches. Located 200 yards off the main road, beside the estuary and close to the new Severn Bridge.

Size 8 acres, 60 touring pitches, 20 with electric hookup, 60 level pitches, 30 static caravans, 6 ♠, 9 WCs, 1 CWP
£ car/tent £7-£7.50, car/caravan £7-£7.50, motorhome £7-£7.50, motorbike/tent £6.50, children £0.90
🛒¼ ✗¼ ☔¼ ⊟ 📞 ⊟ 🔲 ⚠ 🏠 Calor Gaz ♿ 🐾 WS
Last arrival time: 10:00
➜ From M5 junction 17 take B4055 for three miles to Pilning, straight across traffic lights to B4064. Entrance one mile on right.

BRIXHAM Devon   3D4

Galmpton Touring Park
Greenway Road, Galmpton, Brixham TQ5 OEP.
📞 **01803-842066 Fax 01803-844405**
Open Easter-End of Sept 🅰 ⛺ 🚐

A family park enjoying spectacular views over the River Dart from the heart of Torbay. Close to the beach and attractions.

Size 10 acres, 120 touring pitches, 60 with electric hookup, 10 ♠, 18 WCs, 1 CWP
Rental Chalet.
🛒 ✗¼ ⊟ 📞 ⊟ ⚠ 🏠 Calor Gaz ♿
Last arrival time: 10:00
➜ A380 Torbay ring road to A3022 Paignton-Brixham coast road. Right towards Brixham then take second right to Manor Vale Road. Site is 500 yards on right after school park.

Upton Manor Farm Camping Site
St Mary's Road, Brixham TQ5 9QH
📞 **01803-882384 Fax 01803-882384**
Open May-September 🅰 ⛺ 🚐
Size 10 acres, 250 touring pitches, 250 level pitches, 20 ♠, 20 WCs, 1 CWP
£ car/tent £6.20-£8.50, car/caravan £6.20-£8.50, motorhome £6.20-£8.50, motorbike/tent £6.20, children £1-£1.25
🛒 ✗ ☔ ⊟ 📞 ⊟ 🔳 🔲 🏠 🅖🆁 🔲 📺 ⚠ 🏠 🔌 Calor Gaz 🐾
Last arrival time: 9:00
➜ From Brixham town centre, turn right into Bolton Street and continue until the next traffic lights (½ mile). Take the second turning on the left into Castor Road leading to St. Mary's Road.

BROADWAY Worcestershire   7F4

Leedons Park
Childswickham Road, Broadway WR12 7HB
☎ 01386-852423
Open all year 🅰 🚐 🚏
Size 40 acres, 400 touring pitches, 200 with
electric hookup, 400 level pitches, 22 🚿, 22
WCs, 1 CWP
➡ Signposted off A44 Broadway to Evesham
road. 1 mile from Broadway village.

BROMYARD Worcestershire   7E3

Boyce Caravan Park
Stanford Bishop, Bringsty WR6 5UB
☎ 01885-483439
Open March-December 🅰 🚐 🚏

*A peaceful, family run, top grade farm park
ideal for exploring the Heart of England and
the Welsh Border Country. Coarse fishing
available.*

Size 10 acres, 24 touring pitches, 10 with
electric hookup, 24 level pitches, 70 static
caravans, 6 🚿, 12 WCs, 1 CWP
£ car/tent £7.50, car/caravan £7.50,
motorhome £7.50, motorbike/tent £7.50
✗¼ 🔲 📞 🔲 🔲 ⚠ 🔲 Calor Gaz ⚙ ☂
Last arrival time: 6:00
➡ Take B4220 (Bromyard to Malvern). After
1¾ miles turn sharp left at Linley Green
signpost, then turn right and follow the signs.

Budemeadows Touring Holiday Park
Poundstock, Bude EX23 0NA
☎ 01288-361646
Open all year ▲ ⊕ ⇌
Size 10 acres, 100 touring pitches, 52 with electric hookup, 7 🚿, 16 WCs, 1 CWP
£ car/tent £7.20-£10, car/caravan £7.20-£10, motorhome £7.20-£10, motorbike/tent £7.20, children £1.80-£2.50
Rental Chalet. £200 to £350
CC MasterCard Visa
🛒 🚫 🗑 🔌 🗄 🔲 GR 🔍 ⚠ 🎯 Calor Gaz ♿ 🐴 WS
Last arrival time: 12:00
➡ Three miles S of Bude on A39.

Camping & Caravanning Club Site
Gillards Moor, St Gennys, Bude
☎ 01840-230650
Open end March-end September ▲ ⊕ ⇌
Size 100 touring pitches, 9 with electric hookup, 5 🚿, 10 WCs, 1 CWP
£ car/tent £8.75-£11.55, car/caravan £8.75-£11.55, motorhome £8.75-£11.55, motorbike/tent £8.75, children £1.40
CC MasterCard Visa
🗑 🔌 ⚠ 🎯 🐴
Last arrival time: 11:00
➡ From Wadebridge heading N on A39 towards Bude. Site is on left, signposted.

Cornish Coasts Caravan Park
Middle Penlean, Poundstock, Widemouth Bay, Bude EX23 0EE
☎ 01288-361380
Open 1 April-31 October ▲ ⊕ ⇌
Size 4 acres, 78 touring pitches, 12 with electric hookup, 50 level pitches, 3 static caravans, 4 🚿, 5 WCs, 1 CWP
£ car/tent £5.50-£6.50, car/caravan £5.50-£6.50, motorhome £5.50-£6.50, motorbike/tent £5.50, children £0.80-£1
Rental ⊕ £50-£225
🛒 🚫 🗑 🔌 🔲 ⚠ 🎯 Calor Gaz 🐴 WS
Last arrival time: 9:00
➡ On the coastal side of the A39, 5½ miles S of Bude. ½ mile S of Treskinnick Cross. Good access from layby.

Hedley Wood Caravan & Camping Park
Bridgerule, Bude EX22 7ED
☎ 01288-381404 Fax 01288-381909 ➡

← **Hedley Wood Caravan & Camping Park**

Size 16½ acres, 120 touring pitches, 110 with electric hookup, 60 level pitches, 12 static caravans, 12 ⓕ, 14 WCs, 2 CWPs
£ car/tent £5.50-£8.50, car/caravan £5.50-£8.50, motorhome £5.50-£8.50, motorbike/tent £5.50, children £0.75-£1
Rental ⊞
⏚ ✕ ☞ ⊡ ⓚ ⒢⒭ ⑆ ⚊ ✾ Calor Gaz ⌇ WS
➡ From A3072 (midway between Holsworthy and Bude), at red post and roads, turn S on the B3254 for 2½ miles, turn right, the site is in 500 yards.

Red Post Inn & Holiday Park
Launcells, Bude EX23 9NW
☎ **01288-81305**
Open Easter-end October ⚊ ⊞ ☷
Size 4 acres, 50 touring pitches, 11 with electric hookup, 50 level pitches, 4 ⓕ, 5 WCs, 1 CWP
£ car/tent £5-£7.50, car/caravan £5-£7.50, motorhome £5-£7.50, motorbike/tent £5
⒞⒞ Visa

⏚ ⏚¼ ✕ ☞ ⓚ ⊡ ⑆ ⌂ ☷ ♿ ⌇
Last arrival time: 11:00
➡ From junction of A39 and A3072 at Stratton, travel E on A3072 to Red Post (three miles) to site on right.

Widemouth Bay Caravan Park
Widemouth Bay, Bude
☎ **01288-361208**
Open March-October ⚊ ⊞ ☷
Size 56 acres, 80 with electric hookup, 140 static caravans
£ car/tent £4-£8, car/caravan £5-£10.50, motorhome £5-£10.50, motorbike/tent £4
Rental ⊞
⒞⒞ MasterCard Visa
⏚ ✕ ☞ ⊡ ⓚ ⑃ ⌂ ☷ Calor ⌇
Last arrival time: 10:00
➡ Take A39 past Bude and turn right to Widemouth Bay. Turning to Millook in Widemouth Bay.

LADRAM BAY

HOLIDAY CENTRE

BUDLEIGH, SALTERTON, DEVON EX9 7BX
Tel: 01395 568398 Fax: 01395 568338

Ladram Bay is a family owned coastal site situated between Budleigh Salterton and Sidmouth. It offers a very unique setting for a quiet relaxing holiday.

On site facilities include: Private beach, indoor heated pool and toddlers' pool. Supermarket

and Gift Shop, Cafe and take-away. Pub with free family entertainment* and Kiddies Club*, Doctor's Surgery*. Boat launching facility.

Tent sites are on well main-tained grass terraces, most with good sea views. Touring caravans can also take advantage of these

views or book one of our electric hook up sites. Showers and hot water supply are free.

We also have static caravans available for hire.

During peak season only.

For a free colour brochure contact:
LADRAM BAY HOLIDAY CENTRE
BUDLEIGH SALTERTON, DEVON EX9 7BX
Telephone: 01395 568398

Wooda Farm Caravan & Camping Park

Wooda Farm, Poughill, Bude EX23 9HJ
📞 01288-352069 Fax 01288-355258
Open April-October Å ⏴⏵ 🚐

A quiet, family run farm park, overlooking Bude Bay and the countryside. Excellent for touring and camping. Luxury holiday homes for hire. Sandy beaches one and a half miles. 'Splash' indoor pool nearby.

Size 15 acres, 200 touring pitches, 122 with electric hookup, 100 level pitches, 54 static caravans, 22 🏠, 36 WCs, 2 CWPs

£ car/tent £6-£9.50, car/caravan £6-£9.50, motorhome £6-£9.50, motorbike/tent £6, children £0.50-£1
Rental ⏴⏵ £99-£395
℅ MasterCard Visa
🔋 ✗ ⛟ ⊡ 📞 ▶📺 🗂 ♨ 🔲 GR 🔍 📺 🔼 🔲 🔌
Calor Gaz 🐕 WS
Last arrival time: 9:00
➡ From A39 at Stratton take road to Poughill/Coombe Valley. Drive 1 mile through crossroads. Wooda is 200 yards on right.

Ladram Bay Holiday Centre

Budleigh Salterton, Budleigh Salterton EX9 7BX
📞 01395-568398 Fax 01395-568338
Open 1 April-30 September Å ⏴⏵ 🚐
Size 52 acres, 304 touring pitches, 35 with electric hookup, 474 static caravans, 12 🏠, 52 WCs, 1 CWP
£ car/tent £7-£14, car/caravan £8-£12, motorhome £7-£10, motorbike/tent £6
Rental ⏴⏵

CC MasterCard Visa
🦵 ✗ 📭 🖥 📱 📳 🎰 ⚠ 🖾 🔌 Calor Gaz 🛒
Last arrival time: 8:00
➡ Two miles N of Budleigh Salterton on B3178, turn E into Otterton. Ladram Bay is signposted.
See advert on page 31

Outney Meadow Caravan Park
Bungay NR35 1HG
📱 **01986-892338**
Size 8 acres, 45 touring pitches, 45 with electric hookup, 45 level pitches, 4 🚿, 8 WCs, 1 CWP
📱 🗑 Calor Gaz WS
Last arrival time: 10:00
➡ Park is signposted from A144/A143 junction.

Diamond Farm Caravan & Touring Park
Weston Road, Brean, Burnham on Sea
📱 **01278-751041**
Open March-October 🛆 🚐 🚌
Size 5 acres, 100 touring pitches, 100 with electric hookup, 120 level pitches, 12 🚿, 28 WCs, 1 CWP
£ car/tent £4-£8, car/caravan £4-£8, motorhome £4-£8, motorbike/tent £4
🦵 🦵¼ ✗ ✗¼ 📭 📭¼ 🖥 📱 🗑 🖾 ⚠ 🖾 Calor Gaz ♿ 🛒 WS
➡ From M5 junction 22 take B3139 to Brean. Through village and site is 2 miles down coast road.

Home Farm Holidays
Edithmead, Burnham-on-Sea TA9 4HD
📱 **01278-788888** Fax **01278-792365**

Size 40 acres, 850 touring pitches, 750 with electric hookup, 850 level pitches, 34 🚿, 48 WCs, 2 CWPs
CC Visa
🦵 ✗ 📭 🔌 ♿
➡ ½ mile from M5 junction 22.

Cottage Farm Caravan Park
Blackwell In The Peak, Taddington, Buxton SK17 9TQ
📱 **01298-85330**
Open 1 March-31 October 🛆 🚐 🚌
Extra space for tents and motor caravans. 24 level hardstandings. Winter opening with tap and hook-up.

Size 3 acres, 29 touring pitches, 30 with electric hookup, 24 level pitches, 1 static caravans, 5 🚿, 5 WCs, 1 CWP
£ car/tent £5.50-£6.50, car/caravan £6, motorhome £5.50, children £0.50
🦵 📱 Calor Gaz 🛒
➡ Six miles from Buxton on A6 to Bakewell. Turn left on unclassified road. Signposted.

Pomeroy Caravan & Camping Park
Street House Farm, Pomeroy, Flagg, Buxton SK17 9QG
📱 **01298-83259**
Open Easter/April-October 🛆 🚐 🚌

A well maintained level park adjoining the High Peak Trail with a large rally field available. Good access from the A515.

Size 2 acres, 30 touring pitches, 24 with electric hookup, 30 level pitches, 1 static caravans, 4 🚿, 6 WCs, 1 CWP
£ car/tent £4.50-£6, car/caravan £5.50-£6, motorhome £5-£5.50, motorbike/tent £4.50, children £0.50
Rental 🚐
✗¼ 📭¼ 🖥 🗑 Calor Gaz 🛒
Last arrival time: 10:00
➡ On A515 Buxton/Ashbourne road. Five miles from Buxton, 16 miles from Ashbourne. Entrance over double cattle grid with 100 yards of tarmac drive to site.

Old Hall Caravan Park
High Street, Caister-on-Sea NR30 5JL
☎ 01493-720400
Open Easter-October ⚑ 🚐 🚏

*A small family park with outstanding
facilities including free swimming pool.
Close to beach, Great Yarmouth and Norfolk
Broads - an ideal base for touring.*

Size 4 acres, 30 touring pitches, 30 with
electric hookup, 30 level pitches, 33 static
caravans, 6 🚿, 9 WCs, 1 CWP
Rental 🚐 Chalet.
℄ MasterCard Visa
🛁¼ ✗ 🛒 🔲 🛎 🗃 🔳 🖾 GR Ⓜ 🎌 🔌 Calor
Last arrival time: 11:00
➜ Take A149 out of Great Yarmouth, follow
tourist road signs from Yarmouth Stadium.
Park is opposite Caister church.

Scratby Hall Caravan Park
Scratby, Caister-on-Sea NR29 3PH
☎ 01493-730283
Open Easter-mid October ⚑ 🚐 🚏

*Quiet, well-kept, level, grassy site near the
sea with children's playground, shop,
payphone and disabled facilities.*

Size 4½ acres, 108 touring pitches, 64 with
electric hookup, 108 level pitches, 10 🚿, 18
WCs, 1 CWP
£ car/tent £4.25-£9.50, car/caravan £4.25-
£9.50, motorhome £4.25-£9.50,
motorbike/tent £4.25
🛁 ✗¼ 🛒¼ 🔲 🛎 🗃 GR Ⓜ 🎌 Calor Gaz ♿ 🐕
Last arrival time: 10:00
➜ At roundabout, junction of A149 and
B1159, 1½ miles N of Caister, turn N along
B1159 for 1 mile to site on the left.

Blackland Lakes Holiday & Leisure Centre
Stockley Lane, Calne SN11 0NQ
☎ 01249-813672 **Fax** 01249-813672
Open all year ⚑ 🚐 🚏

*An interesting family run site in a scenic
location, ideal children. Bikes, kitchen with
Turkish oven and licensed bar for groups all
available. New 20 x 10m covered swimming
pool, and 15 'Superpitches'. Colour
brochure. Bookings advised.*

Size 17 acres, 180 touring pitches, 120 with
electric hookup, 100 level pitches, 13 🚿, 23
WCs, 2 CWPs
£ car/tent £6.75-£7.80, car/caravan £7-£7.80,
motorhome £7-£7.80, motorbike/tent £6.75,
children £0.55-£0.60
🛁 🔲 🛎 🛎 🗃 🖾🖉 GR 🔍 📺 Ⓜ 🎌 Calor Gaz ♿
🐕 WS
Last arrival time: 11:00
➜ Signposted from the A4 E of Calne.

Moor Farm Trailer Park

Calverton
☎ 01602-652426
Open all year Å ⊕ ⊅
Size 35 acres, 60 touring pitches, 45 with electric hookup, 8 ⁿ, 12 WCs, 2 CWPs
£ car/tent £5.75-£6.80, car/caravan £5.75-£6.80, motorhome £5.75-£6.80, motorbike/tent £5.75
Rental ⊕ from £175 per week, linen £10 a week extra
≗ ✕¼ ✇¼ ▤ ☏ ▱ Calor ⋔
➡ Moor Farm is 6 miles N of Nottingham next to Calverton golf course.

Magor Farm Caravan Site

Tehidy, Cambourne TR14 0JF
☎ 01209-713367
Open April- Easter Å ⊕ ⊅
Size 160 touring pitches, 160 level pitches
£ car/tent £6-£6.50, car/caravan £6
CC Visa
▨ ⋔
➡ At the junction of A30 and A3047, W of Cambourne, travel N on unclassified road for 1½ miles.

Camping & Caravanning Club Site

Behind 19 Cabbage Moor, Great Shelford, Cambridge CB2 5NB
☎ 01223-841185
Open end March-start November Å ⊕ ⊅
Size 12 acres, 120 touring pitches, 58 with electric hookup, 8 ⁿ, 11 WCs, 1 CWP
£ car/tent £9.20-£12.05, car/caravan £9.20-£12.05, motorhome £9.20-£12.05, motorbike/tent £9.20, children £1.40
CC MasterCard Visa
≗ ▤ ☏ ⚠ ⊞ ⧖ ⋔ WS
Last arrival time: 11:00
➡ From M11 junction 11 turn N onto A10. At traffic lights turn right onto A1301 for ¼ mile to site on left.

Highfield Farm Camping Park

Long Road, Comberton, Cambridge CB3 7DG
☎ 01223-262308 **Fax** 01223-262308
Open 1 April-31 October Å ⊕ ⊅

A popular award winning park with an exellent grading, close to the historic university city of Cambridge. Other nearby attractions include the Imperial War Museum at Duxford and Wimpole Hall.

Size 8 acres, 120 touring pitches, 100 with electric hookup, 80 level pitches, 16 ⁿ, 23 WCs, 3 CWPs
£ car/tent £6.75-£8, car/caravan £7-£8.25, motorhome £6.75-£8, motorbike/tent £5.75, children £1-£1.50
≗ ▤ ☏ ☐ ⚠ ⊞ Calor Gaz ⋔
Last arrival time: 10:00
➡ From M11 junction 12 take A603 to Sandy for ½ mile, then turn right on B1046 to Comberton. From A428 leave at Hardwick roundabout and follow signs to Comberton.

Roseberry Tourist Park

Earith Road, Willingham, Cambridge CB4 5LT
☎ 01954-260346
Open Easter-October Å ⊕ ⊅
Size 10 acres, 80 touring pitches, 80 with electric hookup, 80 level pitches, 3 static caravans, 6 ⁿ, 12 WCs, 1 CWP
£ car/tent £6.50, car/caravan £6.50, motorhome £6, motorbike/tent £6, children £1
Rental ⊕ Chalet. £80-£100
≗ ▤ ☏ ☐ ⚠ ⊞ Calor Gaz ⧖ ⋔ WS
➡ Leave M11 at junction 16 (Bar Hill) onto the B1050. Site on left after 6 miles (1 mile after Willingham).

Stanford Park Camping and Caravanning

Weirs Road, Burwell, Cambridge CB5 OBP
☎ 01638-741547 ℻ 01638-743508
Open all year ▲ ⚑ ♨
Size 20 acres, 120 touring pitches, 40 with electric hookup, 120 level pitches, 3 static caravans, 5 ♟, 13 WCs, 1 CWP
£ car/tent £7.50-£9, car/caravan £7.50-£9, motorhome £7.50-£9, motorbike/tent £7.50
Rental ⚑ £100-£120
♨¼ ✗¼ ⬤¼ 🗄 🔌 🗄 ⚠ 🎍 Calor Gaz ♿ 🐾 WS
Last arrival time: 8:00
➜ From Cambridge at Stow Cum Quy roundabout take B1102 to Burwell. From Newmarket turn off A14 onto A142 following the signs to Burwell via Exning.

Camping & Caravanning Club Site

Bekesbourne Lane, Canterbury CT3 4AB
☎ 01227-463216
Open all year ▲ ⚑ ♨
Size 20 acres, 210 touring pitches, 53 with electric hookup, 20 ♟, 23 WCs, 1 CWP
£ car/tent £9.20-£12.05, car/caravan £9.20-£12.05, motorhome £9.20-£12.05, motorbike/tent £9.20, children £1.40
ℂℂ MasterCard Visa
♨ 🗄 🔌 ⚠ 🎍 🐾
Last arrival time: 11:00
➜ At 1½ miles E of Canterbury centre on A257 to Sandwich. Turn opposite Canterbury Golf Club.

Red Lion Caravan Park

Old London Road, Dunkirk, Canterbury ME13 9LL
☎ 01227-750661
⚑ ♨
Size 1 acres, 25 touring pitches, 12 with electric hookup, 11 level pitches, 2 ♟, 5 WCs, 1 CWP
£ car/caravan £7, motorhome £7, children £1
♨¼ ✗¼ ⬤¼ 🔌 🐾 WS
➜ From A2 London bound follow signs. Turn off ½ mile at Dunkirk. From A2 Dover bound take Dunkirk turning immediately after joining from M2 junction 7. Follow signs. Car park 3 miles.

THE COUNTRY CODE

- Enjoy the countryside and respect its life and work
- Guard against all risk of fire
- Keep your dogs under close control
- Keep to the public paths across farmland
- Use gates and stiles to cross fences, hedges and walls
- Leave livestock, crops and machinery alone
- Take your litter home
- Help to keep all water clean
- Protect wildlife, plants and trees
- Take special care on country roads
- Make no unnecessary noise

South View Caravan Park
Maypole Lane, Hoath, Canterbury CT3 4LL
☎ 01227-860280
Open all year ▲ ⬅ ⇋
Size 3 acres, 45 touring pitches, 28 with electric hookup, 45 level pitches, 4 ℟, 8 WCs, 1 CWP
£ car/tent £8.50, car/caravan £8.50, motorhome £8.50, motorbike/tent £8.50, children £1
⯊¼ ✗¼ ⯗¼ ▣ ☎ ▯ Calor ♿ WS
➜ Well signed off the A28 and A299.

Dalston Hall Caravan Park
Dalston Road, Carlisle CA5 7J
☎ 01228-710165
Open 1 March-31 October ▲ ⬅ ⇋
Size 4½ acres, 40 touring pitches, 40 with electric hookup, 40 level pitches, 17 static caravans, 4 ℟, 15 WCs, 1 CWP
£ car/tent £5.50-£6, car/caravan £6.50-£7, motorhome £6.50-£7, motorbike/tent £5.50, children £0.75
⯊ ✗ ⯗ ▣ ☎ ▯ ▣/⚠ ✚ ⊕ Calor Gaz ✝ WS
Last arrival time: 9:00
➜ Leave the M6 at junction 42 and follow the sign for Dalston. Turn right for Carlisle and the site is on the right after 1½ miles.

Dandy Dinmont Caravan & Camping Park
Blackford, Carlisle CA6 4EA
☎ 01228-74611
Open 1 March-31 October ▲ ⬅ ⇋

A quiet rural park yet only 1½ miles north of the M6 (44). A good overnight halt or a base for a longer stay to visit the Lake

District, historic Carlisle, Roman Wall or Romantic Scottish Border.

Size 4½ acres, 27 touring pitches, 20 with electric hookup, 27 level pitches, 4 ℟, 14 WCs, 1 CWP
£ car/tent £5.50-£6, car/caravan £6.75-£7, motorhome £6.75-£7, motorbike/tent £5.50
▣ ☎ ▯ Calor
➜ Just N of Carlisle leave M6 at junction 44 and take A7 Galashiels road. From here the park is approximately 1½ miles on the right. After Blackford village sign, follow the road directional signs to the park.

New House Farm
Newby West, Carlisle CA2 6QZ
☎ 01228-23545
Open Easter-October
Size 1 acre, 2 static caravans, 2 ℟, 2 WCs, 2 CWPs
Rental ⬅ £65-£75
⯊¼ ⯗¼ Calor ✝
➜ 8 miles from M6 (jn 42). Very rural area so please phone or send an S.A.E. for directions in full.

Orton Grange Caravan Park
Wigton Road, Carlisle CA5 6LA
☎ 01228-710252 Fax 01228-710252
Open all year ▲ ⬅ ⇋
Size 7 acres, 50 touring pitches, 30 with electric hookup, 50 level pitches, 22 static caravans, 6 ℟, 11 WCs, 1 CWP
£ car/tent £6.60-£8, car/caravan £6.60-£8, motorhome £6.60-£8, motorbike/tent £4.40, children £0.60-£0.80
Rental ⬅ £99-£175
⣏ MasterCard Visa
⯊ ✗¼ ▣ ☎ ▯ ▣ ⒼⓇ ⓉⓋ ⚠ ✚ Calor Gaz ♿ ✝ WS
Last arrival time: 10:00
➜ 4 miles W of Carlisle on A595.

Detron Gate Caravan Site
Bolton-le-Sands, Carnforth LA5 9TN
☎ 01524-732842
Open 1 March-30 September ▲ ⬅ ⇋
Size 10 acres, 150 touring pitches, 98 with electric hookup, 50 level pitches, 42 static caravans, 12 ℟, 18 WCs, 2 CWPs　　➜

← **Detron Gate Caravan Site**

£ car/tent £4, car/caravan £6, motorhome £6, motorbike/tent £4, children £0.75
⚡ 🔲 📞 🔲 GR 🔲 ⚠ 🗓 Calor Gaz ⚲
Last arrival time: 10:00
➡ 1½ miles S of Carnforth on A6 turn W into Mill Lane, continue to sea, site on left.

Sandside Caravan & Camping Site
The Shore, Bolton-le-Sands, Carnforth LA5 8JS
📞 **01524-822311 Fax 01524-822311**
Open 1 March- 31 October ⛺ 🚐 🚚
Size 6 acres, 130 touring pitches, 100 with electric hookup, 55 level pitches, 35 static caravans, 10 🚿, 18 WCs, 2 CWPs
£ car/tent £8-£12, car/caravan £8-£12, motorhome £8-£12, motorbike/tent £8
Ⅽ MasterCard Visa
⚡ ✗¼ ☂¼ 🔲 📞 🔲 Calor ⚲
Last arrival time: 10:00
➡ From junction 35 follow signs for Morecambe, after 3 miles turn right at Little Chef for a further ½ mile. Entrance on right hand side.

CASTLE DONINGTON Leicestershire 7F2

Park Farmhouse Caravan Site
Melbourne Road, Isley Walton, Castle Donington DE74 2RN
📞 **01332-862409 Fax 01332-862364**
⛺ 🚐 🚚

Well screened grassland site adjacent mature woods in farmhouse hotel grounds. Perfect base for touring southern Derbyshire.

Size 8 acres, 60 touring pitches, 40 with electric hookup, 45 level pitches, 3 🚿, 10 WCs, 2 CWPs

£ car/tent £5-£8, car/caravan £7-£12, motorhome £7-£12, motorbike/tent £5, children £1
Ⅽ MasterCard Visa
✗ ☂ 📞 🔳 🗓 Calor Gaz ⅋ ⚲ WS
Last arrival time: 9:00
➡ Take the Melbourne turn at Isley Walton on the A453 and the site is ½ mile on the right.

CASTLE HOWARD North Yorkshire 11E3

Castle Howard Caravan Site
Coneysthorpe, Castle Howard YO6 7DD
📞 **01653-648444 Fax 01653-648462**
Open 1 March-31 October ⛺ 🚐 🚚
Size 17 acres, 70 touring pitches, 34 with electric hookup, 70 level pitches, 120 static caravans, 6 🚿, 15 WCs, 2 CWPs
£ car/tent £6.80-£7, car/caravan £6.80-£7, motorhome £6.80-£7, motorbike/tent £6.80
⚡ ⚡¼ 🔲 📞 🔳 📋 Calor ⅋ ⚲ WS
Last arrival time: 9:00
➡ 15 miles NE of York off A64 (on York-Scarborough road).

CHARMOUTH Dorset 3E3

Manor Farm Holiday Centre
Charmouth DT6 6QL
📞 **01297-560226 Fax 01297-560429**
Open all year ⛺ 🚐 🚚

A large, open site in an area of outstanding natural beauty at Charmouth. A 10 minute level walk to a beach famous for its fossils and safe for bathing.

Size 32 acres, 302 touring pitches, 30 with electric hookup, 100 level pitches, 15 static caravans, 30 ☔, 42 WCs, 2 CWPs
£ car/tent £6.50-£9, car/caravan £6.50-£9, motorhome £6.50-£9, motorbike/tent £6.50, children £1
Rental ⚅
CC MasterCard Visa
🏕 🏕¼ ✗ ✗¼ ⬤ ⬤¼ ⊟ ⬤ ⊟ ⊡ GR ⌂ ⊞ ⊟
Calor Gaz ♿ ⚓ WS
Last arrival time: 11:00
➜ On A35 travelling west 6 miles W of Bridport enter Charmouth. Manor Farm is ¾ mile on the right in Charmouth.

Wood Farm Caravan & Camping Park
Axminster Road, Charmouth DT6 6BT
📞 01297-560697 **Fax** 01297-560697
Open 21 March-2 November ⚑ ⚅ ⛟

A family run park with exceptional facilities overlooking lovely Marshwood Vale and only threequarters of a mile to Charmouth's safe bathing beach. Tourist board grading - excellent.

Size 20 acres, 216 touring pitches, 175 with electric hookup, 100 level pitches, 80 static caravans, 18 ☔, 18 WCs, 4 CWPs
£ car/tent £7-£11.50, car/caravan £7-£11.50, motorhome £7-£11.50, motorbike/tent £7, children £1.10-£1.20
Rental ⚅ £155-£320
CC MasterCard Visa
🏕 ✗¼ ⬤ ⊟ ⬤ ⊡ ⊟ ⊞ ⊡ GR ⌂ ⊞ Calor Gaz ⚓
Last arrival time: 8:00
➜ 5 miles east of Axminster on A35, entrance off roundabout with A3052.

CHATHAM Kent 5E2

Woolmans Wood Tourist Caravan Park
Bridgewood, Chatham
📞 01634-867685
Open all year ⚑ ⚅ ⛟
Situated close to the London, Dover, Folkestone, Sheerness motorways (M2, M20), the park is a delightful spot from which to explore Kent and the southeast of England.

Size 5 acres, 60 touring pitches, 51 with electric hookup, 60 level pitches, 8 ☔, 10 WCs, 1 CWP
£ car/tent £9-£10.50, car/caravan £9-£10.50, motorhome £9-£10.50, motorbike/tent £8
Rental ⚅
CC MasterCard
🏕 ✗ ⬤ GR ⊡ ⌂ ⊞ ⊟ Calor Gaz ♿ WS
➜ From the M2 and M20, take the A229 towards Chatham. At the large roundabout, take the B2097. The park is ½ mile on the right.

CHEADLE Staffordshire 7E1

Hales Hall Caravan & Camping Park
Oakamoor Road, Cheadle ST10 1BU
📞 01538-753305 **Fax** 01782-202316
Open 1 March-30 October ⚑ ⚅ ⛟
Size 8 acres, 48 touring pitches, 30 with electric hookup, 10 level pitches, 4 ☔, 8 WCs, 3 CWPs
£ car/tent £6-£8, car/caravan £6-£8, motorhome £6-£8, motorbike/tent £6, children £1
🏕 ✗ ⬤ ⊟ ⬤ ⊟ ⊡ ⬤ ⌂ ⊞ ⊟ Calor Gaz ⚓ WS
➜ From Cheadle take the B5417 signposted Oakamoor. The site is ½ mile on the left.

CHEDDAR Somerset 3E1

Broadway House Caravan & Camping Park
Axbridge Road, Cheddar BS27 3DB
📞 01934-742610 **Fax** 01934-744950
Open March-November ⚑ ⚅ ⛟
Size 30 acres, 200 touring pitches, 190 with electric hookup, 200 level pitches, 35 static caravans, 20 ☔, 40 WCs, 2 CWPs ➜

← Broadway House

£ car/tent £4-£10, car/caravan £4-£10, motorhome £4-£10, motorbike/tent £4, children £0.50-£2
Rental 🚐 £105-£385
CC MasterCard Visa
🔌 💧 ▢ 🔋 ▢ 🔲 🔲 CR 🔍 TV 🏔 🔲 ⊑ Calor Gaz & 🐕
➜ Leave M5 at junction 22, and continue for 8 miles to park, following brown tourist signs to Cheddar Gorge and Caves.

Froglands Farm
Cheddar BS27 3RH
📞 01934-742058
Open Easter-October 🏕 🚐 🚍

A small, family site situated in an area of outstanding natural beauty, within walking distance of village shops, pubs, restaurants, swimming pool, leisure centre, gorge and caves.

Size 3 acres, 60 touring pitches, 30 with electric hookup, 50 level pitches, 6 🚿, 12 WCs, 1 CWP
£ car/tent £5-£8, car/caravan £7-£9, motorhome £6-£8
🔌 🔌¼ ✗¼ 🍴¼ ▢ 🔋 ▢ Calor Gaz & 🐕
Last arrival time: 10:30
➜ On the main A371 Wells/Cheddar road, 100 yards past Cheddar Church.

CHELTENHAM Gloucestershire   7E4

Briarfields Caravan & Camping
Gloucester Road, Cheltenham GLS10SX
📞 01242-235324 **Fax** 01242-235324
Open all year 🏕 🚐 🚍

A newly landscaped, six acre, level, grassy site with new toilet and shower blocks, including a custom-built disabled suite. Trees and shrubs afford privacy.

Size 6 acres, 72 touring pitches, 72 with electric hookup, 72 level pitches, 7 ℞, 11 WCs, 3 CWPs
£ car/tent £5-£6, car/caravan £6, motorhome £6, motorbike/tent £5
CC MasterCard Visa
🏊¼ ✕¼ 🍴¼ 🔲 🔌 Calor ♿ 🐕 WS
➜ Leave M5 at junction 11 and take A40 to roundabout. Take first exit off B4063 and Briarfields is 200 yards on left.

Longwillows C&C Park
Station Road, Woodmancote, Cheltenham GL52 4HN
📞 **01242-674113** Fax **01242-678731**
Open March-October ▲ �caravan 🚐
Size 4 acres, 80 touring pitches, 56 with electric hookup, 80 level pitches, 7 ℞, 14 WCs, 2 CWPs
£ car/tent £5.50-£6, car/caravan £5.50-£6, motorhome £5.50-£6, motorbike/tent £5.50
🏊¼ ✕ 🍴 🔲 🔌 🔌 🔲 🏊 🔲 🔳 Calor Gaz ♿ 🐕
Last arrival time: 11:00
➜ Turn off A435 at Bishop's Cleeve or B4632 at Southam, park is next to Staddlestones Restaurant.

Stansby Caravan Park
Reddings Road, The Reddings, Cheltenham GL51 6RS
📞 **01452-712168** Fax **01452-712168**
Open February-end year ▲ �caravan 🚐
Size 2¼ acres, 30 touring pitches, 26 with electric hookup, 30 level pitches, 2 ℞, 4 WCs, 1 CWP
£ car/tent £6-£6.50, car/caravan £6-£6.50, motorhome £6-£6.50, motorbike/tent £6, children £0.50
🏊¼ ✕¼ 🍴¼ 🔌 Calor Gaz 🐕
Last arrival time: 10:30

➜ From M5 junction 11 to Cheltenham. At first roundabout turn right and follow signs to site.

CHERTSEY Surrey 4C2

Camping & Caravanning Club Site
Bridge Road, Chertsey KT16 8JX
📞 **01932-562405**
Open end March-start November ▲ �caravan 🚐
Size 12 acres, 200 touring pitches, 96 with electric hookup, 12 ℞, 21 WCs, 1 CWP
£ car/tent £8.75-£11.55, car/caravan £8.75-£11.55, motorhome £8.75-£11.55, motorbike/tent £8.75, children £1.40
CC MasterCard Visa
🔲 🔌 🏊 🔳 ♿ 🐕 WS
Last arrival time: 11:00
➜ Leave M25 (jn 11) and follow signs to Chertsey. Site is 200 yards from Chertsey Bridge on B375.

CHESTER Cheshire 7D1

Chester Southerly Caravan Park
Balderton Lane, Marlston-cum-Lache, Chester CH4 9LF
📞 **01829-270697**
Open 1 March-30 November ▲ �caravan 🚐
Size 8 acres, 90 touring pitches, 65 with electric hookup, 90 level pitches, 8 ℞, 12 WCs, 1 CWP
£ car/tent £6-£8, car/caravan £6-£8, motorhome £6-£87, motorbike/tent £6, children £1.10-£1.20
🏊 🏊¼ ✕¼ 🍴¼ 🔲 🔌 🔲 🏊 🔳 Calor Gaz ♿ 🐕
Last arrival time: 9:00
➜ Leave A55 at A483 junction towards Wrexham. After 300 yards at roundabout double back to Balderton Lane.

CHICHESTER West Sussex 4C4

Camping & Caravanning Club Site
343 Main Road, Southbourne PO10 8JH
📞 **01243-373202**
Open end March-start November ▲ �caravan 🚐
Size 60 touring pitches
£ car/tent £8.75-£11.55, car/caravan £8.75-£11.55, motorhome £8.75-£11.55, motorbike/tent £8.75, children £1.40
CC MasterCard Visa
🔲 ♿ 🐕

➜

← Camping & Caravanning Club Site

Last arrival time: 11:00
→ From Chichester, heading W on A259, site is on right immediately before Travellers Joy pub.

Red House Farm
Earnley, Chichester PO20 7JG
☎ 01243-512959
Open April-October
Size 4 acres, 100 touring pitches, 100 level pitches, 4 ◉, 12 WCs, 1 CWP
Gaz ♿ WS
→ Take A286 from Chichester to Witterings. Turn left at Birdham garage onto B2198 to Bracklesham Bay. After ½ mile turn left again to Earnley on sharp right hand bend. Site is 500 yards on left.

Southern Leisure Centre
Vinnetrow Road, Chichester PO20 6LB
☎ 01243-787715 **Fax** 01243-533643
Open March-October ⛺ 🚐 🚍

A family holiday park set in 220 acres and amongst 12 lakes, excellent for watersports, heated outdoor pool, kids clubs, tennis and bowling included in the wide range of leisure facilities, restaurants and bars, entertainment. A 'British Holidays Park.'

Size 220 acres, 1500 touring pitches, 420 with electric hookup, 1500 level pitches, 900 static caravans, 32 ◉, 66 WCs, 5 CWPs
£ car/tent £5, car/caravan £6.50-£12.50, motorhome £6.50-£12.50, motorbike/tent £5, children £1.50
CC MasterCard Visa
🛒 🍽 🗑 ☎ 🗒 🌀 🛗 🅿 🍴 Calor Gaz ♿ 🐕 WS

→ At roundabout junction of A27 (Chichester by-pass) and A259, 1 mile SE of Chichester, turn into Vinnetrow Lane and it's ¼ mile to the park.

Camping & Caravanning Club Site
Chipping Norton Road, Chadlington, Chipping Norton
☎ 01608-641993
Open end March-start November ⛺ 🚐 🚍
Size 75 touring pitches, 50 with electric hookup, 4 ◉, 5 WCs, 1 CWP
£ car/tent £9.20-£12.05, car/caravan £9.20-£12.05, motorhome £9.20-£12.05, motorbike/tent £9.20, children £1.40
CC MasterCard Visa
🗑 ☎ ♿ 🐕
Last arrival time: 11:00

Hoburne Park
Christchurch BH23 4HU
☎ 01425-273379 **Fax** 01425-270705
Open March-October 🚐 🚍

A family holiday park with an extensive range of quality family and sporting entertainment facilities. Close to the beach, New Forest and Bournemouth.

Size 40 acres, 285 touring pitches, 285 with electric hookup, 285 level pitches, 287 static caravans, 23 ◉, 38 WCs, 4 CWPs
£ car/caravan £9.50-£22, motorhome £9.50-£22
CC MasterCard Visa
🛒 ✗ 🍽 🗑 ☎ 🗒 🌀 🛗 🅿 GR 📺 🍴 🏠 🅿
Calor ♿
Last arrival time: 9:00

➜ From Lyndhurst, take the A35 signed Bournemouth for 13 miles to the roundabout. Take the first exit left onto the A337, then take the first left at the roundabout. The site is 100 yards on the left.

CHUDLEIGH Devon   3D3

Finlake Leisure Park
Chudleigh TQ13 0EJ
☎ 01626-853833 Fax 01626-854031
Open all year ▲ ⊕ ⊅

Situated in a 130 acre park, encompassing hills, valleys, woodland and lakes. Facilities include indoor and outdoor pools with waterslide, tennis, bar, restaurant and entertainment.

Size 130 acres, 450 touring pitches, 360 with electric hookup, 450 level pitches, 40 ☞, 93 WCs,
£ car/tent £4-£12, car/caravan £5-£16, motorhome £5-£16, motorbike/tent £4
Rental Chalet.
⊄ MasterCard Visa
🐾 ✕ ☞ ⊡ ☎ ⊠ ⊠ ⊡☞ ☒ ⊿ GR ⋔ 🌣 ⊟
Calor Gaz ⛷ WS
➜ From A38 take the Chudleigh/Knighton exit (B3344). Site is 1½ miles on right.

Holmans Wood Tourist Park
Chudleigh TQ13 0DZ
☎ 01626-853785
Open March-end November ▲ ⊕ ⊅

Set amongst beautiful Devon countryside with breathtaking views on all sides, Holmans Wood is an immaculately well kept site. Peaceful and relaxing for all the family. Graded excellent. Winner of 1996 Calor award.

Size 20 acres, 125 touring pitches, 125 with electric hookup, 125 level pitches, 10 ☞, 15 WCs, 3 CWPs
£ car/tent £5.70-£7.95, car/caravan £5.70-£8.95, motorhome £5.70-£8.95, motorbike/tent £5.70, children £1.50
⊄ MasterCard Visa
🐾 ✕¼ ☞¼ ⊡ ⊠ ⊠ ⊡ ⋔ 🌣 Calor Gaz ⛷ ⛷ WS
Last arrival time: 11:00
➜ Follow M5 to Exeter and take A38 towards Plymouth. After the racecourse (about ½ mile on the left) is an exit signposted to Chudleigh. Site entrance is at end of this short slip road.

CHURCH STRETTON Shropshire   7D3

Small Batch Site
Ashes Valley, Little Stretton, Church Stretton SY6 6PW
☎ 01694-723358
Open 17 April-30 September ▲ ⊕ ⊅
Size 32 touring pitches, 1 ☞, 5 WCs, 1 CWP
£ car/tent £6, car/caravan £6, motorhome £6, motorbike/tent £6
🐾¼ ⛷
➜ Off A49 into Little Stretton, onto B4370. Left at Rogleth Inn and site is ¼ mile on right.

Cotswold Hoburne

Broadway Lane, South Cerney, Cirencester
GL7 5UQ
☎ **01285-860216** Fax **01285-862106**
Open Easter-31 October ⚠ 🚐 🚏

*Set in the Cotswold Water Park, this quality
site has fish-stocked lakes, a magnificent
indoor pool and a licensed lakeside lounge
with seasonal entertainment.*

Size 70 acres, 302 touring pitches, 302 with
electric hookup, 302 level pitches, 158 static
caravans, 18 ☂, 54 WCs, 6 CWPs
£ car/tent £9-£20, car/caravan £9-£20,
motorhome £9-£20
Rental 🚐 Chalet.
CC MasterCard Visa
🧺 ✗ 🍴 🖫 📞 🎱 📋 🖥 🎮 📷 📺 🎯 🏸 🔌
Calor Gaz ♿
Last arrival time: 9:00
➡ The park is signposted from A419, 4 miles
S of Cirencester.

Mayfield Touring Park

Cheltenham Road, Perrotts Brook,
Cirencester GL7 7BH
☎ **01285-831301** Fax **01285-831301**
⚠ 🚐 🚏
Size 12 acres, 36 touring pitches, 36 with
electric hookup, 20 level pitches, 2 static
caravans, 4 ☂, 5 WCs, 1 CWP
£ car/tent £5-£8.80, car/caravan £6.50-£8.80,
motorhome £5.50-£8.80, motorbike/tent £5,
children £1.30
Rental 🚐 £70-£160
🧺 ✗¼ 🖫 📞 🔌 Calor Gaz WS
Last arrival time: 10:30
➡ Immediately off main A435 Cirencester to
Cheltenham road, 2 miles N of Cirencester.

Orchards Holiday Park

Point Clear, St Osyth CO16 8CJ
☎ **01255-820651** Fax **01255-820184**
Open March-October ⚠ 🚐 🚏

*A family holiday park surrounded on three
sides by water, ideal for water sports and the
active family. New indoor heated pool,
outdoor pool, kids club, bowling. Included
in the wide range of leisure facilities,
restaurants and bar, excellent cabaret
entertainment. A British Holidays park.*

Size 200 acres, 60 touring pitches, 60 with
electric hookup, 60 level pitches, 1400 static
caravans, 12 ☂, 12 WCs, 2 CWPs
Rental 🚐
CC Mastercard
🧺 ✗ 🍴 📞 🎯 🎱 📋 🖥 🏸 🔌 Calor ♿
➡ From Clacton take B1027 signposted
Colchester and turn left after Pump Hill
petrol station. Go straight over crossroads
and through St Osyth to the park entrance.

Weeley Bridge Holiday Park

Weeley, Clacton-on-Sea CO16 9DH
☎ **01255-830403** Fax **01255-831544**
Open March-October 🚐 🚏
Size 16 acres, 25 touring pitches, 25 with
electric hookup, 25 level pitches, 200 static
caravans, 4 ☂, 4 WCs, 2 CWPs
£ car/caravan £8.50-£11.50, motorhome
£8.50-£11.50
Rental 🚐
CC MasterCard Visa
🧺 ✗ 🍴 🖫 📞 📺 🎯 🏸 🔌 Calor Gaz ♿ 🐕 WS
Last arrival time: 10:00
➡ Take A12 from London onto A133. Follow
signs for Clacton/Weeley.

CLAPHAM Lancashire 10C3

Flying Horseshoe Hotel Caravan Site
Clapham LA2 8ES
☎ 015242-51229 Fax 015242-51229
Open March 31-end September ▲ 🚐 🚏
Size 3½ acres, 30 touring pitches, 30 with electric hookup, 30 level pitches, 2 🚿, 4 WCs, 1 CWP
£ car/tent £3-£8, car/caravan £5-£8, motorhome £5-£8, motorbike/tent £5
✗ 🗲 🔋 🖥 📋 📺 ⚠ 🅿 Calor 🔥 WS
Last arrival time: 10:00
➡ At Clapham on A65, S onto unclassified road, signed Keasden. Site ³/₄ mile.

CLEETHORPES Lincolnshire 11F4

Thorpe Park Holiday Centre
Humberton, Cleethorpes DN36 4HG
☎ 01345-508508
Open March-October 🚐 🚏

A family holiday park close to excellent beaches with a new indoor heated pool, kids clubs, coarse fishing lake, kids pets corner - a wide range of leisure facilities, hot food, bars and cabarets. A 'British Holidays Park'.

Size 279 acres, 115 touring pitches, 115 with electric hookup, 80 static caravans, 78 🚿, 22 WCs, 19 CWPs
℃ MasterCard Visa
🛒 🗲 🖥 🔋 🔲 🔳 🌐 ⚠ 🅿 Calor 🔥
➡ Follow A180 from M180, following signs for Grimsby and Cleethorpes. In Cleethorpes town centre, with seafront on left, follow signs for 'Fitties'. At the mini roundabout you will see Thorpe Park's entrance straight ahead.

CLIPPESBY Norfolk 9F3

Clippesby Holidays
Clippesby, Great Yarmouth NR29 3BJ
☎ 01493-369367 Fax 01493-368181
Open 25 May-30 September ▲ 🚐 🚏

Situated in the wooded grounds of Clippesby Hall, in Broadlands National Park. This family run park, with courtyard cottages (available all year), has won many national awards including the "Best park in England" Calor award. ➡

← **Clippesby Holidays**

Size 34 acres, 100 touring pitches, 70 with electric hookup, 70 level pitches, 10 ℞, 20 WCs, 3 CWPs
£ car/tent £8.50-£15, car/caravan £8.50-£15, motorhome £8.50-£15, motorbike/tent £8.50, children £0.50
Rental Chalet. £100-£495
CC MasterCard Visa
🔌 ✕ 🍴 🖥 🔋 🚿 🔲 🔲 GR 🔲 🅰 🔲 🔲 Calor Gaz ♿ ✱
Last arrival time: 5:30
➡ Take A47 to Acle, then A1064 for 3 miles and turn left at Clippesby. After ½ mile, turn left again and then first right after 200 yards.

CLITHEROE Lancashire   10C3

Camping & Caravanning Club Site
Edisford Bridge, Edisford Road, Clitheroe BB7 3LA
📞 **01200-25294**
Open end March-start November ⛺ 🚐 🚐

CLIPPESBY HOLIDAYS

Family-run Touring Park Camping and Holiday Cottages in the beautiful wooded grounds of Clippesby Hall, with lots of family things to do.
"BEST PARK IN ENGLAND"
1996 CALOR AWARD
"BEST FAMILY PARK" 2 years running,
Practical Caravan

Clippesby,
Nr Gt. Yarmouth NR29 3BJ
Tel: 01493 369367 Fax: 01493 368181

Size 4½ acres, 80 touring pitches, 32 with electric hookup, 6 ℞, 14 WCs, 1 CWP
£ car/tent £8.75-£11.55, car/caravan £8.75-£11.55, motorhome £8.75-£11.55, motorbike/tent £8.75, children £1.40
CC MasterCard Visa
🖥 🔋 Gaz ✱
Last arrival time: 11:00
➡ From A59, take A671 to Clitheroe. In Clitheroe take B6243, Edisford Road, 1 mile to site.

CLOVELLY Devon   2C2

Dyke Green Farm Camping Site
Higher Clovelly, Clovelly
📞 **01237-431279**
Open Easter-October
Size 40 touring pitches, 2 ℞, 3 WCs, 1 CWP
🔌 🔌¼ 🔋 🔲 Calor
➡ On roundabout A39 turn onto Clovelly road and immediately right to site.

COCKERMOUTH Cumbria   10A1

Wyndham Hall Caravan Park
Old Keswick Road, Cockermouth CA13 9SF
📞 **01900-822571**
Open 1 March-15 November 🚐 🚐

A family site. Short walk into the market town (Cockermouth), and quarter of an hour drive to Keswick.

Size 12½ acres, 42 touring pitches, 24 with electric hookup, 42 level pitches, 105 static caravans, 9 ℞, 21 WCs, 2 CWPs
🔌 ✕ 🍴 🔋 🔲 GR 🔲 🅰 🔲 🔲 Calor Gaz WS
➡ Off the A66 on the Old Keswick Road.

Stowford Farm Meadows
Combe Martin, Ilfracombe EX34 0PW
📞 01271-882476 Fax 01271-883053
Open Easter-31 October ▲ 🚐 🚏

Set in the heart of the glorious Devon countryside, on the fringe of Exmoor National Park, the site has large modern amenity blocks and boundries of mature beech and ash trees.

Size 500 acres, 570 touring pitches, 550 with electric hookup, 250 level pitches, 60 🏠, 110 WCs, 10 CWPs
£ car/tent £3.95-£8.85, car/caravan £3.95-£8.85, motorhome £3.95-£8.85, motorbike/tent £3.95
CC MasterCard Visa
🛒 ✗ 🍴 ⊡ 📞 🔧 ▶🔋 🔩 GR TV ⚠ 🔫 🔌 Calor Gaz 🐕 WS
Last arrival time: 8:00
➡ M5 junction 27, follow the North Devon Link to Barnstaple, then A39 (for Lynton) through Barnstaple town centre. One mile from Barnstaple turn left onto the B3230. Turn right at the garage onto the A3123. The site is 1½ miles on the right.

Scarr Head Caravans
Torver, Coniston LA21 8BP
📞 01539-441576
Open Easter-end October ▲ 🚐 🚏   ➡

← **Scarr Head Caravans**

Small working farm at the foot of the Coniston Mountains in a quiet part of the Lake District. A perfect base for exploring the beautiful surrounding countryside by car or foot.

Size 1 acres, 5 touring pitches, 1 with electric hookup, 10 level pitches, 2 static caravans, 1 🐾, 2 WCs, 1 CWP
£ car/tent £6-£6.50, car/caravan £6-£6.50, motorhome £5.50-£6, motorbike/tent £5.50, children £1.50-£2
Rental 🚐 caravans £130-£220
🐕
Last arrival time: 10:00
➜ From Newby Bridge on A590 at Greenodd turn right onto A5902 and follow signs for Coniston. At Torver turn right onto A593 signed Coniston. Take first left up lane. Follow sign to Old Man and Walna Scarr. Proceed up hill to Scarr Head.

Allensford Caravan Park
Castleside, Consett DH8 9BA
☎ **01207-509522**
Open 1 March-31 October

🚽 🔌 📷 ⚡
➜ From Castleside, 21½ miles SW of Consett, travel N on A68 for 2 miles and turn right at Allensford for ¼ mile before crossing river.

Little Trevothan Caravan Park
Coverack, Helston TR12 6SD
☎ **01326-280260**
Open Easter-October 🛡 🚐 🚎
Size 10 acres, 48 touring pitches, 18 with electric hookup, 48 level pitches, 29 static caravans, 4 🐾, 6 WCs, 1 CWP
£ car/tent £5-£6.50, car/caravan £5-£6.50, , motorbike/tent £4.50, children £1-£1.50
Rental 🚐 £95-£275
CC MasterCard Visa
🐾 ✗ 🚽 🔌 📷 🗂 GR ⚡ 🗙 Calor 🐕 WS
Last arrival time: 10:00
➜ From A30 take A39 through Truro, then A394 to Helston. Join A3083 to The Lizard and proceed past Culdrose air base. Turn left at roundabout onto B3293 signposted to Coverack. Follow road past Goonhilly Downs satellite dishes and after 2 miles turn right just before garage following sign to 'Little Trevothan Caravan Park and Fox Club'. Take third turning on left and site is 300 yards on right.

Quarryfield
Crantock TR7 2RE
☎ **01637-872792**
Open March-October 🚐 🚎

An ideal touring site, 15 minutes walk from the beach and close to the village. A level site with all modern amenities.

Size 20 acres, 20 touring pitches, 20 static caravans, 12 🐾, 20 WCs, 2 CWPs
£ car/caravan £4.30-£5.50, motorhome £4.30-£5.50, children £0.50-£1.25
🐾 🚽 📷 🔌 🗂 GR ⚡ 🗙 Calor
Last arrival time: 9:30

➜ Off A3075 Redruth road to Crantock to bottom of village. There is a red telephone kiosk, a road up on right of kiosk. The site is at top.

CREDITON Devon   3D3

Yeatheridge Farm Caravan Park
East Worlington, Crediton EX17 4TN
📞 01884-860330 Fax 01884-860330
Open Easter-30 September ▲ ⛺ 🚐

A genuine working family farm, plenty of animals and panoramic views from a spacious park. Coarse fishing, lakes and horse riding. Two indoor heated swimming pools and 20 acres of woodland.

Size 9 acres, 85 touring pitches, 75 with electric hookup, 2 static caravans, 12 🚿, 17 WCs
£ car/tent £6.50-£7.75, car/caravan £6.50-£7.75, motorhome £6.50-£7.75, motorbike/tent £6.50, children £1.35
CC MasterCard Visa
🛁 🏊¼ 🚽 📞 🍳 🎣 💻 GR 🔍 ♿ 🎫 🐕 Calor Gaz
🐾 WS
➜ Leave M5 at junction 27 onto B3137 out of Finerton. Take B3042 before Witheridge. The site is 3½ miles on the left.

CROMER Norfolk   9F2

Camping & Caravanning Club Site
Holgate Lane, West Runton, Cromer NR27 9NW
📞 01263-837544
Open late March-early November ▲ ⛺ 🚐

A lovely wooded approach brings you to this friendly family site. An ideal base for a seaside holiday with great views towards the coast.

Size 11½ acres, 250 touring pitches, 89 with electric hookup, 20 🚿, 30 WCs, 1 CWP
£ car/tent £9.20-£12.05, car/caravan £9.02-£12.05, motorhome £9.20-£12.05, motorbike/tent £9.20, children £1.40
CC MasterCard Visa
🛁 🚽 📞 ♿ 🎫 🐾 🐕
Last arrival time: 11:00
➜ Towards King's Lynn on A148 towards Cromer, turn left at Roman Camp Inn and follow road, signposted.

Manor Farm Caravan & Camp Site
East Runton, Cromer NR27 9PR
📞 01263-512858 Fax 01263-512858
Open Easter ▲ ⛺ 🚐

Peaceful family run site with glorious sea and woodland views. Well equiped toilet facilites. Separate field for dog owners. Ideal for families. Tents welcome. Beach one mile.
➜

← Manor Farm Caravan & Camp Site

Size 20 acres, 200 touring pitches, 128 with electric hookup, 200 level pitches, 20 🕭, 55 WCs, 5 CWPs

🏊¼ ✕¼ ●¼ 🔋 🗖 ⚠ 🕮 Calor Gaz

Last arrival time: 10:00

➡ 1½ mile W of Cromer. Turn off A148 at signpost East Runton.

Seacroft Camping & Caravan Park
Runton Road, Cromer NR27 9JN
📞 **01263-511722 Fax 01263-511512**
Open 20 March-30 October 🛆 🚐 🚏

The pitches are individually marked with shrubs forming boundaries. Within easy walking distance from Cromer.

Size 7 acres, 120 touring pitches, 110 with electric hookup, 120 level pitches, 15 🕭, 30 WCs, 1 CWP

£ car/tent £7-£11.50, car/caravan £7-£11.50, motorhome £7-£11.50, motorbike/tent £7, children £0.50-£1.50

CC MasterCard Visa

🏊 ✕ ● 🗖 🔋 🗖 🖭 🕮 GR TV ⚠ 🕮 ⊟ Calor Gaz 👬 👬

Last arrival time: 11:00

➡ 1 mile W of Cromer on the A149 Coast Road.

CROSTHWAITE Cumbria   10B2

Lambhowe Caravan Park
Crosthwaite LA8 8JE
📞 **01539-68483**
Open 1 March-31 October 🚐 🚏

Ideal for touring the many attractions of the Lake District National Park. A secluded wooded site located between Lancaster and Windermere.

Size 14 touring pitches, 14 with electric hookup, 14 level pitches, 111 static caravans, 4 🕭, 14 WCs, 1 CWP

£ car/caravan £10, motorhome £10

🏊¼ 🗖 🔋 🕮 ⊟ Calor 👬

Last arrival time: 7:30

➡ Leave M6 N at junction 36 onto A590, then A5074 to Bowness, just opposite Damson Dene hotel.

CROWBOROUGH East Sussex   5D3

Camping & Caravanning Club Site
Goldsmith Recreation Ground,
Crowborough TN6 2TN
📞 **01892-664827**
Open end February-start November 🛆 🚐 🚏
Size 60 touring pitches, 24 with electric hookup, 4 🕭, 7 WCs, 2 CWPs
£ car/tent £8.75-£11.55, car/caravan £8.75-£11.55, motorhome £8.75-£11.55, motorbike/tent £8.75, children £1.40
CC MasterCard Visa
🗖 🔋 ⚠ 🕮 👬 👬
Last arrival time: 11:00
➡ From Tunbridge Wells on A26 S. Before reaching Crowborough town centre, site is adjacent to major sports and leisure centre.

DARLINGTON Co. Durham   11D2

Winston Caravan Park
Winston, Darlington DL2 3RH
📞 **01325-730228 Fax 01325-730228**
Open 1 March-31 October 🛆 🚐 🚏

A pleasant family site ideally situated for exploring the surrounding countryside. Grassy, level and sheltered with tourers and tents welcome. Holiday caravans for hire, one with wheelchair access. ETB grading 4 ticks.

Size 2½ acres, 20 touring pitches, 16 with electric hookup, 20 level pitches, 11 static caravans, 5 ⋔, 5 WCs, 1 CWP
£ car/tent £7-£8.50, car/caravan £7-£8.50, motorhome £7-£8.50, motorbike/tent £7
Rental ⏣ £25-£30 nightly, £145-£190 weekly.
🛁¼ ✕¼ 🚿¼ ▣ 📞 ▣ 🍴 Calor Gaz 🐕
Last arrival time: 11:00
➔ Ten miles W of Darlington on the A67, turn left into Winston Village and the site is 400 yards on the right.

Deer Park Holiday Estate
Stoke Fleming, Dartmouth TQ6 0RF
📞 **01803-770253 Fax 01803-770320**
Open March-November 🅰 ⏣ 🚐

Family site with excellent facilities: adventure playground, pub with family room, games room, swimming pool and

sunbathing area. All facilities are free on site. Four caravans and four flats for hire.

Size 12 acres, 160 touring pitches, 100 with electric hookup, 160 level pitches, 12 ⋔, 18 WCs, 1 CWP
CC Visa
🛁 ✕ 🚿 ▣ 📞 ▣ GR ⚠ 🎣 Calor Gaz 🔥 🐕
Last arrival time: 10:00
➔ Situated 2 miles S of Dartmouth on A379. Observe bus stop at site entrance.

Leonards Cove Holiday Estate
Stoke Fleming, Dartmouth TQ6 0NR
📞 **01803-770206**
Open 15 March-31 October
🛁 ✕ 🚿 ▣
➔ Site on S side of B3207, 1¼ miles W of Dartmouth.
See advert on next page

Cofton Country Holiday Park
Starcross, Dawlish EX6 8RP
📞 **01626-890111 Fax 01626-891572**
Open Easter-31 October 🅰 ⏣ 🚐 ➔

← Cofton Country Holiday Park

Landscaped park with green meadows, bright flower beds, mature trees, woodlands and extensive countryside views. Only a short drive to Dawlish Warren beach.

Size 16 acres, 450 touring pitches, 300 with electric hookup, 62 static caravans, 46 📷, 97 WCs, 2 CWPs
£ car/tent £5-£9.50, car/caravan £5-£9.50, motorhome £5-£9.50, motorbike/tent £5
Rental 🚃 £75-£399, cottages £160-£490.
℃ MasterCard Visa

🛠 ✗ 🍴 🗑 🔌 🔲 🔳 🎫 📷 🅶🆁 🏔 🎯 🔌 Calor Gaz ♿ 🐕 WS
Last arrival time: 8:00
➔ From M5 junction 30 take A379 to Dawlish. Park is on the left, ½ mile after the small harbour at Cockwood Village.

Lady's Mile Touring & Camping Park
Exeter Road, Dawlish EX7 0LX
📞 01626-863411 Fax 01626-888689
Open January-December 🏕 🚃 🚐

Devon's premier holiday park, ideal for families. Indoor and outdoor pools with water slides. ³/₄ mile to sandy beach. Family bar. 9 hole golf course.

Size 20 acres, 300 touring pitches, 300 with electric hookup, 300 level pitches, 1 static caravans, 40 📷, 80 WCs, 3 CWPs
£ car/tent £6-£12, car/caravan £6-£12, motorhome £6-£12, motorbike/tent £6, children £1-£2
Rental Chalet.
℃ MasterCard Visa
🛠 ✗ 🍴 🗑 🔌 🔲 🔳 🔳 📷 🅶🆁 🏔 🎯 🔌 Calor ♿ 🐕 WS
Last arrival time: 8:00
➔ 1 mile N of Dawlish on A379.
See advert on next page

Leadstone Camping
Warren Road, Dawlish EX7 0NG
📞 01626-872239 Fax 01626-873833
Open 20 June-6 September 🏕 🚃 🚐   →

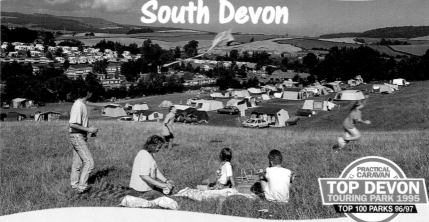

Cofton Country
HOLIDAY PARK
South Devon

PRACTICAL CARAVAN
TOP DEVON
TOURING PARK 1995
TOP 100 PARKS 96/97

Cofton Country – Set in a special corner of Devon in beautiful landscaped grounds, with bright flowers, green meadows, rolling woodlands and countryside views. A unique setting for perfect touring and camping holidays in this attractive part of Devon. Cofton Country Holiday Park – higher standards and excellent facilities.

Heated Swimming Pool • Shop/ Off-Licence • Pub & Family Lounge Woodland Trails & Adventure Play Area • Coarse Fishing Takeaway • Games Room Electric Hook-ups • Launderettes Free Hot Water & Showers

Free colour brochure: Mrs U Jeffery, Cofton Country Holiday Park, Starcross, Nr. Dawlish, South Devon EX6 8RP.

☎ *01626 890111*

RAC SELECTED

AA

DEVON *Swan* HOLIDAYS
The firm family favourite

APPROVED

BRITISH GRADED HOLIDAY PARKS
EXCELLENT

← **Leadstone Camping**

Seven acres of rolling grassland in a natural secluded bowl within ½ mile of Dawlish Warren Beach and nature reserve. Ideally situated for exploring Devon.

Size 8 acres, 15 touring pitches, 15 with electric hookup, 100 level pitches, 12 ⋒, 8 WCs, 1 CWP
£ car/tent £6.40-£7.90, car/caravan £8.40-£10.30, motorhome £6.40-£7.90, motorbike/tent £6.40, children £1-£1.20
🛒 ✗¼ 🗑 🔌 ⚠ 🎣 Calor Gaz 🐕
Last arrival time: 12:00

→ From M5 junction 30 take A379 to Dawlish. As you approach Dawlish, turn left on the brow of hill signposted Dawlish Warren. Site is ½ mile on right.

Peppermint Park
Warren Road, Dawlish Warren EX7 0PQ
☎ **01626-863436**
Open Easter-October 🏕 🚐 🚃

Grassland park with some level terraces, all sheltered by mature trees. Nearest touring park to Dawlish Warren beach (600 yards). Free family entertainment nightly in licensed club.

Size 16 acres, 200 touring pitches, 190 with electric hookup, 200 level pitches, 35 static caravans, 23 ⋒, 22 WCs
£ car/tent £5-£9.50, car/caravan £5-£9.50, motorhome £5-£9.50, motorbike/tent £5
Rental 🚐 holiday homes £55-£399
CC MasterCard Visa
🛒 ✗ ☕ 🗑 🔌 🍴 🅿 🎣 GR ⚠ 🎣 Calor Gaz ♿ 🐕

→ From M5 (jn 30) take A379 to Dawlish. Turn left to Dawlish Warren, 7 miles on, just before entering Dawlish. Park is on left at bottom of hill.

DELABOLE Cornwall　　　2B3

Planet Park
Westdown Road, Delabole
☎ **01840-213361**
Open all year 🏕 🚐 🚃

🛒 ✗ ☕ 🍴

➡ From junction of A395 and A39, travel S for 1½ miles and turn right on unclassified road signed Delabole for 1½ miles to B3314. Travel 2½ miles through village to site on left.

DEVIZES Wiltshire 4A3

Bell Caravan & Camp Site

Andover Road, Lydeway, Devizes SN10 3PS
☎ 01380-840230
Open Easter-31 October Å ⚐ 🚐
Size 3 acres, 30 touring pitches, 24 with electric hookup, 30 level pitches, 5 ℞, 6 WCs, 1 CWP
£ car/tent £6-£7.50, car/caravan £6-£7.50, motorhome £6-£7.50, motorbike/tent £6, children £1.25-£1.75
Rental ⚐
🛒 🍳 🗄 📞 🗇 🔲 GR 🔲 TV 🗃 🖈 🔌 Calor Gaz
🐕 WS
➡ 3 miles SE of Devizes on A342.

Lakeside

Rowde, Devizes SN10 2LX
☎ 01380-722767
Open March-October Å ⚐ 🚐

A beautiful, landscaped, rural setting with excellent facilities surrounding a large well stocked spring fed lake.

Size 6½ acres, 55 touring pitches, 50 with electric hookup, 55 level pitches, 4 ℞, 6 WCs, 1 CWP
£ car/tent £6.50, car/caravan £6.50-£9.45, motorhome £6.50-£9.45, motorbike/tent £6.50
🛒 🛒¼ ✗¼ 🍳¼ 📞 🗇 🖾 Calor Gaz 🚻 🐕
Last arrival time: 11:00
➡ 1 mile N of Devizes on A342.

Lower Foxhangers Farm

Rowde, Devizes
☎ 01380-828254 **Fax** 01380-828254
Open Easter-October Å ⚐ 🚐

Quietly located working farm alongside canal flight of 29 locks. Fishing, boating, walking and cycling. Self catering in 4 holiday homes or farmhouse bed and breakfast.

Size 2 acres, 10 touring pitches, 4 with electric hookup, 10 level pitches, 4 static caravans, 1 ℞, 2 WCs, 1 CWP
£ car/tent £5-£6, car/caravan £5-£6, motorhome £5-£6, motorbike/tent £5
Rental ·Chalet.

➡

← **Lower Foxhangers Farm**

Calor

→ 2 miles W of Devizes on A361. ½ mile E of junction of A361/A365.

DISS Norfolk 9E3

Willows Camping & Caravan Park

Diss Road, Scole IP21 4DH
01379-740271
Open May-September
Size 4 acres, 32 touring pitches, 18 with electric hookup, 32 level pitches, 2, 7 WCs, 2 CWPs
£ car/tent £7, car/caravan £7, motorhome £7, motorbike/tent £7, children £0.25
¼ ¼ ¼ Calor Gaz
Last arrival time: 11:00
→ 200 yards off the A140 roundabout at Scole, in the direction of Diss on A1066.

DORCHESTER Dorset 3E3

Giant's Head Caravan & Camping Park

Old Sherborne Road, Dorchester DT2 7TR
01300-341242
Open 17 April-31 October
Size 3½ acres, 60 touring pitches, 20 with electric hookup, 60 level pitches, 2, 8 WCs, 1 CWP
£ car/tent £5-£6.50, car/caravan £5-£6.50, motorhome £5-£6.50, motorbike/tent £5, children £1
Rental Chalet.
Calor Gaz WS
→ Into Dorchester, avoiding bypass, at Top o' Town roundabout take Sherborne road. After 500 yards take right fork at Loders (BP) Garage and follow signs.

Home Farm Camping & Caravan Site

Puncknowle, Dorchester DT2 9BW
01308-897258
Open April-October

Small secluded site in beautiful area. Good food at village inn. Sea fishing nearby.

Size 5 acres, 5 touring pitches, 22 level pitches, 14 static caravans, 4, 6 WCs, 1 CWP
Rental
¼ Calor Gaz
Last arrival time: 9:00
→ From Dorchester take A35 towards Bridport. Drive through Winterbourne Abbas and turn left just before the dual carriageway to Lilton Cheney. Follow signs to Punchknowle.

DOVER Kent 5F3

Hawthorn Farm

Martin Mill, Dover CT15 5LA
01304-852658 Fax 01304-853417
Open 1 March-31 October

Award winning park set in 28 acres. A quiet, peaceful base from which to discover the delights of Kent and only one hour from France.

Size 250 touring pitches, 100 with electric hookup, 24, 21 WCs, 2 CWPs

CC Visa
🝆 Calor Gaz WS
➡ Well signposted on the A258 from Dover to Deal.

Clifford Bridge Park
Clifford, Drewsteignton EX6 6QE
☎ 01647-24226
Open Easter-end September ▲ ⚬ ♨

A small and level, family run park in a really rural setting within the Dartmoor National Park, surrounded by woodland and bordered by the River Teign.

Size 8 acres, 64 touring pitches, 19 with electric hookup, 64 level pitches, 3 static caravans,
£ car/tent £6.85-£9.95, car/caravan £6.85-£9.95, motorhome £5.95-£9.20
Rental ⚬ Chalet.
🝆 ⬚ ⬚ ⬚ GR Calor Gaz 🏇
➡ From A30, 11 miles W of Exeter, turn to Cheriton Bishop. Left at Old Thatch Inn, 2 miles to crossroads and right to Clifford Bridge. 1 mile over crossroads and bridge. Park is on left.

Woodland Springs Touring Park
Vinton, nr Chagford EX6 6PG
☎ 01647-231695

Cliff House
Minsmere Road, Dunwich IP17 3DQ
☎ 01728-648282 Fax 01728-648282
Open April-October ▲ ⚬ ♨

Size 30 acres acres, 121 touring pitches, 75 with electric hookup, 7 level pitches, 78 static caravans, 8 ⬚, 12 WCs, 4 CWPs
£ car/tent £6.50-£12, car/caravan £8-£12, motorhome £8-£12, motorbike/tent £6.50
Rental ⚬ Chalet. £120-£260
🝆 ✗ ⬚ ⬚ ⬚ ⬚ GR ⬚ ⛰ ⬚ ⬚ Calor Gaz 🏇 WS
Last arrival time: 9:00
➡ From A12, 5 miles N of Saxmundham, follow signs to Dunwich Heath. Site is on the left.

Camping & Caravanning Club Site
Ockham Road North, East Horsley KT24 6PE
☎ 01483-283273
Open end March-start November ▲ ⚬ ♨
Size 12 acres, 135 touring pitches, 47 with electric hookup, 10 ⬚, 15 WCs, 1 CWP
£ car/tent £9.20-£12.05, car/caravan £9.20-£12.05, motorhome £9.20-£12.05, motorbike/tent £9.20, children £1.40
CC MasterCard Visa ➡

← Camping & Caravanning Club Site

🔲 📞 GR ⚠ 🏠 ♿ 🐕 WS
Last arrival time: 11:00
➡ Leave M25 (jn 10) and head S on A3, then take B2039 towards East Horsley, site is signposted.

ELLESMERE Shropshire   7D2

Talbot Caravan Park
2 Willow Street, Ellesmere SY12 0AG
📞 **01691-622285**
Open March-November 🏕 🚐 🚚
Size 2 acres, 21 touring pitches, 21 with electric hookup, 21 level pitches, 3 static caravans, 4 🚿, 6 WCs, 1 CWP
£ car/tent £6, car/caravan £9, motorhome £9, motorbike/tent £6
CC MasterCard Visa
🍴¼ ✗¼ 🍺¼ 🔲 📞 🐕
➡ Site on N side of Ellesmere in Talbot Street.

ESKDALE GREEN Cumbria   10A2

Fisherground Farm
Eskdale Green CA19 1TF
📞 **01946-723319**
Open mid March-mid November 🏕 🚚

Quiet site in beautiful location, adventure playground, children's lake, fishing, canoeing and swimming in adjacent river.

Size 2 acres, 30 touring pitches, 30 level pitches, 4 🚿, 6 WCs, 1 CWP
£ car/tent £7-£8.50, motorhome £7-£8.50, motorbike/tent £7, children £1.50
Rental Chalet.

✗¼ 🔲 📞 🚽 ⚠ 🏠 ♿ 🐕
➡ From Eskdale Green head towards Hadknott Pass, go i mile to King George IV then turn left, site is first left after 400 yards.

EVESHAM Worcestershire   7F4

Ranch Caravan Park
Honeybourne, Evesham WR11 5QG
📞 **01386-830744 Fax 01386-833503**
Open March-November 🚐 🚚
Size 8 acres, 120 touring pitches, 95 with electric hookup, 120 level pitches, 180 static caravans, 10 🚿, 24 WCs, 2 CWPs
£ car/caravan £5.50-£16, motorhome £5.50-£16, children £1.25
Rental 🚐 £180-£350
🍴 ✗ 🍺 🔲 📞 🚽 🏠 ⚠ 🏠 🍺 Calor Gaz 🐕 WS
Last arrival time: 8:00
➡ From Evesham travel E on A44, turn left onto B4035 to Bretforton, then left to Honeybourne, turn left, site on left ¼ mile.

EXETER Devon   3D3

Haldon Lodge Farm Caravan & Camping Park
Kennford, Near Exeter EX6 7YG
📞 **01392-832312**
Open all year 🏕 🚐 🚚

Peaceful family site with beautiful forest scenery, nature walks, fishing lakes, riding holidays, barbecues plus friendly country inns. Excellent facilities with hook-ups. Sea and Exeter 15 minutes.

Size 7½ acres, 40 touring pitches, 80 with electric hookup, 60 level pitches, 4 static caravans, 8 🚿, 14 WCs, 2 CWPs

£ car/tent £5-£7.50, car/caravan £5-£7.50, motorhome £5-£8, motorbike/tent £5
Rental 🛏 Chalet.
🛎 ✗ 🍴 🗄 📞 🚻 ⛳ 🎣 GR TV ⚠ 🔥 Calor Gaz ⚲ WS
Last arrival time: 10:00
➡ Off A38 at Kennford services, follow signs to Haldon Lodge turning left into village. 1½ miles to site.

Springfield Holiday Park
Tedburn Road, Tedburn St Mary, Exeter EX6 6EW
📞 **01647-24242 Fax 01647-24131**
Open 15 March-15 November **A** 🛏 🚐

A quiet family owned park set in nine acres of beautiful countryside on the fringe of Dartmoor National Park. Eight miles west of Exeter and approximately 30 minutes drive to the beaches.

Size 9 acres, 88 touring pitches, 50 with electric hookup, 88 level pitches, 12 static caravans, 8 🚿, 16 WCs, 2 CWPs
£ car/tent £6-£7.50, car/caravan £7-£8, motorhome £6.50-£9.50, motorbike/tent £6
Rental 🛏 £110-£250
🛎 🛎¼ 🍴 🗄 📞 🚻 🎣 GR 🔥 ⚠ 🔥 Calor Gaz ⚲ WS
Last arrival time: 9:30
➡ From M5 (jn 31) take A30 to Okehampton. Leave A30 at second exit, signposted Tedburn St Mary. Turn left at roundabout and drive through village to site on right, 1¾ miles from village.

EXFORD Somerset 3D2

Westermill Farm
Exford, Minehead TA24 7NJ
📞 **01643-831238 Fax 01643-831660**
Open April-October **A** 🚐

Beautiful secluded site for tents by shallow river. Heart of Exmoor National Park. Four waymarked walks over 500 acre working farm. Natural and uncommercialised. Chalets for rent.

Size 6 acres, 60 touring pitches, 60 level pitches, 6 🚿, 8 WCs, 1 CWP
£ car/tent £7, motorhome £7, motorbike/tent £7, children £1
Rental Chalets £140-£350
🛎 🗄 📞 🚻 🎣 Calor Gaz ⚲
➡ Leave Exford on Porlock road, after ½ mile fork left. Continue 2 miles past another campsite until 'Westermill' seen on tree then fork left.

EXMOUTH Devon 3D3

Devon Cliffs Holiday Park
Sandy Bay, Exmouth EX8 5BT
📞 **01395-223000**

Size 150 acres, 200 touring pitches, 100 with electric hookup, 168 level pitches, 25 🚿, 94 WCs
🛎 🍴 ✗ 🔥
➡ From M5 junction 30 take A376 to Exmouth and follow signs to Sandy Bay.

Webbers Farm Caravan Park
Castle Lane, Woodbury, Exeter EX5 1EA
📞 **01395-232276 Fax 01395-233389**
Open Easter-end September **A** 🛏 🚐
Size 7½ acres, 100 touring pitches, 100 with electric hookup, 20 level pitches, 14 🚿, 17 WCs, 6 CWPs
£ car/tent £6.75-£9, car/caravan £6.75-£9, motorhome £6.75-£9, children £1.25 ➡

← Webbers Farm Caravan Park

🏕 🏕¼ ✗¼ 🚐¼ 🔲 📞 🗑 ⚠ 🔲 Calor Gaz ♿ ✝
WS
Last arrival time: 10:00
➡ From M5 junction 5 take A376 to Exmouth. At second roundabout take B3179 to Woodbury and follow signs from village centre.

Honeypot Camp & Caravan Park
Wortham, Eye IP22 1PW
📞 01379-783312 Fax 01379-783293
Open April-September 🏕 🚐 🚍

A quiet, well organised landscaped country site, part of which surrounds two lakes, on well grassed, level, free draining land, facing due south. Under the personal supervision of the owners for over 20 years.

Size 6½ acres, 35 touring pitches, 20 with electric hookup, 35 level pitches, 2 🚿, 4 WCs, 1 CWP
£ car/tent £6.50-£7.50, car/caravan £7.50, motorhome £7.50, motorbike/tent £6.50, children £1
🏕¼ ✗¼ 🚐¼ 🔲 📞 🗑 📄 ⚠ 🔲 Calor Gaz ✝
WS
➡ 4 miles SW of Diss on A143 towards Bury St Edmunds. 18 miles E of Bury St Edmunds on A143.

Crossways Caravan Site
Holt Road, Little Snoring, Fakenham NR21 0AX
📞 01328-878335 Fax 01328-878335
Open March-October

A quiet caravan site with provision for some tents. Handy for touring the north Norfolk coast.

Size 2 acres, 30 touring pitches, 22 with electric hookup, 2 🚿, 7 WCs, 1 CWP
CC MasterCard Visa
🏕 📞 Calor Gaz
➡ On A148, 3 miles N of Fakenham.

Fakenham Racecourse Caravan Club Site
Fakenham NR21 7NY
📞 01328-862388 Fax 01328-855908
Open all year 🏕 🚐 🚍

Size 12 acres, 150 touring pitches, 150 with electric hookup, 150 level pitches, 12 ℞, 36 WCs, 3 CWPs
£ car/tent £8-£10, car/caravan £8-£10, motorhome £8-£10, motorbike/tent £7.50, children £1.10-£1.20
℅ MasterCard Visa
⚒ ✕ ☛ ▣ ▣ ▤ ▶ ▨ ▨ ▨ GR ▣ ⊕ Calor Gaz
⚓ ⚐ WS
➜ Approaching Fakenham from all directions follow campsite directions to racecourse.

FALMOUTH Cornwall   2A4

Calamankey Farm
Longdowns, Penryn TR10 9DL
☎ **01209-860314**
⚑ ⛺
Size 4 static caravans, 3 ℞, 12 WCs, 1 CWP
£ car/tent £5, motorhome £5, motorbike/tent £5, children £2.50
Rental ⛴
⚒¼ ☎ ▣ ⚐
Last arrival time: 10:00
➜ From Truro, take the A39 to Treluswell roundabout and go straight across onto the A394 towards Hilston Calamankey. Farm is in Longdowns village, opposite the Evoco filling station.

Menallack Farm Caravan & Camping Site
Treverva, Penryn, Falmouth TR10 9BP
☎ **01326-340333** Fax **01326-340333**
Open April-October ⚑ ⛴ ⛺
Size 1½ acres, 30 touring pitches, 4 with electric hookup, 30 level pitches, 2 ℞, 6 WCs, 1 CWP
£ car/tent £4.30-£5, car/caravan £4.30-£5, motorhome £4.30-£5, motorbike/tent £4.30, children £0.70-£0.80
⚒ ☛ ▣ Calor Gaz ⚐
Last arrival time: 9:00
➜ From Truro go towards Falmouth for 10 miles. Follow A39 over double mini roundabouts. At next roundabouts go straight across first roundabout and take second exit from second roundabout. Do not take the Helston road. In Mabe Burnthouse go straight over crossroads. 2 miles further on at next crossroads turn right towards Gweek. Go through Lamanva and Treverva. Farm is ¾ mile beyond Trevera on left going towards Gweek.

Pennance Mill Farm
Maenporth, Falmouth TR11 5HJ
☎ 01326-312616
Open Easter-November
Size 4 acres, 50 touring pitches, 15 with electric hookup, 40 level pitches, 4 static caravans, 4 ☂, 7 WCs, 1 CWP
£ car/tent £8.50, car/caravan £7-£8.50
🚿 ✕¼ ▣ ◧ ⚠ ⊞ Calor ♿
Last arrival time: 21
➤ Take A39 from Truro to Falmouth and follow Brown International Camping Caravan Signs to Maenporth. Farm site at bottom of hill to left. Clearly signposted.

Ellerslie Camping & Caravan Park
Down End Road, Fareham PO16 8TS
☎ 01329-822248 Fax 01329-822248
Open March-October 🏕 ⛺ ⛺

A small, attractive wooded site on the southern slopes of Portsdown Hill with space for approxiately 40 caravans and cars. Positioned close to the M27.

Size 4 acres, 40 touring pitches, 30 with electric hookup, 4 level pitches, 14 ☂, 7 WCs, 1 CWP
£ car/tent £6, car/caravan £6.50, motorhome £6.50, motorbike/tent £5.50, children £0.50
CC MasterCard Visa
🚿¼ ✕ ▣ ▣¼ ▣ ⊟ ⊞⚫▣ ⊞ ⊞ GR TV ⊞ ♿ 🐕 WS
Last arrival time: 10:00
➤ From M27 junction 11 take A27 to Portsmouth. After ½ mile turn left at traffic lights into Dannend Road. Site ½ mile on right.

Suffolk Sands Caravan Park
Carr Road, Felixstowe IP11 8TS
☎ 01394-273434 Fax 01394-671269
🏕 ⛺ ⛺
Size 18 acres, 60 touring pitches, 36 with electric hookup, 60 level pitches, 8 ☂, 20 WCs
🚿 ☕ ⊟ ♿
➤ Take A45 into Felixstowe and turn right at first roundabout. Go across next roundabout and continue along Walton Avenue to traffic lights. Turn right and after 200 yards bear right into Carr Road. Park is on left.

Blue Dolphin Holiday Centre
Gristhorpe Bay, Filey YO14 9PU
☎ 01723-515155 Fax 01723-512059
🏕 ⛺
Size 87 acres, 416 touring pitches, 169 with electric hookup, 116 level pitches, 380 static caravans, 34 ☂, 101 WCs
🚿 ☕ ▣ ▣ ♿
➤ Off A165 1½ miles N of Filey. Turn right at roundabout signposted to Blue Dolphin.

Primrose Valley Holiday Estate
Primrose Valley, Filey YO14 9RF
☎ 01723-513771 Fax 01723-513777
⛺
Size 150 acres, 90 touring pitches, 70 with electric hookup, 80 level pitches, 423 static caravans, 8 ☂, 21 WCs
🚿 ✕ ☕ ▣ ▣ ▣ ⊟
➤ 3 miles S of Filey off main A165 Scarborough to Bridlington road.

Reighton Sands Holiday Village
Reighton Gap, Filey YO14 9SJ
☎ 01723-890476 Fax 01723-891043
🏕 ⛺
Size 140 acres, 327 touring pitches, 78 with electric hookup, 195 level pitches, 135 static caravans, 30 ☂, 90 WCs
🚿 ☕ ▣ ⊟
➤ One mile off main A165 Filey to Bridlington road. Signposted opposite a garage.

Black Horse Farm Caravan & Camping Park
385 Canterbury Road, Densole, Folkestone
CT18 7BG
☎ 01303-892665
Open all year **Å ⚏ ⚏**

Quiet family touring park in a rural location with excellent facilities. Ideal base for East Kent, Canterbury, Channel ferries and Tunnel.

Size 5 acres, 70 touring pitches, 40 with electric hookup, 45 level pitches, 7 ⚏, 10 WCs, 1 CWP
£ car/tent £7.40, car/caravan £7.40, motorhome £7.40, motorbike/tent £7.40, children £1-£1.70
⚏¼ ✕¼ ⚏¼ ⚏ ⚏ ⚏ Calor Gaz ⚏ ⚏ WS
Last arrival time: 10:00
➡ From A20 follow signs towards Canterbury on A260. Site is on left, 2 miles from junction.

Camping & Caravanning Club Site
The Warren, Folkestone CT19 6PT
☎ 01303-255093
Open end March-end September **Å ⚏ ⚏**
Size 4 acres, 82 touring pitches, 6 ⚏, 17 WCs, 1 CWP
£ car/tent £8.20-£10.40, car/caravan £8.20-£10.40, motorhome £8.20-£10.40, motorbike/tent £8.20, children £1.30
⚏ MasterCard Visa
⚏ ⚏
Last arrival time: 11:00
➡ From M20 and A20 turn S to Folkestone and follow signs to site.

Little Satmar Holiday Park
Winehouse Lane, Capel-le-Ferne, Folkestone
CT18 7JF
☎ 01303-251188 Fax 01303-251188
Open April-October **Å ⚏ ⚏**

Situated inland of the B2011. Quiet country setting. Holiday homes for hire, excellent facilities for touring caravans and camping. Rose award winning park. Satisfaction guaranteed.

Size 8 acres, 60 touring pitches, 60 with electric hookup, 60 level pitches, 70 static caravans, 6 ⚏, 15 WCs, 2 CWPs
£ car/tent £6.25-£8.25, car/caravan £6.25-£8.25, motorhome £6.25-£8.25, motorbike/tent £4.50, children £0.75
Rental Chalet. £130-£235
⚏ ✕¼ ⚏¼ ⚏ ⚏ ⚏ ⚏ ⚏ ⚏ Calor Gaz ⚏ ⚏ WS
Last arrival time: 11:00
➡ Leave A20 at junction of B2011, signposted Capel-le-Ferne. In Capel-le-Ferne, turn into Winehouse Lane and site is immediately ahead.

Little Switzerland Caravan Site
Wear Bay Road, Folkestone CT19 6PS
☎ 01303-52168
Open 1 March-31 October **Å ⚏ ⚏**
Size 2 acres, 18 touring pitches, 12 with electric hookup, 13 static caravans, 4 ⚏, 12 WCs, 1 CWP
£ car/tent £8.85, car/caravan £9.50, motorhome £9.50, motorbike/tent £8.50
⚏¼ ✕ ⚏ ⚏ ⚏ ⚏ ⚏ ⚏ Calor Gaz ⚏
➡ On A20 over first two roundabouts. At third roundabout at foot of Folkestone Hill turn right along A2033 (Hill Road), then ½ mile further continue ahead into Wear Bay Road for ¼ mile, site on left.

Low Farm Touring Park

Spring Lane, Folkingham NG34 0SJ
☎ **01529-497322**
Open Easter-end October Å ⊕ ⊋
Size 2½ acres, 36 touring pitches, 25 with
electric hookup, 36 level pitches, 4 ₨, 6
WCs, 1 CWP
£ car/tent £6.50-£7.50, car/caravan £6.50-
£7.50, motorhome £6.50-£7.50,
motorbike/tent £6.50
₤¼ ✗¼ ⬤¼ ☐ ⊟ ⅙ ↟ WS
➡ Signposted from A15. Folkingham is
midway between towns of Bourne and
Sleaford. Turn opposite petrol station.

Yeate Farm Campsite

Bodinnick, Fowey PL23 1LZ
☎ **01726-870256**
Open 1 April-31 October
Size 1 acre, 33 touring pitches, 12 with
electric hookup, 33 level pitches, 2 static
caravans, 2 ₨, 3 WCs, 1 CWP
☐ ⋀ ⊠ Calor Gaz ⅙
Last arrival time: 11:00
➡ From A38 Liskeard bypass fork left onto
A390. Turn left on B3359 and follow signs
to Bodinnick, signposted from there.

Eilands Caravan Park

Landieu, Frosterley DL13 2SJ
☎ **01388-527230**
Open March-October
Size 10 touring pitches

Bridge House Marina & Caravan Park

Nateby Crossing Lane, Nateby, Garstang PR3
0JJ
☎ **01995-603207** ℻ **01995-601612**
Open March-January Å ⊕ ⊋

*Family owned, sheltered level grassy site,
with centrally heated toilet block. Close to
Blackpool, the Lake District and Bowland
Fells. An 18 hole golf course is just one mile
away.*

Size 6 acres, 50 touring pitches, 50 with
electric hookup, 50 level pitches, 20 static
caravans, 8 ₨, 12 WCs, 2 CWPs
£ car/caravan £7.70, motorhome £7.70
₡ MasterCard Visa
₤ ✗¼ ☐ ◖ ⋀ ⊠ Calor Gaz ↟ WS
Last arrival time: 10:30
➡ From M6 junction 32 take A6 to N. After 9
miles turn left at Chequered Flag. After 100
yards turn left to site 400 yards on left.

Claylands Caravan Park

Claylands Farm, Cabus, Garstang PR3 1AJ
☎ **01524-791242**
Open 1 March-mid September Å ⊕ ⊋
Size 14 acres, 56 touring pitches, 56 with
electric hookup, 56 level pitches, 39 static
caravans, 5 ₨, 12 WCs, 2 CWPs
£ car/tent £8.25, car/caravan £8.25,
motorhome £8.25, motorbike/tent £5,
children £0.75
₡ MasterCard Visa
₤ ✗ ⬤ ☐ ⬛ ☐ ▱ GR ▣ TV ⋀ ⊠ ⊟ Calor
Gaz ⅙ ↟ WS
➡ Turn E off A6, 1¼ miles N of junction
with B6430. Site is signposted.

Six Arches Holiday Caravan Park

Scorton, Garstang PR3 1AC
☎ **01524-791683**
Open 1 March-31 October ⊕ ⊋

*Family run riverside park within easy reach
of Blackpool, Morecambe, Lake District and
Bowland. Family entertainment in club
house. Colour brochure available on request.*

Size 16 acres, 16 touring pitches, 16 with electric hookup, 16 level pitches, 275 static caravans, 4 ⋒, 8 WCs, 1 CWP
£ car/caravan £9-£10, motorhome £9-£10
Rental ⇔ Chalet. 6 berth caravans/flats £125-£250
⚑ ✕¼ ☛ ⊟ ☏ ⊟ ⊿ ◙ ⋀ ⊞ ⊕ Calor ☛
Last arrival time: 10:00
➡ Turn E off A6 by Little Chef, ¼ mile N of junction with B6430. After 200 yards turn left under railway bridge to site.

Derwent Park Caravan and Camping Park

Dept. of Leisure Services, Gateshead
☎ **01207-543383**
Open 1 April-30 September ▲ ⇔ ☷

Situated seven miles south west of Newcastle at the junction of the A694 and B6314, this beautiful riverside park offers tennis, crazy golf, bowling green and adventure playground. Ideally placed for touring Northumbria and near to the Gateshead Metro Centre and Beamish museum.

Size 9 acres, 47 touring pitches, 35 with electric hookup, 25 static caravans, 12 ⋒, 13 WCs, 1 CWP
£ car/tent £6.50-£8, car/caravan £8-£9, motorhome £6.75-£8, motorbike/tent £6.50, children £1.05-£1.10
℀ MasterCard Visa
⚑¼ ☛ ⊟ ☏ ⊟ ◙ ⊿ ⋀ ⊞ Calor Gaz ⅊ ☛ WS
Last arrival time: 10:30
➡ On A694 and B6314, 3 miles from A1 and near to Gateshead Metro Centre and Beamish Museum.

Old Oaks Touring Park

Wick Farm, Wick, Glastonbury BA6 0JS
☎ **01458-831437**
Open 1 March-31 October ▲ ⇔ ☷

A family run park, set in delightfully tranquil and unspoilt countryside with lovely views and walks, offering excellent amenities in an outstanding environment.

Size 4 acres, 40 touring pitches, 40 with electric hookup, 40 level pitches, 6 ⋒, 9 WCs, 2 CWPs
£ car/tent £6.50-£8, car/caravan £6.50-£8, motorhome £6.50-£8, motorbike/tent £6.50, children £1.25-£1.75
⚑ ⊟ ☏ ⊟ ⊿ GR ◙ ⋀ ⊞ Calor Gaz ⅊ ☛
Last arrival time: 9:00
➡ 1½ miles from Glastonbury on A361 Shepton Mallet road, turn left at sign for Wick. Park on left in 1 mile.

Camping & Caravanning Club Site

Crowden, Hadfield, Hyde
☎ **01457-866057**
Open end February-start November ▲ ⇔ ☷
Size 2½ acres, 46 touring pitches, 2 ⋒, 6 WCs, 1 CWP
£ car/tent £8.75-£11.55, car/caravan £8.75-£11.55, motorhome £8.75-£11.55, motorbike/tent £8.75, children £1.30
℀ MasterCard Visa
☏ ☛
Last arrival time: 1:00
➡ From M67 (Hyde) take A628. Site is on left.

Brow House Farm
Goathland YO22 5NP
☎ 01947-896274
Open March-October Å ⊕ ⏻

Excellent location for exploring the National park and the Moors.

Size 3 acres, 50 touring pitches, 50 level pitches, 1 ᐠ, 2 WCs
£ car/tent £4, car/caravan £4, motorhome £4, motorbike/tent £4, children £4
⛿¼ ✗¼ ⛲¼ ▣ ᐠ
Last arrival time: 11:00

→ Turn W off A169 at ¼ mile N of Eller Beck Bridge. Site 1 mile S of Goathland.

Rose Hill Farm Tourist Park
Goonhavern TR4 9LA
☎ 01872-572448
Open Easter-September Å ⊕ ⏻
Size 7 acres, 65 touring pitches, 36 with electric hookup, 65 level pitches, 7 ᐠ, 9 WCs, 1 CWP
£ car/tent £5-£8.50, car/caravan £5-£8.50, motorhome £5-£8.50, motorbike/tent £5, children £0.75
⛿ ✗¼ ⛲¼ ▣ ᐠ ▣ GR ▣ TV ⛰ ✚ Calor Gaz ⚘
Last arrival time: 9:00
→ From A30 take B3285 signposted Perranporth to village of Goonhavern. Turn right at New Inn. Site is on the right.

Silverbow Park
Goonhavern TR4 9NX
☎ 01872-572347
Size 24 acres, 90 touring pitches, 54 with electric hookup, 80 level pitches, 12 ᐠ, 15 WCs, 1 CWP
⛿ ᐠ ▣ ▣ ▣ GR ▣ ⛰ ✚ Calor Gaz ⚿
Last arrival time: 10:30
→ From A30 take B3285 Perranporth road. At the T junction in Goonhavern village, turn left on the A3075 for ½ mile. Silverbow entrance is on the left.

Tregarton Farm Caravan & Camping Park
Gorran, St Austell PL26 6NF
☎ 01726-843666
Open 1 April-31 October Å ⊕ ⏻
Size 8 acres, 150 touring pitches, 40 with electric hookup, 60 level pitches, 10 ᐠ, 15 WCs, 1 CWP
£ car/tent £8-£11, car/caravan £8-£11, motorhome £8-£11, motorbike/tent £8, children £1.20-£2.20
CC MasterCard Visa
⛿ ⛲ ▣ ᐠ ▣ ▣ ⛰ ✚ Calor Gaz ⚘
Last arrival time: 10:00
→ From St Austell take B3273 to Mevagissey. After Pentwan turn right to Gorran.

Trelispen Camping & Caravaning Park

Gorran, St Austell PL26 6NS
📞 01726-843501 Fax 01726-843501
Open 1 April-31 October A 🚐 🚏
Size 2 acres, 40 touring pitches, 8 with electric hookup, 40 level pitches, 2 🚿, 7 WCs, 1 CWP
£ car/tent £7-£9, car/caravan £8-£9, motorhome £8-£9, motorbike/tent £7, children £1-£3
🚿¼ ✗¼ 🚻¼ 🔲 📞 🗔 🏧 🅟 🛒
➡ From St Austell take B3273 for Mevagissey. Follow signs for park.

Set on a working family farm within easy reach of Scafell and many other mountains. An ideal walking and climbing area.

GOSFORTH Cumbria   10A2

Church Stile Camp Site

Wasdale, Seascale, Gosforth CA20 1ET
📞 01946-726388
Open March-October A 🚏

Size 4 acres, 50 level pitches, 30 static caravans, 4 🚿, 9 WCs, 1 CWP
£ car/tent £5-£6, motorhome £5-£6, motorbike/tent £5
✗¼ 🚐¼ 🏧 🅟 Calor 🛒 WS
Last arrival time: 10:00
➡ Off A595, 4½ miles E of Gosforth to Nether Wasdale village.

Kingfisher Caravan Park

Browndown Road, Stokes Bay, Gosport
PO13 9BE
☎ 01705-502611 Fax 01705-583583
Open February-November ▲ 🚐 🚏

A family run site situated on the South Coast within easy reach of Portsmouth with ferries to the continent and Isle of Wight.

Size 14 acres, 120 touring pitches, 100 with electric hookup, 120 level pitches, 100 static caravans, 12 🚿, 17 WCs, 2 CWPs
£ car/tent £13-£15, car/caravan £13-£15, motorhome £13-£15, motorbike/tent £9
Rental 🚐 £40 per night.
℄ MasterCard Visa
🔋 ✗ 🍴 🅾 🔌 GR ⚠ ⌧ 🔒 Calor & 🐕 WS
Last arrival time: 11:00
➡ From M27 junction 11 take A32 to Gosport. Seafront road into Browndown Road.

Lakeland Leisure Park

Moor Lane, Flookburgh LA11 7LT
☎ 01345-508508
Open March-October ▲ 🚐 🚏

A family holiday park just a few minutes drive from picturesque Grange Over Sands and within easy driving distance of the Lakes. Indoor/outdoor pools, kids clubs, tennis and bowling. Live family entertainment, bars, great food. A 'British Holidays Park'.

Size 108 acres, 100 touring pitches, 150 static caravans, 7 🚿, 1 CWP
℄ MasterCard Visa
🔋 🍴 🅾 🔌 🔧 🔲 🔍 GR 🔍 ⚠ ⌧ 🔌 Calor 🐕
Last arrival time: 9:00
➡ From M6 junction 36 take A590 to Barrow-in-Furness. Then take the B5277 through Grange-over-Sands and into Flookburgh. Turn left at the village square and travel 2 miles down this road to site.

Hawkswick Cote Farm Caravan Park

Arncliffe, Skipton BD23 5PX
☎ 01756-770226 Fax 01756-770327
Open March-October ▲ 🚐 🚏
Size 50 touring pitches, 50 with electric hookup, 50 level pitches, 90 static caravans, 5 🚿, 6 WCs, 1 CWP
£ car/tent £8, car/caravan £8-£12, motorhome £8-£12, motorbike/tent £8, children £1.50
🔋 🅾 🔌 🔲 Calor Gaz & 🐕
➡ B6160 Threshfield to Grassington Road. Half a mile north of Kilnsey take the road to Arncliffe. The park is on the left, 1½ miles.

Camping & Caravanning Club Site

Clent Hills, Fieldhouse Lane, Romsey, Halesowen B62 0NH
☎ 01562-710015
Open end March-start November ▲ 🚐 🚏
Size 6½ acres, 130 touring pitches, 48 with electric hookup, 8 🚿, 13 WCs, 1 CWP
£ car/tent £8.75-£11.75, car/caravan £8.75-£11.75, motorhome £8.75-£11.75, motorbike/tent £8.75, children £1.40
℄ MasterCard Visa
🅾 🔌 GR ⚠ ⌧ & 🐕 WS
Last arrival time: 11:00

→ Take B4551, then road by Sun Hotel, turn left at Bell End Brougthen junction. Left turn after ¼ mile. Site on left.

Bluebell Holiday Park

The Broyle, Shortgate, Halland BN8 6PJ

📞 01825-840407

Open 1 April-31 October ▲ 🚐 🚐

Quiet rural park sheltered by trees. No club, swimming pool or playground, just peace and quiet, and an abundance of wild life. Luxury caravans for hire.

Size 2½ acres, 10 touring pitches, 10 with electric hookup, 20 level pitches, 4 static caravans, 4 🚿, 7 WCs, 1 CWP
£ car/tent £7.50, car/caravan £7.50, motorhome £7.50, motorbike/tent £7.50
Rental 🚐 £90-£250
✗¼ 🚐¼ 📞 🔌 Calor 🐕
Last arrival time: 9:00
→ From A22 Halland roundabout take B2192 to Ringmer. Site is 1½ miles on left behind Bluebell Inn.

Camping & Caravanning Club Site

Burnfoot Park Village, Haltwhistle NE49 0JP

📞 01434-320106

Open end September-start November ▲ 🚐 🚐

Size 3 acres, 60 touring pitches, 36 with electric hookup, 4 🚿, 9 WCs, 1 CWP
£ car/tent £8.75-£11.55, car/caravan £8.75-£11.55, motorhome £8.75-£11.55, motorbike/tent £8.75, children £1.40

CC MasterCard Visa
🔲 📞 🐕
Last arrival time: 11:00
→ Turn S of A69 immediately W of Haltwhistle, site is on right.

Lone Pine Camping

Low Road, Wortwell, Harleston IP20 0HJ

📞 01379-852423

Open 1 May-30 September ▲ 🚐

Size 2 acres, 24 touring pitches, 24 level pitches, 2 🚿, 4 WCs
£ car/tent £4, motorhome £4, motorbike/tent £4, children £0.50
🔲 Calor Gaz 🐕
→ Turn off A143 to Wortwell. In village turn into Low Road by pub. Site is ½ mile on right.

Hogbarn Caravan Park

Hogbarn Lane, Stede Hill, Harrietsham ME17 1NZ

📞 01622-859648

Open April-October 🚐 🚐

Size 23 acres, 45 touring pitches, 45 with electric hookup, 70 static caravans, 10 🚿, 12 WCs, 3 CWPs
🔌 ✗ 🔲 ♿ WS
→ On A20 between Maidstone and Charing. Signposted from Harrietsham.

High Moor Farm Park

Skipton Road, Harrogate HG3 2LZ

📞 01423-563637

Open 1 April-31 October ▲ 🚐 🚐

Size 22 acres, 250 touring pitches, 200 with electric hookup, 250 level pitches, 151 static caravans, 25 🚿, 10 WCs, 2 CWPs
£ car/tent £8.75-£9, car/caravan £8.75-£9, motorhome £8.75-£9, motorbike/tent £8.75
Rental 🚐
CC MasterCard Visa
🔌 ✗ 🚐 🔲 📞 🔲 🔳 📺 📻 🗑 GR ⚠ 🎣 🔌 Calor Gaz ♿ 🐕 WS →

← **High Moor Farm Park**

Last arrival time: 11:00
➜ On A59, 4 miles W of Harrogate.

Maustin Caravan Park
The Riddings, Spring Lane, Kearby-with-Netherby, Wetherby LS22 4DP
📞 **0113-288 6234**
Open March-October **A 🚐 🚙**
Size 6 acres, 13 touring pitches, 13 with electric hookup, 13 level pitches, 75 static caravans, 2 📷, 6 WCs, 1 CWP
£ car/tent £8-£8.50, car/caravan £8.50-£9, motorhome £8.50
Rental 🚐 from £195 per week
CC Visa
🛒 ✗ 🍴 📞 🔌 Calor 🐕
➜ From A61, after crossing River Wharfe, bottom of Harewood Bank, take first right signposted Kirkby Overblow. Then right again to Kearby, then right to caravan park.

Ripley Caravan Park
Ripley, Harrogate HG3 3AU
📞 **01423-770050 Fax 01423-770050**

Ripley Caravan Park
Ripley, Harrogate HG3 3AU
Tel: 01423-770050

Luxury touring park in the countryside. First class facilities: Indoor heated swimming pool, sauna, sunbed, games room, nursery playroom, playground, tennis net, football pitch, shop, laundry and disabled unit. At a crossroads for the Yorkshire Dales, only three miles to Harrogate and the Yorkshire Dales. At junction of A61/B6165. Park 300 yards towards Knaresborough.

Open Easter-31 October **A 🚐 🚙**
Size 18 acres, 100 touring pitches, 75 with electric hookup, 100 level pitches, 15 📷, 18 WCs, 1 CWP
£ car/tent £5.60-£6.60, car/caravan £5.60-£6.60, motorhome £5.60-£6.60, motorbike/tent £5.60, children £1
🛒 🛒¼ ✗¼ 🚐¼ 📷 📞 🔌 🔲 🏧 GR 📷 ⛰ 🎯
Calor Gaz ♿ 🐕 WS
Last arrival time: 9:00
➜ About 3 miles N of Harrogate, access is 300 yards down B6165 Knaresborough Road from roundabout junction with A61.

Rudding Holiday Park
Follifoot, Harrogate HG3 1JH
📞 **01423-870439**
Open March-November **A 🚐 🚙**
Size 50 acres, 141 touring pitches, 141 with electric hookup, 76 level pitches, 16 📷, 24 WCs, 2 CWPs
£ car/tent £7-£10, car/caravan £9-£20, motorhome £9-£20, motorbike/tent £7
Rental Cottages & lodges available from £150 p.w.
CC MasterCard Visa
🛒 ✗ 🍴 📷 📞 🔌 🔲 GR ⛰ 🎯 🔌 Calor Gaz ♿
🐕 WS
Last arrival time: 10:00
➜ Between A61 and A661 on A658, 1½ miles SE of Harrogate, turn NW ½ mile on right.

HARTLEPOOL Cleveland   11D1

Ash Vale Holiday Homes Park
Easington Rd, Hartlepool TS24 9RF
📞 **01429-86211 Fax 01429-86211**
Open 1 April-31 October **A**
Size 22 acres, 40 touring pitches, 30 with electric hookup, 90 level pitches, 50 static caravans, 6 📷, 10 WCs, 1 CWP
£ car/tent £5-£6
Rental 🚐
🛒 🛒¼ ✗¼ 📷 📞 🔌 ⛰ 🎯 Calor Gaz 🐕 WS
Last arrival time: 24 hrs
➜ From A19 take A179 towards Hartlepool, at the third roundabout turn left onto A1086 to Peterlee. Through next roundabout 300 yards on left.

Spindlewood Country Holiday Park
Rock Lane, Ore, Hastings TN35 4JN
📞 **01424-720825 Fax 01424-442105**
Open 1 March-31 October ▲ �"🚗 🚐
Size 12 acres, 49 touring pitches, 40 with
electric hookup, 49 level pitches, 75 static
caravans, 4 🛁, 11 WCs, 1 CWP
£ car/tent £4.50-£8, car/caravan £4.50-£8,
motorhome £4.50-£8, motorbike/tent £4.50
Rental 🚐 £95-£195 per week
🛒¼ ✗ 📮 🗑 🔌 🍴 🍽 ♿ 🐕
Last arrival time: 10.30
➡ Off A1 onto B2093, 3 miles until A259,
turn left for 100 yards. Left again on
Redlake Terrace for 50 yards. Then into
Rock Lane 50 yards on left.

Upwood Holiday Park
Blackmoor Road, Oxenhope, Haworth BD22
9SS
📞 **01535-643254 Fax 01535-643254**
Open 1 March-31 October ▲ 🚗 🚐
Size 13 acres, 70 touring pitches, 70 with
electric hookup, 70 level pitches, 30 static
caravans, 8 🛁, 10 WCs, 1 CWP
£ car/tent £7.50-£9.50, car/caravan £7.50-
£9.50, motorhome £7.50-£9.50,
motorbike/tent £5.50
Rental 🚐 £90-£225
✗ 📮 🗑 🔌 🗑 📶 🌐 🍴 🌐 🅿 🏬 Calor Gaz ♿ 🐕
WS
Last arrival time: 10:00
➡ 1 mile from Haworth, follow signs.

Camping & Caravanning Club Site
Kinder Road, Hayfield SK12 5LE
📞 **01663-745394**
Open end March-start November ▲ 🚗 🚐
Size 7 acres, 90 touring pitches, 6 🛁, 12
WCs, 1 CWP
£ car/tent £8.75-£11.55, car/caravan £8.75-
£11.55, motorhome £8.75-£11.55,
motorbike/tent £8.75, children £1.40
Rental ▲ Chalet.
CC MasterCard Visa
♿
Last arrival time: 11:00

➡ From A624 follow signs for Hayfield and
then international camping signs.

Callouse Caravan & Camping Park
Leedstown, Paythorne, Hayle TR27 5ET
📞 **01736-850431 Fax 01736-850431**
Open 30 March-28 Septembe ▲ 🚗 🚐

*Award winning secluded family park in
suntrap valley offering, superb facilities for
tourers.*

Size 12½ acres, 120 touring pitches, 99 with
electric hookup, 120 level pitches, 17 static
caravans, 15 🛁, 21 WCs, 2 CWPs
£ car/tent £6-£10, car/caravan £6-£10,
motorhome £6-£10, motorbike/tent £6,
children £0.75-£1.75
Rental 🚐 £100-£450
CC MasterCard Visa
🛒 ✗ 📮 🗑 🔌 🗑 📶 🌐 🏪 🍴 🌐 📺 🏬 🅿 🍴 Calor
Gaz ♿ 🐕
Last arrival time: 10:00
➡ Take B3302 towards Helston. Turn left at
approach to Leedstown opposite village
hall.

Parbola Holiday Park
Wall, Gwinear, Nr Hayle TR27 5LE
📞 **01209-831503 Fax 01209-831503**
Open Easter-October ▲ 🚗 🚐
Size 17½ acres, 115 touring pitches, 55 with
electric hookup, 115 level pitches, 19 static
caravans, 12 🛁, 16 WCs, 2 CWPs
£ car/tent £6.50-£10, car/caravan £6.50-£10,
motorhome £6.50-£10, motorbike/tent £6.50
Rental ▲ 🚐 Chalet. £99-£369
CC MasterCard Visa
🛒 📮 🗑 🔌 🍴 🅿 🌐 📺 🏬 🅿 Calor Gaz ♿ WS
Last arrival time: 10:00
➡ Take A30 to Hayle. At roundabout leave
first exit to Connor Downs. At end of village
turn right to Carnhell Green and turn right
at T junction. Parbola is 1 mile on the left.

St Ives Bay Holiday Park
73 Loggans Road, Upton Towans, Hayle
TR27 5BH
☎ **01736-752274 Fax 01736-754523**
Open 1 May-1 October 🅰 ⏀ ⏁

Set in sand dunes with private access to a fabulous sandy beach. Two bars and a large indoor pool. Family and children oriented.

Size 75 acres, 250 touring pitches, 130 with electric hookup, 200 level pitches, 250 static caravans, 26 ♛, 38 WCs, 5 CWPs
£ car/tent £5-£18, car/caravan £5-£18, motorhome £5-£18, motorbike/tent £5
Rental ⏀ Chalet. £99-£450
CC MasterCard Visa
⛽ ● ⊡ ⛃ ⊞ ⊠ GR ⊡ TV ⋀ ⊞ ⊟ Calor Gaz
🐕
➔ Exit A30 at Hayle and take B3301 coastroad. Park entrance is 600 yards on left.

HAYLING ISLAND Hampshire   4B4

Lower Tye Farm Camp Site
Copse Lane, Hayling Island PO11 0RQ
☎ **01705-462479**
Open 1 March-1 November 🅰 ⏀ ⏁

Quiet family site near family pub. An excellent touring base for Portsmouth, Isle of Wight, and the New Forest. Long term parking is available on site.

Size 5 acres, 150 touring pitches, 75 with electric hookup, 150 level pitches, 13 ♛, 18 WCs, 1 CWP

£ car/tent £7, car/caravan £7, motorhome £7, motorbike/tent £7, children £0.50
Rental 🅰 ⏀ Chalet.
⛽ ⛽¼ ✕ ● ⊡ ⛃ ⊟ ⊡ GR ⋀ ⊞ Calor Gaz 🐕
WS
Last arrival time: 12:00
➔ Exit M27 and A317 at Havant. Follow A3023 from Havant. 1½ miles after crossing the bridge to Hayling Island, turn left into Copse Lane. Site entrance 1 mile on right.

HEACHAM Norfolk   9D2

Heacham Beach Holiday Park
South Beach Road, Heacham PE31 7BD
☎ **01485-570270**
Open Easter-October 🅰 ⏀
Size 23 acres, 24 touring pitches, 18 with electric hookup, 18 level pitches, 400 static caravans, 8 ♛, 12 WCs
⛽ ● ⊡ ⊠ ⊟
➔ Take A149 from King's Lynn to Hunstanton. After Snettisham village turn left at sign for Heacham Beaches and fork left 1 mile along the road.

HELMSLEY North Yorkshire   11D2

Foxholme Touring Caravan Park
Harome, Helmsley YO6 5JG
☎ **01439-770416**
Open 1 March-31 October 🅰 ⏀ ⏁

Quiet, sheltered and level wooded site. All pitches attractively situated among evergreen trees and well spaced to ensure peace, quiet and privacy. Hard roads throughout the site give good all-weather access.

Size 6 acres, 60 touring pitches, 60 with electric hookup, 60 level pitches, 8 ♛, 16 WCs, 2 CWPs

£ car/tent £6.50-£7, car/caravan £6.50-£7, motorhome £6.50-£7, motorbike/tent £6.50
🗤 🖸 📞 🗗 Calor Gaz 🕭 🛏 WS
➜ On A170 for ½ mile, turn right on road to Harome, 2 miles turn left at church, ½ mile further keep left, then take first turn on left to site in 350 yards.

Golden Square Caravan Park
Oswaldkirk, Helmsley YO6 5YQ
📞 **01439-788269**
Open 1 March-31 October 🛆 🚐 🚛

A quiet secluded site with excellent facilities, hidden from the outside world.

Size 12 acres, 129 touring pitches, 100 with electric hookup, 129 level pitches, 14 🗤, 18 WCs, 2 CWPs
£ car/tent £6-£7.50, car/caravan £6-£7.50, motorhome £6-£7.50, motorbike/tent £6
Rental 🚐 Chalet. £90-£300
🗤 ✕¼ 🖘 🖸 📞 🗗 GR 🔍 🗚 🗚 Calor Gaz 🕭 🛏 WS
Last arrival time: 10:00
➜ From A19 follow 'caravan' route to Coxwold, Wass and Ampleforth. Site is 1 mile from Ampleforth going towards Helmsley.

Wrens Of Ryedale Caravan Site
Gale Lane, Nawton, Helmsley YO6 5SD
📞 **01439-771260**
Open 1 April-31 October 🛆 🚐 🚛

Very attractive, well-sheltered, level site. Ideal for North York National Park, Dales, York and the coast. 5% discount with this advert.

Size 2½ acres, 45 touring pitches, 21 with electric hookup, 45 level pitches, 4 🗤, 10 WCs, 1 CWP
£ car/tent £5-£6.50, car/caravan £5-£6.50, motorhome £5-£6.50, motorbike/tent £5, children £0.50
🗤 📞 🗗 🗚 🗚 Calor Gaz 🛏 WS
Last arrival time: 10:00
➜ Take A170 from Helmsley to Pickering. 3 miles E of Helmsley in Beadlam turn right into Gale Lane. Site is 600 yards on right.

HELSTON Cornwall   2A4

Franchis Holiday Park
Cury Cross Lanes, Nr Mullion, Helston TR12 7AZ
📞 **01326-240301**
Open 1 March-31 October 🛆 🚐 🚛

Rose award park in an area of outstanding natural beauty. Close mown grass and woodland. Excellent facilities.   ➜

← **Franchis Holiday Park**

Size 17 acres, 70 touring pitches, 37 with electric hookup, 65 level pitches, 7 static caravans, 11 🅟, 11 WCs, 1 CWP
£ car/tent £6-£7, car/caravan £6-£7, motorhome £6-£7, motorbike/tent £6, children £0.50
Rental 🚐 Bungalows £105-£298, caravans £105-£380
🅟 🔌 ☕ Calor Gaz 🐕
Last arrival time: 10:00
➜ 6 miles from Helston on A3083, 1 mile past Wheel Inn pub.

Mullion Holiday Park

Penhale Cross, Ruan Minor, Helston TR12 7LJ
📞 **01326-240000** Fax **01326-241141**
Open Easter-September ▲ 🚐 🚐
Size 49 acres, 159 touring pitches, 87 with electric hookup, 295 static caravans, 15 🅟, 15 WCs, 1 CWP
£ car/tent £7.50-£14.50, car/caravan £7.50-£14.50, motorhome £7.50-£14.50, motorbike/tent £7.50
Rental 🚐 Chalet. £105-£599
CC MasterCard Visa

🅟 ✖ 💧 ☕ 🔌 📞 📶 📶 🍴 GR 🔍 TV 🅰 🅇 🔌 Calor Gaz 🐕
Last arrival time: 9:00
➜ From the A30, take the A39 from Fraddon to Truro and continue on the Falmouth road. Take the A394 to Helston, then the A3083 for the Lizard. After 7 miles site is on left opposite Mullion turning.

Long Beach Estate

Hemsby, Great Yarmouth NR29 4JD
📞 **01493-730023** Fax **01493-730188**
Open 22 March-21 October ▲ 🚐 🚐
Size 30 acres, 30 touring pitches, 30 with electric hookup, 30 level pitches, 120 static caravans, 10 🅟, 25 WCs, 2 CWPs
£ car/tent £5-£11, car/caravan £7-£11, motorhome £7-£11, motorbike/tent £5
Rental 🚐 Chalet.
🅟 ✖ ✖¼ 💧 💧¼ ☕ 🔌 ☕ GR TV 🅰 🅇 🔌 Calor Gaz 🦽 🐕 WS
Last arrival time: 11:00
➜ From B1159 at Hemsby, turn right on Beach Road, then 2nd left (signposted Longbeach).

Harwoods Farm

West End Lane, Henfield BN5 9RF
📞 **01273-492820**
Open Easter-end October ▲ 🚐
Size 1¾ acres, 35 touring pitches, 35 level pitches, 2 CWPs
£ car/tent £3.50, motorhome £3.50, motorbike/tent £3.50, children £0.50
🖊 🐕
Last arrival time: 12:00
➜ On A251 to Henfield turn into Church Road opposite White Hart pub in High Street. Continue 2 miles to end of road. Site is on right.

Swiss Farm Camping International

Marlow Road, Henley-on-Thames RG9 2HY
📞 **01491-573419**
▲ 🚐 🚐

Size 7 acres, 200 touring pitches, 10 ⋔, 21 WCs
🐕 ✗ ☕
➡ Site ½ mile N of Henley, W side of A4155.

Poston Mill Park
Golden Valley, Peterchurch HR2 0SF
📞 **01981-550225 Fax 01981-550885**
Open all year Å 🚐 🚍

One of Britain's best parks. Set in the beautiful countryside of the Golden Valley, the site provides an ideal location for a peaceful holiday.

Size 25 acres, 60 touring pitches, 60 with electric hookup, 60 level pitches, 40 static caravans, 8 ⋔, 12 WCs, 2 CWPs
£ car/tent £5-£6, car/caravan £6.50-£7.50, motorhome £6.50-£7.50, motorbike/tent £5
Rental 🚐 holiday home £120-£185
🐕¼ ✗ ✗¼ ☕ ☕¼ 🔘 📞 🖥 🔋 🔳 ⚠ 🔲 🔌
Calor Gaz ♿ 🐾 WS

Last arrival time: 10:00
➡ Site on B4348 Hereford to Hay-on-Wye road.

Hillborough Caravan Park
Reculver Road, Herne Bay CT6 6SR
📞 **01227-374618**
Open 22 March-October 🚐 🚍
Size 35 touring pitches, 35 with electric hookup, 380 static caravans, 4 ⋔, 4 WCs, 1 CWP
🐕 ✗ ☕ 📞 🖥 GR 🔲 ⚠ 🔲 🔌 Calor Gaz ♿ WS
Last arrival time: 12:00
➡ From A299 turn off to Reculver.

Camping & Caravanning Club Site
Mangrove Road, Hertford SG13 8QF
📞 **01663-745394**
Open end March-start November Å 🚐 🚍
Size 32 acres, 150 touring pitches, 65 with electric hookup, 2 ⋔, 10 WCs, 1 CWP
£ car/tent £8.20-£10.40, car/caravan £8.20-£10.40, motorhome £8.20-£10.40, motorbike/tent £8.20, children £1.30
CC MasterCard Visa
📞 ⚠ 🔲 🐾 WS
Last arrival time: 11:00
➡ Leave the A1(M) (jn4) and follow the A414. In Hertford take Mangrove Road on left by fire station. Site is ¾ mile.

Causey Hill Caravan Park
Bensonsfell Farm, Hexham NE46 2JN
📞 **01434-602834**
Open 1 April-31 October Å 🚐 🚍
Size 7½ acres, 35 touring pitches, 22 with electric hookup, 22 level pitches, 68 static caravans, 6 ⋔, 32 WCs, 2 CWPs
£ car/tent £7.50-£8.50, car/caravan £5, motorhome £7.50, motorbike/tent £7.50
🐕 🔘 📞 Calor 🐾
Last arrival time: 8:00

Riverside Leisure
Tyne Green, Hexham NE46 3RY
☎ 01434-604705
Open March-January ⚊ 🚐 🚐

Nestling in the heart of Roman Wall country, this beautiful country garden park offers peace and tranquillity. Riverside leisure is truly 'where holidays begin!'

Size 5.8 acres, 30 touring pitches, 30 with electric hookup, 30 level pitches, 100 static caravans, 8 🚿, 12 WCs, 1 CWP
£ car/tent £9-£10, car/caravan £12-£13.50, motorhome £12-£13.50, motorbike/tent £9, children £1.50
Rental 🚐 Chalet. £135-£300
🛒¼ ▣ ☎ ▣ Calor Gaz ♿ ⛓
Last arrival time: 7:00
➡ From roundabout on A69 over the river and railway bridges, straight on at two mini roundabouts to town centre. Follow round the right hand bend and take second lane on right after the Shell Garage. Turn left at the bottom. Park is in 200 yards.

Melbreak Caravan Park
Carr Lane, Middleton, Heysham LA3 3LH
☎ 01524-852430
Open 1 March-30 October ⚊ 🚐 🚐

Small family site with modern fully-tiled toilet blocks situated four miles from Morecambe and six miles from Lancaster, within reach of the Lake District and Yorkshire Dales.

Size 2 acres, 30 touring pitches, 40 with electric hookup, 40 level pitches, 10 static caravans, 4 🚿, 7 WCs, 1 CWP
£ car/tent £5.75-£6, car/caravan £6.45-£7, motorhome £6.75-£7, motorbike/tent £5.75
🛒 🛒 ▣ Calor Gaz ⛓
Last arrival time: 9:00
➡ Take A589 S from Lancaster. At second large roundabout turn left to Middleton. Follow signs for site.

New House Farm Caravan Site
Walrow, Highbridge TA9 4RA
☎ 01278-782218
⚊ 🚐 🚐

Peace and tranquillity on a level country site with easy access. Country pubs and coarse fishing within one mile. Play area for children.

Size 8 acres, 30 touring pitches, 30 with electric hookup, 30 level pitches, 4 🚿, 5 WCs, 1 CWP
£ car/tent £6, car/caravan £6, motorhome £5
🛒 ✕¼ 🛒¼ ▣ ▣ ⚠ 🔀 Calor ⛓ WS
Last arrival time: 11:00
➡ 2½ miles from M5 junction 22, 3 miles from Burnham-on-Sea.

HINKLEY Leicestershire 8B3

Wolvey Villa Farm Caravan & Camp Site

Wolvey, Hinkley LE10 3HF
☎ 01455-220493
Open all year ▲ ⬤ ⬤

A quiet site on the border of Warwickshire and Leicestershire. Ideally located to explore the many places of interest in the Midlands.

Size 7 acres, 50 with electric hookup, 110 level pitches, 4 ⬤, 11 WCs, 1 CWP
£ car/tent £5-£5.20, car/caravan £5.10-£5.30, motorhome £5.10-£5.30, motorbike/tent £5, children £1
⬤ Calor Gaz ⬤ WS
➤ M6 junction 2 to B4065 and follow Wolvey signs. M69 junction 1, then follow Wolvey signs.

HODDESDON Hertfordshire 5D2

Lee Valley Caravan Park

Charlton Meadows, Essex Road, Dobbs Weir, Hoddesdon EN11 0AS
☎ 01992-462090
Open March (Easter)-October ▲ ⬤ ⬤
Size 23 acres, 100 touring pitches, 36 with electric hookup, 100 level pitches, 100 static caravans, 20 ⬤, 16 WCs, 2 CWPs
£ car/tent £9.20, car/caravan £9.20, motorhome £9.20, motorbike/tent £9.20, children £1.90
⬤ MasterCard Visa
⬤¼ ⬤¼ ⬤ ⬤ ⬤ Calor Gaz ⬤ ⬤ WS
➤ Take Hoddesdon turn off A10. At second roundabout turn left and site is 1½ miles on right.

HOLBEACH Lincolnshire 9D2

Matopos Touring Park

Main Street, Fleet Hargate, Holbeach, Spalding PE12 8LL
☎ 01406-22910
Open 16 March-16 October ▲ ⬤ ⬤
Size 7 acres, 45 touring pitches, 8 with electric hookup, 45 level pitches, 4 ⬤, 5 WCs, 1 CWP
£ car/tent £6, car/caravan £6, motorhome £6, children £0.80
⬤¼ ⬤¼ ⬤¼ ⬤ ⬤ ⬤ Calor Gaz ⬤ WS
Last arrival time: 12:00
➤ From Spalding take A151 to Holbeach. Continue further 3 miles to Fleet Hargate. Turn right into village just before A151 joins A17.

HOLMFIRTH West Yorkshire 10C4

Holme Valley Camping & Caravan Park

Thongsbridge, Holmfirth HO7 2TD
☎ 01484-665819 Fax 01484-663870
▲ ⬤ ⬤

In the heart of beautiful 'Summerwine' country. The park is regularly chosen by the BBC for water and woodland shots. See display advert for description.

Size 8½ acres, 62 touring pitches, 62 with electric hookup, 56 level pitches, 4 ⬤, 8 WCs, 1 CWP
£ car/tent £5.50-£6.50, car/caravan £6.50-£7.50, motorhome £5.50-£6.50, motorbike/tent £4.50, children £0.50
Rental ⬤ £75-£180
⬤ ⬤¼ ⬤ ⬤ ⬤ ⬤ ⬤ ⬤ Calor Gaz ⬤ ⬤
Last arrival time: 10:00
➤ Entrance to private lane is off A6024, one mile N of Holmfirth.
See advert on next page

HONITON Devon   3D3

Camping & Caravanning Club Site
Otter Valley Park, Northcote, Honiton EX14 8SS
☎ 01404-44546
Open end March-start November 🏕 🚐 🚛
Size 6 acres, 90 touring pitches, 36 with electric hookup, 10 🚿, 15 WCs, 2 CWPs
£ car/tent £8.20-£10.40, car/caravan £8.20-£10.40, motorhome £8.20-£10.40, motorbike/tent £8.20, children £1.30
CC MasterCard Visa
☎ 🐕
Last arrival time: 11:00
➜ From A30 follow Honiton signposts, then follow caravan and tent signs. Drive through public site to reach Club site.

HOPE Derbyshire   8A1

Laneside Caravan Site
Laneside Farm, Hope S30 2RR
☎ 01433-620215 Fax 01433-620214
Open 31 March-31 October 🏕 🚐 🚛

Breathtaking scenery, spotless, well equipped, manicured level valley site surrounded by hills. Adjoins Hope, so seven day late shopping, pubs, restaurants, etc are all within five minutes walk.

Size 7 acres, 100 touring pitches, 100 with electric hookup, 95 level pitches, 24 static caravans, 6 🚿, 14 WCs, 2 CWPs
£ car/tent £6.25-£7.25, car/caravan £6.25-£7.25, motorhome £6.25-£7.25, children £0.75
Rental Cottages from £60 w/e to £350 weekly.
🛒 🛒¼ ✗¼ ♨¼ 🔥 ☎ 🗑 🗿 🎯 Calor Gaz 🐕

Last arrival time: 9:00
➡ Site on A625, ½ mile E of Hope village.

5D4
HORAM East Sussex

Horam Manor Touring Park
Horam, Near Heathfield TN21 0YD
☎ 01435-813662
Open March-mid October ▲ 🚐 🚏

A tranquil rural site in an area of outstanding natural beauty. Plenty of space. Special mother and toddler room. Free hot water and showers.

Size 7 acres, 90 touring pitches, 46 with electric hookup, 75 level pitches, 7 🚿, 10 WCs, 1 CWP
£ car/tent £9-£11, car/caravan £9-£11, motorhome £9-£11, motorbike/tent £9
🚻¼ ✗¼ 🚰¼ 🗑 🛒 🗑 🎣 🧺 Calor Gaz 🚾 🐕
➡ Site is on the A267 S of Horam village. 3 miles S of Heathfield, 13 miles N of Eastbourne.

HORRABRIDGE Devon   2C3

Magpie Leisure Dartmoor Country Holidays
Bedford Bridge, Horrabridge PL20 7RY
☎ 01822-852651
Open 15 March-15 November ▲ 🚐 🚏

Peaceful woodland park bordered by the River Walkham in Dartmoor National Park. Ideal for walkers, bird-watchers and all lovers of unspoiled countryside.

Size 8 acres, 30 touring pitches, 26 with electric hookup, 30 level pitches, 18 static caravans, 4 🚿, 4 WCs, 1 CWP
£ car/tent £5-£7.50, car/caravan £5-£7.50, motorhome £5-£7.50
🚻¼ ✗¼ 🚰¼ 🗑 🛒 🗑 Calor 🐕
Last arrival time: 11:00
➡ 2¾ miles SE of Tavistock off the A386 Plymouth Road.

HUNSTANTON Norfolk   9D2

Searles Holiday Centre
3 South Beach Road, Hunstanton PE36 5BB
☎ 01485-534211 **Fax** 01485-533815
Open March-October ▲ 🚐 🚏
Size 60 acres, 350 touring pitches, 200 static caravans
£ car/tent £7-£16, car/caravan £7-£20, motorhome £7-£20, motorbike/tent £7
Rental 🚐 Chalet.
(C MasterCard Visa
🚻 ✗ 🚰 🗑 🛒 🗑 🗑 🎣 🗑 🗑 🗑 GR 🗑 🗑 🗑
Calor 🚾
Last arrival time: 9:00
➡ From King's Lynn take A149 to Hunstanton. Turn left at roundabout signposted South Beach.
See advert on next page

HUNTINGDON Cambridgeshire   8C4

Old Manor Caravan Park
Church Lane, Grafham, Huntingdon PE18 0BB
☎ 01480-810264
Open February-November ▲ 🚐 🚏   ➡

← **Old Manor Caravan Park**

Size 6½ acres, 80 touring pitches, 60 with electric hookup, 80 level pitches, 20 static caravans, 6 ♠, 10 WCs, 1 CWP
£ car/tent £9, car/caravan £9, motorhome £9, motorbike/tent £6, children £1
♁ ✕¼ ▣ ▌ ▣ ▣ ⚠ ▣ Calor Gaz ♿ ♞
Last arrival time: 10:00
➡ Leave A1 at Buckden for B661. Take A14 to Ellington.

Park Lane Touring Park
Park Lane, Godmanchester, Huntingdon PE18 8AF
☎ **01480-453740** Fax **01480-453740**
Open March-October ⚊ ⛺ 🚐
Size 2½ acres, 50 touring pitches, 50 with electric hookup, 50 level pitches, 4 ♠, 8 WCs, 1 CWP
£ car/tent £7.50, car/caravan £7.50, motorhome £7.50, motorbike/tent £7.50, children £1
♁¼ ✕¼ ⛽¼ ▣ ▌ ▣ Calor Gaz ♿ ♞ WS
Last arrival time: 10:30
➡ From A14 turn off to Godmanchester and pick up camp signs on lamp post. Turn right at Black Bull Pub. Entrance on left.

Quiet Waters Caravan Park
Hemingford Abbots, Huntingdon PE18 9AJ
☎ **01480-463405**
Open April-October ⚊ ⛺ 🚐
Size 5 acres, 20 touring pitches, 20 with electric hookup, 20 level pitches, 9 static caravans, 6 ♠, 6 WCs, 1 CWP
£ car/tent £7.50-£8.50, car/caravan £7.50-£8.50, motorhome £7.50-£8.50, motorbike/tent £7.50
Rental ⛺
℃ Visa
♁ ✕¼ ▌ Calor Gaz ♞
Last arrival time: 8:00
➡ From A14 turn off at Hemingford Abbotts. 1 mile into village follow signs.

ILFRACOMBE Devon   2C2

Hidden Valley Touring & Camping Park
West Down, Ilfracombe EX34 8NU
☎ **01271-813837** Fax **01271-814041**
Open 15 March-5 November ⚊ ⛺ 🚐

Set in a beautiful wooded valley with hard standing and grass pitches, plus immaculate first class facilities including free showers and hot water, and free TV hook-ups. Woodland walks, play parks, dog walks.

Size 25 acres, 134 touring pitches, 124 with electric hookup, 134 level pitches, 10 ⛾, 27 WCs, 4 CWPs
£ car/tent £3.50-£10, car/caravan £3.50-£14, motorhome £3.50-£10, motorbike/tent £3.50
CC MasterCard Visa
⛄ ✗ 🛒 ⊟ 🔋 🚿 ⚠ 🏕 🛗 Calor Gaz ♿ 🐕 WS
Last arrival time: 10:00
➡ From M5 turn off at junction 27 and follow A361 to Barnstaple. Continue for 8 miles towards Ilfracombe to site on left.

Napps Camp Site
Old Coast Road, Berrynarbor, Ilfracombe EX34 9SW
📞 **01271-882557**
Open 1 April-31 October 🏕 🚐 🚙

A well kept site in a peaceful setting right on the beautiful North Devon coast, with woodland and coastal footpaths to the beach. Breathtaking coastal views and excellent facilities.

➡

← Napps Camp Site

Size 15 acres, 200 touring pitches, 80 with electric hookup, 200 level pitches, 2 static caravans, 10 ⋔, 20 WCs, 1 CWP
℃ Visa
⧓ ✕ ☎ ⊡ ▧ ▦ GR ◐ ⚠ ⊞ ⊟ Calor Gaz ♿ WS
➜ Take A399 1½ miles W of Combe Martin. Site is signposted on your right. and is approximately 300 yards along old coast road.

ILMINSTER Somerset   3E2

Thornleigh Caravan Park
Horton, Ilminster TA19 9QH
☎ **01460-53450 Fax 01460-53450**
Open March-October ⊼ ⊡ ⊞
Size 1½ acres, 20 touring pitches, 11 with electric hookup, 20 level pitches, 2 ⋔, 4 WCs, 1 CWP
£ car/tent £5.50, car/caravan £5.50, motorhome £5.50, motorbike/tent £5.50
Rental Chalet. £180-£220
⧓¼ ✕¼ ⬤¼ ▦ ♿ ⚲
➜ At A303 roundabout W of Ilminster take A358 signposted Chard. ¼ mile turn right opposite Lambs Inn. Site is on left in ¾ mile, opposite Horton filling station.

IPSWICH Suffolk   5E1

Low House Touring Caravan Centre
Bucklesham Road, Foxhall, Ipswich IP10 OAU
☎ **01473-659437**
Open all year ⊼ ⊡ ⊞
Size 3 acres, 30 touring pitches, 30 with electric hookup, 3 level pitches, 4 ⋔, 5 WCs, 1 CWP
£ car/tent £4.25-£6.50
✕¼ ▣ ☎ ⊡ ▧ ▦ ◐ ⚠ ⊞ ♿ ⚲
➜ Turn off A14 Ipswich ring road onto A1156 (signposted Ipswich East). Follow road over bridge which crosses the A14 and almost immediately turn right (no sign). After ½ mile turn right again (signposted Bucklesham) and site is on left after ¼ mile.

Priory Park
Off Nacton Road, Ipswich IP10 0JT
☎ **01473-727393**
Open all year ⊼ ⊡ ⊞

Set in 85 acres on the banks of the River Orwell, with woodland, a golf course, swimming pool, tennis and foreshore access for small boats. Bar with food. Open all year.

Size 85 acres, 110 touring pitches, 110 with electric hookup, 80 level pitches, 50 static caravans, 16 ⋔, 15 WCs, 3 CWPs
£ car/tent £11-£13, car/caravan £11-£13, motorhome £11-£13, motorbike/tent £11
Rental Chalet. From £200 per week.
⧓¼ ✕ ▣ ☎ ⊡ ▧ P ▧ ▦ GR ◐ ⚠ ⊞ ⊟ Calor Gaz ⚲
➜ Leave A14 at Nalton/Ransomet Europark interchange and follow signs to airport/town centre. Turn left after 400 yards and follow signs to Priory Park.

ISLE OF WIGHT   4B4

Adgestone Camping Park
Lower Road, Adgestone, Sandown PO36 OHL
☎ **01983-403432 Fax 01983-404955**
Open Easter-September ⊼ ⊡ ⊞

Superb family run park in glorious countryside 1½ miles from beach. Facilities include swimming pool, take-away, adventure playgrounds, and river fishing. All-season package holidays and retired couples concessions available.

Size 15½ acres, 200 touring pitches, 200 with electric hookup, 200 level pitches, 15 ℞, 30 WCs, 2 CWPs
£ car/tent £6.40-£9.90, car/caravan £6.40-£9.90, motorhome £6.40-£9.90, motorbike/tent £6.40, children £1.60-£2.75
CC MasterCard Visa
🦺 🖤 🔘 🔋 🗇 🔲 🔲 🔍 /📐 🔲 Calor Gaz ♿ ♉
Last arrival time: dusk
➡ Turn off A3055 at Manor House pub in Lake. Go past golf club to T-junction and turn right. Site is 200 yards on right.

Comforts Farm
Pallance Road, Northwood, Cowes
☎ **01983-293888**
Open March-October ⋏ 🚐 🚎

Set on a 60 acre working farm near the sea at Cowes, with excellent views and good amenities. No charge for children or dogs.

Size 9 acres, 50 touring pitches, 25 with electric hookup, 25 level pitches, 6 ℞, 12 WCs, 1 CWP
£ car/tent £2-£2.50, car/caravan £5.30-£6.30, motorhome £5.30-£6.30, motorbike/tent £2
🦺 🔘 🗇 🔲 🔍 🔲 Calor Gaz ♉
➡ From Cowes take A3020, turn right into Three Gates Road at Plessy Road and after ¼ mile, right into Pallance Road.

Heathfield Farm Camping Site
Heathfield Road, Freshwater PO40 9SH
☎ **01983-752480** Fax **01983-752480**

Open May-end September ⋏ 🚐 🚎

Peaceful family site with sea and downland views. High standard of cleanliness maintained in modern toilet block. Close to the beach, shops and buses. Ferry inclusive holidays.

Size 5 acres, 60 touring pitches, 16 with electric hookup, 60 level pitches, 4 ℞, 7 WCs, 1 CWP
£ car/tent £5.50-£6.50, car/caravan £5.50-£6.50, motorhome £5.50-£6.50, motorbike/tent £5.50, children £1-£1.50
🦺¼ ✗ 🖤 🗇 Gaz ♉
Last arrival time: 10:00
➡ Two miles W from Yarmouth ferry port on A3054. Turn left into Heathfield Road. Site entrance is 200 yards on right.

Landguard Camping Park
Landguard Manor Road, Shanklin PO37 7PH
☎ **01983-867028**
Open May-September ⋏ 🚐 🚎
Size 6 acres, 150 touring pitches, 150 with electric hookup, 140 level pitches, 10 ℞, 16 WCs, 1 CWP
£ car/tent £6-£10, car/caravan £6-£10, motorhome £6-£10, motorbike/tent £6, children £1.80-£2.75
CC MasterCard Visa
🦺 ✗ 🖤 🔘 🔋 🗇 🔲 🔍 GR /📐 🔲 🔲 Calor Gaz ♿
Last arrival time: 9:00
➡ From Newport take A3056 to Sandown. Do not turn off at A3020 to Shanklin. Continue on the Sandown road past Safeway and take next turning right into Whitecross Lane. Follow signs.

Lower Hyde Character Holiday Village
Shanklin PO37 7LL
☎ **01983-866131**   ➡

← Lower Hyde Character Holiday Village

Open April-October ▲ ⊞
Size 20 acres, 128 touring pitches, 72 with electric hookup, 128 level pitches, 228 static caravans, 12 ⚐, 21 WCs,
⚑ ⛽ ⊟ ⊟ ⚐ ⊟ &
➔ In Shanklin town - ½ mile from train station.

Ninham Country Holidays
Shanklin PO37 7PL
☎ 01983-864243 Fax 01983-868881
Open Easter-September ▲ ⊞ ⊞

Country park setting overlooking a wooded valley and small lakes. Adjacent to the island's main resort of Shanklin.

Size 5 acres, 98 touring pitches, 40 with electric hookup, 90 level pitches, 4 static caravans, 8 ⚐, 12 WCs, 1 CWP
£ car/tent £7.20-£9.50, car/caravan £7.20-£9.50, motorhome £7.20-£9.50, motorbike/tent £7.20, children £1.80-£2.50
Rental ⊞ £185-£345
℅ MasterCard Visa
⚑¼ ✗¼ ⚐¼ ⊟ ⛽ ⊟ ⊟ ⊟ GR ⊟ ⊞ ⊞ Calor Gaz WS
Last arrival time: 10:00
➔ Main site entrance is 1½ miles W of Lake on Newport-Sandown road (A3056). Private drive on left past mini-roundabout outside 'Safeway' superstore.

Nodes Point Holiday Village
St Helens, Ryde PO33 1YA
☎ 01983-872401 Fax 01983-874696
Open 4 May-September
Size 65 acres, 30 touring pitches, 18 ⚐, 31 WCs, 1 CWP
℅ MasterCard Visa
⚑ ✗¼ ☕ ⚑ ⛽ ⊟ ⊟ GR ⊟ ⊟ TV ⊟ ⊞ ⚐
Last arrival time: 10:00
➔ Approach Ryde on A3054 to join A3055 in town at Bishop Lovett School (on left). Straight ahead onto B330 to St Helens and Nodes Point.

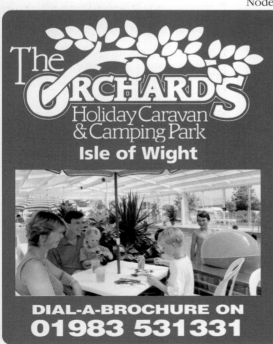

Orchards Holiday Caravan & Camping Park

Newbridge, Yarmouth PO41 0TS

☎ **01983-531331 Fax 01983-531666**

Open Easter-31 October ▲ ⊕ ☎

Size 100 touring pitches

➜ From B3401 Yarmouth to Neport road, follow signs to Newbridge.

Pondwell Caravan & Camping Park

Pondwell Hill, Ryde

☎ **01983-612100 Fax 01983-613511**

Open April-September ▲ ⊕ ☎

A rural park within easy walking distance of the beach and village. Special ferry fares for caravans and trailers can be arranged.

Size 8 acres, 150 touring pitches, 20 with electric hookup, 45 level pitches, 20 🏠, 30 WCs, 2 CWPs

£ car/tent £4-£7, car/caravan £4-£7, motorhome £4-£7, children £1-£1.75

Rental Chalet. £73-£381

℃ MasterCard Visa

🍴 ✗¼ 🍺¼ 🗑 📞 🗑 📶 🕳 📺 🚿 🗑 Calor

Last arrival time: 11:30

➜ Take A3054 to Ryde, then A3055 turning left along B3330 to Seaview. Park is next to Well pub.

Southland Camping Park

Newchurch, Sandown PO36 0LZ

☎ **01983-865385 Fax 01983-867663**

Open late March-end September ▲ ⊕ ☎

Size 6 acres, 100 touring pitches, 100 with electric hookup, 100 level pitches, 7 🏠, 14 WCs, 1 CWP

£ car/tent £6.20-£8.50, car/caravan £6.20-£8.50, motorhome £6.20-£8.50, motorbike/tent £6.20, children £1.10-£1.60

℃ MasterCard Visa

🍴 ✗¼ 🗑 📞 📶 🗑 Calor Gaz 🚻 🐕

Last arrival time: 10:30 ➜

← **Southland Camping Park**

→ Park is signposted from the A3055/6 Newport to Sandown road, SE of Arreton.

Thorness Bay Holiday Park
Thorness PO31 8NJ
📞 **01983-523109 Fax 01983-822213**
Open Easter-September 🅰 ⊞
Size 158 acres, 100 touring pitches, 45 with electric hookup, 275 static caravans, 18 🕭, 38 WCs
🗲 📦 🗊 🗊 🍴
→ Turn off A3054 at signpost. The park is 5 miles further on left.

Waverley Park Holiday Centre
Old Road, East Cowes
📞 **01983-293452 Fax 01983-200494**
Open Easter-October 🅰 ⊞ 🚐
Size 12 acres, 45 touring pitches, 28 with electric hookup, 42 static caravans, 12 🕭, 15 WCs, 1 CWP
£ car/tent £6.40-£9.50, car/caravan £6.40-£9.50, motorhome £6.40-£9.50, motorbike/tent £6.40, children £1.60-£2

Rental ⊞ £100-£345
CC MasterCard Visa
🗲 ✗ 📦 🗊 🗊 🗊 🗊 🗊 🗊 🗊 🗊 🗊 🗊 Calor 🐾 WS
Last arrival time: 10:30
→ Signposted from the Red Funnel terminal, East Cowes and also from York Avenue, coming from Newport or Ryde.
See advert on previous page

Whitecliff Bay Holiday Park
Hillway, Bembridge PO35 5PL
📞 **01983-872671 Fax 01983-872941**
Open March-31 October 🅰 ⊞ 🚐
Size 40 acres, 400 touring pitches, 130 with electric hookup, 200 level pitches, 14 static caravans, 38 🕭, 68 WCs, 15 CWPs
£ car/tent £5.80-£8, car/caravan £5.80-£8, motorhome £5.80-£8, motorbike/tent £5.80, children £1.70-£2.40
Rental 🅰 ⊞ Chalet.
CC MasterCard Visa
🗲 ✗ 📦 🗊 🗊 🗊 🗊 🗊 🗊 🗊 🗊 🗊 🗊 Calor Gaz WS
Last arrival time: 10:00
→ Take A3055, turn onto B3395 at Brading and follow the signs to Whitecliff Bay

IVYBRIDGE Devon 2C4

Whiteoaks Caravan Site
Davey's Cross, Filham, Ivybridge PL21 0DW
☎ 01752-892340
Open April-October ⚑ 🚐 🚛
Size 1½ acres, 20 touring pitches, 6 with electric hookup, 20 level pitches, 2 ☂, 6 WCs, 1 CWP
£ car/tent £6-£7, car/caravan £6-£7, motorhome £6-£7, motorbike/tent £6, children £0.75
📞 🗑 🔌 🐕 WS
Last arrival time: 10:00
➡ From Exeter come off A38 at first Ivybridge sign. Then follow B3213 to David's Lane and roads. Turn left 200 yards on right. From Plymouth drive through Ivybridge and continue 1 mile to David's Lane, then turn right. Signed both ways.

KENDAL Cumbria 10B2

Camping & Caravanning Club Site
Millcrest, Shap Road, Kendal
☎ 01539-741363
Open end March-start November ⚑ 🚐 🚛
Size 55 touring pitches, 31 with electric hookup, 4 ☂, 6 WCs, 1 CWP
£ car/tent £8.75-£11.55, car/caravan £8.75-£11.55, motorhome £8.75-£11.55, motorbike/tent £8.75, children £1.40
℃ MasterCard Visa
🗑 🔌 ⚠ 🎋 🐕
Last arrival time: 11:00
➡ Situated on A6, 1½ miles N of Kendal.

Ings Caravan Park
Mill Cottage, Ings, Kendal LA8 9QF
☎ 01539-821426
Open March-November 🚐 🚛
Size 5 acres, 14 touring pitches, 14 with electric hookup, 14 level pitches, 57 static caravans, 6 ☂, 8 WCs, 1 CWP
£ car/caravan £7.50-£9, motorhome £7.50-£9, children £1.50
Rental 🚐
🛒¼ ✗¼ 🗑 🔌 ⚠ 🎋 Calor ♿ 🐕 WS
Last arrival time: 10:00
➡ 300 yards off A591, 5 miles W of Kendal and 2 miles E of Windermere.

Millness Hill Park
Preston Patrick, Crooklands, Kendal LA7 7NU
☎ 01539-567306 Fax 01539-567306
Open 1 March-mid November ⚑ 🚐 🚛
Size 5 acres, 15 touring pitches, 15 with electric hookup, 15 level pitches, 6 static caravans, 2 ☂, 5 WCs, 1 CWP
£ car/tent £6-£7.50, car/caravan £6-£7.50, motorhome £6-£7.50, motorbike/tent £6
Rental 🚐 Chalet. caravans £125-£300, chalets £195-£530
✗¼ 📞¼ 🗑 🔌 📺 ⚠ 🎋 Calor 🐕
Last arrival time: 9:00
➡ Exit M6 junction 36 onto A65 to Kirkby Lonsdale. Turn left at the next roundabout signposted Endmoor and Crooklands. Site is 100 yards on left.

Waters Edge Caravan Park
Crooklands, Kendal LA7 7NN
☎ 015395-67708 Fax 015395-67610
Open 1 March-14 November ⚑ 🚐 🚛
Size 3 acres, 30 touring pitches, 30 with electric hookup, 30 level pitches, 5 ☂, 8 WCs, 1 CWP
£ car/tent £6.50, car/caravan £7.95-£13.50, motorhome £7.95-£13.50, motorbike/tent £6.50
Rental 🚐 £150-£230
℃ MasterCard Visa
🛒 ✗¼ 🗑 🔌 🗑 🔶 📺 🍴 Calor Gaz ♿ 🐕 WS
Last arrival time: 11:00
➡ Located at Crooklands ¾ miles along A65, M6 junction 36.

KENNACK SANDS Cornwall 2A4

Silver Sands Holiday Park
Gwendreath, Kennack Sands, Helston TR12 7LZ
☎ 01326-290631
Open May-September ⚑ 🚐 🚛
Size 6 acres, 34 touring pitches, 18 with electric hookup, 34 level pitches, 16 static caravans, 4 ☂, 9 WCs, 1 CWP
£ car/tent £5-£6.50, car/caravan £5-£6.50, motorhome £5-£6.50, motorbike/tent £5, children £1-£1.40
Rental 🚐 £75-£295
🛒¼ ✗¼ 📞¼ 🗑 🔌 🗑 ⚠ 🎋 Calor Gaz 🐕
Last arrival time: 10:00

➡

← **Silver Sands Holiday Park**

➜ Take A3083 "The Lizard" out of Helston. Past Naval Air Station Culdrose, turn left onto B3293 (St Keverne) past Goonhilly Satellite Station. Turn right at crossroads, after 1½ miles sign on left indicating "Gwendreath." Site is about 1 mile down lane on right.

KESSINGLAND Suffolk   9F3

Heathland Beach Caravan Park
London Road, Kessingland NR33 7PJ
☎ 01502-740337 Fax 01502-742355
Open Easter-October Å 🚐 🚚

Flat, grassy park surrounded by farmland, with private beach access.

Size 30 acres, 106 touring pitches, 65 with electric hookup, 106 level pitches, 168 static caravans, 25 🚿, 44 WCs, 2 CWPs
£ car/tent £9.50-£11.50, car/caravan £9.50-£11.50, motorhome £9.50-£11.50, motorbike/tent £9.50, children £0.50
Rental 🚐 £185-£335
CC Visa
🛒 ✕ 🛟 🔲 📞 🗄 🗼 🔲 ⚠ 🖾 🔌 Calor Gaz 🍴 WS
Last arrival time: 10:00
➜ 1 mile N of Kessingland on B1437. 3 miles S of Lowestoft off A12.

KESWICK Cumbria   10B2

Camping & Caravanning Club Site
Derwentwater, Keswick CA12 5EP
☎ 01768-772392

Open start February-start December Å 🚐 🚚
Size 11 acres, 250 touring pitches, 97 with electric hookup, 17 🚿, 35 WCs, 2 CWPs
£ car/tent £9.20-£12.05, car/caravan £9.20-£12.05, motorhome £9.20-£12.05, motorbike/tent £9.20, children £1.40
CC MasterCard Visa
🔲 📞 ⚠ 🖾 🚻 🍴
Last arrival time: 11:00
➜ From Penrith take A66, ignore Keswick signs and follow road to roundabout, turn right onto A5271, take first right at bottom of road, site is adjacent to Rugby Club.

Castlerigg Hall
Keswick
☎ 017687-72437 Fax 017687-72437
Open Easter-mid November Å 🚐 🚚

Castlerigg Hall Caravan & Camping Park overlooks Derwentwater with panoramic views of the surrounding fells. Fully serviced touring pitches available. Luxury holiday caravan for hire.

Size 53 touring pitches, 53 with electric hookup, 53 level pitches, 30 static caravans, 12 🚿, 26 WCs, 1 CWP
£ car/tent £6-£6.80, car/caravan £8.75, motorhome £7, motorbike/tent £5.70, children £1.60-£1.90
🛒 ✕¼ 🔲 📞 🗄 Calor Gaz 🍴
Last arrival time: 9:00
➜ 1½ miles SE of Keswick. Turn right off A591, 50 yards past Heights Hotel on the right.

Derwentwater Caravan Park
Crowe Park Road, Keswick CA12 5EN
☎ 017687-72579
Open 1 March-14 November 🚐 🚚

Situated on the shores of Derwentwater, with its own lake frontage and excellent views of the surrounding fells, yet convenient for the town.

Size 17½ acres, 50 touring pitches, 50 with electric hookup, 50 level pitches, 160 static caravans, 10 🅐, 15 WCs, 2 CWPs
£ car/caravan £8-£8.80, motorhome £8-£8.80, children £2
🅐¼ ✗¼ 🅐¼ 🅐 🅐 🅐 🅐 🅐 Calor Gaz ⅍ ⅏
Last arrival time: 10:00
➜ From the M6 (jn 40) take A66 signposted Keswick for 13 miles and at roundabout signed Keswick turn left. At the T-junction turn left to Keswick town centre. At the mini roundabout turn right. In 200 yards bear right, and in 400 yards turn right. Park is right after the bend in the road.

Scotgate Holiday Park
Braithwaite, Keswick
📞 **017687-78343**
Open March-October 🅐 🅐 🅐
Size 9 acres, 15 touring pitches, 15 with electric hookup, 15 level pitches, 27 static caravans, 8 🅐, 32 WCs, 1 CWP
£ car/tent £6.70-£7, car/caravan £10-£13, motorhome £5.25-£5.50, motorbike/tent £6.70, children £1.50-£1.60
Rental 🅐 Chalet.
🅐 ✗ 🅐 🅐 🅐 🅐 🅐 Calor Gaz ⅏
➜ 2 miles W of Keswick, just off A66 (Keswick-Cockermouth Road) on B5292.

Camp Easy
The Old Vicarage Activity Centre,
Stottesdon, Kidderminster DY14 8UH
📞 **01746-718436 Fax 01746-718420**
🅐

Camp Easy is based in Ginny Hole Nature Reserve, situated on the outskirts of the village of Stottesdon. When you arrive a tent can be pitched and ready for you.

Size 27 acres

Camping & Caravanning Club Site
Brown Westhead Park, Wolverley, Kidderminster
☎ 01562-850909
Open late March-early November A ⛺ 🚐

A quiet, secluded site within easy reach of the M5. Take a trip on the Severn Valley Railway, or a walk along the nearby canal.

Size 8.2 acres, 130 touring pitches, 62 with electric hookup
£ car/tent £8.75-£11.55, car/caravan £8.75-£11.55, motorhome £8.75-£11.55, motorbike/tent £8.75, children £1.40
CC MasterCard Visa
🛢 📞 GR 🔥 🚻 ♿ 🐕
Last arrival time: 11:00
➡ Off A449 onto B4189 near to Canal and Lock Inn.

Shorthill Caravan & Camping Centre
Worcester Road, Crossway Green, Stourport, Kidderminster DY13 9SH
☎ 01299-250571
A ⛺ 🚐
Size 7 acres, 30 touring pitches, 20 with electric hookup, 30 level pitches, 3 🔥, 5 WCs, 1 CWP
£ car/tent £6.50-£8.50, car/caravan £6.50-£10, motorhome £6.50-£10, motorbike/tent £6.50
🍴 🍴¼ ✕ 🛒 🛒¼ 🔲 🔥 🔥 🐕 WS
Last arrival time: 10:00
➡ On A1449 Kidderminster to Worcester road, 200 yards after Hartlebury service station island is Little Chef restaurant. Turn into restaurant entrance and site is located at rear.

Kielder Campsite
Hexham, Kielder NE48 1EL
☎ 01434-250291 Fax 01434-220756
Open Easter-end September A ⛺ 🚐
Size 10 acres, 70 touring pitches, 36 with electric hookup, 70 level pitches, 6 🔥, 9 WCs, 1 CWP
£ car/tent £5-£6, car/caravan £8-£9, motorhome £8-£9, motorbike/tent £5
CC MasterCard Visa
🍴 🍴¼ ✕¼ 🛒¼ 🛢 📞 🔥 🔲 ♿ 🐕
Last arrival time: 9:00
➡ Follow C200 from Bellingham to Kielder. Site is 400 yards N of Kielder village.

Diglea Camping & Caravan Park
Beach Road, Snettisham, King's Lynn PE31 7RB
☎ 01485-541367
Open 1 April-31 October A ⛺ 🚐

Attractive, level, quiet, family run park in a peaceful rural setting, ½ mile from the beach. Ideally situated for exploring the north Norfolk coast and the historic town of King's Lynn.

Size 200 touring pitches, 50 with electric hookup, 150 static caravans, 19 🔥, 35 WCs, 3 CWPs
£ car/tent £5-£8, car/caravan £5-£8, motorhome £5-£8, motorbike/tent £5
🍴¼ ✕¼ 🛒¼ 🛢 📞 🔲 GR 🔥 🔲 🔌 Calor Gaz 🐕
➡ From King's Lynn take A149 Hunstanton Road to Snettisham. Turn left at sign marked Snettisham Beach. Site is on left 1¼ miles from turning.

Pentney Park Caravan Site

Gayton Road, Narborough, King's Lynn
PE32 1HU
📞 **01760-337479 Fax 01760-338118**
Å 🚐 🚏

Sixteen acres of woodland and clearings in the heart of true Norfolk countryside. Near to Sandringham and within easy reach of the coast and Broads.

Size 16 acres, 200 touring pitches, 156 with electric hookup, 190 level pitches, 16 ⬥, 44 WCs, 3 CWPs
£ car/tent £8-£10, car/caravan £8-£10, motorhome £8-£10, motorbike/tent £8, children £1.10-£1.40
Rental Å 🚐 from £100
℃ MasterCard Visa
⬥ ✕ 🗪 ⬥ 📞 ⬥ 🔲 🔲 GR ⬥ ⬥ 🔲 Calor Gaz ⬥ 🐕 WS
Last arrival time: 10:00
➡ On A47, midway between King's Lynn and Swaffham. Entrance on B1153, 150 yards from junction.

Rickels Caravan Site

Bircham Road, Stanhoe, King's Lynn PE31 8PU
📞 **01485-518671 Fax 01485-518671**
Open March-October Å 🚐 🚏
Size 2 acres, 30 touring pitches, 26 with electric hookup, 20 level pitches, 4 ⬥, 7 WCs, 1 CWP
£ car/tent £7.50-£8.50, car/caravan £7.50-£8.50, motorhome £7.50-£8.50, motorbike/tent £7.50, children £0.50
Rental 🚐
⬥ 📞 ⬥ 🔲 🔲 Calor Gaz 🐕 WS
Last arrival time: 10:00

➡ Take A148 (Cromer road) for 4 miles to Hillington. Continue through village and turn left onto B1153 to Great Bircham. Proceed through Bircham and on a left hand bend fork right onto B1155, follow to main crossroads (Fakenham right, Docking left). Continue straight over and site is situated 150 yards on left.

KINGSBRIDGE Devon 2C4

Camping & Caravanning Club Site

Middle Grounds, Slapton, Kingsbridge
📞 **01548-580538**
Open late March-early November Å 🚐 🚏
Size 5½ acres, 115 touring pitches, 18 with electric hookup, 6 ⬥, 9 WCs, 1 CWP
£ car/tent £9.20-£12.05, car/caravan £9.20-£12.05, motorhome £9.20-£12.05, motorbike/tent £9.20, children £1.40
℃ MasterCard Visa
⬥ 📞 ⬥ 🔲 ⬥ 🐕
Last arrival time: 11:00
➡ A381 to Totnes, left onto B3207 to Dartmouth, right onto A379 to Street, right to Slapton.

Karrageen Camping & Caravan Park
Bolberry, Malborough, Kingsbridge TQ7 3EN
☎ 01548-561230 Fax 01548-560192
Open 15 March-15 November ⚊ 🚐 🚛

A small family park offering panoramic rural and sea views - the closest park to the beaches at Hope Cove and only ¾ mile from the National Trust Coastal Path.

Size 8 acres, 75 touring pitches, 54 with electric hookup, 75 level pitches, 20 static caravans, 8 🚿, 9 WCs, 1 CWP
£ car/tent £6-£8, car/caravan £6-£9.50, motorhome £7-£8, motorbike/tent £6, children £0.50
⚑ 🛒 🔲 Calor Gaz ♿ ⚓
➜ Take A381 from Kingsbridge towards Salcombe and at Malborough turn sharp right. After ½ mile turn right to Bolberry and site is on right.

Scotton Holiday Park
New Road, Scotton, Knaresborough HG5 9HH
☎ 01423-864413
Open 1 March-7 January ⚊ 🚐 🚛
Size 8½ acres, 100 touring pitches, 85 with electric hookup, 60 level pitches, 10 🚿, 16 WCs
£ car/caravan £6.50
⚑ ✕ 🔲 ⚠ 🔲 Calor Gaz ⚓
➜ 1½ miles NW of Knaresborough on B6165.

Piccadilly Caravan Site
Folly Lane West, Lacock SN15 2LP
☎ 01249-730260
Open 1 April-31 October ⚊ 🚐 🚛

Located in countryside half a mile from the historic National Trust village of Lacock, the site is an ideal touring centre for Bath and the Cotswolds.

Size 2½ acres, 40 touring pitches, 34 with electric hookup, 40 level pitches, 4 🚿, 6 WCs, 1 CWP
£ car/tent £7-£8.50, car/caravan £7-£8.50, motorhome £7-£8.50, motorbike/tent £7
⚑¼ ✕¼ 🔲 ⚑ 🔲 ⚠ 🔲 Calor Gaz ⚓
Last arrival time: 10:00
➜ Turn right off A350 Chippenham to Melksham road signposted Gastard (with caravan symbol) into Folly Lane West. Site on left in 300 yards.

Inglenook Caravan Park
Lamplugh CA14 4SH
☎ 01946-861240
Open all year ⚊ 🚐 🚛
Size 3½ acres, 36 touring pitches, 12 with electric hookup, 36 level pitches, 22 static caravans, 4 🚿, 8 WCs, 1 CWP
£ car/tent £6.50-£8, car/caravan £7.50-£8, motorhome £7.50-£8, motorbike/tent £6.50, children £1
Rental 🚐 £140-£250
⚑ 🛒 ⚑ 🔲 ⚠ 🔲 Calor Gaz ⚓ WS
Last arrival time: 8:00
➜ Leave A5086 at sign for Lampugh Green. Site ½ mile on the right-hand corner.

Cockerham Sands Caravan Park
Cockerham, Lancaster LA2 0BB
☏ 01524-751387
Open March-October
Size 9 touring pitches
A country club and caravan park with a cabaret suite, lounge bar, snooker, TV room, play area and pool.

➡ From M6 junction 33 take A6 to Glasson Dock for 1¼ miles. Turn right onto Cockerham Road and right again for Thurnham Hall. Turn left opposite hall at signpost.

Roselands Caravan Park
St Just, Land's End TR197RS
☏ 01736-788571
Open April-October ⚑ ⛺ 🚐
Size 4 acres, 20 touring pitches, 10 with electric hookup, 20 level pitches, 15 static caravans, 2 ☂, 3 WCs, 1 CWP
£ car/tent £5-£7, car/caravan £5-£7, motorhome £5-£7, motorbike/tent £5
⚡ ✗ 🍴 ☏ ⌂ 🏠 ♨ WS
➡ From Penzance take the bypass and turn right on A3071 to St Just. 1 mile from St Just turn left to site 800 yards.

Thorney Lakes Caravan Park
Muchelney., Langport
☏ 01458-250811
Open March-November ⚑ ⛺ 🚐
Size 7 acres, 16 touring pitches, 16 with electric hookup, 16 level pitches, 4 ☂, 5 WCs, 1 CWP
£ car/tent £6, car/caravan £6, motorhome £6, motorbike/tent £6
📷 ♿ 🐕
➡ 2 miles S of Langport on Crewekerne road follow sign to Muchelney Pottery. Farmhouse is opposite the pottery.

Moor Lodge Caravan Park
Blackmoor Lane, Bardsey, Leeds LS17 9DZ
☏ 01937-572424
⚑ ⛺ 🚐

Peaceful, immaculate, countryside park.

Size 7½ acres, 12 touring pitches, 12 with electric hookup, 12 level pitches, 60 static caravans, 4 ☂, 4 WCs, 1 CWP
£ car/tent £6.50, car/caravan £6.50, motorhome £6.50, motorbike/tent £6.50
⚡¼ ✗¼ 🍴¼ ☏ ⌂ Calor Gaz ♿ 🐕 WS
➡ Take A58 from Leeds towards Wetherby. Cross over roundabout on outskirts of Leeds. After one third of a mile when street lights finish, turn left at next cross road and follow caravan signs.

Roundhay Caravan & Camping Park
Elmete Lane, Leeds LS8 2LQ
☏ 0113-265 9354 Fax 0113-237 0077
Open 1 March-end November ⚑ ⛺ 🚐

In 700 acres of glorious parkland, including the top free attraction in England, Tropical World. The site is an ideal touring base for

➡

← **Roundhay Caravan & Camping Park**

the city of Leeds, Royal Armouries, York, Harrogate and the Yorkshire Dales.

Size 6 acres, 60 touring pitches, 50 with electric hookup, 60 level pitches, 4 ℟, 6 WCs, 1 CWP
£ car/tent £6, car/caravan £9.50, motorhome £9, motorbike/tent £6
🐂 �¼ ▣ 📞 🔲 ⚠ 🔲 Calor Gaz ♿ ♞
Last arrival time: 10:00
➔ Signposted from A58.

Size 6 acres, 48 touring pitches, 60 with electric hookup, 60 level pitches, 6 static caravans, 7 ℟, 8 WCs, 3 CWPs
£ car/tent £8, car/caravan £8, motorhome £8, motorbike/tent £8, children £1.50
Rental 🚐
℀ Visa
✕¼ ▣ 📞 🔲 ⚠ 🔲 Calor Gaz ♞ WS
Last arrival time: 9:30
➔ Turn left off A520 (Leek-Stone) at foot of hill in Cheddleton into Station Road (sign-N. Staffs Rly Museum). Park is on right in ¾ mile.

LEEK Staffordshire   7E1

Camping & Caravanning Club Site
Blackshaw Grange, Blackshaw Moor, Leek
📞 **01538-300285**
Open end March-start November Å 🚐 🚏
Size 60 touring pitches,
£ car/tent £8.75-£11.55, car/caravan £8.75-£11.55, motorhome £8.75-£11.55, motorbike/tent £8.75, children £1.40
℀ MasterCard Visa
▣ ⚠ 🔲 ♿ ♞
Last arrival time: 11:00

Glencote Caravan Park
Churnet Valley, Station Road, Cheddleton, Leek ST13 7EE
📞 **01538-360745** Fax **01538-361788**
Open April-October Å 🚐 🚏

A pleasant, well sheltered, level park to the south of Leek to the Churnet Valley. Railway museum and canal-side pub close by. Central for the Potteries, Alton Towers, Staffordshire moorlands and Peak District.

LEISTON Suffolk   9F4

Cakes & Ale Park
Abbey Lane, Theberton, Leiston IP16 4TE
📞 **01728-831655** Fax **01473-736270**
Open 1 April-31 October Å 🚐 🚏

A fully serviced site in tranquil parkland with a golf driving range and practice nets, and a large mown recreation area. Nearby is an indoor pool, and the area offers superb walking and cycling. Minsmere, Dunwich, Southwold, Aldeburgh and Snape are within easy distance.

Size 45 acres, 50 touring pitches, 50 with electric hookup, 50 level pitches, 150 static caravans, 20 ℟, 20 WCs, 2 CWPs
£ car/tent £8-£10, car/caravan £8-£10, motorhome £8-£10, motorbike/tent £8
🐂 ▣ 📞 ▣ 🔲 🔲 🔲 ⚠ 🔲 🔲 Calor Gaz ♞ WS
Last arrival time: 9:00
➔ From A12 take B1121 to Saxmundham. At the crossroads in Saxmundham, take B1119 to Leiston. Turn onto minor road 3 miles from Saxmundham and follow signs.

LEOMINSTER Herefordshire   7D3

Shobdon Airfield Touring Site
Leominster HR6 9NR
☎ 01568-708369 Fax 01568-708935
Open February-6 January ▲ ⊕ ⊞
Size 5 acres, 35 touring pitches, 4 with
electric hookup, 35 level pitches, 12 static
caravans, 8 ♠, 8 WCs, 1 CWP
£ car/tent £2-£6, car/caravan £3.50-£5,
motorhome £3.50-£5, motorbike/tent £2,
children £2-£6
㏄ MasterCard Visa
♣¼ ✗ ☞ ▣ ᕦ ☛ WS
Last arrival time: 9:00

LEYBURN North Yorkshire   10C2

Constable Burton Hall Caravan Park
Leyburn DL8 5LJ
☎ 01677-450428 Fax 01677-450622
Open April-October ⊕ ⊞
Size 10 acres, 120 touring pitches, 114 with
electric hookup, 120 level pitches, 9 ♠, 13
WCs, 3 CWPs
£ car/caravan £6.50-£7.50, motorhome
£6.50-£7.50, children £0.70
✗¼ ☞¼ ▣ ᕦ ▢ Calor Gaz ☛ WS
Last arrival time: 10:00
➡ 8 miles W of A1 on the A684 between
Bedale and Leyburn.

LEYSDOWN-ON-SEA Kent   5E2

Priory Hill Holiday Park
Wing Road, Leysdown-on-Sea, Sheerness
ME12 4QT
☎ 01795-510267 Fax 01795-510267
▲ ⊕ ⊞

*Located adjacent to the beach and coastal
park, a family run site with excellent*

*facilities, including pitch and putt, and
entertainment.*

Size 15 acres, 55 touring pitches, 34 with
electric hookup, 55 level pitches, 8 ♠, 5
WCs, 1 CWP
£ car/tent £9-£12, car/caravan £9-£12,
motorhome £8-£12, motorbike/tent £8
Rental ⊕ Chalet. £50-£200
㏄ Visa
♣ ☞ ▣ ᕦ ▢ ᕦ ▦ ㏕ ㏑ ᕦ Calor Gaz ᕦ ☛
WS
Last arrival time: 11:00
➡ Take A2, M2 or M20 from London and
then A249 signposted to Sheerness. B2231
to Leysdown.

LINCOLN Lincolnshire   8C1

White Horse Inn Holiday Park
Dunston Fen, Lincoln LN4 3AP
☎ 01526-398341 Fax 01526-398341
Open 1 February-31 December ▲ ⊕ ⊞
Size 3 acres, 18 touring pitches, 34 static
caravans, 2 ♠, 10 WCs, 1 CWP   ➡

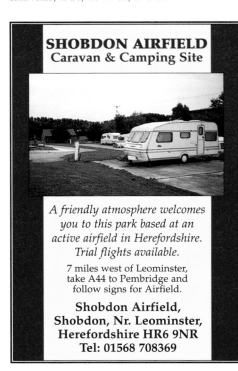

← **White Horse Inn Holiday Park**

£ car/tent £5-£7.50
🐾 ✕ 📳 🗑 ⚠ 🎌 🍴 Calor Gaz ☗ ☗
Last arrival time: 11:00
➡ From Lincoln take B1188 and turn left into Dunston. Follow road through village and then signs to River Witham and Dunston Fen.

LINGFIELD Surrey   5D3

Long Acres Caravan & Camping Park

Newchapel Road., Lingfield RH7 6LE
📞 **01342-833205**
Open all year 🛆 🚐 🚍
Size 40 acres, 60 touring pitches, 60 with electric hookup, 50 level pitches, 6 🍴, 10 WCs, 2 CWPs
£ car/tent £7.50, car/caravan £7.50, motorhome £7.50, motorbike/tent £7.50, children £1.25
🐾 🐾¼ ✕¼ ☗¼ 🗑 📳 🗑 📷 ⚠ 🎌 Calor Gaz ☗ WS
➡ From M25 junction 6 take A22 to East Grinstead. At Newchapel roundabout turn left onto B2028 to Linchfield. Site is on right (700 yards).

LISKEARD Cornwall   2B3

Colliford Tavern

Colliford Lake, Liskeard PL14 6PZ
📞 **01208-821335** Fax **01208-821335**
Open Easter-September 🛆 🚐 🚍

An oasis on Bodmin Moor. Small, sheltered site, ideal for couples, with a country pub

serving excellent food and ale. Booking recommended. ETB graded Excellent.

Size 3¼ acres, 40 touring pitches, 15 with electric hookup, 25 level pitches, 4 🍴, 7 WCs, 1 CWP
£ car/tent £7-£9, car/caravan £7-£9, motorhome £7-£9, motorbike/tent £7, children £1.25-£1.75
⊄ MasterCard Visa
✕ ☗ 📳 🗑 ⚠ 🎌 🍴 Calor Gaz ☗
Last arrival time: 10:00
➡ From A30 between Bodmin and Launceston, turn left at Collingford Lake signpost and then take the first left to the campsite. Site is at end of lane.

Pine Green Caravan Park

Doublebois, Liskeard PL14 6LD
📞 **01274-328981**
Open Easter-31 October 🛆 🚐 🚍

Off the A38, near Dobwalls, an elevated site tastefully landscaped with rural views, and within easy reach of Plymouth, the sea and the moors. Warden on site.

Size 2 acres, 50 touring pitches, 20 with electric hookup, 16 level pitches, 1 static caravans, 4 🍴, 6 WCs, 1 CWP
£ car/tent £4-£7, car/caravan £5-£9, motorhome £5-£9, motorbike/tent £4
Rental 🚐 £80-£210
🗑 📳 Calor ☗ WS
➡ From Liskeard W on A38 to Dobwalls. Keep right and ¾ mile further turn left onto B3360, site ¼ mile on right.

Hackney Camping
Millfields Road, Hackney, London E5
☎ 0181-985 7656 Fax 0181-749 9074
Open 1 June-30 August A ⚌ 🚐
Size 3 acres, 60 touring pitches, 200 level pitches, 20 ⁂, 12 WCs
£ car/tent £10, car/caravan £10, motorhome £10, motorbike/tent £10, children £5
Rental A
🛎 ✕¼ 🍴 🖻 🛒 🛗 GR TV 🛆 🖂 Calor ☂
➜ A102 or A104 to Lower Clapton Road. Down Millfields Road, over hump bridge to Hackney Camping.

Lee Valley Campsite
Sewardstone Road, Chingford, London E4 7RA
☎ 0181-529 5689 Fax 0181-559 4070
Open Easter-October A ⚌ 🚐
Size 13 acres, 200 touring pitches, 100 with electric hookup, 100 level pitches, 28 ⁂, 30 WCs, 3 CWPs
£ car/tent £10, car/caravan £10, motorhome £10, motorbike/tent £10, children £2.10

CC Visa
🛎 🍴 🖻 🛒 🛆 🖂 ⚲ ☂ WS
➜ Leave M25 junction 26, follow signs to Waltham Abbey, turn left at traffic lights. Site 2 miles on right.

Lee Valley Cycle Circuit
Lee Valley Sports Centre, Temple Mills Lane, Leyton, London E15 2EN
☎ 0181-534 6085 Fax 0181-534 6085
Open March (Easter)-October A ⚌ 🚐
Size 2 acres, 80 touring pitches, 80 level pitches, 20 ⁂, 10 WCs, 1 CWP
£ car/tent £10, car/caravan £10, motorhome £10, motorbike/tent £10, children £2
CC MasterCard Visa
🛎¼ ✕¼ 🍴¼ 🖻 🛒 🖂 🖳 🖂 ☂

Lee Valley Leisure Centre
Picketts Lock Lane, Edmonton, London N9 0AS
☎ 0181-345 6666 Fax 0181-884 4975
Open all year A ⚌ 🚐
Size 6 acres, 200 touring pitches, 60 with electric hookup, 200 level pitches, 6 ⁂, 17 WCs, 2 CWPs ➜

← **Lee Valley Leisure Centre**

£ car/tent £10, car/caravan £10, motorhome £10, motorbike/tent £10, children £2.10
CC MasterCard Visa
🐾 ✕ 🛒 🗑 🔌 🔄 🔂 🎌 📶 🛗 🔲 🔀 🔀 🔀 GR 🔍
🔺 🎌 ⛽ Calor Gaz ♿ WS
➡ From M25 junction 25 follow signs for City. At first set of traffic lights take slip road signposted 'Feezywater', continue along this road (A1055) for 6 miles, site is at rear of Leisure Centre complex.

LONGRIDGE Lancashire   10B3

Beacon Fell View Caravan Park
110 Higher Road, Longridge PR3 2TY
📞 **01772-785434**
Open 23 March-19 October 🅰 🚐
Size 33 acres, 100 touring pitches, 66 with electric hookup, 97 level pitches, 20 static caravans, 10 🚿, 28 WCs
🐾 🛒 🔄 ⛽
➡ From M6 junction 32 take A6 Garstang road. Turn right at traffic lights and head for Longridge (not Beacon Fell). Go straight across the roundabout at the White Bull and keep left. Park is 1 mile on right.

LONGTOWN Cumbria   13E4

Camelot Caravan Park
Sandysike, Longtown CA6 5SZ
📞 **01228-791248**
Open March-October 🅰 🚐 🚋
Size 5 acres, 20 touring pitches, 6 with electric hookup, 20 level pitches, 1 static caravan, 2 🚿, 4 WCs, 1 CWP
£ car/tent £5.50, car/caravan £6.50, motorhome £6.50, motorbike/tent £5.50, children £0.50
🐾 🔲 🔄 ⛽ Calor Gaz ♀ WS
Last arrival time: flexible
➡ Leave M6 at junction 44. Site on right off A7 in four miles, 1 mile S of Longtown.

LOOE Cornwall   2B4

Camping Caradon
Trelawne Gardens, Looe PL13 2NA
📞 **01503-272388**
Open Easter-end October 🅰 🚐 🚋

Size 3½ acres, 85 touring pitches, 37 with electric hookup, 85 level pitches, 1 static caravan, 4 🚿, 12 WCs, 1 CWP
£ car/tent £5-£8, car/caravan £5-£8, motorhome £5-£8, children £0.30-£1
🐾 🛒 🔲 🔄 🔍 🔺 🎌 ⛽ Calor Gaz ♀
Last arrival time: 10:00
➡ 2¼ miles W of Looe on the A387, turn N on the B3359 and take first on right. Site ¼ mile on left.

Polborder House Caravan & Camping Park
Bucklawren Road, St Martins, Looe PL13 1QR
📞 **01503-240265**
Open April-October 🅰 🚐 🚋
Size 3 acres, 31 touring pitches, 28 with electric hookup, 36 level pitches, 5 static caravans, 9 🚿, 16 WCs, 1 CWP
£ car/tent £6-£8, car/caravan £6-£8, motorhome £6-£8, motorbike/tent £4, children £0.75-£1
Rental 🚐 £120-£265
🐾 🔲 🔄 🔲 Calor Gaz ♿ ♀
Last arrival time: 10:00
➡ 2½ miles E of Looe, turn off B3253 signposted Polborder, Monkey Sanctuary & Seaton Site ¾ mile on the right.

Tencreek Caravan Park
Looe PL13 2JR
📞 **01503-262447 Fax 01503-262447**
Open all year 🅰 🚐 🚋
Size 16 acres, 250 touring pitches, 163 with electric hookup, 250 level pitches, 45 static caravans, 24 🚿, 40 WCs, 2 CWPs
£ car/tent £6.75-£11, car/caravan £6.75-£11, motorhome £6.75-£11, motorbike/tent £6.75, children £1.10-£1.65
Rental 🚐
CC MasterCard Visa
🐾 🛒 🔲 🔄 🔲 🔀 GR 🔺 🎌 ⛽ Calor Gaz ♿ ♀ WS
Last arrival time: 11:00
➡ From A38 turn right onto A387 for Looe. Travel through Looe town, over the bridge and up the hill. Approximately 1½ miles from bridge.

Treble B Holiday Centre
Polperro Road, Looe PL12 2JS
📞 01503-262425 Fax 01503-262425
Open May-end September **A** 🚐 🏕
Size 22 acres, 557 touring pitches, 265 with electric hookup, 450 level pitches, 30 static caravans, 44 🚿, 100 WCs, 4 CWPs
£ car/tent £6.80-£10, car/caravan £6.80-£10, motorhome £6.80-£10, motorbike/tent £6.80, children £0.75-£1.50
Rental 🏠 Chalet. £63-£350
CC MasterCard Visa
🧍 ✕ 🛒 🖥 🔌 🖬 🔲 GR 🔍 TV 🏍 🎯 🍴 Calor Gaz 🚿 WS
Last arrival time: 11:00
➡ 2 miles W of Looe on A387. Observe sign.

Trelawne Manor Character Holiday Village
Looe PL13 2NA
📞 01503-272151
Open May-September
Size 40 acres, 40 touring pitches, 20 with electric hookup, 40 level pitches, 200 static caravans, 6 🚿, 16 WCs
🧍 🛒 🔲 🔲 🔍 🍴
➡ Take the A390 for St Austell. Go through Taphouse, then turn left onto the B3359. Trelawne is on the left, after 8½ miles.

Trelay Farmpark
Pelynt, Looe PL13 2JX
📞 01503-220 900
Open Easter-end October **A** 🚐 🏕
Size 5 acres, 55 touring pitches, 23 with electric hookup, 27 level pitches, 20 static caravans, 5 🚿, 10 WCs, 1 CWP
£ car/tent £6.80-£8, car/caravan £6.80-£8, motorhome £6.80-£8, motorbike/tent £6.80, children £1-£1.50
Rental 🏠
🖥 📞 🔲 Calor 🚿 🐴
Last arrival time: 11:00
➡ From A38 2 miles W of Liskeard at Dobwales turn onto A390 for Lostwithiel. Shortly after E Taphouse turn left onto B3359 to Pelynt. Trelay is ½ mile past Pelynt on left. Or from A387 Polperro/Looe road, take A3359 ½ mile before Pelynt on right.

Powderham Castle Touring Park
Lanlivery, Lostwithiel PL30 5BU
📞 01208-872277
Open 1 April-31 October **A** 🚐 🏕

A quiet, select uncommercialised park appealing to the more discerning camper. Spacious pitches in enclosed paddocks. Approved and recommended by all revelant touring authorities.

Size 10 acres, 75 touring pitches, 75 with electric hookup, 75 level pitches, 38 static caravans, 8 🚿, 20 WCs, 1 CWP ➡

← **Powderham Castle Touring Park**

£ car/tent £6.30-£8, car/caravan £6.30-£8, motorhome £6.30-£8, motorbike/tent £4, children £0.50-£1

✕¼ 🚐¼ 🔲 📞 🗑 🔲 🎣 GR 🔲 📺 ⚠ 🏥 Calor Gaz ♿ 🐾 WS

Last arrival time: 10:00

➡ 1½ miles SW of Lostwithiel on A390 turn right at signpost to Lanlivery. Go up the road for 400 yards.

LOTHERSDALE North Yorkshire   10C3

Springs Farm Caravan Park
Lothersdale, Nr Skipton BD20 8HH
📞 **01535-632533**
Open 1 April-15 October 🏕 🚐 🚛
Size 4 acres, 17 touring pitches, 17 with electric hookup, 10 level pitches, 2 🚿, 5 WCs, 1 CWP
Calor Gaz WS
➡ From A629 Keighley-Skipton road, take A6068 at Crosshills. Turn right onto Lothersdale road. After 2 miles, turn left at crossroads, go through the village, past the church, shop and school. Then take the next left, then first left and continue past lakes up the hill to Springs.

LOUGHTON Essex   5D2

Debden House Campsite
Debden Green, Loughton IG10 2PA
📞 **0181-508 3008** Fax **0181-508 0284**

Set within the beautiful countryside of Epping Forest, but within easy reach of London by road or Underground. Newly refurbished toilet blocks on site.

Size 48½ acres, 150 touring pitches, 60 with electric hookup, 150 level pitches, 10 🚿, 18 WCs, 2 CWPs

🅿 🅿¼ 🚐 📞 🗑 🔲 ⚠ 🏥 Calor Gaz ♿

Last arrival time: 11:30

➡ From M25 junction 26 take A121 to Loughton. At double mini roundabout, turn left onto A1168 Rectory Lane, then take second left into Pyrles Lane.

LOUTH Lincolnshire   11F4

West End Farm
Carlton Road, South Reston, Louth LN13 0NS
📞 **01507-450705** Fax **01507-450705**
Open Easter-November 🏕 🚐 🚛
Size 7 acres, 12 touring pitches, 8 with electric hookup, 1 🚿, 2 WCs, 1 CWP
£ car/tent £4.50-£6, car/caravan £4.50-£6, motorhome £4.50-£6, motorbike/tent £4.50
✕ ✕¼ 🚐 🚐¼ 🗑 🐾 WS
Last arrival time: 12:00

➜ Take the A157 from Louth to Mablethorpe. In 5 miles through South Reston take Manby sign into Carlton Road and site.

LOWESTOFT Suffolk 9F3

Camping & Caravanning Club Site
Suffolk Wildlife Park, Whites Lane, Kessingland, Lowestoft
☎ 01502-742040
Open end March-start November 𝗔 🚐 🚎
Size 6½ acres, 90 touring pitches, 53 with electric hookup, 10 🚿, 9 WCs, 1 CWP
£ car/tent £9.20-£12.05, car/caravan £9.20-£12.05, motorhome £9.20-£12.05, motorbike/tent £9.20, children £1.40
CC MasterCard Visa
▣ 🔌 ⚗ 🔲 ♿ 🐕
Last arrival time: 11:00
➜ From Lowestoft towards London on A12 follow signs to Wildlife Park.

Carlton Manor Caravan Site
Chapel Road, Carlton Colville, Lowestoft NR33 8BL
☎ 01502-566511 Fax 01502-573949
Open 1 April-October 𝗔 🚐 🚎
Size 9½ acres, 90 touring pitches, 60 with electric hookup, 6 🚿, 10 WCs, 2 CWPs
£ car/tent £5.50-£8.25, car/caravan £7-£9.75, motorhome £7.50, motorbike/tent £5.50
CC MasterCard Visa
✕ 🛒 🔌 🔲 ⚗ 🔲 Calor 🐕 WS
➜ From A12 or A146 follow signs to Transport Museum. Site next door on B1384.

LYME REGIS Dorset 3E3

Hook Farm Camping & Caravan Park
Gole Lane, Uplyme, Lyme Regis DT7 3UU
☎ 01297-442801 Fax 01297-442801
Open all year 𝗔 🚐 🚎
Size 10 acres, 100 touring pitches, 24 with electric hookup, 50 level pitches, 17 static caravans, 8 🚿, 24 WCs, 1 CWP
£ car/tent £6-£8, car/caravan £6-£9, motorhome £6-£8, motorbike/tent £5.50, children £1
Rental 𝗔 🚐 tents £15 night, caravans £110-£175 week
🛒 ▣ 🔌 🔲 ⚗ 🔲 Calor Gaz ♿ 🐕 ➜

West End Farm

Our peaceful 4 acres touring site is secluded by trees and 1 mile from the main road. The site is also situated 6 miles from the beautiful coast. There is a Fish Smoker, Fish Bistro/Restaurant and a Trout Lake available with rods. The site has 8 hookups, public toilets and shower.

For more information Ring:

**CARLTON ROAD, LOUTH
Tel: 01507-450705 or 450949
Fax: 01507-450705**

CARLTON MANOR

The touring caravan park is set in 9 acres of beautiful parkland, with childrens play area bouncy castle. The park is open from Easter through to October 31st, licensed for 90 units and has ample electric hook up and wash room facilities.

Facilities at a glance: Easily accessible and level siting. Full use of the hotel facilities. Restaurant. Bar/TV lounge.

Places of interest nearby: Oulton Broad, Gateway to the Broads network. Lowestoft (centre), all major shops in the high street. Beach (2 miles) holds the EC Blue flag award. East Anglian Transport Museum situated next door to our hotel.

**Carlton Colville, Lowestoft, Suffolk NR33 8BL
Tel: (01502) 566511 Fax: (01502) 573949**

← **Hook Farm Camping & Caravan Park**

Last arrival time: Flexible
➜ From A3052 turn right 2 miles W of Lyme Regis.

Shrubbery Caravan Park
Rousdon, Lyme Regis DT7 3XW
☎ **01297-442227**
Open March-November A ⊕ ⇌
Size 10½ acres, 120 touring pitches, 90 with electric hookup, 120 level pitches, 14 ⚲, 21 WCs, 1 CWP
£ car/tent £5.75-£7.25, car/caravan £5.75-£7.25, motorhome £5.75-£7.25, motorbike/tent £5, children £4.50-£6.50
⚑ ⊡ ☎ ⊟ ⚠ ☒ ⊟ Calor Gaz ⚐ ⍭ WS
Last arrival time: 9:00
➜ 3 miles W of Lyme Regis on the A3052 at village of Rousdon.

LYMINGTON Hampshire　　4B4

Lytton Lawn Camping & Caravan Park
Lymore, Milford-on-Sea, Lymington
☎ **01590-642513 Fax 01590-645610**
Open 1 March-5 January A ⊕ ⇌
Size 5 acres, 126 touring pitches, 126 with electric hookup, 126 level pitches, 24 ⚲, 24 WCs, 24 CWPs
£ car/tent £9.50-£22, car/caravan £9.50-£22, motorhome £9.50-£22, motorbike/tent £9.50, children £9.50-£22
℗ MasterCard Visa
⚑ ✕¼ ●¼ ⊡ ☎ ⊟ ☒ ☒ ☒ ⌨ GR ◙ ⚠ ☒
Calor Gaz ⚐ ⍭
Last arrival time: 10:00
➜ From Lymington take the A337 towards Everton, then left onto B3058 towards Milford-on-Sea, second left into Lymore Lande for Lytton Lawn.

LYNTON Devon　　2C2

Camping & Caravanning Club Site
Caffyns Cross, Lynton EX35 6JS
☎ **01598-752379**
Open end March-start November A ⊕ ⇌
Size 5½ acres, 105 touring pitches, 50 with electric hookup, 10 ⚲, 17 WCs, 1 CWP

£ car/tent £9.20-£12.05, car/caravan £9.20-£12.05, motorhome £9.20-£12.05, motorbike/tent £9.20, children £1.40
℗ MasterCard Visa
⊡ ☎ ⚠ ☒ ⍭
Last arrival time: 11:00
➜ Turn N off A39, signposted Caffyns, then turn right.

Channel View Caravan Park
Manor Farm, Barbrook, Lynton EX35 6LD
☎ **01598-753349**
Open March-October A ⊕ ⇌

A warm welcome awaits you from Robin & Pat Wren at this quiet family run site. Situated on the edge of Exmoor National Park with spectacular views.

Size 9 acres, 70 touring pitches, 40 with electric hookup, 40 level pitches, 29 static caravans, 11 ⚲, 20 WCs, 1 CWP
£ car/tent £7-£7.50, car/caravan £7.50-£8, motorhome £7-£7.50, motorbike/tent £7, children £0.50
Rental ⊕ £30 per night
℗ MasterCard Visa
⚑ ✕¼ ●¼ ⊡ ☎ ⚠ ☒ Calor Gaz ⚐ ⍭
Last arrival time: 10:00
➜ On main A39, ¾ mile from Barbrook village.

LYTHAM ST ANNES Lancashire　　10B4

Bank Lane Caravan Park
Warton, Preston
☎ **01772-633513**
Open March-October A ⊕ ⇌　　➜

Escape

At the RAC we can release you from
the worries of motoring

But did you know that we can also
give you invaluable peace of mind
when you go on holiday,

Or arrange your hotel bookings,

Or even organise your entire
holiday, all over the phone?

RAC Travel Insurance	0800 550 055
RAC Hotel Reservations	0345 056 042
RAC Holiday Reservations	0161 480 4810

Call us

RAC

← Bank Lane Caravan Park

Bank Lane Caravan Park has been architecturally designed, popular and highly praised by visitors. With modern facilities all holiday homes are situated in spacious cul-de-sacs. Tourers very welcome.

Size 15 acres, 50 touring pitches, 50 with electric hookup, 40 level pitches, 160 static caravans, 5 ⌂, 8 WCs, 2 CWPs
£ car/tent £7-£8, car/caravan £7, motorhome £7, motorbike/tent £7, children £7
⚡ ✕¼ ☕¼ 🔲 🔳 🔳 ⚠ 🔯 Calor ♿ 🐕 WS
Last arrival time: 8:00
➡ M6 (jn 31) to Blackpool. Join A584 Freckleton/Lytham, past BAE. Turn left at art gallery/ladies hairdressers. Follow the lane to site.

Eastham Hall Caravan Park
Saltcotes Road, Lytham St Annes FY8 4LS
📞 **01253-737907**
Open 1 March-31 October ⌂ 🚐
Size 25 acres, 140 touring pitches, 72 with electric hookup, 140 level pitches, 250 static caravans, 10 ⌂, 52 WCs, 10 CWPs
£ car/caravan £8-£9, motorhome £8-£9, children £0.75-£1
⚡ 🔲 🔳 ⚠ 🔯 Calor Gaz ♿ 🐕 WS
➡ Take A584 from Preston, turn right onto B5259 and site is ¾ mile on the right.

MABLETHORPE Lincolnshire   11F4

Camping & Caravanning Club Site
Highfield, Church Lane, Mablethorpe LN12 2NU
📞 **01507-472374**
Open end March-end September ⌂ 🚐 🚐

Size 6 acres, 105 touring pitches, 48 with electric hookup, 4 ⌂, 11 WCs, 1 CWP
£ car/tent £8.20-£10.40, car/caravan £8.20-£10.40, motorhome £8.20-£10.40, motorbike/tent £8.20, children £1.30
CC MasterCard Visa
🔲 🔳 ⚠ 🔯 🐕 WS
Last arrival time: 11:00
➡ From A1104 turn into Church Lane. Site is ¼ mile on right.

Golden Sands Holiday Park
Quebec Road, Mablethorpe LN12 1QJ
📞 **01507-477871**
Open Easter-October ⌂ 🚐 🚐
Size 320 touring pitches, 70 with electric hookup, 1,300 static caravans
CC MasterCard Visa
⚡ ✕ ☕ 🔲 🔳 🔳 🔯 ⚠ 🔯 🔳 Calor Gaz ♿
➡ From Mablethorpe town centre follow the seafront road to the N end for Golden Sands. About 1 mile.

Kirkstead Holiday Park
North Road, Trusthorpe, Mablethorpe LN12 2QD
📞 **01507-441483**
Open March-December ⌂ 🚐 🚐
Size 6 acres, 60 touring pitches, 40 with electric hookup, 60 level pitches, 45 static caravans, 6 ⌂, 10 WCs, 1 CWP
£ car/tent £5, car/caravan £6.50-£9, motorhome £6.50-£9, motorbike/tent £5
Rental 🚐 caravan £80-£200
⚡ ⚡¼ ✕ ✕¼ ☕ ☕¼ 🔲 🔳 🔳 🔯 🔯 🔳 🔳
Calor ♿ 🐕 WS
➡ On A52 coast road between Mablethorpe and Sutton-on-Sea. Turn off Trusthorpe Island for signs to Kirkstead Holiday Park.

Trusthorpe Springs Leisure Park
Trusthorpe Hall, Mile Lane, Trusthorpe, Mablethorpe LN12 2QQ
📞 **01507-441333** Fax **01507-441333**
Open 1 March-30 November 🚐 🚐
Size 4 acres, 22 touring pitches, 22 with electric hookup, 22 level pitches, 109 static caravans, 8 ⌂, 30 WCs, 5 CWPs
£ car/caravan £5.50-£7.50
Rental ⌂ 🚐 £25 daily, £185 weekly.
CC MasterCard Visa
⚡ ✕ ☕ 🔲 🔳 🔳 ⚠ 🔯 🔳 Calor ♿ 🐕
Last arrival time: 5:00

➔ Enter Mablethorpe on A1104, right at Cross Inn public house into Mile Lane. Site on corner, 1 mile from Cross Inn.

MAIDSTONE Kent	5E3

Pine Lodge Touring Park

Ashford Road, Hollingbourne, Maidstone
ME17 1XH
📞 **01622-730018** Fax **01622-734498**
Open all year ▲ 🚐 🚎

Ideally placed for touring Kent (Leeds Castle is only a mile away) and within easy reach of the Channel ports and the Channel Tunnel. New facilities block. Open all year. Sorry no dogs.

Size 7 acres, 100 touring pitches, 95 with electric hookup, 100 level pitches, 8 🚿, 11 WCs, 1 CWP
£ car/tent £7.50-£8.50, car/caravan £7.50-£8.50, motorhome £7.50-£8.50, motorbike/tent £6, children £0.50
🛒 ✕¼ 🔲 📞 🔲 ⚠ 🔲 Calor Gaz 🚹 WS
Last arrival time: 11:00
➔ From junction 8 on A20 roundabout turn off towards Bearsted and Maidstone. Pine Lodge is on left after 1 mile.

MALMESBURY Wiltshire	4A2

Burton Hill Caravan & Camping Park

Burton Hill, Malmesbury SN16 0EH
📞 **01666-822585** Fax **01666-822585**
Open 1 April-30 November ▲ 🚐 🚎
Size 2 acres, 30 touring pitches, 18 with electric hookup, 30 level pitches, 2 🚿, 4 WCs, 1 CWP
£ car/tent £6.50, car/caravan £6.50, motorhome £6.50, motorbike/tent £6.50, children £0.50
🔲 📞 🔲 🔲 Calor Gaz 🚹 WS

Last arrival time: 12:00
➔ 200 yards S of roundabout at junction of A429, B4014 and B4042, turn W off A429 opposite Malmesbury Hospital (Arches Lane) and follow signs.

MALVERN Worcestershire	7E4

Camping & Caravanning Club Site

Blackmore Camp Site No. 2, Hanley, Swan
WR8 0EE
📞 **01684-310280**
Open end March-end November ▲ 🚐 🚎
Size 12 acres, 200 touring pitches, 104 with electric hookup, 12 🚿, 14 WCs, 2 CWPs
£ car/tent £9.20-£12.05, car/caravan £9.20-£12.05, motorhome £9.20-£12.05, motorbike/tent £9.20, children £1.30
CC MasterCard Visa
🔲 GR ⚠ 🔲 ⚖ 🚹 WS
Last arrival time: 11:00
➔ Watch for Blackmore camp sign at junction of B4211. All approaches to site are well signposted.

Riverside Caravan Park

Little Clevelode, Malvern WR13 6PE

☎ **01684-310475 Fax 01684-310475**

Open March-December Å 🚐 🚏

Size 25 acres, 60 touring pitches, 60 with electric hookup, 60 level pitches, 130 static caravans, 13 WCs, 1 CWP

£ car/tent £6, car/caravan £6, motorhome £6, motorbike/tent £6, children £1

Rental 🚐 caravan £150-£185

🛒 🗇 📞 ▨ 🖨 GR TV ⚠ 🎎 Calor Gaz ✝ WS

Last arrival time: 9:00

➡ On B4424 in between Upton-upon-Severn and Callow End.

Strangers Home Inn

The Street, Bradfield, Manningtree CO11 2US

☎ **01255-870304**

Open 1 March-31 October Å 🚐 🚏

Size 2 acres, 65 touring pitches, 14 with electric hookup, 65 level pitches, 4 🛁, 9 WCs, 1 CWP

SHERWOOD FOREST
CARAVAN PARK

Sherwood Forest provides visitors with a superb location and beautiful scenery making it an ideal place for a relaxing break. The Park is a perfect base for visiting the many interesting and historical sites the area has to offer.

Sherwood Forest has 200 touring pitches of which 137 have electrical hook-up points. There are washing-up points, modern toilet and shower blocks, a laundry and hair washing room. Small service points are located close to the groups of pitches.

CAVENDISH LODGE, OLD CLIPSTONE, MANSFIELD NG21 9HW

Tel: 01623-823132

£ car/tent £7, car/caravan £7, motorhome £7, motorbike/tent £7, children £2.50

Rental 🚐

🛒¼ ✗ 🍺 📞 🗇 🍴 Calor Gaz ♿ ✝

➡ From A120 Colchester-Harwich road take the left turn at Horsley Cross to the television mast. Turn right through village diagonally opposite parish church.

Sherwood Forest Caravan Park

Near Edwinstowe, Mansfield NG21 9HW

☎ **01623-823132**

Open March-October Å 🚐 🚏

Quiet country park in the heart of Robin Hood country. Some pitches overlook lake and river. Rural atmosphere with wildlife around. Excellent area for walking and cycling.

Size 22 acres, 200 touring pitches, 137 with electric hookup, 200 🛁, 35 WCs, 4 CWPs

£ car/tent £9-£9.75, car/caravan £9-£9.75, motorhome £9-£9.75, motorbike/tent £9, children £1.10

CC MasterCard Visa

🛒 🗇 📞 🖨 GR 🔍 TV ⚠ 🎎 Calor Gaz ♿ ✝

➡ Best approach is via the Ollerton-Mansfield road A6075; turn S towards Old Clipstone opposite turning to Warsop and ½ mile to park. From M1 take exit 27 from S and 30 from N.

Pine Meadow Caravan Park

Spratling Court Farm, Manston CT12 5AN

☎ **01843-587770 Fax 01843-851177**

Open April-end September Å 🚐 🚏

Size 3 acres, 40 touring pitches, 40 with electric hookup, 40 level pitches, 4 ⛺, 4 WCs, 1 CWP
£ car/tent £7-£10.20, car/caravan £7-£10.20, motorhome £7-£10.20
🚾¼ ✗¼ ⛟¼ 🔌 ⚠ 🔳 Calor
Last arrival time: 10:00
➡ From A256 junction take B2050 west towards Manston village, in 300 yards turn right, signposted Greensole Lane Pine Meadow.

MARAZION Cornwall　　　　　2A4

Wayfarers Camping Site
St Hilary, Marazion TR20 9EF
📞 01736-763326
Open March-November 🏕 ⛺ 🚐
Size 4 acres, 60 touring pitches, 20 with electric hookup, 56 level pitches, 4 static caravans, 5 ⛺, 8 WCs, 1 CWP
£ car/tent £6-£7, car/caravan £6-£7, motorhome £6-£7, motorbike/tent £6, children £1
Rental 🚐
🚾 🖾 🔌 🛢 ⚠ 🔳 Calor Gaz 🐕 WS
Last arrival time: 11:00
➡ Turn left off A30 onto A394 to Helston. Proceed 2 miles to roundabout, left on B3280 to Goldsithney, ½ mile further site on left.

MARDEN Kent　　　　　5E3

Tanner Farm Caravan & Camping Park
Goudhurst Road, Marden TN12 9ND
📞 01622-832399 **Fax** 01622-832472
Open all year 🏕 ⛺ 🚐

Secluded park in centre of 150 acre farm. Ideal touring centre. Shire horses in use.

Size 15 acres, 100 touring pitches, 100 with electric hookup, 95 level pitches, 7 ⛺, 13 WCs, 3 CWPs
£ car/tent £7.50-£10, car/caravan £6-£10, motorhome £6-£10, motorbike/tent £7.50, children £1.10-£1.20
CC MasterCard Visa
🚾 🖾 🔌 🛢 ⚠ 🔳 Calor Gaz 🚻 🐕 WS
Last arrival time: 8:00
➡ From A229 or A262 onto B2079 midway between villages of Marden and Goudhurst.

MARGATE Kent　　　　　5F2

Frost Farm Caravan Site
St Nicholas-at-Wade, Birchington, Margate
📞 01843-847219
Open March-October 🏕 ⛺ 🚐
Size 3 acres, 12 touring pitches, 8 with electric hookup, 6 level pitches, 48 static caravans, 2 ⛺, 8 WCs, 1 CWP
£ car/tent £6-£8, car/caravan £6-£8, motorhome £6-£8
🚾¼ ✗¼ ⛟¼ 🔌 ⚠ 🔳 Calor 🐕 WS
Last arrival time: 10:00
➡ Site on A299, just before St Nicholas roundabout on London side.

St Nicholas Camping Site
Court Road, St Nicholas-at-Wade, Birchington, Margate
📞 01843-847245
Open 1 March-31 October 🏕 ⛺ 🚐
Size 3 acres, 75 touring pitches, 16 with electric hookup, 75 level pitches, 4 ⛺, 8 WCs, 1 CWP
£ car/tent £7-£7.50, car/caravan £6.50-£8.50, motorhome £6.50-£7.50, motorbike/tent £7
🚾 🚾¼ ✗¼ ⛟¼ 🛢 ⚠ 🔳 Calor Gaz ♿ 🐕
➡ The village is signposted off A299 and off A28 near Birchington.

MARKET RASEN Lincolnshire　　　　　8C1

Market Rasen Racecourse
Legsby Road, Market Rasen LN8 3EA
📞 01673-842307 **Fax** 01673-844532
Open 27 March-5 October 🏕 ⛺ 🚐　　　➡

← Market Rasen Racecourse

Rural site, with phone, TV room, playground, games area, reduced admission to racing, 9 hole pay and play golf course. Shop and restaurant one mile.

Size 2 acres, 55 touring pitches, 32 with electric hookup, 55 level pitches, 6 ⏣, 6 WCs, 1 CWP
CC MasterCard Visa
⚡ ▣ ☎ ▣ GR ▣ TV ⏢ ⊞ Calor ♿ ♞
Last arrival time: 8:00
➜ S off A631 on E outskirts of Market Rasen. Site is on left after ¾ mile.

Walesby Woodlands

Walesby, Market Rasen LN8 3UN
☎ **01673-843285**
Open 1 March-1 November 🏕 🚐 🚚

A family owned, sheltered, well-drained, level site. Bordered by forests, giving many woodland walks. Quality site offering peace and quiet. Calor Environmental Award runner-up 1993.

Size 2½ acres, 64 touring pitches, 60 with electric hookup, 64 level pitches, 14 ⏣, 12 WCs, 2 CWPs
£ car/tent £6.50, car/caravan £6.50, motorhome £6.50, motorbike/tent £6.50, children £1-£1.25

⚡ ▣ ☎ ⏢ ⊞ Calor Gaz ♿ ♞ WS
Last arrival time: 9:30
➜ In Market Rasen, adjacent to the railway bridge, take the B1203 to Tealby. After ¾ mile turn left onto an unclassified road to Walesby. After ¼ mile the site is signposted on left.

Bolberry House Farm

Camping and Caravan Park, Bolberry, Marlborough TQ7 3DY
☎ **01548-561251**
Open Easter-October 🏕 🚐 🚚

A friendly family run park in a peaceful setting on a farm which adjoins spectacular National Trust coastline, with superb sea views and cliff walks nearby. First class facilities on a well maintained park.

Size 5½ acres, 20 touring pitches, 36 with electric hookup, 50 level pitches, 10 static caravans, 8 ⏣, 12 WCs, 1 CWP
£ car/caravan £6.50
Rental 🚐
⚡¼ ✕¼ 🍴¼ ▣ ☎ ⏢ ⊞ Calor Gaz ♞ WS
➜ Take A381 from Kingsbridge towards Salcombe. Turn sharp right, through village of Malborough and follow signs to Bolberry. Park is on right on outskirts of hamlet.

Hillview Caravan Park

Oare, Marlborough SN8 4JE
☎ **01672-563151**
Open April-September 🏕 🚐 🚚
Size 6 acres, 10 touring pitches, 10 with electric hookup, 10 level pitches, 36 static caravans, 4 ⏣, 3 WCs, 1 CWP
£ car/tent £6.50-£7.50, car/caravan £7-£10, motorhome £7-£10, motorbike/tent £5

✕¼ ▯ ⋔
Last arrival time: 10:00
→ S from Marlborough on A345 Marlborough to Pewsey road. Junction of Sunnyhill Lane.

Second Chance Touring Park
Marston Meysey SN6 6SZ
☎ **01285-810675**
Open 1 March-30 November Å ⊕ ⊞
Size 2 acres, 26 touring pitches, 26 with electric hookup, 26 level pitches, 4 ▮, 5 WCs, 1 CWP
£ car/tent £6
✕¼ ⬤¼ ▯ ▨ Calor ⋔
Last arrival time: 9:00
→ Follow A419 from Cirencester or Swindon, turn off at Fairford signpost and proceed 3 miles. Turn left at first Castle Eaton signpost. Site is 200 yards on left.

Southfork Caravan Park
Parrett Works, Martock TA12 6AE
☎ **01935-825661** Fax **01935-825122**
Open all year Å ⊕ ⊞

A small family-run park in beautiful countryside near the River Parrett, clean and well-maintained with a modern toilet block and free hot showers. Numerous places of interest are nearby for all ages.

Size 2 acres, 30 touring pitches, 18 with electric hookup, 30 level pitches, 2 static caravans, 4 ▮, 5 WCs, 1 CWP
£ car/tent £7, car/caravan £7, motorhome £7, motorbike/tent £7, children £1
Rental ⊕ caravans £90-£220
⛟ ▯ ☎ ▯ ⚟ ▨ Calor Gaz ♿ ⋔
Last arrival time: 10:00

Darwin Forest Country Park
Two Dales, Matlock DE4 5LN
☎ **01629-732428** Fax **01629-735015**
Open March-December Å ⊕ ⊞

→

← **Darwin Forest Country Park**

A luxurious family park set in 44 acres of magnificent woodland, featuring every comfort in a spacious and peaceful environment.

Size 44 acres, 58 touring pitches, 58 with electric hookup, 58 level pitches, 16 ☗, 21 WCs, 1 CWP
£ car/tent £10-£12, car/caravan £10-£12, motorhome £10-£12, motorbike/tent £10
Rental Chalet. £190
℄ MasterCard Visa
☡ ✕ ♥ ⬚ ◪ ⬚ ⬚ GR TV ⚠ ✕ ⬚ Calor ♿ ☂
➡ From A63, turn right onto B5057 and park is on right.

Packhorse Farm
Tansley, Matlock DE4 5LF
☏ **01629-582781 Fax 01629-580950**
Å ⊕ ⊕
Size 2 acres, 30 touring pitches, 17 with electric hookup, 30 level pitches, 2 ☗, 4 WCs, 1 CWP
£ car/tent £6-£8, car/caravan £6-£8, motorhome £6-£8, motorbike/tent £6
☡ ☡¼ ♥ ♥¼ ◪ ⬚ ♿ ☂
➡ On A615 Alfreton to Matlock road. Turn right in Tansley village.

Wayside Farm Caravan Site
Matlock Moor, Matlock DE4 5LF
☏ **01629-582967**
Open all year ⊕ ⊕

A working farm, with a hard road around a well-kept site and trees and hedges beginning to establish. B&B and holiday cottages also available.

Size 1¾ acres, 30 touring pitches, 19 with electric hookup, 6 ☗, 10 WCs, 1 CWP
℄ MasterCard Visa
☡ ✕ ♥ ◪ ⬚ ⬚ ⬚ ✕ GR ⬚ Calor Gaz WS
➡ Wayside Farm is 2 miles from Matlock, just off A632, well signposted from main road.

MERSEA ISLAND Essex   **5E1**

Waldegraves Farm Holiday Park
West Mersea, Mersea Island CO5 8SE
☏ **01206-382898 Fax 01206-385359**
Open March-October Å ⊕ ⊕

Family park, scenic with a private beach. Three fishing lakes, pool, golf driving range, games areas. Entertainment, bar and shop. Something to suit everyone. All up-to-date facilities. Holiday homes for hire.

Size 25 acres, 120 touring pitches, 120 with electric hookup, 120 level pitches, 205 static caravans, 20 ☗, 20 WCs, 4 CWPs
£ car/tent £7-£11, car/caravan £7-£11, motorhome £7-£11, motorbike/tent £7
Rental ⊕ £140-290
℄ MasterCard Visa
☡ ✕ ♥ ⬚ ◪ ⬚ ⬚ ✕ ⬚ GR ⬚ TV ⚠ ✕ ⬚
Calor Gaz ♿ ☂ WS
Last arrival time: 10:00
➡ B1025 from Colchester to Mersea. Follow brown tourist signs to East Mersea and on to Waldegraves.

MEVAGISSEY Cornwall   **2B4**

Penhaven Touring Park
Pentewan PL26 6DL
☏ **01726-843687 Fax 01726-843**
Open Easter-31 October Å ⊕ ⊕

Size 13 acres, 105 touring pitches, 78 with electric hookup, 105 level pitches, 10 ⋒, 17 WCs, 2 CWPs
£ car/tent £7-£12, car/caravan £7-£16.50, motorhome £7-£16.50, motorbike/tent £7, children £1.30
℃ MasterCard Visa
🐾 ✕ 🗪 ◙ 🔋 🗂 ▣ 🔍 🄼 🔳 Calor Gaz & 🐦 WS
Last arrival time: 9:00
➡ S of St Austell, on the B3273 turning on left.

Sea View International
Boswinger, Gorran, St Austell PL26 6LL
📞 01726-843425 Fax 01726-843358
Open April-October **Å ⛺ 🚐**

A peaceful, landscaped, level park close to beautiful beaches. Acres of recreational space with badminton, tennis court, volleyball and putting green.

Size 16 acres, 165 touring pitches, 150 with electric hookup, 165 level pitches, 39 static caravans, 13 ⋒, 30 WCs,
£ car/tent £6-£15.50, car/caravan £6-£15.50, motorhome £6-£15.50
Rental Å ⛺ Chalet.
℃ MasterCard Visa
🐾 🗪 ◙ 🔋 🗂 ▣ 🔍 🄶🄡 🔳 ▣ 🄼 🔳 Calor Gaz &
🐦
Last arrival time: 12:00
➡ From St Austell take B3273 signed Mevagissey. Prior to village turn right signed Gorran. After 6 miles follow directional signs on right.

Fell End Caravan Park
Slackhead Road, Near Hale, Milnthorpe LA7 7BS
📞 015395-62122
Open all year **Å ⛺ 🚐**

Rural park in an area of outstanding natural beauty, ETB graded five ticks. Free luxury facilities, lounge bar and restaurant, TV and satellite hook-ups, sports.

Size 28 acres, 68 touring pitches, 68 with electric hookup, 60 level pitches, 215 static caravans, 13 ⋒, 44 WCs, 3 CWPs
🐾 ✕ 🗪 &
➡ Leave M6 at junction 35 and head N up A6 for 3¼ miles. Turn left on to unclassified road at brown sites sign and follow road ¾ mile, pick up Fell End Caravan Park signs.

Blue Anchor Bay Caravan Park
Minehead TA24 6JT
📞 01643-821360 Fax 01643-821572
Open March-October **Å ⛺ 🚐**   ➡

← **Blue Anchor Bay Caravan Park**

Peaceful beach side location bordered by the West Somerset Railway. Ideal for exploring Exmoor and the beautiful Somerset coast.

Size 29 acres, 103 touring pitches, 103 with electric hookup, 103 level pitches, 300 static caravans, 8 ☂, 15 WCs, 1 CWP
£ car/caravan £7.50-£18, motorhome £7.52-£18
Rental ⛺
CC MasterCard Visa
🐄 🐄¼ ✗¼ ⊡ 🔌 🔲 ⚠ 🎣 Calor Gaz ♿
Last arrival time: 11:00
➔ From junction 25 on M5, take A358 signed Minehead. After about 12 miles, turn left onto A39 at Williton. After about four miles, turn right onto B3191 at Carhampton. Park is 1½ miles on the right.

Camping & Caravanning Club Site
Hill Road, North Hill, Minehead TA24 5RY
📞 **01643-704138**
Open end March-end September ⚓ ⛺ 🚐
Size 3¾ acres, 60 touring pitches, 2 ☂, 10 WCs, 1 CWP
£ car/tent £8.20-£10.40, car/caravan £8.20-£10.40, motorhome £8.20-£10.40, motorbike/tent £8.20, children £1.30
CC MasterCard Visa
⊡ 🔌 🐕
Last arrival time: 11:00
➔ From A39 turn into The Parade, then left into Blenheim Road and left again into Martlett Road. Follow road past church into Moor Road and then Hill Road. Site is ¼ mile on right.

MODBURY Devon   2C4

Camping & Caravanning Club Site
California Cross, Modbury PL21 0SG
📞 **01548-821297**
Open end March-start November ⚓ ⛺ 🚐
Size 3.66 acres, 80 touring pitches, 40 with electric hookup, 6 ☂, 9 WCs, 1 CWP
£ car/tent £8.75-£11.55, car/caravan £8.75-£11.55, motorhome £8.75-£11.55, motorbike/tent £8.75, children £1.40
CC MasterCard Visa
⊡ ⚠ 🎣 ♿ 🐕
Last arrival time: 11:00
➔ On B3196 towards Kingsbridge. Site is behind Gulf service station.

Moor View Touring Park
California Cross, Modbury PL21 0SG
📞 **01548-821485**
Open Easter-end September ⚓ ⛺ 🚐

Quiet country park, superb moorland views, sheltered spacious level pitches, modern and scrupulously clean toilets and showers with free hot water. Shop and take-away. Dogs welcome.

Size 5½ acres, 68 touring pitches, 68 with electric hookup, 68 level pitches, 6 ☂, 9 WCs, 1 CWP
£ car/tent £6-£9.50, car/caravan £6-£9.50, motorhome £6-£9.50, motorbike/tent £6, children £0.75
CC MasterCard Visa
🐄 ✗ 🛒 ⊡ 🔌 GR ⚠ 🎣 Gaz 🐕 WS
Last arrival time: 10:00
➔ From A38, 25 miles W of Exeter, leave at Wrangaton Cross (A3121). After 3 miles leave Mobil garage on left and follow Modbury (B3107) road. Park is ½ mile on left.

MORECAMBE Lancashire   10B3

Broadfields Caravan & Camping Park
276 Oxcliffe Road, Morecambe
📞 **01524-410 278 Fax 01524-410 278**
Open March-December ⚓ ⛺ 🚐
Size 2 acres, 25 touring pitches, 25 with electric hookup, 25 level pitches, 16 static caravans, 2 ☂, 7 WCs, 1 CWP
£ car/tent £5-£6.25, car/caravan £6.25, motorhome £6.25, motorbike/tent £5
Rental ⛺ Static 6 berth £150
🐄¼ ✗¼ 🛒¼ 🔌 ⊡ GR ⚠ 🎣 Calor ♿ 🐕 WS
Last arrival time: 10:00
➔ Take B59 from Lancaster, then B5273 to Heysham.

Regent Leisure Park

Westgate, Morecambe LA3 3DF
☎ 01524-413940 Fax 01524-832247
Open March-January 🚐 🚛

A level, grassy site in town, half a mile from the beach, with a club, disco, family room and children's play area, plus two swimming pools. 120 caravans with own WCs for hire.

Size 12 acres, 23 touring pitches, 23 with electric hookup, 23 level pitches, 299 static caravans, 6 🍴, 7 WCs, 1 CWP
£ car/caravan £9-£15, motorhome £9-£15
Rental 🚐 £85-£385
CC MasterCard Visa
🛒 ✗ 🍺 🖥 🛄 🔲 🔲 🔲 ⚠ 🔲 Calor ♿
Last arrival time: 12:00
➜ Leave the M6 (jn34), turn left, follow Morecambe into Lancaster, over River Lune, turn left at third roundabout into Westgate. The park is 1 mile on left.

Riverside Caravan Park

Oxcliffe Hill Farm, Heaton-with-Oxcliffe, Morecambe LA3 3ER
☎ 01524-844193
Open March-October
Size 2½ acres, 50 touring pitches, 50 with electric hookup, 50 level pitches, 4 🍴, 8 WCs, 1 CWP
CC MasterCard Visa
🛒¼ ✗¼ 🔲 ⚠ 🔲 ⊟ Calor
➜ Leave M6 junction 34, follow signs for Morecambe. Cross river and follow signs for Overton and Middleton. Site gate next to Golden Ball Inn, where river and road run next to each other.

Venture Caravan Park

Langridge Way, Westgate, Morecambe LA4 4TQ
☎ 01524-412986 Fax 01524-855884
Open all year 🅰 🚐 🚛

18 acre site with level grass pitches. Quiet, but only three quarters of a mile to all town amenities.

Size 18 acres, 100 touring pitches, 70 with electric hookup, 100 level pitches, 200 static caravans, 16 🍴, 24 WCs, 2 CWPs
🛒 ✗ 🖥 Calor Gaz ♿ WS
➜ M6 junction 34 to Lancaster, then A589 to Morecambe. At the third roundabout by the Shrimp Public House, take the left along Westgate, ½ mile right at the school into Langridge Way. Straight on ahead for the site.

Percy Wood Caravan Park

Swanland, Morpeth NE65 9JW
☎ 01670-787649 Fax 01670-787034
Open March 1-January 31 🅰 🚐 🚛
Size 67 acres, 60 touring pitches, 60 with electric hookup, 60 level pitches, 60 static caravans, 6 🍴, 10 WCs, 1 CWP
£ car/tent £8, car/caravan £9.50, motorhome £9.50, motorbike/tent £8, children £1   ➜

← Percy Wood Caravan Park

Rental 🚐 £85-£290
CC MasterCard Visa
🛁 🛁¼ ✕¼ 🍴¼ 🔲 🔌 🔲 GR 🔲 ⚠ 🔲 Calor Gaz
🐕
Last arrival time: 10:00
➡ 2 miles off A1 to Swarland, 6 miles S of
Alnwick.

Mill Farm Holiday Park
Hughley, Much Wenlock SY5 6NT
📞 0174636-208
Open 1 March-31 October ⛺ 🚐 🚚

*Family run site in an area of outstanding
natural beauty. Mill Farm offers peace,
tranquillity, an abundance of bird and
wildlife, excellent walking, riding and
fishing.*

Size 10 acres, 40 touring pitches, 35 with
electric hookup, 30 level pitches, 85 static
caravans, 6 🚿, 12 WCs, 2 CWPs
£ car/tent £7.05, car/caravan £7.05,
motorhome £7.05, children £1
🔲 🔌 🔲 🔲 🔲 Calor Gaz ♿ 🐕 WS
Last arrival time: 8:00
➡ A4169 from Telford to Much Wenlock.
From Much Wenlock take B4731. Turn right
for Hughley, go through village, past the
church and the site is signposted on left.

Sandy Gulls Clifftop Touring Park
Cromer Road, Mundesley-on-Sea NR11 8DF
📞 01263-720513
Open March-November ⛺ 🚐 🚚

*Set on a clifftop with panoramic sea views,
half a mile from the village. Only a ten
minute drive to the Broads National Park
and centrally situated for all attractions.*

Size 20 acres, 40 touring pitches, 40 with
electric hookup, 20 level pitches, 100 static
caravans, 10 🚿, 20 WCs, 2 CWPs
£ car/tent £5-£10, car/caravan £5-£10,
motorhome £5-£10
Rental 🚐 Chalet. £140-£200
🛁¼ ✕¼ 🍴¼ 🔲 🔌 🔲 TV ⚠ 🔲 Calor ♿ 🐕
Last arrival time: 10:00
➡ At Cromer take coast road S for 5 miles.

Woodland Caravan Park
Trimingham, Mundesley NR11 8AL
📞 01263-579208 Fax 01263-833071
Open March-October 🚐 🚚

*Surrounded by mature woodland, peace
and tranquillity in conjunction with up to
date facilities including beautiful bar and
restaurant.*

Size 43 acres, 150 touring pitches, 80 with
electric hookup, 100 level pitches, 150 static
caravans, 14 🚿, 30 WCs, 2 CWPs

£ car/caravan £6.50-£10.50, motorhome £5.50-£7
℃ MasterCard Visa
🦽 ✕ 📞 🗑 🔋 🗓 GR 🔍 ⚠ ✖ Calor Gaz ♿ ✝
WS
➜ On coast road between Cromer and Mundesley.

Brookfield Caravan Park
Shrewbridge Road, Nantwich
📞 01270-69176 Fax 01270-650756
Open Easter-end September ⛺ 🚐 🚲
Touring caravans and tents are welcome at this site, which is situated only 5 minutes walk away from the historical town of Nantwich and the shops.

Size 12 touring pitches, 12 with electric hookup, 24 level pitches, 2 🚿, 4 WCs,
£ car/caravan £6, motorhome £3.50, motorbike/tent £1.50
🦽¼ ✕¼ 📞¼ 🔋 🗓 🗂 🔍 ⚠ ✖ ♿ ✝
➜ From M6 junction 16 take A500 into Nantwich.

Forestry Commission Aldridge Hill
Brockenhurst SO42 7QD
📞 01703-283771 Fax 01703-283929
Open 22 May-1 September
Size 40 acres, 200 level pitches, 2 CWPs
£ car/tent £6.50
Calor Gaz
➜ Off A337, 1 mile NW of Brockenhurst village.

Forestry Commission Longbeech Campsite
New Forest
📞 01703-283771
Size 400 touring pitches, 1 CWP
➜ From Lyndhurst take A337 to Cadnam, turn NW onto B3079 and take first left. Site signposted on left.

Forestry Commission Ocknell Campsite
Fritham, Lyndhurst SO43 7NH
📞 01703-283771 Fax 01703-283929
Open 21 March-29 September
Size 48 acres, 480 touring pitches, 17 WCs, 6 CWPs
£ car/tent £6-£8.50
℃ MasterCard Visa
🦽 📞 Calor Gaz ♿
Last arrival time: 11:00
➜ From A31 at Cadnam take B3079 and then B3078 via Brook and Fritham.

Forestry Commission Setthorns Campsite
Wootton, New Milton BH25 5UA
📞 01703-283771 Fax 01703-283929
Size 60 acres, 120 with electric hookup, 320 level pitches, 5 CWPs
£ car/tent £6-£11
℃ MasterCard Visa
📞 Calor Gaz
➜ From Brockenhurst take B3055 to Sway. After 2 miles take unclassified signposted road to site.

Bashley Park

Sway Road, New Milton BH25 5QR
☎ 01425-612340 Fax 01425-612602
Open 1 March-31 October 🚐 🚙

Set in a wooded country estate close to Bournemouth, the New Forest and Solent Beaches, this family park has a vast range of sporting and entertainment facilities.

Size 100 acres, 420 touring pitches, 420 with electric hookup, 350 level pitches, 380 static caravans, 37 🍴, 72 WCs, 4 CWPs
£ car/caravan £9.50-£22, motorhome £9.50-£22
Rental 🚐
CC MasterCard Visa
🛒✕🐕🔯📞🔒📷📶📺▶🎣🎯🆖📵📺⛰✦
🔥 Calor
Last arrival time: 9:00
➡ From A35 Lyndhurst to Bournemouth for 10 miles. Take the B3055 signed Swayford for 2½ miles, then straight over at the crossroads. Park is ¼ mile on left.

Marlie Farm Holiday Village

Dymchurch Road, New Romney TN28 8UE
☎ 01797-363036
Open Easter-end October
An ideal base for touring Kent and Sussex situated only a quarter of a mile from New Romney. Safe sandy beaches only 1½ miles away.

Size 450 touring pitches
➡ On A259, ¼ mile E of New Romney.

Newby Bridge Caravan Park

Canny Hill, Newby Bridge LA12 8NF
☎ 015395-31030 Fax 015395-30105
Open March-October 🚐 🚙
Size 25 acres, 20 touring pitches, 20 with electric hookup, 20 level pitches, 69 static caravans, 4 🍴, 8 WCs, 1 CWP
£ car/caravan £8-£10.50, motorhome £8-£10.50
Rental 🚐 Chalet. £150-£365
🛒¼ ✕¼ 🐕¼ 🔯 📞 Calor ♿ 🐾 WS
Last arrival time: 8:00
➡ Just before entering Newby Bridge from motorway turn left at Canny Hill signpost. Park entrance is 200 yards on right.

Oak Head Caravan Park

Ayside, Newby Bridge LA11 6JA
☎ 01539-531475
Open March-October 🏕 🚐 🚙
Size 3½ acres, 60 touring pitches, 30 with electric hookup, 50 level pitches, 71 static caravans, 8 🍴, 33 WCs, 1 CWP
£ car/tent £5-£7, car/caravan £7-£8, motorhome £5-£7, motorbike/tent £5
Rental 🚐
🔯 📞 🔯 Calor Gaz ♿ 🐾 WS
Last arrival time: flexible
➡ M6 motorway junction 36 onto A590. Follow signs for Newby Bridge for 14 miles. The caravan sign is on the left side of A590. Site is 1½ miles S of Newby Bridge.

Newhaven Caravan & Camping Park

Newhaven SK17 0DT
☎ 01298-84300
Open 1 March-31 October 🏕 🚐 🚙

Delightful site in the heart of the Peak District with excellent facilities and free hot water. Alton Towers, Chatsworth House, Haddon Hall, Harwick Hall, all within easy reach.

Size 13 acres, 95 touring pitches, 62 with electric hookup, 80 level pitches, 70 static caravans, 8 📷, 18 WCs, 1 CWP
£ car/tent £6.75, car/caravan £6.75, motorhome £6.75, motorbike/tent £6.75
🐃 ✕¼ 🗐 🔃 🗓 GR 🗚 ⊠ Calor Gaz 🏇 WS
➜ Halfway between Ashbourne and Buxton on A515 at the junction with the A5012.

NEWMARKET Suffolk 9D4

Camping & Caravanning Club Site
Rowley Mile Racecourse, Newmarket CB8 8JL
📞 **01638-663235**
Open end March-end September 🅰 🚐 🚍
Size 90 touring pitches, 36 with electric hookup, 6 📷, 13 WCs, 1 CWP
£ car/tent £8.75-£11.55, car/caravan £8.75-£11.55, motorhome £8.75-£11.55, motorbike/tent £8.75, children £1.40
CC MasterCard Visa
🗐 GR 🗚 ⊠ 🏇
Last arrival time: 11:00
➜ On A1304 in Newmarket, follow signs for Hospital Racecourse.

NEWQUAY Cornwall 2A3

Camping & Caravanning Club Site
Tregurrian, Watergate Bay, Newquay TR8 4AE
📞 **01637-860448**
Open late March-late September 🅰 🚐 🚍
Size 4½ acres, 106 touring pitches, 14 with electric hookup, 6 📷, 16 WCs, 2 CWPs
£ car/tent £8.20-£10.40, car/caravan £8.20-£10.40, motorhome £8.20-£10.40, motorbike/tent £8.20, children £1.30
CC MasterCard Visa
🗐 🔃 🏇
Last arrival time: 11:00
➜ From B3056 take road signed Airport, left at B3276 then follow signs.

Gwills Holiday Park
Newquay TR8 4PE
📞 **01637-873617** Fax **01637-873617**
Open Easter-December 🅰 🚐 🚍
Size 14 acres, 150 touring pitches, 45 with electric hookup, 150 level pitches, 32 static caravans, 13 📷, 10 WCs, 1 CWP
£ car/tent £5.20-£9, car/caravan £5.20-£9, motorhome £4.60-£8, motorbike/tent £4.90, children £1.20-£2.10
Rental 🚐 Chalet. £90-£500
CC MasterCard Visa
🐃 ✕ 🦯 🗐 🔃 🖥 🗓 GR 📺 🗚 ⊠ 🍴 Calor ♿ 🏇
WS
Last arrival time: 10:00
➜ Take M5 to Exeter, then A30, then A392 to Newquay. At Quintrell Downs go straight across at roundabout, then take second turning on left signposted 'Gwills'. Go past Lane Theatre, turn right at crossroads and site is 400 yards on right.

Hendra Holiday Park
Newquay TR8 4NY
📞 **01637-875778** Fax **01637-879017**
Open April-October 🅰 🚐 🚍   →

← **Hendra Holiday Park**

Size 49 acres, 600 touring pitches, 250 with electric hookup, 600 level pitches, 160 static caravans, 3 CWPs
Rental 🚐
℀ MasterCard Visa
🅟 ✕ 📖 🔌 🔦 📶 📞 ⊞ 🅶🅡 🔲 📺 ⚠ ✗ 🔌
Calor Gaz ♿ 🐕 WS
➡ A30 to Indian Queens, A392 to Newquay. Hendra is 1½ miles before Newquay town centre.

Newquay Holiday Park
Newquay TR8 4HS
📞 **01637-871111 Fax 01637-850818**
Open 11 May-14 September ▲ 🚐 🚏
Size 23 acres, 259 touring pitches, 156 with electric hookup, 10 level pitches, 112 static caravans, 24 ⋔, 30 WCs, 4 CWPs
£ car/tent £6.80-£11, car/caravan £6.80-£14.50, motorhome £6.80-£14.50, motorbike/tent £6.80, children £3.50
Rental 🚐 £112-£417
℀ MasterCard Visa
🅟 ☕ 🅞 🔌 🔦 ⊞ 🅶🅡 🔲 📺 ⚠ ✗ 🔌 Calor Gaz
Last arrival time: 10:00

TREKENNING
TOURIST PARK

An exclusive family run park set in beautiful quiet countryside but only minutes away from sandy beaches.

Facilities include:
Swimming Pools, Bar, Restaurant, TV and Games Room, Play Area, Family Bathrooms/Showers, Shop and Laundry.

Contact John Dave or Tracey.
NEWQUAY, CORNWALL TR8 4JF
Tel/Fax: 01637 880462

➡ 2 miles from Newquay on A3059 toward St Columb, signposted.

Resparva House Camping & Caravanning
Summercourt, Newquay TR8 5AH
📞 **01872-510332 Fax 01872-510332**
Open Easter-October ▲ 🚐 🚏
Size 1 acre, 15 touring pitches, 12 with electric hookup, 15 level pitches, 2 ⋔, 4 WCs, 1 CWP
£ car/tent £5-£8, car/caravan £5-£8, motorhome £5-£8, motorbike/tent £5, children £1.25-£2
🅞 Calor Gaz 🐕
Last arrival time: 9:00
➡ From the A30 passing Bodmin, proceed SW past Indian Queens. Take second exit to Summercourt (marked Chapel Town and Summercourt). The site entrance is opposite.

Trekenning Manor Tourist Park
Newquay TR8 4JF
📞 **01637-880462 Fax 01637-880462**
Open March-October ▲ 🚐 🚏
Size 6½ acres, 75 touring pitches, 68 with electric hookup, 9 ⋔, 11 WCs, 1 CWP
£ car/tent £6.80-£9.40, car/caravan £6.80-£9.40, motorhome £6.80-£9.40, motorbike/tent £6.80, children £2.30-£3.40
Rental ▲ 🚐
℀ MasterCard Visa
🅟 ✕ 📖 🅞 🔌 🅞 ⊞ 🅶🅡 📺 ⚠ ✗ 🔌 Calor Gaz WS
➡ Adjacent to A39 by the St Columb Major roundabout.

Treloy Farm Tourist Park
Newquay TR8 4JN
📞 **01637-872063**
Open April-end September ▲ 🚐 🚏
Size 11½ acres, 141 touring pitches, 98 with electric hookup, 100 level pitches, 14 ⋔, 24 WCs, 1 CWP
£ car/tent £5-£8.60, car/caravan £5-£8.60, children £2.15
℀ MasterCard Visa
🅟 ✕ 📖 🅞 🔌 🅞 ⊞ 🅶🅡 🔲 📺 ⚠ ✗ 🔌 Calor Gaz 🐕
Last arrival time: 11:00   ➡

Newquay Holiday Park
CORNWALL

JUST WHAT YOU'RE LOOKING FOR !

If you want a high quality Holiday Park in a beautiful country setting yet only 3 miles from some of the finest beaches in Cornwall then Newquay Holiday Park is just what you're looking for...

EXCELLENT FACILITIES

You'll find all the high standard facilities you would expect from an RAC appointed holiday park.

- *Free electric hook-ups**
- *Children Free** • *Free showers* • *Launderette*
- *Self-service shop* • *Takeaway foods*

* At selected times, see our brochure for details

GREAT FAMILY VALUE

Great value holidays and so much to enjoy...

- *Free childrens club* • *Free 3 heated swimming pools & 200ft waterslide* • *Free nightly entertainment for all the family* • *Amusements* • *Snooker & pool* • *Crazy golf* • *Pitch & putt* • *Children's playgrounds* • *Recreation field* • *Golf course adjacent*

PERFECT LOCATION

A beautiful scenic park ideally situated for exploring the magical county of Cornwall...

- *Superb holiday caravans are also available*

01637 871111 (ext: 30)

30 Newquay Holiday Park, Newquay, Cornwall TR8 4HS

Fabulous Family Fun !

← **Treloy Farm Tourist Park**

➡ Just off the A3059 (the main St Columb Major to Newquay road). 5 minutes to Newquay.

Trenance Caravan Park
Edgcumbe Avenue, Newquay TR7 2JY
📞 **01637-873447**
Open 1 April-31 October ⚊ ⏏ ⛺
Size 12 acres, 50 touring pitches, 36 with electric hookup, 16 level pitches, 134 static caravans, 22 ☞, 3 CWPs
£ car/tent £5-£9.50, car/caravan £5-£9.50, motorhome £5-£9.50, motorbike/tent £5, children £1-£2.25
Rental ⏏ Chalet. £80-£340
ℂℂ MasterCard Visa
🐕 ✕ ☕ ⊚ 📞 ⊟ 𝔾ℝ Calor Gaz
Last arrival time: 9:00
➡ On the main A3075 Newquay/Truro road. 1 mile from Newquay town centre.

Trethiggey Touring Park
Quintrell Downs, Newquay TR8 4LG
📞 **01637-877672**
Open 1 March-1 January ⚊ ⏏ ⛺
Size 15 acres, 145 touring pitches, 100 with electric hookup, 145 level pitches, 12 static caravans, 8 ☞, 21 WCs, 1 CWP
£ car/tent £5.15-£7.75, car/caravan £5.15-£7.75, motorhome £4.40-£7, motorbike/tent £4.40, children £1-£1.75
Rental ⏏ £80-£300
ℂℂ MasterCard Visa
🐕 🐕¼ ✕¼ ☕ ☕¼ ⊚ 📞 ⊟ ☜ 🅰 𝔾ℝ 𝕋𝕍 ⚠ ✕
Calor Gaz ♿ ↑ WS
Last arrival time: 10:30
➡ From A30 at Indian Queens take A392 Newquay Road. Follow this road for 5 miles to Quintrell Downs roundabout. The site is signposted left on A3058 ½ mile.

Trevornick Holiday Park
Holywell Bay, Newquay TR8 5PW
📞 **01637-8360531 Fax 01637-831000**
Open 1 May-14 September ⚊ ⏏ ⛺

Just ½ mile from beach, stunning sea views from immaculately maintained 5 tick park. Daytime/evening entertainment programme. Fully equiped tents to sleep 6, to rent.

Size 30 acres, 450 touring pitches, 250 with electric hookup, 200 level pitches, 40 🅿, 70 WCs, 8 CWPs
£ car/tent £5.50-£10.40, car/caravan £5.50-£10.40, motorhome £5.50-£10.40, motorbike/tent £5.50, children £2.90
Rental ⚠ Eurotents, fully equipped £80-£250 weekly.
CC MasterCard Visa
🐾 ✕ ⛟ 🗑 📞 🔃 📠 🛝 🔍 🏕 🏷 🔍 📺 🅿 🏕 ⚱ Calor ♿ 🐕
➔ Take A3075 Newquay to Perranporth road. Turn left for Cubert/Holywell. Go through Cubert and site is ½ mile on the right.

Watergate Bay Holiday Park
Tregurrian, Watergate Bay, Newquay TR8 4AD
📞 **01637-860387** Fax **01637-860387**
Open 1 March-30 November ⚠ 🚐 🚍

For a relaxing holiday in beautiful countryside by the sea. Heated pool, licensed club, cafeteria, electronics, laundrette, adventure playground and evening entertainment.

Size 15 acres, 171 touring pitches, 100 with electric hookup, 171 level pitches, 20 🅿, 32 WCs, 6 CWPs
£ car/tent £6-£10, car/caravan £6-£10, motorhome £6-£10, motorbike/tent £6
CC MasterCard Visa
🐾 ✕ ⛟ 🗑 📞 🔃 🔃 📠 📺 🅿 🏕 ⚱ Calor ♿ 🐕 WS
➔ 4 miles N of Newquay on B3276 coast road to Newquay.

NEWTON ABBOT Devon   **3D3**

Dornafield Caravan Park
Two Mile Oak, Newton Abbot TQ12 6DD
📞 **01803-812732**
Open 20 March-31 October ⚠ 🚐 🚍   ➔

← **Dornafield Caravan Park**

Beautiful 14th century farmhouse located in peaceful Devon countryside. Superb facilities for discerning caravanners with 135 pitches (including 64 full service). Tennis, games room, children's adventure areas and shop.

Size 13 acres, 135 touring pitches, 135 with electric hookup, 135 level pitches, 19 ⬆, 28 WCs, 32 CWPs
£ car/tent £6.50-£11.50, car/caravan £6.50-£11.50, motorhome £6.50-£11.50, motorbike/tent £6.50
⛴ ✕¼ ➥¼ 🔲 📞 ⭕ 🔲 GR 🔲 🅰 🔲 Calor Gaz ⛄ ⛄ WS
Last arrival time: 10:00
➡ Take A381, Newton Abbot to Totnes road. From Newton Abbot after 2½ miles turn right at 'Two Mile Oak Inn'. After 5 miles take first turning on left and site is 200 yards on right.

Lemonford Caravan Park
Bickington, Newton Abbot TQ12 6JR
📞 **01626-821242**
Open March-October 🅰 ➥ ➥

One of the prettiest parks in South Devon, landscaped with hedges and trees, with easy

access to Torbay, Dartmoor and many major attractions.

Size 7½ acres, 86 touring pitches, 56 with electric hookup, 86 level pitches, 17 static caravans, 6 ⬆, 12 WCs, 3 CWPs
£ car/tent £5-£8, car/caravan £5-£8, motorhome £5-£8, motorbike/tent £5, children £1.10
⛴ ✕¼ 🔲 📞 🔲 🅰 🔲 Calor Gaz ⛄ WS
➡ From Exeter take the A38 towards Plymouth to the B382. At the roundabout, take the third exit to Bickington. From Plymouth take the A383 turn off to Bickington.

Ross Park
Park Hill Farm, Ipplepen, Newton Abbot TQ12 5TT
📞 **01803-812983** Fax **01803-812983**
🅰 ➥ ➥

Welcoming, tranquil, rural site with private pitches and splendid views of Dartmoor. Easy access from all major routes. Magnificent floral displays. Heated tropical conservatory. Restaurant.

Size 26 acres, 110 touring pitches, 110 with electric hookup, 110 level pitches, 11 ⬆, 19 WCs, 1 CWP
£ car/tent £6.50-£9.60, car/caravan £6.50-£9.60, motorhome £6.50-£9.60, motorbike/tent £6.50, children £1.50
⛴ ✕ ➥ 🔲 📞 🔲 GR 🔲 TV 🅰 🔲 Calor Gaz ⛄ ⛄ WS
Last arrival time: 9:00

➜ 3 miles from Newton Abbot, 6 miles from Totnes on A381. At Park Hill crossroads and BP filling station, take road sign to Woodlands and brown tourist road sign Ross Park.

Stover International Caravan Park
Lower Staple Hill, Newton Abbot TQ12 6JD
☎ 01626-821446 Fax 01626-821606
Open Easter-31 October ⋏ ⊕ ⌷

Quiet secluded touring park on the edge of Dartmoor. Excellent facilities including free indoor heated swimming pool. Also holiday homes for sale or rent.

Size 15 acres, 220 touring pitches, 200 with electric hookup, 200 level pitches, 4 static caravans, 26 ℟, 60 WCs, 3 CWPs
£ car/tent £4.25-£8.25, car/caravan £4.25-£8.25, motorhome £4.25-£8.25, children £1.20
Rental Chalet.
℃ MasterCard Visa
⚍ ⬤ ▣ ☏ ⊡ ▦ ⊞ ⬟ ⚠ ⊠ ⬡ Calor Gaz ♿ ♈ WS
Last arrival time: dusk
➜ From A38 take A382 signed Newton Abbot. 800 yards follow signs to Stover International and Trago Mills.

Cote Ghyll Caravan Park
Osmotherley, Northallerton OL6 3AH
☎ 01609-883425
Open April-October ⋏ ⊕ ⌷
Size 7 acres, 57 touring pitches, 47 with electric hookup, 57 level pitches, 17 static caravans, 10 ℟, 17 WCs, 2 CWPs

£ car/tent £5.25-£6, car/caravan £6, motorhome £5.50, motorbike/tent £5, children £0.50
⚍¼ ✗¼ ▣ ⊡ Calor Gaz ♈
Last arrival time: 11:00
➜ Take A19 to A68. Follow signpost for Osmotherley to village centre. Turn left up hill. Site is ½ mile on right.

Camping & Caravanning Club Site
Martineau Lane, Lakenham, Norwich NR1 2HX
☎ 01603-620060
Open end March-start September ⋏ ⊕ ⌷
Size 2½ acres, 50 touring pitches, 4 ℟, 6 WCs, 1 CWP
£ car/tent £8.75-£11.55, car/caravan £8.75-£11.55, motorhome £8.75-£11.55, motorbike/tent £8.75, children £1.40
℃ MasterCard Visa
⚍ ♈
Last arrival time: 11:00 ➜

← **Camping & Caravanning Club Site**

➜ From A47 turn into Long John Hill (under low bridge 10' 6"), left into Martineau Lane and site is on right.

Dower House Touring Park
East Harling, Norwich NR16 2SE
📞 **01953-717314 Fax 01953-717843**
Open 15 March-31 October ⛺ 🚐 🚍

This family run touring park deep in the heart of the Thetford Forest provides the ideal break. Set in rural tranquillity with excellent facilities, including a pub and outdoor pool.

Size 20 acres, 80 with electric hookup, 160 level pitches, 11 🚿, 20 WCs, 3 CWPs
£ car/tent £6.95-£9.40, car/caravan £6.95-£9.40, motorhome £6.95-£9.40, motorbike/tent £6.95
CC MasterCard Visa
🖫 ✗ 🍺 🗄 📞 🍴 🎱 🔍 📺 ⛽ Calor Gaz ♿ ☂ WS
Last arrival time: 9:00
➜ From Thetford, take A1066 E for 5 miles, fork left at camping sign onto East Harling road. Site is on left after 2 miles.

Haveringland Hall Caravan Park
Cawston, Norwich NR10 4PN
📞 **01603-871302**
Open March-October ⛺ 🚐 🚍
Size 35 acres, 24 touring pitches, 16 with electric hookup, 20 level pitches, 55 static caravans, 12 🚿, 18 WCs, 1 CWP
£ car/tent £6.50-£7.50, car/caravan £7-£8.50, motorhome £7-£8.50, motorbike/tent £6.50, children £1

🖫¼ ✗¼ 🔍 🍴 ⚠ 🔍 Calor Gaz ♿ ☂ WS
Last arrival time: 8:00
➜ From Norwich N on A140 for 3¾ miles, fork left on B1149 for 2¾ miles. 3 miles past turn left into unclassified road, after 1¼ miles turn right and continue to site on right in ½ mile.

Orchard Farm Camping & Caravanning
Cherry Tree Road, Tibenham, Norwich NR16 1PQ
📞 **01953-860365 Fax 01953-860365**
Open all year ⛺ 🚐 🚍
Size 1½ acres, 5 touring pitches, 5 with electric hookup, 5 level pitches, 2 🚿, 2 WCs, 1 CWP
£ car/tent £5, car/caravan £6, motorhome £6, motorbike/tent £5, children £0.50
🔍 🅶🆁 ♿ ☂
➜ From Diss take B1077 where you see a signpost to Attleborough. Go N for 5 miles, then turn right onto B1134. At sign to Marlston go ¾ mile, then turn left into Cherry Tree Road. Site is ¼ mile on right.

Swans Harbour Caravan Park
Barford Road, Marlingford, Norwich NR9 4BE
📞 **01603-759658**
Open all year ⛺ 🚐 🚍
Size 4 acres, 25 touring pitches, 25 with electric hookup, 25 level pitches, 2 🚿, 6 WCs, 1 CWP
£ car/tent £5, car/caravan £5, motorhome £5, motorbike/tent £5, children £0.50
🖫¼ ✗¼ 🍺¼ 🔍 🍴 Calor Gaz ☂
➜ Take B1108 Norwich-Watton. 2½ miles past Norwich southern bypass, turn right at crossroads to Marlingford. Follow tourist signs to site.

Thornton's Holt Camping Park
Stragglethorpe, Radcliffe-on-Trent, Nottingham NG12 2JZ
📞 **0115-933 2125 Fax 0115-933 3318**
Open all year ⛺ 🚐 🚍

A country park appealing to families who enjoy the countryside but also the good camp facilities, such as the indoor heated swimming pool and the family pub and restuarant, within 150 metres.

Size 14 acres, 90 touring pitches, 64 with electric hookup, 90 level pitches, 9 🐾, 12 WCs, 1 CWP
£ car/tent £6.50-£7.50, car/caravan £6.50-£7.50, motorhome £6.50-£7.50, motorbike/tent £6.50, children £0.50-£0.75
🛒 🛒¼ ✕¼ 🗓 🔧 🗓 GR 🔍 ⚠ 🔝 🔌 Calor Gaz ♿ 🕭 WS
Last arrival time: 9:00
➡ From A52, 3 miles E of Nottingham, turn S at traffic lights towards Cropwell Bishop. Park is ½ mile on the left. From A46, 5 miles SE of Nottingham turn N signposted Stragglethorpe. Park is 2½ miles on the right.

Ranksborough Hall Camping & Caravan Park

Langham, Oakham
📞 01572-722984
Open all year 🛆 🚐 🚃
Size 34 acres, 140 touring pitches, 100 with electric hookup, 260 level pitches, 65 static caravans, 12 🐾, 16 WCs, 2 CWPs
£ car/tent £7.50-£10.50, car/caravan £7.50-£10.50, motorhome £6.50, motorbike/tent £7.50
Rental Chalet. £30-£55 per day
🛒 ✕ 🌐 🗓 🔧 🗓 🔝 🔝 GR ⚠ 🔝 🔌 Calor Gaz 🕭 WS
Last arrival time: 11:00
➡ Main A606 from Oakham towards Melton Mowbray. 1½ miles from Oakham.

Bridestow Caravan Park

Bridestowe, Okehampton EX20 4ER
📞 01837-86261
Open March-end December 🛆 🚐 🚃
Size 5½ acres, 13 touring pitches, 13 with electric hookup, 13 level pitches, 36 static caravans, 4 🐾, 9 WCs, 1 CWP
£ car/tent £6, car/caravan £6, motorhome £6, motorbike/tent £4.50, children £0.50
Rental 🚐 caravans from £85
🛒 🛒¼ ✕¼ 🍵¼ 🗓 🔧 🗓 GR 🔍 ⚠ 🔝 Calor Gaz 🕭 WS
Last arrival time: 10:30
➡ Turn off A30 at Sourton Cross junction, follow signs to Bridestowe Village. In the village follow signs to the park.

Camping & Caravanning Club Site

Lydford, Nr Okehampton EX20 4BE
📞 01822-820275
Open end March-end September 🛆 🚐 🚃
Size 4 acres, 70 touring pitches, 30 with electric hookup, 8 🐾, 18 WCs, 1 CWP ➡

← Camping & Caravanning Club Site

£ car/tent £8.75-£11.55, car/caravan £8.75-£11.55, motorhome £8.75-£11.55, motorbike/tent £8.75, children £1.40
CC MasterCard Visa
▣ 🗲 ⚠ 🗶 🛏
Last arrival time: 11:00
➜ From Okehampton on A386 turn right at Lydford, follow road past school and turn right past war memorial. Site is on left.

Dartmoor View Caravan & Camping Park
Whiddon Down, Okehampton EX20 2QL
🗲 01647-231545 Fax 01647-231654
Open March-November ▲ ⛟ 🚐

A quiet, friendly and superbly maintained family holiday park within easy reach of the A30 and the perfect base for touring glorious Devon and Cornwall. Letterboxing centre with licensed bar, heated outdoor pool and take-away.

Size 5½ acres, 75 touring pitches, 40 with electric hookup, 31 static caravans, 4 🐾, 8 WCs, 1 CWP
£ car/tent £6.50-£8.80, car/caravan £6.50-£8.80, motorhome £6.50-£8.80, motorbike/tent £6.50, children £1.50-£8.80
Rental ⛟ Chalet. £110-£295
CC MasterCard Visa
🛒 ✕¼ 🍴 ▣ 🗲 🔲 GR TV ⚠ 🗶 🔌 Calor Gaz 🛏
Last arrival time: 10:00
➜ A30 from Exeter to Merry Meet roundabout (17 miles) turn left. Caravan park ½ mile from roundabout on right.

Olditch Farm Caravan & Camping Park
Sticklepath, Okehampton EX20 2NT
🗲 01837-840734 Fax 01837-840877
Open 14 March-14 November ▲ ⛟ 🚐

A small family run site, within the Dartmoor National Park - direct walking access to the moor, small play area for children, dogs welcome approximately one hour from the coast.

Size 5 acres, 35 touring pitches, 15 with electric hookup, 12 level pitches, 20 static caravans, 4 🐾, 12 WCs, 1 CWP
£ car/tent £5.50-£6.50, car/caravan £5.50-£6.50, motorhome £5.50-£6.50, motorbike/tent £5.50
Rental ⛟ £75-£195
🛒¼ ✕ ✕¼ ▣ 🗲 🔲 GR 🔳 TV ⚠ 🗶 Calor Gaz 🛏 WS
Last arrival time: 10:00
➜ 3 miles E of Okehampton turn off A30 at Merry Meet roundabout. Site is 3 miles down Old Road.

Yertiz Caravan and Camping Park
Exeter Road, Okehampton EX20 1QF
🗲 01837-52281
Open all year ▲ ⛟ 🚐
Size 3½ acres, 30 touring pitches, 22 with electric hookup, 8 level pitches, 4 static caravans, 3 🐾, 5 WCs, 1 CWP
£ car/tent £3.75-£4.50, car/caravan £3.75-£4.50, motorhome £3.25-£4, motorbike/tent £2.60
Rental ⛟ £70-£155
🛒¼ ✕¼ ▣ 🗲 🔲 ⚠ 🗶 Calor Gaz ♿ 🛏

OLNEY Buckinghamshire   4C1

Emberton Country Park
Olney MK46 5DB
🗲 01234-711575
Open 1 April-31 October ▲ ⛟ 🚐

Size 195 acres, 59 touring pitches, 200 level pitches, 115 static caravans, 10 🅁, 4 WCs, **£** car/tent £6.50, car/caravan £8, motorhome £8-£9, motorbike/tent £6.50

🛁 🚐 📷 🔲🅿🎿 ⚠ 🎌 ♿ 🐕

➡ From M1 junction 14 take A509 to Bedford/Olney. Site is 1 mile S of Olney.

ORMSKIRK Lancashire 10B4

Abbey Farm Caravan Park
Dark Lane, Ormskirk L40 5TX
📞 **01695-572686** Fax **01695-572686**
Open all year Å 🚐 🚏
Size 6 acres, 104 touring pitches, 104 with electric hookup, 104 level pitches, 12 static caravans, 13 🅁, 20 WCs, 1 CWP
£ car/tent £5-£8, car/caravan £6.50-£8, motorhome £6.50-£8, motorbike/tent £5, children £1
🛁 ✕¼ 🚐¼ 📷 📞 🗄 ⚠ 🎌 Calor Gaz ♿ 🐕
Last arrival time: 10:00
➡ M6 junction 27 take A5209 to B5240 and then an immediate right into Hobcross Lane. Site is 1½ miles on right.

OWERMOIGNE Dorset 3F3

Sandyholme Holiday Park
Moreton Road, Owermoigne DT2 8HZ
📞 **01305-852677**
Open 1 April-31 October Å 🚐 🚏
Size 6 acres, 65 touring pitches, 58 with electric hookup, 65 level pitches, 35 static caravans, 8 🅁, 20 WCs, 1 CWP
£ car/tent £5-£10, car/caravan £5-£10, motorhome £5-£10, motorbike/tent £5
Rental 🚐 caravans £95-£295
€€ MasterCard Visa
🛁 ✕ 🚐 🗄 📞 🗄 🅿 GR 🔍 ⚠ 🎌 🔌 Calor Gaz
🐕 WS
Last arrival time: 10:00
➡ Turn off A352 Dorchester/Wareham road through village of Owermoig for 1 mile.

OXFORD Oxfordshire 4B2

Cassington Mill Caravan Park
Eynsham Road, Cassington, Oxford OX8 1DB
📞 **01865-881081** Fax **01865-880577**   ➡

← **Cassington Mill Caravan Park**

Open 1 April-31 October ▲ 🚐 🚙

A quiet, grassy site, with the River Evenlode running through the park. Restaurant one mile. Swimming pool seven miles.

Size 4 acres, 83 touring pitches, 70 with electric hookup, 83 level pitches, 35 static caravans, 4 🕭, 30 WCs, 2 CWPs
£ car/tent £7, car/caravan £7, motorhome £7, motorbike/tent £5, children £1.50
CC MasterCard Visa
🛱 🔌 ⚠ 🔞 Calor Gaz ⚲ ⚘ WS
Last arrival time: 9:00
➡ A40 W of Oxford, second left, signposted.

Diamond Farm Caravan & Camping Park
Bletchingdon, Oxford OX5 3DR
📞 **01869-350909** Fax **01869-350918**
Open all year ▲ 🚐 🚙
Size 3 acres, 37 touring pitches, 26 with electric hookup, 37 level pitches, 4 🕭, 8 WCs, 1 CWP
£ car/tent £7-£9, car/caravan £7-£9, motorhome £7-£9, motorbike/tent £7, children £1-£1.50
🛱 ✗ ☕ 🔞 🔌 🔲 🔞 GR ⚠ 🔞 ⊟ Calor Gaz ⚘
WS
Last arrival time: 10:00
➡ From M40 take junction 9 and follow A34 for about 1 mile towards Oxford. Take the second exit off A34 and follow signs for Bletchingdon.

Oxford Camping International
426 Abingdon Road, Oxford OX1 4XN
📞 **01865-246551** Fax **01865-240145**
Open all year ▲ 🚐 🚙

Situated on the edge of Oxford, just over one mile from the historic centre and ½ mile from the River Thames, with good access to the M4/M40.

Size 5 acres, 129 touring pitches, 90 with electric hookup, 129 level pitches, 10 🕭, 21 WCs, 1 CWP
£ car/tent £7.85, car/caravan £7.85, motorhome £7.85, motorbike/tent £6.85
CC MasterCard Visa
🛱 🛱¼ ✗¼ 🚐¼ 🔞 🔌 Calor Gaz ⚲ ⚘
Last arrival time: 10:00
➡ On S side of Oxford, take A4144 to city centre from ring road, ¼ mile on left. Rear of Touchwoods Outdoor Life Centre.

PADDOCK WOOD Kent   **5D3**

Whitbread Hop Farm
Beltring, Paddock Wood TN12 6PY
📞 **01622-872068** Fax **01622-872630**
Open 10 months ▲ 🚐 🚙

Campers and Caravanners are welcome to stay in the beautiful surroundings of this top tourist attraction. For further enquiries and reservations call the Whitbread Hop Farm.

Size 10 acres, 300 touring pitches, 18 with electric hookup, 2 🚿, 4 WCs, 1 CWP
£ car/tent £16, car/caravan £16
℄ MasterCard Visa
🏊¼ ✗ ♥ 🛈 🛗 ✕ ♿ ⛽
➜ On the A228, 20 minutes from junction 5 of M25, 20 minutes junction 4 of M20.

PADSTOW Cornwall 2B3

Carnevas Holiday Park
St. Merryn, Padstow PL28 8PN
📞 01841-520230 **Fax** 01841-520230
Open April-October **A** ⛺ 🚐
Size 12 acres, 195 touring pitches, 20 with electric hookup, 75 level pitches, 9 static caravans, 10 🚿, 21 WCs, 1 CWP
£ car/tent £5-£8, car/caravan £5-£8, motorhome £4.50-£7.50, motorbike/tent £5, children £0.80
Rental ⛺ Chalet. £95-£375
🏊 🛈 📞 🛈 ⓖ ⋀ ✕ Calor Gaz ⛽
➜ From village of St Merryn take B3276 towards Porthcothan Bay, turn right off Tredrea Inn and park is ¼ mile on right.

Dennis Cove Camping
Padstow PL28 8DR
📞 01841-532349
Open Easter-30 September **A** ⛺ 🚐

Site with estuary views, ten minutes walk from Padstow town. Touring caravans must book in advance.

Size 5 acres, 62 touring pitches, 22 level pitches, 7 🚿, 18 WCs, 1 CWP
£ car/tent £7.20-£10.10, car/caravan £7.20-£10.10, motorhome £7.20-£10.10, motorbike/tent £7.20
🏊¼ ✗ ✗¼ ♥ ♥¼ 🛈 📞 ✕ ⋀ ✕ ⛽ Calor Gaz ⛽
Last arrival time: 11:00

➜ From A389 turn right at town sign, then second right into Dennis Lane. Camp site is at the end of lane.

Maribou Holidays
St Merryn, Padstow PL28 8QA
📞 01841-520520 **Fax** 01841-521154
Open Easter-October **A** ⛺ 🚐
Size 22 acres, 100 touring pitches, 20 with electric hookup, 80 level pitches, 100 static caravans, 6 🚿, 20 WCs, 1 CWP
£ car/tent £6-£8, car/caravan £6-£8, motorhome £6-£8, motorbike/tent £6
Rental ⛺ Chalet. £95-£295
🏊 ♥ 🛈 📞 ✕ ✕ ⓖ ⋀ ✕ ⛽
Last arrival time: 9:00
➜ From Wadebridge SW on A39 to first roundabout. Right on to B3274. Second left to St Merryn, over crossroads to site in 1 mile.

Music Water Touring Site
Rumford, Padstow PL27 7SJ
📞 01841-540257
A ⛺ 🚐
Size 8 acres, 140 touring pitches, 40 with electric hookup, 130 level pitches, 7 static caravans, 8 🚿, 18 WCs, 2 CWPs
£ car/tent £4-£6.95, car/caravan £4-£6.95
Rental ⛺
🏊 ✗ ♥ 🛈 📞 🛈 ⓖ ✕ ⋀ ✕ Calor Gaz ⛽ WS
➜ From junction of A39 and B3274 (N of St Columb Major), N on B3274 signed Padstow for 2 miles, turn left to site on right in just over ¼ mile.

Trevean Farm Caravan & Camping Site
St Merryn, Padstow PL28 8PR
📞 01841-520772
Open 1 April-31 October **A** ⛺ 🚐

A quiet, family run site, with a new toilet and amenity block, including laundry ➜

← Trevean Farm Caravan & Camping Site

facilities. Situated near several shady surfing beaches, with pleasant coastal walks nearby.

Size 2 acres, 36 touring pitches, 12 with electric hookup, 36 level pitches, 3 static caravans, 4 ☔, 7 WCs, 1 CWP
£ car/tent £5, car/caravan £5, motorhome £5, motorbike/tent £4
Rental 🚐 £100-£260
🛒 🖥 📞 🖲 ⚠ 🎌 Calor Gaz ⚓ WS
Last arrival time: 10:00
➡ From St. Merryn village take the B3246 Newquay road for 1 mile. Turn left for Rumford. Site is ¼ mile right.

PAIGNTON Devon   3D3

Beverley Park Holiday Centre
Goodrington Road, Paignton TQ4 7JE
📞 **01803-843887** Fax **01803-845427**
Open Easter-October 🛖 🚐 🚎

Superb holiday park overlooking Torbay, offering the very best in touring park facilities. The perfect centre for exploring Devon.

Size 21 acres, 194 touring pitches, 190 with electric hookup, 40 level pitches, 203 static caravans, 24 ☔, 48 WCs, 3 CWPs
£ car/tent £7-£11.50, car/caravan £8.50-£13, motorhome £7-£11.50, motorbike/tent £7, children £1.60
Rental 🚐
℃ MasterCard Visa
🛒 ✗ 📺 🖥 📞 🖲 🎛 🎌 📟 🎥 📠 📷 ⚠ 🎌 🔌 Calor Gaz ♿
Last arrival time: 10:00
➡ 2 miles S of Paignton on the A380, then take the A3022 and turn left into Goodrington Road.

Byslades Camping & Caravan Park
Totnes Road, Paignton TQ4 7PY
📞 **01803-555072** Fax **01803-555072**
Open April - October 🛖 🚐 🚎
Size 23½ acres, 170 touring pitches, 100 with electric hookup, 170 level pitches, 17 ☔, 17 WCs, 2 CWPs
£ car/tent £5.50-£9.50, car/caravan £6-£10.50, motorhome £5.50-£9.50, motorbike/tent £5.50, children £0.80-£1.50
🛒 ✗ 🖥 📞 🖲 🎛 📟 🎌 ⚠ 🎌 🔌 Calor Gaz ♿ ⚓ WS
Last arrival time: 10:00
➡ On the main Paignton-Totnes road (A385). 2 miles from Paignton, 4 miles from Totnes.

Grange Court Holiday Centre
Grange Road, Goodrington, Paignton TQ4 7JP
📞 **01803-558010** Fax **01803-663336**
Open 15 February-15 January 🛖 🚐 🚎

Superb family park with extensive entertainment and leisure facilities including a new indoor pool complex and licensed club. Panoramic view across Torbay.

Size 65 acres, 157 touring pitches, 157 with electric hookup, 90 level pitches, 530 static caravans, 33 ☔, 35 WCs, 3 CWPs
£ car/tent £9-£20, car/caravan £9-£20, motorhome £9-£20
Rental 🚐
℃ MasterCard Visa
🛒 ✗ 📺 🖥 📞 🎛 🎛 📟 🎥 📠 🎥 📷 ⚠ 🎌 🔌 Calor Gaz
Last arrival time: 10:00
➡ From junction of A380 (Paignton ring road) and A385, travel S on A380 for 1 mile. Turn left into Goodrington Road. After ¾ mile turn left into Grange Road. The park is signposted.

Higher Well Farm Holiday Park
Stoke Gabriel, Paignton TQ9 6RN
☎ **01803-782289**
Open Easter-October 🛆 ⬝ ⬝
Size 12 acres, 30 touring pitches, 30 with electric hookup, 30 level pitches, 18 static caravans, 12 🚿, 18 WCs, 1 CWP
£ car/tent £5.80, car/caravan £5.80, motorhome £5.80
Rental ⬝ £115-£285 weekly. £17 nightly.
⬝ ⬝ ⬝ ⬝ Calor Gaz 🐕
➡ Take A385 from Paignton to Totnes and turn left at Parker Arms pub. Head straight on for 1½ miles and turn left.

Holly Gruit Camp
Brixham Road, Paignton TQ4 7BA
☎ **01803-550763**
Open end May-end September 🛆
Size 3 acres, 70 touring pitches, 70 level pitches, 4 🚿, 11 WCs,
£ car/tent £8-£9, motorbike/tent £8
⬝ ⬝ ⬝ ⬝ ⬝ GR ⬝ TV ⬝ ⬝ ⬝ Calor Gaz 🐕
Last arrival time: 11:00
➡ From junction of A3022 and A385 (1 mile W of Paignton), travel S on A3022 for ¾ mile. Site signposted.

Lower Yalberton Holiday Park
Long Road, Lower Yalberton, Paignton TQ4 7PQ
☎ **01803-558127**
Open May-September 🛆 ⬝ ⬝
Size 80 with electric hookup, 8 static caravans, 3 CWPs
£ car/tent £6.50-£8, car/caravan £7.50-£10, motorhome £6.75-£8.25, motorbike/tent £6.50, children £1.25-£1.75
Rental ⬝ caravans £125-£325 weekly.
⬝ ⬝ ⬝ ⬝ ⬝ ⬝ TV ⬝ ⬝ ⬝ Calor Gaz
Last arrival time: 8:30
➡ 2½ miles from Paignton. 5 miles from Torquay. 3 miles from Brixham. 1 mile S of intersection of A385 and A3022 Paignton ring road. Turn W off the A3022 into Long Road for ¾ mile

Ramslade Touring Park
Stoke Road, Stoke Gabriel TQ9 6QB
☎ **01803-782575** Fax **01803-782828**
Open mid March-31 October 🛆 ⬝ ⬝   ➡

← **Ramslade Touring Park**

Size 8½ acres, 135 touring pitches, 135 with electric hookup, 135 level pitches, 12 🚿, 20 WCs, 4 CWPs
£ car/tent £7.50-£10.50, car/caravan £7.50-£10.25, motorhome £7.50-£10.50, motorbike/tent £7.50, children £1.10-£1.20
🛒 🛒¼ 🚻¼ 🚽 🛁 🖥 GR 🔍 📺 ⚠ 🅿 Calor Gaz
♿ WS
Last arrival time: 9:00
➜ Turn off A385 Paignton to Totnes road at Parkers Arms, Ramslade is 1½ miles on right, near Stoke Gabriel.

Whitehill Farm Holiday Park
Stoke Road, Paignton TQ4 7PF
📞 01803-782338 Fax 01803-782722
Open May-September 🏕 🚐 🚏
Size 30 acres, 400 touring pitches, 225 with electric hookup, 200 level pitches, 63 static caravans, 52 🚿, 81 WCs, 3 CWPs
£ car/tent £6.50-£9, car/caravan £6.50-£9, motorhome £6.50-£9, motorbike/tent £6.50
Rental 🚐
CC Visa
🛒 ✖ 🛒 🗄 🍴 Calor Gaz

➜ Turn off A385 at the Parkers Arms pub and the site is ½ mile from Paignton Zoo.

Widend Touring Park
Berry Pomeroy Road, Marldon, Paignton TQ3 1RT
📞 01830-550116

Open April-October 🏕 🚐 🚏
Size 22 acres, 184 touring pitches, 119 with electric hookup, 174 level pitches, 17 🚿, 28 WCs, 3 CWPs
£ car/tent £5.50-£9, car/caravan £5.50-£9.50, motorhome £5.50-£9, children £1-£1.50
CC MasterCard Visa
🛒 🛒 🚽 🛁 🗄 🅿 GR 🔍 ⚠ 🅿 🍴 Calor Gaz
♿
Last arrival time: 10:00
➜ Follow A380 Torbay ring road. At second roundabout turn towards Marldon. At next roundabout turn second left into Five Lanes - Singmore Hotel on corner. Head towards Berry Pomeroy and Totnes following camping signs. Widend is 1 mile from ring road.

Par Sands Holiday Park

Par Beach, Par PL24 2AS
☎ 01726-812868 Fax 01726-817899
Open 1 April-31 October **⛺ ⚏ ⚐**

A flat, grassy site alongside a large, safe, sandy beach. Ideal position for touring Cornwall. Modern toilet and shower facilities, electric hook-ups, super pitches and baby's bathroom.

Size 23 acres, 199 touring pitches, 114 with electric hookup, 199 level pitches, 210 static caravans, 20 ♒, 26 WCs, 2 CWPs
CC MasterCard Visa
⚡ ✗ ⚑ ⊡ 🔌 ⊟ 🔄 ▦ ▣ ⚠ ☒ Calor Gaz 🚿
🐕
➡ Signposted ½ mile E of Par on the A3082, heading towards Fowey.

Studfold Farm

Lofthouse, Harrogate HG3 5SG
☎ 01423-755210
Open April-October **⛺ ⚏ ⚐**
Size 3 acres, 20 touring pitches, 6 with electric hookup, 20 level pitches, 60 static caravans, 8 ♒, 15 WCs, 1 CWP
£ car/tent £5, car/caravan £6
Rental ⚏ £100
⚡ ✗¼ ⚑¼ 🔌 ⊟ Calor Gaz 🚿 🐕 WS
➡ 7 miles from Pateley Bridge.

Gill Head Farm

Troutbeck, Penrith CA11 0ST
☎ 01768-779652

Open 1 April-10 November **⛺ ⚏ ⚐**

Pleasant, very well kept rural site containing a small stream with ducks. Bed & breakfast available at farm. Dog walk alongside adjacent river.

Size 1½ acres, 17 touring pitches, 17 with electric hookup, 17 level pitches, 17 static caravans, 4 ♒, 8 WCs, 1 CWP
£ car/tent £7-£10, car/caravan £7-£10, motorhome £7, motorbike/tent £7, children £3.50
⚡ ✗¼ ⚑¼ ⊡ 🔌 ⊟ Calor Gaz 🚿 🐕
Last arrival time: 10:00
➡ Take A5091 off A66. After 200 yards turn right. Site is first on right in ¼ mile.

Lowther Caravan Park
Eamont Bridge, Penrith CA10 2JB
📞 01768-63631 Fax 01768-868126
Open March-November ▲ 🚐 🚏
Size 50 acres, 225 touring pitches, 175 with electric hookup, 200 level pitches, 397 static caravans, 25 🚿, 30 WCs, 2 CWPs
£ car/tent £7.50-£11, car/caravan £7.50-£11, motorhome £7.50-£11, motorbike/tent £7.50
CC MasterCard Visa
🛒 ✕ 🍴 🗄 📞 🗄 📠 GR 📶 🎏 Calor Gaz ⚓ 🐾 WS
Last arrival time: 11:00
➔ From roundabout (junction of A6, A66 and A686) S of Penrith, travel on A6 for ½ mile, then right along W bank of River Lowther to site.

Thacka Lea Caravan Site
Penrith CA11 9HX
📞 01768-863319
Open March-October 🚐 🚏
Size 25 touring pitches, 24 with electric hookup, 25 level pitches, 2 🚿, 7 WCs, 1 CWP
£ car/caravan £6, motorhome £6
🛒¼ Calor Gaz 🐾
➔ Off A6 N of Penrith.

Thanet Well Caravan Park
Greystoke, Penrith CA11 0XX
📞 01768-484262
Open March-October ▲ 🚐 🚏
Size 10 acres, 20 touring pitches, 10 with electric hookup, 10 level pitches, 60 static caravans, 6 🚿, 8 WCs, 2 CWPs
£ car/tent £7, car/caravan £7, motorhome £7, motorbike/tent £6, children £1
🛒 🗄 📞 🗄 📠 🎏 Calor Gaz 🐾 WS
Last arrival time: 9:00
➔ Leave M6 junction 41 onto B5305. Leave B5305 at the junction signed to Lamonby and follow the caravan direction signs to the park. Approx. 2 miles.

PENRUDDOCK Cumbria   10B1

Beckses Caravan Site
Penruddock CA11 ORX
📞 01768-483224 Fax 01768-483830
Open Easter-31 October ▲ 🚐 🚏

A small pleasant site on the fringe of the Lake District National Park, offering modern facilities to pitch tents or caravans. Hire of luxury caravans available.

Size 20 acres, 23 touring pitches, 23 with electric hookup, 18 static caravans, 6 🚿, 12 WCs, 1 CWP
£ car/tent £4.50, car/caravan £6, motorhome £6, motorbike/tent £4.50
Rental 🚐
🛒¼ 🗄 📞 🗄 📠 🎏 Calor Gaz 🐾
➔ From M6 junction 40 take A66 W to Keswick. Take B5288 on the right.

PENZANCE Cornwall   2A4

Bone Valley Caravan Park
Heamoor, Penzance TR20 8UJ
📞 01736-60313
Open March-December ▲ 🚐 🚏
Size 17 touring pitches, 17 with electric hookup, 17 level pitches, 2 🚿, 3 WCs, 1 CWP
£ car/tent £7-£8, car/caravan £7-£8, motorhome £6-£7, motorbike/tent £7, children £1
🛒 ✕¼ 🍴¼ 🗄 Calor Gaz
Last arrival time: 10:00
➔ From A30 Penzance by-pass turn off to Heamoor. Drive through village to caravan/camp sign on right. To next caravan/camp sign on left. Site is 200 yds on left.

Camping & Caravanning Club Site
Higher Tregiffian Farm, St Buryan, Penzance
📞 01736-871588
Open end March-end September ▲ 🚐 🚏

A great family site, perfect for Visiting Land's End, exploring Cornwall's picturesque coves, or just relaxing on the Blue Flag beach at nearby Sennen Cove.

Size 4 acres, 75 touring pitches, 24 with electric hookup, 6 🚿, 9 WCs, 1 CWP
£ car/tent £8.20-£10.40, car/caravan £8.20-£10.40, motorhome £8.20-£10.40, motorbike/tent £8.20, children £1.30
CC MasterCard Visa
🖬 📞 ♿ ✴
Last arrival time: 11:00
➡ Follow A30 from Penzance to Land's End, site is signed off B3306 (St Just Airport road).

Kenneggy Cove Holiday Park
Higher Kenneggy, Rosudgeon, Penzance TR20 9AU
📞 **01736-763453 Fax 01736-763453**
Open 31 March-31 October ⛺ 🚐 🚃

In a superb location overlooking Mount's Bay and The Lizard Penninsula this is a quiet family site ideally situated for walking and exploring West Cornwall.

Size 4 acres, 60 touring pitches, 21 with electric hookup, 50 level pitches, 9 static caravans, 6 🚿, 12 WCs, 1 CWP

£ car/tent £4.30-£7.50, car/caravan £4.30-£7.50, motorhome £4.30-£7.50, motorbike/tent £4.30, children £0.75
Rental 🚐 £110-£285
👥 ✂ 🍽 🖬 📞 🖬 GR ⚠ ✴ Calor Gaz ✴ WS
Last arrival time: 11:00
➡ 3 miles E of Marazion on the A394 just E of Rosudgeon. Turn S for ½ mile to the site.

River Valley Caravan Park
Relubbus, Penzance TR20 9ER.
📞 **01736-763398**
Open 1 March-6 January ⛺ 🚐 🚃

➡

← **River Valley Caravan Park**

Set in a sheltered valley with a small trout stream half mile from any main road. All roads on site are tarmac and all the pitches are level. Separate dog area near to the footpath.

Size 18 acres, 90 touring pitches, 60 with electric hookup, 90 level pitches, 12 🅵, 30 WCs, 1 CWP
£ car/tent £7.75-£8.70, car/caravan £7.75-£8.70, motorhome £7.75-£8.70, motorbike/tent £7.75
CC MasterCard Visa
🅿 🔲 📱 📁 Calor Gaz 🐕 WS
Last arrival time: 8:00
➜ From Hayle B3302 to Leeds, turn right onto B3280 and straight on to Relubbus. From Marazion, B3280 to Goldsithney and Relubbus.

Tower Farm Camping and Caravanning Park
St. Buryan, Penzance TR19 6BZ
📞 **01736-810286**
Open March-October 🅰 🚐 🚍
Size 12 acres, 102 touring pitches, 33 with electric hookup, 102 level pitches, 5 static caravans, 11 🅵, 20 WCs, 2 CWPs
£ car/tent £5-£7.50, car/caravan £5-£7.50, motorhome £5-£7.50, motorbike/tent £5, children £0.50
Rental 🚐 £98-£250
🅿 ✕¼ 📱 🔲 📱 🔲 GR 🔲 TV 🅰 ✕ Calor Gaz &
🐕
Last arrival time: 10:00
➜ At Catchall, on A30 Penzance to Lands End road, turn left onto B3283 to St Buryan. Turn right at church and park is 300 yards on right.

PERRANPORTH Cornwall   2A4

Blue Seas Holidays
Newquay Road, Goonhavern TR4 9QD
📞 **01872-572176**
Open Easter-October

Twelve static luxury caravans with sea and beach views on a quiet family park, overlooking Perranporth. Only ten minutes walk to golden sands, lake and shops.

Size 12 static caravans,
Rental 🚐 £70-£320 weekly
🅿 🔲 📱 Calor
➜ In Perranporth on B3285, 800 yards on right from town centre.

Perran Sands Holiday Super Centre
Perranporth TR6A OAQ
📞 **01872-573551** Fax **01872-571158**
Open 1 May-1st week October 🅰 🚐
Size 550 acres, 450 touring pitches, 240 with electric hookup, 400 level pitches, 398 static caravans, 35 🅵, 74 WCs,
🅿 ✕ 📱 🔲 🔲 🔲 &
➜ A30 to Cornwall, 3 miles after Mitchell turn right onto B3285 to Perranporth. The park is on the right just before Perranporth.

PETWORTH West Sussex   4C3

Camping & Caravanning Club Site
Great Bury, Graffham, Petworth GU28 0QJ
📞 **01798-867476**
Open end March-start November 🅰 🚐 🚍
Size 20 acres, 90 touring pitches, 18 with electric hookup, 6 🅵, 11 WCs, 2 CWPs
£ car/tent £8.75-£11.55, car/caravan £8.75-£11.55, motorhome £8.75-£11.55, motorbike/tent £8.75, children £1.40
CC MasterCard Visa
🔲 📱 &
Last arrival time: 11:00
➜ From A285 follow signs for Graffham, site is 1½ to 2 miles on left.

Bay View Caravan and Camping Park

Old Martello Road, Pevensey Bay BN24 6DX
☎ **01323-768688**
Open March-October A ⊟ ⊞
Size 3½ acres, 49 touring pitches, 34 with electric hookup, 49 level pitches, 6 static caravans, 4 ☌, 6 WCs, 1 CWP
£ car/tent £6.65-£7.15, car/caravan £7.15-£7.70, motorhome £7.15-£7.70, motorbike/tent £6.65, children £1.20-£1.30
Rental ⊟ £105-£225
🛢 ✕¼ ●¼ ⊟ 🛢 ⊟ ⚠ ✗ Calor ♁ WS
Last arrival time: 10:00
➡ Situated on the A259 between Pevensey Bay and Eastbourne. Signpost at entrance of private road. Site is ¼ mile on the left. Adjacent to the beach.

Camping & Caravanning Club Site

Norman's Bay, Pevensey Bay BN24 6PP
☎ **01323-761190**
Open end March-start November A ⊟ ⊞
Size 1 acre, 200 touring pitches, 100 with electric hookup, 14 ☌, 23 WCs, 2 CWPs
£ car/tent £9.20-£12.05, car/caravan £9.20-£12.05, motorhome £9.20-£12.05, motorbike/tent £9.20, children £1.40
CC MasterCard Visa
⊟ ☎ GR ⚠ ✗ ♿ ♁
Last arrival time: 11:00
➡ From A295 follow signs for Eastbourne, over level crossing, then turn left signed Beachland.

Castle View Caravan Site

Eastbourne Road, Pevensey Bay BN24 6DT
☎ **01323-763038**
Open 1 March-31 October A ⊟ ⊞
Size 15 acres, 100 touring pitches, 70 with electric hookup, 100 level pitches, 32 static caravans, 20 ☌, 33 WCs, 1 CWP
£ car/tent £7.20-£9.20, car/caravan £7.20-£9.20, motorhome £6.60-£8.60, motorbike/tent £7, children £0.50-£1.20
Rental ⊟ statics £120-£195.
CC MasterCard Visa
🛢 ● ⊟ ☎ ⊟ 📺 Calor Gaz ♿ ♁ WS
Last arrival time: 9:00
➡ On N side of A259, almost 1 mile SW of Pevensey Bay and 3½ miles NE of Eastbourne.

Wayside Caravan Park

Wrelton, Pickering YO18 8PG
☎ **01751-472608** Fax **01751-472608**
Open Easter-early October A ⊟ ⊞

Quiet, south facing, sheltered park with country views, with modern toilet facilites and cubicled wash basins. Ideal centre for the North York Moors and the coast.

Size 10 acres, 72 touring pitches, 35 with electric hookup, 72 level pitches, 10 ☌, 21 WCs, 1 CWP ➡

← **Wayside Caravan Park**

£ car/tent £7, car/caravan £7.50, motorhome £7
⚡ ✕¼ 🔲 🔋 ▯ Calor Gaz ♿ ✝
Last arrival time: 11:00
➜ 2½ miles W of Pickering off the A170 signposted at Wrelton.

POOLE Dorset   3F3

Beacon Hill Touring Park
Blandford Road North, Poole BH16 6AB
📞 **01202-631631**
Open Easter-end September 🏕 🚐 🚍

A secluded, peaceful site, yet close to the main routes. An ideal touring base for Dorset, Bournemouth and the New Forest, and only three miles from the Poole ferry terminal. Fishing, tennis, bar (entertainment and take-away during the high season).

Size 30 acres, 170 touring pitches, 140 with electric hookup, 150 level pitches, 22 🚿, 25 WCs, 2 CWPs
£ car/tent £6.60-£14, car/caravan £7.40-£14, motorhome £6.60-£14, motorbike/tent £6.60, children £1
⚡ ✕¼ 🚿 🔲 🔋 🔷 🔳 🔲 🔳 🔲 GR 🔲 📺 ⚠ ✕ 🔲
Calor Gaz ♿ ✝
Last arrival time: 11:00
➜ ¼ mile N of the junction of A35 and A350 towards Blandford. 3 miles N of Poole.

Huntick Farm
Lytchett Matravers, Poole
📞 **01202-622222**
Open Easter-30 September 🏕 🚐 🚍

Small, quiet, level grass site for 30 pitches in wooded surroundings and well away from the nearest road. This site has hot and cold water, showers and flushing lavatories with hook-ups available.

Size 3 acres, 30 touring pitches, 23 with electric hookup, 30 level pitches, 4 🚿, 6 WCs, 1 CWP
£ car/tent £4.50-£6, car/caravan £4.50-£7, motorhome £4.50-£7, motorbike/tent £4, children £0.50
⚡¼ ✕¼ 🚐¼ 🔲 🔋 ▯ ⚠ ✕ Calor Gaz ✝ WS
Last arrival time: 10:30
➜ Off the A350 Blandford to Poole road, turn right into Lytchett Matravers and take the Huntick road at the Rose and Crown pub. The site is situated ¾ mile on right.

Organford Manor Caravans & Holidays
Poole BH16 6ES
📞 **01202-622202**
Open 15 March-31 October 🏕 🚐 🚍

Quiet secluded site in wooded grounds of the manor house. Touring field is level, sheltered and well-drained with good amenities.

Size 3 acres, 75 touring pitches, 34 with electric hookup, 75 level pitches, 45 static caravans, 6 🚿, 8 WCs, 1 CWP

⊡ █ ❏ ⚠ ✕ Calor Gaz ⊩
➡ From A35/A351 junction, continue on A35 for ¼ mile towards Dorchester, and take first left and then first right.

Pear Tree Caravan Park
Organford, Poole BH16 6LA
█ 01202-622434
Open April-October ▲ ⊕ ⊞
Size 7½ acres, 125 touring pitches, 94 with electric hookup, 125 level pitches, 10 ℞, 20 WCs, 2 CWPs
£ car/tent £6.50-£8.50, car/caravan £6.50-£8.50, motorhome £6.50-£8.50, motorbike/tent £6.50, children £1.25
CC MasterCard Visa
🛉 ✕¼ ●¼ ⊡ █ ❏ ⚠ ✕ Calor Gaz ♿ ⊩ WS
Last arrival time: 9:00
➡ The park lies between A351 at Holton Heath and the A35 at Lytchett Minster. Take A351 signposted to Wareham. At the Holton Heath crossroads, turn right down the road beside the garage signposted Organford. About ½ mile down the road on the left is the wide entrance to the park.

Rockley Park
Napier Road, Hamworthy, Poole BH15 4LZ
█ 01345-508508
Open March-October ▲ ⊕ ⊞

A family holiday park in a lovely location overlooking Poole Harbour. Indoor/outdoor heated pools, kids clubs, sailing and scuba diving included in the wide range of leisure facilities. Restaurants and bars, excellent cabaret entertainment. A 'British Holidays Park'.

Size 88 acres, 74 touring pitches, 58 with electric hookup, 16 level pitches, 1,077 static caravans, 20 ℞, 24 WCs, 1 CWP

£ car/tent £7-£14, car/caravan £7-£14, motorhome £10.50-£17.50, motorbike/tent £4, children £1.50
Rental ⊕ from £154
CC MasterCard Visa
🛉 ✕ ● ⊡ █ ❏ ▤ ▤ ▦ ▨ GR ▣ ⚠ ✕ ⊕
Calor ⊩
Last arrival time: 12:00
➡ Leave M27 for Poole and follow signs for Poole town centre. Once in the town centre Rockley Park is signposted.

Sandford Park
Holton Heath, Poole BH16 6JZ
█ 01202-631600 Fax 01202-625678
Open Easter-end October ▲ ⊕ ⊞
Size 60 acres, 505 touring pitches, 460 with electric hookup, 505 level pitches, 268 static caravans, 27 ℞, 60 WCs, 2 CWPs
£ car/tent £7.90-£13.40, car/caravan £7.90-£13.40, motorhome £7.90-£13.40, motorbike/tent £7.90, children £1.50-£2.50
Rental ⊕ Chalet. £99-£476
CC MasterCard Visa
🛉 ✕ ● ⊡ █ ▤ ▣ ▣ GR ▣ ⚡ ⚠ ✕ Calor ♿
WS   ➡

← Sandford Park

Last arrival time: 10:00
➡ 2½ miles NE of Wareham on A351 turn into Organford Road at Holton Heath crossroads. Site is 50 yards on left.

South Lytchett Manor Caravan Park
Lytchett Minster, Poole BH16 6JB
☎ 01202-622577
Open Easter-13 October 🏕 🚐 🚍

Popular rural site situated in lovely parkland surroundings. Ideal base for beautiful beaches, sailing, windsurfing and touring the Purbeck area.

Size 10 acres, 150 touring pitches, 68 with electric hookup, 150 level pitches, 21 🚿, 26 WCs, 1 CWP
£ car/tent £6.30-£7.90, car/caravan £6.30-£7.90, motorhome £6.30-£7.90, motorbike/tent £6.30, children £0.95-£1.25
℄ MasterCard Visa
🛒 ✗¼ 🍴¼ 🔥 🔌 📺 🛝 🎣 Calor Gaz ♿ 🐕 WS
Last arrival time: 11:00
➡ From the junction of A35 and A350, travel S on A350 to Upton. Turn right onto B3067 for 1 mile and the site is on right.

Burrowhayes Farm Camping & Caravan Site
West Luccombe, Porlock TA24 8HU
☎ 01643-862463
Open 15 March-31 October 🏕 🚐 🚍

Ideally situated for walkers and riders in the glorious Horner Valley, part of the National Trust's Holnicote Estate, the site is surrounded by moors and woods and contains a stream.

Size 9 acres, 54 touring pitches, 40 with electric hookup, 40 level pitches, 19 static caravans, 8 🚿, 17 WCs, 2 CWPs
£ car/tent £5.50-£7, car/caravan £5.50-£7, motorhome £5.50-£7, motorbike/tent £5.50, children £1
Rental 🚐 £90-£225
🛒 🔥 🔌 🎣 Calor Gaz ♿ 🐕
➡ Take M5 to Bridgwater, A39 to Minehead, then towards Porlock. 5 miles W of Minehead, take left toward West Luccombe. Site in ½ mile on right.

Porlock Caravan Park
Near Minehead, Porlock TA24 8NS
📞 01643- 862269
🏕 ⛺ 🚐

Grassy, level site with children's play area. Convenient for the sea. No single-sex groups. Open March-October.

Size 5 acres, 40 touring pitches, 32 with electric hookup, 40 level pitches, 55 static caravans, 6 🚿, 20 WCs, 2 CWPs
£ car/tent £5-£6.50, car/caravan £6-£6.50, motorhome £5-£5.50, motorbike/tent £4
Rental ⛺ Chalet. £164.50-£293.75
🛁 🔧 🔌 ⊟ Calor Gaz 🐕 WS
➡ Minehead to Porlock: take B3225 turning to right, signed Porlock Weir. After 50 yards turn right signed Porlock Caravan Park.

Sparkhayes Farm
Sparkhayes Lane, Porlock TA24 8NE
📞 01643-862470
Open 1 April-October 🏕 ⛺

Three acres of level camping overlooking Bristol Channel. 100 yards from village centre, pubs, shops and restaurants. Near SW coast path. Children and dogs welcome.

Size 6 acres, 50 touring pitches, 50 level pitches, 4 🚿, 9 WCs, 1 CWP
£ car/tent £6-£8, motorhome £6-£8, motorbike/tent £6, children £1.50
🛁¼ ✗¼ 🛒¼ 🔧 🔌 ⊟ 🐕
➡ Signposted Sparkhayes Lane, N off A39 in village centre. 6 miles W of Minehead.

Porthtowan Tourist Park
Mile Hill, Truro, Porthtowan TR4 8TY
📞 01209-890256 **Fax** 01209-890256
Open Easter-October 🏕 ⛺ 🚐
Size 5½ acres, 50 touring pitches, 22 with electric hookup, 50 level pitches, 6 🚿, 9 WCs, 1 CWP
£ car/tent £6-£8.50, car/caravan £6-£8.50, motorhome £6-£8.50, motorbike/tent £6, children £1-£1.25
🛁 ✗¼ 🛒¼ 🔧 🔌 ⊟ 🎮 📺 🛝 🎯 Calor Gaz 🐕
➡ Take A30 until you reach the exit 'Redruth/Porthtowan', cross the A30 and continue through north country to 'T' junction, turn right up the hill. Pass Woodlands Restaurant and park is on left.

Southsea Leisure Park

Melville Road, Southsea PO4 9TB
☎ 01705-735070 Fax 01705-821302
Open all year
Size 12 acres, 188 touring pitches, 45 static
caravans
🛒 ✕ 🚐 ♿
➜ From M27 take A2030 S for 3 miles, then
turn left on to A288, following caravan
signs, turn left into Bransbury Road. Site on
left, signed.

High Compley Park

Garstang Road West, Poulton-le-Fylde FY6
8AR
☎ 01253-890831 Fax 01253-892832
Open 1 March-4 January
Size 14 acres, 50 touring pitches, 50 with
electric hookup, 50 level pitches, 150 static
caravans, 8 🚿, 10 WCs, 1 CWP
✕¼ 🚐¼ 🔌 🔥 🍴 Calor

You could'nt get closer to the beach. A fully equipped
12 acre site right by the Solent. Touring and luxury
holiday caravans. Heated outdoor pool, restaurant
and 2 bars, park, shop, all modern facilities. An ideal
stopover for the cross channel ferries
(only 10 minutes' drive).
Special off-season rates.
Discounts for OAP's and
CC members.

Southsea Leisure Park, Quote RAC C&C 97
Melville Road, Southsea, Hampshire PO4 9TB
Tel: 01705 735070 Fax: 01705 821302

Last arrival time: 9:00
➜ From M55 turn right onto A588 to
Fleetwood and turn left at traffic lights.
Follow Blackpool sign onto A586, park on
left.

Loddon Court Farm

Beech Hill Road, Spencers Wood, Reading
RG7 1HT
☎ 01734-883153
🏕 🚐 🚏
Size 4 acres, 30 touring pitches, 4 level
pitches, 4 🚿, 8 WCs, 1 CWP
£ car/tent £5.50, car/caravan £5.50,
motorhome £5.50, motorbike/tent £5.50,
children £1
🛒¼ 🗑 🔌 Calor 🛒 WS
Last arrival time: 10:00

Wellington Country Park

Riseby, Reading R67 1SP
☎ 01734-326444 Fax 01734-326445
Open March-November 🏕 🚐 🚏

Luxury new caravans for sale & hire.
17 acres of secluded country park.
1 mile from Blackpool, ½ mile from the
ancient market town of Poulton-le-Fylde.
Touring park with new facilities
open March to 4th January.
GARSTANG ROAD WEST,
POULTON-LE-FYLDE,
LANCASHIRE FY6 8AR
TEL: 01253 890831

Size 350 acres, 58 touring pitches, 45 with electric hookup, 6 ⋒, 16 WCs, £ car/tent £7-£12, car/caravan £7-£12, motorhome £7-£12, motorbike/tent £7
Rental ⋏ ⊞ Chalet.
⅀ ✕ ⊡ ⦿ ⊟ ⚠ ⊞ ⍭
Last arrival time: 5:30
➡ Between Reading and Basingstoke off B3349.

Tresaddern Holiday Park
St Day, Redruth TR16 5JR
☎ 01209-820459
Open 1 April-31 October ⋏ ⊞ ⊞

Small, quiet park in tranquil surroundings. Dog exercise area, free showers and use of microwave. Individually hedged pitches.

Size 6 acres, 27 touring pitches, 21 with electric hookup, 27 level pitches, 17 static caravans, 4 ⋒, 7 WCs, 1 CWP
£ car/tent £4.75-£5.75, car/caravan £4.75-£5.75, motorhome £4.75-£5.75, motorbike/tent £4.75, children £1
Rental ⊞ Chalet.
⅀ ⅀¼ ✕¼ ⍟¼ ⊡ ⦿ ⊟ Calor Gaz ⍭ WS
Last arrival time: 10:00
➡ From A30 turn off at A3047 (Scorrier). After 400 yards turn left at Crossroads Hotel onto B3298 (St. Day). The park is signposted, 1¾ miles on right.

Brompton-on-Swale Caravan Park
Brompton, Richmond DL10 7EZ
☎ 01748-824629

Open 1 April-31 October ⋏ ⊞ ⊞
Size 10 acres, 150 touring pitches, 140 with electric hookup, 150 level pitches, 23 static caravans, 15 ⋒, 23 WCs, 2 CWPs
£ car/tent £4.70-£8.75, car/caravan £6.40, motorhome £6.40, motorbike/tent £4.70
Rental Chalet. £145-£220
⅀ ⊡ ⦿ ⊟ ⍰ ▦ ⚠ ⊞ Calor ⅃ ⍭
Last arrival time: 10:00
➡ Exit A1 at Catterick onto A6136. Follow B6271 through Brompton-on-Swale towards Richmond. Park on left, 1½ SE of Richmond.

Swaleview Caravan Park
Reeth Road, Richmond DL10 4SF
☎ 01748-823106
Open March-October ⋏ ⊞ ⊞

Situated beside River Swale in a wooded valley in Yorkshire Dales National Park.

Size 12 acres, 25 touring pitches, 25 with electric hookup, 50 level pitches, 100 static caravans, 10 ⋒, 20 WCs, 1 CWP
£ car/tent £5.50-£6.50, car/caravan £6.50-£6.80, motorhome £6.20-£6.50, motorbike/tent £5.50, children £0.40-£0.80
Rental ⊞ £110-£175
⅀ ⊡ ⦿ ⊟ ⍰ ⅁ ⍂ ⚠ ⊞ Calor Gaz
Last arrival time: 9:00
➡ 3 miles W of Richmond on A6108. 7 miles from A1/A1M at Scotch Corner.

Oakdene Holiday Park
Ringwood BH24 2RZ
☎ 01202-875422 **Fax** 01202-894152
Open mid February-end December ⋏ ⊞ ⊞
Size 55 acres, 435 touring pitches, 220 with electric hookup, 435 level pitches, 210 static caravans, 80 ⋒, 80 WCs, 4 CWPs
ℂℂ Mastercard, Visa
➡ On A31 at St Leonards, 3 miles W of Ringwood, next to St Leonards Hospital.
See advert on next page

Oakhill Farm Caravan Park
St. Leonards, Ringwood BH24 2SB
☎ 01202-876968
Open 1 April-31 October ⋏ ⊞ ⊞ ➡

A Holiday Park that all the family will love, offering a wealth of things to see and do, with excitement & all-weather fun for the kids and perfect relaxation for mum & dad.

The Village is situated in 55 acres of beautiful forest, just 9 miles from Bournemouth's safe Blue Flag beaches, bustling shopping centre & entertainment complex making an ideal base for your holiday. With 2 superb heated pools, indoor & outdoor, our own 'Forest Edge' riding stables, Children's adventure playground, licensed clubhouse incorporating teens disco, solarium, mini gym & sauna. You'll be spoilt for choice.

All pitches are level with plug in mains electric & water and with easy access to modern service blocks. Pre-booking service available. On site cafeteria and takeaway, barbeque, general store and laundrette for your day to day requirements.

(Some facilities only availble at peak times. Small charge for sauna, solarium & gym).

RAC Approved

Also static Holiday Homes for sale, ask for details

24hrs FREEPHONE 0500 202216 ASK FOR EXT 21

Village Holidays, Oakdene, St Leonards, Ringwood, Hampshire BH24 2RZ.

ROSE AWARD CARAVAN HOLIDAY PARK

← Oakhill Farm Caravan Park

Secluded quiet ten acre site in private woodland. Clean toilets with hot water to wash basins, laundry room. Easy reach of the New Forest and Bournemouth.

Size 10 acres, 80 touring pitches, 80 level pitches, 10 🚿, 16 WCs, 1 CWP
£ car/tent £4, car/caravan £4.50, motorhome £4, motorbike/tent £3.50, children £0.75
🔲 📞 📠 ⚠ 🎣 Calor Gaz 🐕 WS
➜ ¾ mile off main A31 at roundabout opposite Boundary Lane, St Leonards. Near hospital.

Red Shoot Camping Site
Linwood, Ringwood BH24 3QT
📞 **01425-473789**
Open March-October ⚊ ⛟ ⛺

Situated just outside Ringwood, this site is an ideal centre for visiting the New Forest.

Size 4 acres, 105 touring pitches, 45 with electric hookup, 105 level pitches, 6 🚿, 18 WCs, 1 CWP
🐾 ✕ 🍴 📞 🔲 ⚠ 🎣 🔌 Calor Gaz 🐾
Last arrival time: 10:30
➜ Off A338, 2 miles N of Ringwood, turn right and follow signs to Linwood. Site signed.

River Laver Holiday Park
Studley Road, Ripon HG4 2QR
📞 **01765-690508** Fax **01748-811393**
Open 1 March-31 December ⛟ ⛺

A five acre park with 50 touring pitches, situated one mile from the city centre and ideally located for touring the Yorkshire Dales. Open March to October.

Size 5 acres, 50 touring pitches, 50 with electric hookup, 50 level pitches, 50 static caravans, 8 🚿, 10 WCs, 1 CWP
£ car/tent £8.50-£10.50, car/caravan £8.50-£10.50, motorhome £8.50-£10.50, motorbike/tent £8.50
Rental ⛟ statics £120-£395
℃ Visa
🐾 ✕ 🍴 🔲 📞 Calor Gaz ♿ 🐕 WS
Last arrival time: 9:00
➜ From A1 take A61 or B6265 to Ripon (following signs for Fountains Abbey). Park is situated off B6265, 1 mile from Ripon Centre.

Slennigford Watermill Caravan & Camping Park
North Stainley, Ripon HG4 3HQ
📞 **01765-635201**
Open 1 April-31 October ⚊ ⛟ ⛺
Size 14 acres, 65 touring pitches, 25 with electric hookup, 25 level pitches, 25 static caravans, 4 🚿, 9 WCs
£ car/tent £6.50-£10.50, car/caravan £6.50-£10.50, motorhome £6.50-£10.50, motorbike/tent £6.50
Rental Chalet. £135-£165
🐾 🔲 📞 GR ⚠ 🎣 Calor Gaz ♿ 🐕 WS
Last arrival time: 10:00
➜ 5 miles from Ripon on A6108.

Ure Bank Caravan Park
Ripon HG4 1JD
☎ 01765-602964
Open 1 March-31 October ⚊ 🚐 🚛
Size 26 acres, 175 touring pitches, 60 with
electric hookup, 200 static caravans, 12 �📷,
24 WCs, 2 CWPs
🍴 ✗ 🏫
➡ Leave Ripon N on A61. Cross River Ure
and turn W and ahead bear right to site.

Lordine Court Caravan Park
Ewhurst Green, Staplecross, Robertsbridge
TN32 5TS
☎ 01580-830209 Fax 01550-830091
Open Easter-31 October ⚊ 🚐 🚛

*An inland site with good access to the main
coastal resorts. Close to Bodiam Castle and
the pretty town of Battle. Shop, licensed bar,
pay-phone, children's playground, outdoor
pool, restaurant. All year storage.*

Size 40 acres, 200 touring pitches, 50 with
electric hookup, 60 level pitches, 120 static
caravans, 17 ⏲, 25 WCs, 2 CWPs
£ car/tent £5.50-£15, car/caravan £5.50-£15,
motorhome £5.50-£15, motorbike/tent £5.50
🍴 ✗ 🛒 🗄 🎱 🏫 🌂 🐕 Calor Gaz 🐕 WS
Last arrival time: 10:00
➡ A21 from London, left at Flimwell to
Hawkhurst. B2244 at Hawkhurst to Cripps
Corner. Left onto B2165 (Northam
direction).

Hollingworth Lake Caravan Park
Rakewood, Littleborough, Rochdale OL15
0AT
☎ 01706-378661
Open all year ⚊ 🚐 🚛
Size 7 acres, 45 touring pitches, 35 with
electric hookup, 45 level pitches, 8 ⏲, 8
WCs, 2 CWPs
£ car/tent £6-£7, car/caravan £6-£7,
motorhome £5-£8, motorbike/tent £4
🍴 🗄 🏫 🗄 🌂 🎱 Calor Gaz 🐕 WS
Last arrival time: 8:00
➡ From M62 junction 21 take B6225 from
Hollingworth Lake Country Park, at the
Fisherman's Inn. Take Rakenwood Road,
then second on the right.

Symonds Yat Camping & Caravan Park
Symonds Yat West, Ross-on-Wye HR9 6DA
☎ 01600-891069/89088
Open 1 March-end October ⚊ 🚐 🚛

*Situated in an area of outstanding natural
beauty on the banks of the river Wye. Ideal
for walking, fishing, canoeing. Small family
site, 35 pitches.*

Size 2 acres, 35 touring pitches, 28 with
electric hookup, 35 level pitches, 4 ⏲, 7
WCs, 1 CWP
£ car/tent £6.25-£7, car/caravan £6.25-£7.50,
motorhome £5.50-£7.50, motorbike/tent
£6.25, children £0.75
🍴¼ ✗¼ 🛒¼ 🗄 🎱 🏫 🐕
Last arrival time: 9:30

→ Turn off A40 7 miles from Ross-on-Wye or 4 miles from Monmouth. Follow signs for Leisure Park. ¼ mile off A40. Signed Symonds Yat West.

ROTHBURY Northumberland   13F3

Coquetdale Caravan Park
Whitton, Rothbury NE65 7RU
☎ **01669-620549**
Open Easter-31 October ▲ ⛟ 🚐
Size 14 acres, 55 touring pitches, 30 with electric hookup, 30 level pitches, 180 static caravans, 10 🚿, 15 WCs, 2 CWPs
£ car/tent £8-£10, car/caravan £8-£10, motorhome £8-£10, motorbike/tent £8
⊡ ☏ ☐ ⚠ 🔀 Calor Gaz 🐾 WS
→ ½ mile SW of Rothbury on Newton road.

ROYDON Essex   5D2

Roydon Mill Leisure Park
Roydon, Harlow CM19 5EJ
☎ **01279-792777 Fax 01279-792695**
Open all year ▲ ⛟ 🚐
Size 58 acres, 110 touring pitches, 72 with electric hookup, 106 static caravans, 8 🚿, 14 WCs, 2 CWPs
£ car/tent £8.90-£10.70, car/caravan £8.90-£10.70, motorhome £8.90-£10.70, motorbike/tent £8.90, children £1.65
Rental ⛟ caravan £150-£280
C MasterCard Visa
🛒 ⅟₄ ✗ ✗¼ 🍴 ⊡ ☏ 🔀 🔀 🔀 GR 🔍 ⚠ 🔀 🔀
Calor Gaz ♿ WS
Last arrival time: 24 hrs
→ From N via A1 or M1/M25/M11. From S take junction 7 off M11 and follow signs to Harlow, then A414 and B181 to Roydon. At end of High Street, just before level crossing.

ROYSTON Hertfordshire   9D4

Apple Acre Park
London Road, Fowlmere, Royston SG8 7RU
☎ **01763-208354**
▲ ⛟ 🚐
Size 3½ acres, 20 touring pitches, 20 with electric hookup, 20 level pitches, 12 static caravans, 2 🚿, 4 WCs, 1 CWP
£ car/tent £4-£5, car/caravan £6.50, motorhome £5-£6, motorbike/tent £4

🛒¼ ✗¼ 🍴¼ ⊡ ☏ ☐ ⚠ 🔀 🐾
Last arrival time: 10:00
→ From Cambridge, A10 to Harston, turn left onto B1368 to site through village of Fowlmere on left. From Royston, A505 to Flint Cross Road, turn left onto B1358, site is on right after Fowlmere village sign.

RUAN MINOR Cornwall   2A4

Gwendreath Farm Caravan Park
Kennack Sands, Ruan Minor, Helston TR12 7LZ
☎ **01326-290666**
Open Easter-October ▲ ⛟ 🚐

← **Gwendreath Farm Caravan Park**

Quiet, friendly, family run park overlooking the sea in an area of outstanding natural beauty. Short woodland walk to clean safe sandy beaches. Close to village pub and restaurant.

Size 7 acres, 10 touring pitches, 10 with electric hookup, 16 level pitches, 30 static caravans, 4 🅫, 8 WCs, 1 CWP
£ car/tent £4.80-£6, car/caravan £4.80-£6, motorhome £4.80-£6, motorbike/tent £4.80
Rental 🚐 Static caravans £79-£ 275
🐄 ✕¼ 🛁¼ ▣ 🔋 ⊟ ⚠ ⊞ Calor Gaz 🐾
➔ From Helston take A3083, then left on to B3293 signposted St Keverne. Continue 4 miles to Goonhilly Earth station and take next right then next left. At end of lane turn right over cattle grid and drive through Seaview and stop at second shop.

Set in the heart of Cannock Chase, Silvertrees is an idyllically peaceful park, set in 30 acres of natural woodlands, graded '4 ticks' and Rose Awarded by the ETB.

Size 30 acres, 50 touring pitches, 40 with electric hookup, 50 level pitches, 50 static caravans, 4 🅫, 9 WCs, 1 CWP
£ car/caravan £6-£9, motorhome £6-£9
Rental 🚐 £110-£350 (short breaks from £75)
CC MasterCard Visa
▣ 🔋 ⊟ 🔲 🔲 ⊠ GR TV ⚠ ⊞ Calor 🐾
➔ 2 miles W of Rugeley off A51 on unclassified road signposted Penkridge. Turn right at bottom of hill by white fence. Entrance 100 yards on left.

RUGELEY Staffordshire   7F2

Camping & Caravanning Club Site
Old Youth Hostel, Wandon, Rugeley WS15 1QW
📞 **01889-42166**
Open end March-start November ⋀ 🚐 🚏
Size 5 acres, 60 touring pitches, 36 with electric hookup, 6 🅫, 6 WCs, 1 CWP
£ car/tent £8.75-£11.55, car/caravan £8.75-£11.55, motorhome £8.75-£11.55, motorbike/tent £8.75, children £1.40
Rental ⋀ 🚐 Chalet.
CC MasterCard Visa
▣ 🔋 ♿ 🐾
Last arrival time: 11:00
➔ From Cannock follow A460 and signs to Hednesford. At traffic lights turn right. After 1 mile turn left. Site is on left ½ mile from Hazelslade.

Silvertrees Caravan Park
Stafford Brook Road, Rugeley WS15 2TX
📞 **01889-582185** Fax **01889-582185**
Open 1 April-31 October 🚐 🚏

Tackeroo Forest Enterprise
Midlands District Office, Birches, Valley, Rugeley WS15 2UQ
📞 **01889-586593** Fax **01889-574217**
Open April-October ⋀ 🚐 🚏
70 touring pitches, 2 CWPs
£ car/tent £5, car/caravan £5, motorhome £5
🐄¼ ✕¼ 🛁¼ 🔋 ⊠ 🔲 ⚠ ⊞ ♿ 🐾
➔ Take A34 (Cannock-Stafford) E of junctions 12 and 13 of M6. Turn E 1 mile N of Huntington for Rugeley. Site is 2½ miles on right.

RYE East Sussex   5E3

Cock Horse Inn
Main Street, Peasmarsh, Rye
📞 **01797-230281**
Open March-October ⋀ 🚐 🚏

Quiet caravan park behind a traditional country inn serving good food and real ales. Near to Rye, Romney Marsh and the beautiful Sussex countryside.

Size 1 acre, 5 touring pitches, 5 with electric hookup, 5 level pitches, 20 static caravans, 2 ⌂, 5 WCs
£ car/tent £12, car/caravan £12, motorhome £12
CC MasterCard Visa
⬛¼ ✕ ⬤ 🔋 🔌 🐕
Last arrival time: 11:30
➨ On A268, 4 miles W of Rye.

SALCOMBE Devon   2C4

Alston Farm Caravan Site
Salcombe TQ7 3BJ
📞 01548-561260 Fax 01548-551260
Open Easter-end October ⛺ 🚐 🚚
Size 12 acres, 104 touring pitches, 104 with electric hookup, 104 level pitches, 40 static caravans, 18 ⌂, 35 WCs, 1 CWP
£ car/tent £5-£6.50, car/caravan £6-£8, motorhome £5-£6.50, motorbike/tent £5, children £0.50
⬛ 🔋 ⬛ 🔲 ⬺ 🔲 Calor Gaz ♿ WS
➨ Signposted on left on A381 Kingsbridge to Salcombe main road.

Higher Rew Caravan Park
Malborough, Kingsbridge, Salcombe TQ7 3DW
📞 01548-842681
Open Easter-October ⛺ 🚐 🚚

Quiet family park in area of outstanding natural beauty, adjoining National Trust land. Only one mile from South Sands and Salcombe Estuary with cliff walks nearby.

Size 5 acres, 75 touring pitches, 27 with electric hookup, 75 level pitches, 8 ⌂, 10 WCs, 1 CWP
£ car/tent £5-£6.50, car/caravan £5-£6.50, motorhome £5-£6.50, motorbike/tent £5
⬛ 🔋 ⬛ 🔲 ⬛ Calor Gaz 🐕
Last arrival time: 10:00
➨ From A381 at Malborough turn right and follow signs to Soar for 1 mile, then turn left at Rew Cross signpost to Higher Rew.

Sun Park Caravan & Camping Park
Soar Mill Cove, Malborough, TQ7 3DS
📞 01548-561378
Open Easter-31 October ⛺ 🚐 🚚
Size 5 acres, 60 touring pitches, 18 with electric hookup, 60 level pitches, 33 static caravans, 8 ⌂, 10 WCs, 1 CWP
£ car/tent £5-£9, car/caravan £5-£9, motorhome £5-£9, motorbike/tent £5
Rental 🚐 £70-£265
⬛ 🔋 ⬛ 🔲 📺 ⬺ 🔲 Calor Gaz 🐕
Last arrival time: 8:00
➨ From A38, turn left at the Totnes and Kingsbridge sign. Bypass Kingsbridge by following signs to Salcombe. On entering the village of Malborough turn sharp right signposted Soar. Pass through village and keep on road following signs to Soar Mill Cove and Sun Park. Site is 1½ miles on right.

SALISBURY Wiltshire   3F2

Alderbury Caravan and Camping Park
Old Southampton Road, Whaddon, Salisbury
📞 01722-710125   ➨

← **Alderbury Caravan and Camping Park**

Open all year Å 🚐 🚍

A new, pleasant and friendly site set in a pretty village opposite the local pub. Close to local shops and bus stop. Three miles from Salisbury and a short drive from the New Forest.

Size 1½ acres, 39 touring pitches, 20 with electric hookup, 39 level pitches, 1 static caravan, 4 🅿, 6 WCs, 2 CWPs
£ car/tent £6.50, car/caravan £6.50, motorhome £6.50, motorbike/tent £6.50, children £1
🛒¼ ✗¼ 🍴¼ 🔌 🐾 ♿
Last arrival time: 11:00
➜ From Salisbury take A36 Southampton road for 3 miles. Along dual carriageway take slip road marked Alderbury/Whaddon, turn right over flyover then left for site opposite Three Crowns pub.

Camping & Caravanning Club Site
Hudson's Field, Castle Road, Salisbury
📞 **01722-320713**
Open end March-end September Å 🚐 🚍
Size 4½ acres, 100 touring pitches, 23 with electric hookup, 4 🅿, 12 WCs, 1 CWP
£ car/tent £8.75-£11.55, car/caravan £8.75-£11.55, motorhome £8.75-£11.55, motorbike/tent £8.75, children £1.40
🐾
Last arrival time: 11:00
➜ From Amesbury take B342 to Salisbury, site is on right before town.

Coombe Touring Caravan Park
Race Plain, Netherhampton, Salisbury SP2 8PN
📞 **01722-328451**

Open all year Å 🚐 🚍
Size 3 acres, 50 touring pitches, 48 with electric hookup, 50 level pitches, 6 🅿, 12 WCs, 2 CWPs
£ car/tent £5-£7.50, car/caravan £5-£7.50, motorhome £5-£7.50, motorbike/tent £5, children £0.50-£1
🛒 🔌 🍴 🔌 🐾 ⚠ 🖼 Calor Gaz ♿ 🐾
Last arrival time: 9:00
➜ A36 Salisbury to Warminster road. Turn onto A3094 at traffic lights. Cross on bend at top of hill. Take third left behind the racecourse. Site is on the right.

Stonehenge Touring Park
Orcheston, Salisbury SP3 4SH
📞 **01980-620304** Fax **01980-621121**
Open all year Å 🚐 🚍
Size 2 acres, 30 touring pitches, 20 with electric hookup, 30 level pitches, 4 🅿, 5 WCs, 1 CWP
£ car/tent £6.75-£8.60, car/caravan £6.75-£8.60, motorhome £6.75-£8.60, motorbike/tent £6.75, children £0.75-£1
🛒 ✗ 🍴 🔌 🔌 ⚠ 🖼 Calor Gaz 🐾
Last arrival time: 9:30
➜ Off A360 Salisbury to Devizes road.

SALTASH Cornwall   2C4

Dolbeare Caravan & Camping Park
St Ive Road, Landrake, Saltash PL12 5AF
📞 **01752-851332**
Å 🚐 🚍

A quality touring park in peaceful countryside ideally placed for south east Cornwall and south west Devon. The site is close to the coast and Plymouth, Looe, the Tamar Valley, Dartmoor and the Brittany ferries are easily accessible.

Size 9 acres, 60 touring pitches, 38 with electric hookup, 58 level pitches, 4 🚿, 6 WCs, 1 CWP
£ car/tent £5.50-£7.50, car/caravan £6.50-£7.50, motorhome £6.50-£7.50, motorbike/tent £5, children £1
🐕 🅿 🔌 ⊟ ⚠ ✕ Calor Gas 🚻 WS
Last arrival time: 10:00
➡ 4 miles W of Saltash turn right off A38 at Landsrake into Pound Hill (signposted Blunts). Follow signs to site for ¾ mile.

Notter Bridge Camping & Caravaning Park
Notter Bridge, Saltash PL12 4RW
📞 **01752-842318**
Open April-November 🏕 🚐 🚛

Small, family run site, sheltered by trees, with a river running through it. Open April - November.

Size 4 acres, 55 touring pitches, 12 with electric hookup, 55 level pitches, 12 static caravans, 4 🚿, 12 WCs, 2 CWPs
£ car/tent £4.50-£6, car/caravan £5.50-£7
Rental 🚐 £95-£190 per week
🐕 ✕¼ 🅿 🔌 ⊟ 🔣 Calor Gas 🚻 WS
➡ 3 miles W of Saltash (Tamar Bridge) on A38, opposite Notter Bridge Inn.

SANDRINGHAM Norfolk 9D2

Camping & Caravanning Club Site
The Sandringham Estate, Double Lodges, Sandringham PE35 6EA
📞 **01485-542555**
Open end September-start December 🏕 🚐 🚛
Size 22 acres, 250 touring pitches, 152 with electric hookup, 15 🚿, 28 WCs, 2 CWPs

£ car/tent £9.20-£12.05, car/caravan £9.20-£12.05, motorhome £9.20-£12.05, motorbike/tent £9.20, children £1.40
CC MasterCard Visa
🅿 🔌 ⚠ ✕ ♿ 🚻
Last arrival time: 11:00
➡ From A42 turn right onto A149, 1 mile after Babingley turn right, right again at next crossroads. Site is on left.

SAXMUNDHAM Suffolk 9F4

Marsh Farm Caravan Site
Sternfield, Saxmundham IP17 1HW
📞 **01728-602168**
Open all year 🚐 🚛
Size 6 acres, 30 touring pitches, 40 with electric hookup, 30 level pitches, 2 CWPs
£ car/caravan £6
🐕 🔌 🔣 ♿ 🚻 WS
➡ Turn off A12 onto A1094 to Aldeburgh. After 1 mile turn left to Sternefield and in ½ mile caravan signs will direct you left for the site.

Whitearch Touring Park
Main Road, Benhall, Saxmundham IP17 1NA
📞 **01728-604646** Fax **01728-604646**
Open April-October 🏕 🚐 🚛

Set in Suffolk, with all its rural charm, on 14½ acres offering 30 pitches and close to Heritage Conservation land and Snape Concert Hall

Size 14½ acres, 30 touring pitches, 30 with electric hookup, 30 level pitches, 4 🚿, 6 WCs, 2 CWPs
£ car/tent £8.50, car/caravan £8.50, motorhome £8.50, motorbike/tent £8.50, children £0.50

➡

← Whitearch Touring Park

⚡ 📞 🔲 🔳 ⚠ 🔲 Calor Gaz ♿ 🐕
➡ From Ipswich on A12 towards Lowestoft turn off onto B1121 to Saxmundham. Entrance 20 yards on right.

SCARBOROUGH North Yorkshire   **11E2**

Cayton Village Caravan Park
D14 Mill Lane, Cayton Bay, Scarborough YO11 3NN
📞 **01723-583171**
Open 1 April-1 October 🏕 🚐 🚎
Size 11 acres, 200 touring pitches, 170 with electric hookup, 200 level pitches, 18 ⛱, 37 WCs, 3 CWPs
£ car/tent £5-£8, car/caravan £5-£8, motorhome £5-£8, motorbike/tent £5
⚡ ✕¼ 🛒¼ 🔲 📞 🔲 ⚠ 🔲 Calor Gaz ♿
Last arrival time: 8:00
➡ On A165 turn right at Cayton Bay traffic lights onto Mill Lane. The park is ½ mile on right hand side. On A64 take B1261 signposted Filey. At Cayton Village turn second left after Blacksmiths Arms onto Mill Lane. Park is on left in 500 yards.

Flower Of May Caravan Park
Lebberston Cliff, Scarborough YO11 3NU
📞 **01723-582324**
Open Easter-end October 🏕 🚐 🚎

Acclaimed privately owned park, constantly being updated to provide the most comprehensive facilities. Located on the coast between Scarborough and Filey. Fifty caravans for hire (own WCs). No single-sex groups.

Size 20 acres, 300 touring pitches, 270 with electric hookup, 300 level pitches, 184 static caravans, 36 ⛱, 36 WCs, 3 CWPs
£ car/tent £6.50-£10, car/caravan £6.50-£10, motorhome £6.50-£10, motorbike/tent £6.50
Rental 🚐 £85-£305
⚡ ✕¼ 🛒 🔲 📞 🔳 🔲 🔲 🔲 🔲 GR TV ⚠ 🔲 🍺 Calor ♿ WS
Last arrival time: dusk
➡ 2¼ miles NW of Filey, 5 miles SE of Scarborough on A165. Turn left, then NE to site.

Jacob's Mount Caravan Park
Stepney Road, Scarborough YO12 5NL
📞 **01723-361178 Fax 01723-361178**
Open 1 March-31 October 🏕 🚐 🚎

A small family run park with excellent on site facilities, surrounded by mature woodland yet only two miles from Scarborough on the A170. Highly Recommended.

Size 7 acres, 44 touring pitches, 12 with electric hookup, 12 level pitches, 44 static caravans, 4 ⛱, 14 WCs, 1 CWP
£ car/tent £5.75-£8.50, car/caravan £5.75-£8.50, motorhome £5.75-£8.50, motorbike/tent £5.75, children £1
Rental 🚐 caravans £110-£295.
⚡ ✕ 🛒 🔲 📞 🔲 GR TV ⚠ 🔲 🍺 Calor Gaz 🐕 WS
Last arrival time: 10:00
➡ On the A170 within Scarborough boundary, 2 miles from Scarborough.

Lowfield
Down Dale Road, Staintondale, Scarborough YO13 0EZ
📞 **01723-870574**
Open all year 🏕 🚐 🚎

Size 2 acres acres, 33 touring pitches, 11 with electric hookup, 33 level pitches, 2 , 5 WCs, 1 CWP
£ car/tent £5.50-£8, car/caravan £7, motorhome £5.50-£6.50, motorbike/tent £5, children £0.50
☖ ✕¼ ⏻¼ ⊡ 🔋 ⊟ ⚠ ⊠ Calor Gaz ♿ ⊶
Last arrival time: 10:00
➡ A171 Whitby road to Cloughton, then Ravenscar road for 2 miles to site.

Scalby Close Camping Park
Burniston Road, Scarborough YO13 0DA
📞 **01723-365908**
Open March-October 🅰 ⏚ 🚐

Sheltered by mature trees with all pitches on level ground, ideal for touring North York Moors. Three caravans for hire (own WCs). Restaurant half a mile. Swimming pool 1½ miles.

Size 2 acres, 42 touring pitches, 30 with electric hookup, 5 static caravans, 4 , 10 WCs, 1 CWP
£ car/tent £4-£8, car/caravan £4-£8, motorhome £4-£8, motorbike/tent £4
Rental ⏚ £115-£275
CC MasterCard Visa
☖ ✕¼ ⊡ 🔋 ⊟ Calor Gaz ⊶ WS
Last arrival time: 10:00
➡ Site is on the A165 2½ miles N of Scarborough.

Spring Willows Touring Caravan & Camping
Main Road, Staxton, Scarborough YO12 4SB
📞 **01723-891505**
Open March-January 4th 🅰 ⏚ 🚐
Size 12 acres, 184 touring pitches, 164 with electric hookup, 184 level pitches, 13 , 29 WCs, 3 CWPs

☖ ✕ ⏻ ⊡ 🔋 ⊟ 🗐 Ⓖ GR TV ⚠ ⊠ J Calor Gaz ♿ ⊶ WS
Last arrival time: 7:00
➡ A64 towards Scarborough. Right at Staxton onto A1039 to Filey. Site entrance on right.

Scotch Corner Caravan Park
Richmond, Scotch Corner DL10 6NS
📞 **01748-822530 Fax 01748-850370**
Open April-October 🅰 ⏚ 🚐

← Scotch Corner Caravan Park

Landscaped, level, grassed, well-spaced pitches. Booking advisable July/August and bank holiday weekends.

Size 7 acres, 75 touring pitches, 43 with electric hookup, 75 level pitches, 1 static caravan, 6 ⏣, 14 WCs, 1 CWP
£ car/tent £8-£10, car/caravan £8-£10, motorhome £8-£10, motorbike/tent £7, children £1
🛒 ✗¼ ♨¼ ▣ 🔌 ⊟ Calor Gaz ⚿ ⚲ WS
Last arrival time: 10:30
➜ Leave A1 at Scotch Corner and take A6108 Richmond exit. Proceed 150 yards on dual carriageway, then cross central reservation and return 200 yards to site entrance.

Manor Farm Camping & Caravan Site
Seaton EX12 2JA
📞 01297-21524

Open March-end October ⚿ 🚐 🚏

Quiet family run site with beautiful views of Axe Valley and Lyme Bay. An ideal centre for exploring glorious East Devon. Modern facilities, electric hook-ups.

Size 20 acres, 280 touring pitches, 48 with electric hookup, 50 level pitches, 16 ⏣, 36 WCs, 2 CWPs
£ car/tent £6-£7, car/caravan £7-£8, motorhome £6-£7, children £0.50
🛒¼ ▣ 🔌 ⊟ ⚠ ⊠ ⚿ ⚲ WS
➜ 3 miles W of Lyme Regis on A3052. Left at Tower petrol station on Seaton Down hill. ¼ mile on left to entrance.

Pinfold Caravan Park
Garsdale Road, Sedbergh
📞 01539-620576
Open 1 March-31 October ⚿ 🚐 🚏
Size 6 acres, 30 touring pitches, 22 with electric hookup, 30 level pitches, 56 static caravans, 4 ⏣, 9 WCs, 1 CWP
Calor Gaz
➜ Leave M6 junction 37 onto A684 to Sedbergh (five miles) and turn right at MOT caravan sign. Over Dales Bridge. Park on left side.

Warner Farm Touring Park
Warner Lane., Selsey
📞 01243-604499 Fax 01243-604499
Open 1 March-31 October ⚿ 🚐 🚏

Situated in beautiful Sussex, with top family entertainment and two swimming pools. Special offers with great savings in June, July, September and October.

Size 10 acres, 200 touring pitches, 130 with electric hookup, 180 level pitches, 150 static caravans, 20 🐾, 30 WCs, 4 CWPs
£ car/tent £5.50-£16.50, car/caravan £5.50-£16.50, motorhome £5.50-£16.50, motorbike/tent £5.50
Rental 🚐
CC MasterCard Visa
🐾 ✕ 🐕 🔲 🔋 🔳 🔲 🔲 🔲 🔲 🔲 GR TV ⚠ 🔲 🔲
Calor Gaz ⚐ 🐕
Last arrival time: 8:00
➡ From Chichester A27 take B2145 to Selsey. At Selsey turn right into school lane and follow signs for park.

SENNEN Cornwall   2A4

Lower Treave Caravan and Camping Park

Crows-an-Wra, Sennen TR19 6HZ
📞 **01736-810559**
Open April-October ⛺ 🚐 🚍

Quiet family site at the heart of the Land's End peninsula with sheltered grass terraces and panoramic views to the sea, only 2½ miles from Sennen Blue Flag Beach.

Size 4½ acres, 80 touring pitches, 26 with electric hookup, 80 level pitches, 5 static caravans, 6 🐾, 10 WCs, 1 CWP
£ car/tent £4.50-£6.50, car/caravan £4.50-£6.50, motorhome £4.50-£6.50, motorbike/tent £4.50, children £1
🐾 ✕¼ 🐕¼ 🔲 🔋 🔲 Calor Gaz 🐕
Last arrival time: 10:30
➡ Lower Treave is located on the edge of village of Crows-An-Wra, midway between Penzance and Lands End on A30. From Penzance continue through Crows-An-Wra on the A30 and site is ½ mile beyond village on left.

SETTLE North Yorkshire   10C3

Knight Stainforth Hall Camping & Caravan Park

Little Stainforth, Settle BD24 ODP
📞 **01729-822200 Fax 01729-823387**   ➡

← **Knight Stainforth Hall**

Open March-October Δ ⊕ ⊞

Family run camping park catering mainly for families. Situated in the Yorkshire Dales National Park on the west bank of the River Ribble, near waterfall and Pack-horse Bridge.

Size 10 acres, 50 touring pitches, 50 with electric hookup, 80 level pitches, 60 static caravans, 8 ⧉, 21 WCs, 1 CWP
£ car/tent £8, car/caravan £8, motorhome £8, motorbike/tent £8, children £1
CC Visa
⚡ ✗¼ ⊡ 🔧 ⊟ 🔲 GR 🔳 TV ⚠ 🔲 Calor Gaz ⛺
Last arrival time: 9:30
➜ Take A65 Settle to Kendal. Turn off opposite Settle High School on Stackhouse Lane. Site is 2½ miles.

SEVENOAKS Kent　　5D3

Camping & Caravanning Club Site
Styants Bottom, Seal, Sevenoaks
☎ 01732-762728
Open end March-early November Δ ⊕ ⊞
Size 4 acres, 60 touring pitches, 24 with electric hookup, 4 ⧉, 7 WCs, 1 CWP
£ car/tent £8.75-£11.55, car/caravan £8.75-£11.55, motorhome £8.75-£11.55, motorbike/tent £8.75, children £1.40
CC MasterCard Visa
⊡ 🔧 ⚠ 🔲 ⛐ ⛺
Last arrival time: 11:00
➜ On A25 from Sevenoaks turn right into Styants Bottom Road. Site is signposted just before Crown Point Inn.

SHEERNESS Kent　　5E2

Sheerness Holiday Park
Isle of Sheppey, Sheerness ME12 3AA
☎ 01795-662638
Open Easter-end September Δ ⊕
Size 5½ acres, 80 touring pitches, 16 with electric hookup, 25 static caravans, 6 ⧉, 15 WCs,
⚡ 🔧 📺 ⊞
➜ Take A249 from M2. Over bridge turn left and follow signs to Sheerness. The park is ¼ mile from town centre.

SHEFFIELD South Yorkshire　　8B1

Fox Hagg Farm Caravan Site
Lodge Lane, Rivelin, Sheffield S6 5SN
☎ 0114-230-5589
Open 1 April-31 October Δ ⊕ ⊞
Size 2 acres, 10 touring pitches, 10 with electric hookup, 30 level pitches, 20 static caravans, 4 ⧉, 6 WCs, 1 CWP
£ car/tent £4, car/caravan £5, motorhome £5, motorbike/tent £4
⚡ ⚡¼ ✗¼ ⊞¼ ⊡ ⛐ ⛺ WS
Last arrival time: 12:00
➜ Take A57 to Lodge Lane. Site is 300 yards before Rivelin post office.

SHEPTON MALLET Somerset　　3E2

Batcombe Vale Caravan Park
Batcombe, Shepton Mallet BA4 6BW
☎ 01749-830246
Open 1 May-30 September Δ ⊕ ⊞

Small, peaceful site in a secluded valley of lakes and wild gardens. Close to Longleat, Stourhead, Wells and Glastonbury.

Size 5 acres, 32 touring pitches, 16 with electric hookup, 32 level pitches, 2 ⌂, 4 WCs, 1 CWP
£ car/tent £7-£8, car/caravan £7-£8, motorhome £7-£8, motorbike/tent £6, children £1-£2
⌂ ⌂ Calor Gaz ⌂ WS
➡ Off the B3081 between Bruton and Evercreech, from where it is well-signed.

Manleaze Caravan Park
Cannards Grave, Shepton Mallet BA4 4LY
☎ 01749-342404
Open all year ⌂ ⌂ ⌂
Size 1 acre, 25 touring pitches, 10 with electric hookup, 25 level pitches, 3 static caravans, 2 ⌂, 4 WCs, 1 CWP
£ car/tent £3-£4, car/caravan £3-£4, motorhome £3-£4, motorbike/tent £2
Rental Chalet.
✗¼ ⌂¼ ⌂ ⌂ ⌂
➡ At the Cannards Grave roundabout, junction A371 and A37, and Fosse Way, follow site signs (300 yards).

Quiet family-run park, situated on the edge of the picturesque village of Salcombe Regis in an area of outstanding natural beauty. Ideal base for exploring east Devon. Colour brochure available on request.

Size 16 acres, 100 touring pitches, 60 with electric hookup, 60 level pitches, 10 static caravans, 14 ⌂, 14 WCs, 2 CWPs
£ car/tent £6-£8.75, car/caravan £6-£8.75, motorhome £6-£8.75, motorbike/tent £6
Rental ⌂ £99-£315
⌂ MasterCard Visa ➡

Woodlands Caravan Park
Holt Road, Sheringham NR26 8TU
☎ 01263-823802
Open March-October ⌂ ⌂
Size 21 acres, 286 touring pitches, 216 with electric hookup, 250 level pitches, 133 static caravans, 28 ⌂, 74 WCs, 4 CWPs
£ car/caravan £7.20-£10.75, motorhome £7.20-£10.75
⌂ ✗ ⌂ ⌂ ⌂ ⌂ ⌂ ⌂ ⌂ ⌂ ⌂ ⌂ ⌂ Calor Gaz ⌂ ⌂
Last arrival time: 12:00
➡ On N side of A148. 4 miles E of Holt.

Salcombe Regis Camping & Caravan Park
Salcombe Regis, Sidmouth EX10 0JH
☎ 01395-514303 Fax 01395-514303
Open April-October ⌂ ⌂ ⌂

← Salcombe Regis Camping & Caravan Park

🗲 🗲¼ ✗¼ ▦¼ ▣ 🗐 🗗 ⚠ 🎇 Calor Gaz & ⌇ WS

Last arrival time: 10:00

➜ Signposted off the A3052 Exeter to Lyme Regis coast road, 1½ miles E of Sidmouth.

SILLOTH Cumbria   **10A1**

Solway Holiday Village
Silloth CA5 4QQ
🕻 016973-31236 Fax 016973-32553
Open all year 🛆 🚐 🚛

Discover nearby Lake District and Borders. Quality accomodation and spacious touring area. Indoor pool, bowling alley, deer farm, bars, kiddies club. O.A.P. and Rally discounts.

Size 130 acres, 100 touring pitches, 50 with electric hookup, 100 level pitches, 200 static caravans, 5 🚿, 10 WCs, 1 CWP
£ car/tent £7-£11, car/caravan £7-£11, motorhome £7-£11, motorbike/tent £7
Rental 🚐 Chalet. £90-£395 weekly (family of four)
CC MasterCard Visa
🗲 ✗ ➲ ▣ 🕻 🗗 🖫 🎇 🖳 ▣ 🖽 🔍 📺 ⚠ 🎇 🍷 Calor Gaz & ⌇ WS
Last arrival time: 10:00
➜ From S: leave M6 junction 41. From N: leave A74 junction 44 - take B5305 to Silloth, turning right on reaching sea front towards Skinburness. The park is about a mile on right.

Stanwix Park Holiday Centre
Greenrow, Silloth CA5 4HH
🕻 016973-31671 Fax 016973-32555
Open March-October 🛆 🚐 🚛
Size 20 acres, 121 touring pitches, 121 with electric hookup, 121 level pitches, 186 static caravans, 15 🚿, 20 WCs, 2 CWPs
£ car/tent £8.60-£12.60, car/caravan £8.60-£12.60, motorhome £8.60-£12.60, motorbike/tent £8.60
Rental 🚐 Chalet. £135-£370
CC MasterCard Visa
🗲 ✗ ➲ ▣ 🕻 🗗 🖫 🎇 🖳 ▣ 🎇 🍷 🍷 GR ⚠ 🎇
🍷 Calor Gaz & ⌇ WS
Last arrival time: 10:00
➜ 1 mile S of Silloth on B5300.

Tanglewood Caravan Park
Causeway Head, Silloth CA5 4PE
🕻 016973-31253
Open March-October 🛆 🚐 🚛

Natural, tree-sheltered, friendly park, ideal for touring the lakes and the Borders. Large modern holiday homes for hire with colour TV.

Size 7 acres, 21 touring pitches, 17 with electric hookup, 21 level pitches, 56 static caravans, 4 🚿, 12 WCs, 2 CWPs
£ car/tent £6, car/caravan £6, motorhome £6, motorbike/tent £6, children £1-£2
Rental 🚐
▣ 🕻 🗗 GR 📺 ⚠ 🎇 🍷 Calor ⌇
Last arrival time: 11:00
➜ On B5302, 4 miles on from Abbeytown on left, or, on B5302, 1 mile from Silloth on right.

Dales Bank Holiday Park
Low Lane, Silsden BD20 9JH
☎ **01535-656523**
Open April-October ▲ 🚐 🚎
Size 5 acres, 52 touring pitches, 20 with electric hookup, 52 level pitches, 10 WCs, 1 CWP
£ car/tent £6, car/caravan £6, motorhome £6, motorbike/tent £6
🏊 ✕ 🗑 📺 🆖 🏕 🖾 🍴 Calor Gaz ♿ ⚓ WS
Last arrival time: 11:00
➤ Follow signs from police station for 1½ miles.

Holgates Caravan Park
Cove Road, Silverdale, Carnforth LA5 0SH
☎ **01524-701508 Fax 01524-701580**
Open 22 December-3 November ▲ 🚐 🚎

A superb award winning holiday centre set in wooded countryside adjacent to the sea.

Size 11 acres, 70 touring pitches, 70 with electric hookup, 350 static caravans, 10 🍴, 18 WCs, 2 CWPs
£ car/tent £13.50-£15, car/caravan £13.50-£15, motorhome £13.50-£15
CC MasterCard Visa
🏊 ✕ 🍴 🗑 🆖 📺 📺 🆖 🏕 🖾 🍴 Calor Gaz ♿ ⚓
Last arrival time: 10:30
➤ NW of Carnforth, 5 miles from junction 45.

Shaw Ghyll Farm
Simonstone, Hawes DL8 3LY
☎ **01969-667359 Fax 01969-667894**
Open 1 March-31 October ▲ 🚐 🚎
Size 3 acres, 30 touring pitches, 18 with electric hookup, 30 level pitches, 6 static caravans, 2 🍴, 7 WCs, 2 CWPs
£ car/tent £7, car/caravan £7, motorhome £7
Rental Chalet.
🆖 Calor ⚓
➤ Follow signs from Hawes to Muker. Turn left and then right through Simonstone.

Richmond Holiday Centre
Richmond Drive, Skegness PE25 3TQ
☎ **01754-762097 Fax 01754-765631**
Open 1 March-30 November 🚐 🚎

Family owned park, with on-site facilities including a Post Office, arcade, launderette, hair salon, leisure complex and heated indoor pool. Live nightly entertainment subject to season.

Size 46 acres, 175 touring pitches, 107 with electric hookup, 107 level pitches, 600 static caravans, 24 🍴, 100 WCs, 3 CWPs
£ car/caravan £7-£12.50, motorhome £7-£12.50
Rental 🚐 £90-£270
CC Visa
🏊 🏊¼ ✕ ✕¼ 🍴 🍴¼ 🗑 🆖 🗑 🖾 📺 📺 🆖 📺
🏕 🖾 🍴 Calor Gaz ♿ ⚓ WS
➤ Follow signs to bus station. Site is 400 yards beyond coach station on right.

Riverside Caravan Park
Wainfleet Bank, Wainfleet, Skegness PE24 4ND
☎ **01754-880205**
Open March-October
Size 1¼ acres, 30 touring pitches, 30 with electric hookup, 30 level pitches, 2 , 6 WCs, 1 CWP
£ car/tent £4.50, car/caravan £4.50, motorhome £4.50, motorbike/tent £4.50
Calor Gaz WS
➔ A52 Boston to Skegness, turn left onto B1195 Wainfleet All Saints, follow brown signs.

SKIPSEA East Yorkshire 11F3

Far Grange Park
Windhook, Hornsea Road, Skipsea YO25 8SY
☎ **01262-468293 Fax 01262-468648**
Open March-October

Full facilities for touring caravans, tents and motorhomes. Luxury rose award holiday homes for hire. Holiday homes for sale. Leisure centre and indoor swimming pool.

Size 60 acres, 170 touring pitches, 170 with electric hookup, 170 level pitches, 327 static caravans, 20 , 76 WCs, 4 CWPs
£ car/tent £7-£11, car/caravan £7-£11, motorhome £7-£11
Rental £110-£295
CC MasterCard Visa
Calor Gaz
➔ Halfway between Skipsea and Hornsea on B1242.

Skirlington Leisure Park
Low Skirlington, Skipsea YO25 8SY
☎ **01262-468213 Fax 01262-468105**
Open 1 March-31 October

Situated on the East Yorkshire coast, a family run business with a reputation for high standards and constant updating of all facilities. Please call for a brochure.

Size 80 acres, 275 touring pitches, 275 with electric hookup, 275 level pitches, 465 static caravans, 45 , 55 WCs, 5 CWPs ➔

← **Skirlington Leisure Park**

£ car/tent £8-£14, car/caravan £8-£14, motorhome £8-£14, motorbike/tent £8
CC MasterCard Visa
🦮 ✕ 🗣 🖥 🔋 📷 🖊 ▶ 🔲 🔲 🔲 GR TV ⚠ 🔲 🔲
Calor Gaz 🚻 🐕 WS
➜ M62 signposted to Beverley, follow signs to Hornsea. Brown signposts direct to site once in Hornsea.

SLAPTON Devon   3D4

Newlands Farm Camp Site

Newlands Farm, Slapton, Dartmouth TQ7 2RB
📞 **01548-580366**
Open Whitsun-mid September 🏕 🚐 🚚
Size 10 acres, 30 touring pitches, 4 with electric hookup, 30 level pitches, 1 static caravans, 2 📷, 5 WCs, 1 CWP
£ car/tent £5-£6, car/caravan £5-£6, motorhome £5-£6, motorbike/tent £5
Rental 🏕
🔲 🚻 🐕 WS
Last arrival time: 10:00
➜ Midway along beach road A379, turn inland signposted Slapton, pass through village and go up hill. Newlands Farm is ¼ mile on right.

SLIMBRIDGE Gloucestershire   7E4

Tudor Caravan & Camping

Shepherds Patch, Slimbridge GL2 7BP
📞 **01453-890483**
Open all year 🏕 🚐 🚚

Behind a pub in farming country, this orchard site is bordered by the Gloucester to Sharpness canal, with the Wild Fowl Trust on the far bank.

Size 7½ acres, 75 touring pitches, 45 with electric hookup, 75 level pitches, 4 📷, 12 WCs, 1 CWP
£ car/tent £6-£6.50, car/caravan £7-£7.50, motorhome £7-£7.50, motorbike/tent £6, children £0.75
CC MasterCard
🦮 ✕¼ 🚐¼ 🔋 🔲 🔲 Calor 🐕
Last arrival time: 10:00
➜ From junction of A4135 and A38, 11 miles SW of Gloucester, take road through Slimbridge towards Wild Fowl Trust for 1½ miles. On left immediately before canal bridge.

SLINGSBY North Yorkshire   11E3

Camping & Caravanning Club Site

Railway Street, Slingsby YO6 7AA
📞 **01653-628335**
Open late March-early November 🏕 🚐 🚚
Size 3½ acres, 60 touring pitches, 41 with electric hookup, 4 📷, 9 WCs, 1 CWP
£ car/tent £8.20-£10.40, car/caravan £8.20-£10.40, motorhome £8.20-£10.40, motorbike/tent £8.20, children £1.30
CC MasterCard Visa
🔋 🚻 🐕
Last arrival time: 11:00
➜ From A64 Scarborough to York road, take B1257 at Maltby to Slingsby. Follow signs to site.

SNAINTON North Yorkshire   11E2

Jasmine Caravan Park

Cross Lane, Snainton YO13 9BE
📞 **01723-859240** Fax **01723-859240**
Open March-January 🏕 🚐 🚚
Size 5 acres, 70 touring pitches, 70 with electric hookup, 70 level pitches, 1 static caravan, 4 📷, 14 WCs, 1 CWP
£ car/tent £6-£8.50, car/caravan £6-£8.50, motorhome £6-£8.50, motorbike/tent £6, children £0.75
Rental 🚐 Chalet.
🦮 🖥 🔋 🔲 Calor Gaz 🚻 🐕 WS
➜ Turn off A170 in Snainton village opposite junior school. After ¾ mile signposted. Midway between Scarborough and Pickering.

SOUTH BRENT Devon 2C3

Edeswell Farm Country Caravan Park
Rattery, South Brent TQ10 9LN
01364-72177
Open 1 April-31 October Å 🚐 🚲
Size 21 acres, 46 touring pitches, 22 with electric hookup, 40 level pitches, 18 static caravans, 10 �🛁, 10 WCs, 1 CWP
£ car/tent £6.50-£8.50, car/caravan £6.50-£8.50, motorhome £6.50-£8.50, motorbike/tent £6.50, children £1
🛒 ✕ 🗑 📞 🗂 🗄 🔍 🐾 🅖🅡 🎮 📺 ⚠ 🎯 🔌
Calor Gaz 🐾 WS
Last arrival time: 8:30
➡ From A38 to Marley Head junction take A385 to Paignton. Site ½ mile on right.

SOUTH MOLTON Devon 2C2

Black Cock Inn & Camping Park
Molland, South Molton EX36 3NW
01769-550297 **fax** 01769-550297
Open March-November Å 🚐 🚲
Size 7 acres, 64 touring pitches, 24 with electric hookup, 48 level pitches, 2 static caravans, 8 🛁, 15 WCs, 1 CWP
£ car/tent £5.50-£7.50, car/caravan £6.50-£9, motorhome £6.50-£8.50, motorbike/tent £5.50
Rental 🚐 Chalet. From £25 per day.
🛒 ✕ 🚰 🗑 📞 🗂 🗄 📂 🅖🅡 📺 ⚠ 🎯 🔌 Calor ♿ 🐾 WS
Last arrival time: 11:00
➡ Signed from A361, 4 miles E of South Molton.

SOUTH SHIELDS Tyne & Wear 11D1

Lizard Lane Caravan & Camping Site
Marsden, South Shields NE34 7AB
0191-454 4982
Open 1 March-26 October Å 🚐 🚲
Size 4¼ acres, 45 touring pitches, 45 level pitches, 70 static caravans, 6 🛁, 14 WCs, 1 CWP
➡ 2 miles S of South Shields on A183.

Sandhaven Caravan Park
Sea Road, South Shields
0191-454 5594
Å 🚐 🚲
Size 7 acres, 94 touring pitches, 94 with electric hookup, 94 level pitches, 52 static caravans, 6 🛁, 14 WCs, 1 CWP
ℂℂ Visa
Calor Gaz ♿ WS
➡ Site ¾ mile E of town centre on coast road.

SOUTHAMPTON Hampshire 4B4

Dibles Park Caravan Site
Dibles Road, Warsash, Southampton SO3 9SA
01703-575232
Open 1 March-30 November Å 🚐 🚲
Size 5 acres, 15 touring pitches, 15 with electric hookup, 15 level pitches, 4 🛁, 7 WCs, 1 CWP
£ car/tent £6.70, car/caravan £6.70, motorhome £6.70, motorbike/tent £5
🛒¼ ✕¼ 🚐¼ 🗑 📞 🗄 🗂 Calor 🐾 WS
➡ Junction 8 M27 turn left A27 to Sarisbury Green. Right into Barnes Lane, right into Brook Lane, left at Warsash Village then the third turning on right.

SOUTHMINSTER Essex 5E2

Beacon Hill Leisure Park
St Lawrence Bay, Southminster CM10 7LS
01621-779248
Open 1 April-31 October Å 🚐 🚲

A quiet park situated beside the River Blackwater on level ground with its own slipway to the river. Lake for children's boating and fishing, excellent for sailing, water skiing, windsurfing and bird watching. Restaurant ¼ mile.

Size 25 acres, 50 touring pitches, 20 with electric hookup, 50 level pitches, 88 static caravans, 10 🛁, 24 WCs, 2 CWPs
🛒 ✕¼
➡ B1010 to Latchingdon. At mini roundabout take Bradwell Road. At St Lawrence take left turn at sign for St Lawrence Bay. ¼ mile to site.

Steeple Bay Caravan Park

Steeple, Southminster CM0 7RS

☎ 01621-773991 Fax 01621-773967

🅰 ⏚

Size 65 acres, 51 touring pitches, 19 with electric hookup, 51 level pitches

⚑ ✕ 🛒 ▣ ⏦ ♿

➡ A12 onto A414 (Maldon) followed by B1010 & B1018 (Latchingdon, Mayland). On entering Steeple village, park is signposted first left.

SOUTHPORT Lancashire   10B4

Leisure Lakes Caravan Park

Mere Brow, Tarleton, Southport PR4 JX

☎ 01772-813446 Fax 01772-816250

🅰 ⏚ 🚐

A 90 acre site with two lakes for fishing, windsurfing, canoeing and jet skis. Also mountain bike hire. Pub on site serving meals.

Size 90 acres, 87 touring pitches, 80 with electric hookup, 87 level pitches, 6 ⏣, 11 WCs, 2 CWPs

£ car/tent £9, car/caravan £9, motorhome £9, motorbike/tent £9

⚑¼ ✕ 🛒 ▣ ☎ ⟨⟩ ⏧ ▦ ⚙ ▥ ⏦ Calor Gaz 🐕

Last arrival time: 9:00

➡ From Southport, take A565 N for 3½ miles, then turn right onto B5246 to Mere Brow village, site entrance is 500 yards on right.

SPALDING Lincolnshire   8C2

Lake Ross Caravan Park

Dozens Bank, West Pinchbeck, Spalding PE11 3NA

☎ 01775-761690

Open 1 April-31 October 🅰 ⏚ 🚐

Size 2½ acres, 20 touring pitches, 12 with electric hookup, 20 level pitches, 4 static caravans, 2 ⏣, 3 WCs, 1 CWP

£ car/tent £7.50, car/caravan £7.50, motorhome £7.50, motorbike/tent £7.50, children £0.50

Rental ⏚ £90-£160

⚑ ⚑¼ ✕¼ 🛒¼ ☎ ⏧ ▥ ⏦ Calor Gaz ♿ 🐕

Last arrival time: 11:30

➡ On A151 Spalding-Bourne road.

ST AGNES Cornwall   2A4

Beacon Cottage Farm

Beacon Drive, St Agnes TR5 0NU

☎ 01872-552347

Open May-October 🅰 ⏚ 🚐

Small secluded park on a working family farm set in six landscaped paddocks covering two acres. Ten minutes walk to the sandy beach. Beautiful scenery, lovely walks. Quiet and uncommercialised.

50 touring pitches, 27 with electric hookup, 45 level pitches, 4 ⏣, 9 WCs, 1 CWP

£ car/tent £5-£11, car/caravan £5-£11, motorhome £5-£11, motorbike/tent £5, children £1.50-£2.50

⚑ ⏧ ☎ ⏦ ▦ ▥ Calor Gaz 🐕 WS

Last arrival time: 8:00

➡ Leave the A30 at Chiverton roundabout and take B3277 to St Agnes. On reaching the village, turn left, signposted The Beacon, and follow signs to the park.

Trevarth Holiday Park

Blackwater, St Agnes TR4 8HR

☎ 01872-560266 Fax 01872-560266

Open Easter-mid October 🅰 ⏚ 🚐

Small family run park in rural area, conveniently situated for the north and south coast resorts.

Size 4½ acres, 30 touring pitches, 27 with electric hookup, 30 level pitches, 20 static caravans, 3 ℞, 4 WCs, 1 CWP
CC MasterCard Visa
🐾¼ ✗¼ ⬤¼ 🔌 🗑 GR ⚠ 🔭 Calor Gaz WS
Last arrival time: 10:00
➜ 300 yards down Blackwater road, from Cliverton roundabout which is on A30, 4½ miles N of Redruth.

ST AUSTELL Cornwall   2B4

River Valley Holiday Park
London Apprentice, St Austell PL26 7AP
📞 01726-73533 **Fax** 01726-73533
Open April-September ⛺ 🚐 🚍

A small family owned Rose Award Park set in the sheltered Penlewan Valley. Covered heated pool, pets paddock and woodland cycle trail to the beach.

Size 8 acres, 45 touring pitches, 25 with electric hookup, 45 level pitches, 40 static caravans, 6 ℞, 9 WCs, 1 CWP

£ car/tent £6-£13.50, car/caravan £6-£13.50, motorhome £6-£13.50, motorbike/tent £6
Rental 🚐 £70-£345
CC MasterCard Visa
🐾 🗑 🔌 🗑 🔲 ⚠ 🔭 Calor ➜ WS
Last arrival time: 10:00
➜ Situated in London Apprentice. Take B3273 from St Austell to Mevagissey. Continue for 1½ miles to park on left.

Trevor Farm Camping & Caravan Site
Gorran, St Austell PL26 6LW
📞 01726-842387
Open 1 April-end October ⛺ 🚐 🚍
Size 4 acres, 50 touring pitches, 24 with electric hookup, 50 level pitches, 4 ℞, 12 WCs, 1 CWP
£ car/tent £5-£11, car/caravan £5-£11, motorhome £5-£11, motorbike/tent £5
🗑 🔌 🗑 📋 ⚠ 🔭 ➜
Last arrival time: 8:00
➜ From St Austell S on B3273, 3¼ miles past Pentewan, turn right signed Gorran. After 4½ miles bear right. After ¼ mile turn right to site.

Trewhiddle Holiday Estate

Trewhiddle, Pentewan Road, St Austell PL26 7AD

☎ 01726-67011 Fax 01726-67011
🅰 🚐 🚚

A country park in the peaceful Pentewan Valley, with the sea nearby. 16 acre family site ideally situated for exploring Cornwall. Excellent facilities for family holidays.

Size 16 acres, 105 touring pitches, 50 with electric hookup, 50 static caravans, 9 🚿, 16 WCs, 1 CWP
£ car/tent £6-£10, car/caravan £6-£10, motorhome £6-£10, motorbike/tent £6, children £1
Rental 🚐 Chalet. £130-£360
CC MasterCard Visa
🛒 ✗ 🍴 🍵 🔟 🎫 🚾 GR 🅰 🏯 🍺 Calor Gaz 🐎
Last arrival time: 10:00
➡ From St Austell take B3273 to Mevagissey. Site entrance is ¾ mile on right from roundabout.

ST BURYAN Cornwall   2A4

Tower Park

St Buryan TR19 6BZ
☎ 01736-810286
Open April-October 🅰 🚐 🚚

Quiet, friendly site in peaceful rural setting, near sandy beaches and Minack open air theatre. Ideal for touring, walking, diving, etc. Spotless facilities ensured by resident owners.

Size 12 acres, 102 touring pitches, 30 with electric hookup, 102 level pitches, 5 static caravans, 10 🚿, 12 WCs
£ car/tent £5-£7.50, car/caravan £5-£8, motorhome £5-£8, motorbike/tent £5, children £1
🛒 ✗¼ 🍴 🍵 🔟 🎫 GR 🎫 🚾 🅰 🏯 Calor Gaz ♿ 🐎
Last arrival time: 10:00
➡ From Penzance take Land's End road (A30). After 3 miles fork left on B3283 signed to St Buryan. On entering village turn right. Tower Park is 300 yards on right.

ST IVES Cornwall   2A4

Ayr Holiday Park

Higher Ayr, St Ives TR26 1EJ
☎ 01736-795855 Fax 01736-798797
Open 1 April-31 October 🅰 🚐 🚚

The only holiday park in St Ives itself, with easy access to the beaches, town centre and coastal footpath. Beautiful views over St Ives Bay.

Size 4 acres, 40 touring pitches, 35 with electric hookup, 20 level pitches, 43 static caravans, 10 🚿, 11 WCs, 1 CWP
£ car/tent £9-£14, car/caravan £9-£14, motorhome £8.20-£13, motorbike/tent £9, children £1-£1.75

Rental ⚌ Chalet. £140-£525
ℂℂ MasterCard Visa
🏕¼ ✕¼ ⛟¼ ▣ 🔋 ▯ GR ⚠ ✠ Calor Gaz ⵜ
Last arrival time: 8:00
➡ From the A30 follow the holiday route to St Ives joining B3311 and B3306. ½ mile from St Ives turn left at Menz roundabout following signs to Ayr and Porthmeon Beach.

Balnoon Camp Site
Halsetown, St Ives TR26 3JA
📞 **01736-795431**
Open Easter-31 October 🇦 ⚌ 🚐

Small, quiet, level sheltered site, pleasantly situated with tree and hedge screening, just 2 miles from St Ives town centre and beaches.

Size ¾ acre, 24 touring pitches, 24 level pitches, 2 🚿, 4 WCs, 1 CWP
£ car/tent £5-£8, car/caravan £5-£8, motorhome £5-£8, motorbike/tent £5, children £0.50-£1
🏕 ✕¼ ▯ Calor Gaz ♿ ⵜ
Last arrival time: 8:00
➡ Leave A30 W of Hayle at large roundabout and take A3074 for St Ives. At second mini roundabout take first left (signposted Holiday Route). Continue for 3 miles taking second right (not Carbis Bay).

Polmanter Tourist Park
Halsetown, St Ives TR26 3LX
📞 **01736-795640** Fax **01736-795640**
Open Easter-31 October 🇦 ⚌ 🚐   ➡

← Polmanter Tourist Park

Award winning park, with excellent facilities including a heated swimming pool, located within easy walking distance of St Ives and its glorious beaches just one mile away.

Size 13 acres, 240 touring pitches, 188 with electric hookup, 34 ⚲, 40 WCs, 4 CWPs
£ car/tent £6-£12.50, car/caravan £6-£12.50, motorhome £6-£12.50, motorbike/tent £6, children £1.50-£1.75
CC Visa

⚲ ✕ 🛒 ⊡ ⚙ ⊡ ⊡ ⊞ ⊞ GR ⊡ Ⓜ ⊞ ⚐ Calor Gaz ✹
Last arrival time: 9:00
➔ Off A30 to St Ives (A3074). First left at mini-roundabout. Take holiday route (HR) to St Ives (Halsetown). Right at Halsetown Inn, then first left.

Trevalgan Family Camping Park
St Ives TR26 3BJ
📞 **01736-796433 Fax 01736-796433**
Open 1 May-30 September ⚑ ⚐ ⚑

Friendly, family run park with modern, clean facilities. Just 1½ miles from St Ives' beaches. Superb scenery and our own stretch of Cornish coast.

Size 5 acres, 120 touring pitches, 22 with electric hookup, 120 level pitches, 10 ⚲, 15 WCs, 1 CWP
£ car/tent £6-£10, car/caravan £6-£10, motorhome £6-£10, motorbike/tent £6, children £2-£4
CC MasterCard Visa
⚲ 🛒 ⊡ ⚙ ⊡ GR ⊡ TV Ⓜ ⊞ Calor Gaz ⚬ ✹
➔ Take A30 to B3306 and follow signs for park.

ST LEONARDS Hampshire   4A4

Camping International
229 Ringwood Road, St Leonards BH24 2SD
📞 **01202-872817 Fax 01202-861292**
Open 1 March-October ⚑ ⚐ ⚑
Size 9 acres, 205 touring pitches, 165 with electric hookup, 205 level pitches, 16 ⚲, 22 WCs, 2 CWPs
£ car/tent £7-£10.80, car/caravan £7-£10.80, motorhome £7-£10.80, motorbike/tent £7, children £1.20-£1.50
CC MasterCard Visa

ⓩ ✖ ➧ 🏕 🔋 ▯ ▣ 🅖🅡 🔲 📺 ⚠ 🈲 ⚡ Calor
Gaz ♿ ♒ WS
Last arrival time: 10:00
➜ On main A31 2½ miles W of Ringwood.
Entrance in Boundary Lane.

ST MAWES Cornwall   2B4

Trethem Mill Touring Park
St Just-in-Roseland, St Mawes TR2 5JF
📞 01872-580504 Fax 01872-580968
Open 1 April-31 October ▲ 🚐 🚌

Discover the beautiful Roseland, staying on our exclusive, peaceful park, offering immaculate facilties in tranquil countryside setting. Ideal for beaches, walking, watersports, gardens and touring Cornwall.

Size 11 acres, 84 touring pitches, 37 with electric hookup, 40 level pitches, 8 🚿, 16 WCs, 1 CWP
£ car/tent £5.50-£8.50, car/caravan £5.50-£8.50, motorhome £5.50-£8.50, motorbike/tent £5.50, children £1-£2
℃ MasterCard Visa
ⓩ ▯ 🔋 🅖🅡 📺 ⚠ 🈲 Calor Gaz ♿
Last arrival time: 10:00
➜ From Tregony follow the A3078 to St Mawes. 2 miles after passing through Trewithian look for sign.

ST NEOTS Cambridgeshire   8C4

Camping & Caravanning Club Site
Rush Meadow, St Neots PE19 2UD
📞 01480-474404
Open end March-early November ▲ 🚐 🚌
Size 10 acres, 180 touring pitches, 53 with electric hookup, 12 🚿, 18 WCs, 2 CWPs

£ car/tent £9.20-£12.05, car/caravan £9.20-£12.05, motorhome £9.20-£12.05, motorbike/tent £9.20, children £1.40
℃ Visa
▯ 🔋 ♿ ♒
Last arrival time: 11:00
➜ Site signposted from B1043 in St Neots.

STAMFORD Lincolnshire   8C3

Casterton Caravan Site
Casterton Hill, Casterton, Stamford PE9 4DE
📞 01780-481481 Fax 01780-55753
Open all year ▲ 🚐 🚌
Size 4 acres, 32 touring pitches, 32 with electric hookup, 32 level pitches, 3 static caravans, 2 🚿, 4 WCs, 2 CWPs
£ car/tent £4.95-£5.95, car/caravan £4.95-£5.95, motorhome £4.95-£5.95, motorbike/tent £4.95, children £1.20-£1.30
Rental ▲ Chalet. chalet £69-£128
℃ MasterCard Visa
ⓩ ✖ ➧ ▯ 🔋 ▯ 🈲 🅖🅡 📺 ⚠ 🈲 ⚡ Calor Gaz
♿ ♒ WS
Last arrival time: 12:00
➜ From the A1/A606 junction, follow the Ministry signs for the services.

Tallington Lakes
Barholm Road, Tallington, Stamford PE9 4RT
📞 01778-347000 Fax 01778-346213
Open all year ▲ 🚐 🚌

Bring your own touring caravan or tent to Tallington Lakes, and enjoy the water during your visit. Landscaped area for 90/100 caravans. Hook up, toilet/showers, chemical disposal, washing, launderette available.   ➜

← **Tallington Lakes**

Size 100 touring pitches, 60 with electric hookup, 100 level pitches, 3 🍴, 5 WCs, 1 CWP
£ car/tent £7.50, car/caravan £8.50, motorhome £8.50, motorbike/tent £7.50
Rental ⏚
🚐¼ ✕ 📧 ⊡ 🔋 🔲 🔲 🔲 🔲 ⚠ 🎪 ⻤ WS
Last arrival time: 8:00

Heather View Caravan Park
Stanhope DL13 2PS
📞 **01388-528728**
Open 1 March-31 October
Size 30 touring pitches

Hardwick Parks
Downs Road, Off Witney Road, Standlake OX8 7PZ
📞 **01865-300501 Fax 01865-300037**
Open 1 April-31 October ▲ ⏚ 🚐
Size 180 acres, 250 touring pitches, 76 with electric hookup, 250 level pitches, 117 static caravans, 20 🍴, 18 WCs, 1 CWP
£ car/tent £7.25-£9.25, car/caravan £7.25-£9.25, motorhome £7.25-£9.25, motorbike/tent £4
CC MasterCard Visa
🚐 ✕ 📧 ⊡ 🔋 🔲 🔲 Calor Gaz ⟁ ⻤ WS
Last arrival time: 8:00
➜ Signposted from A415, 4½ miles S of Witney.

Trentham Caravan & Camping Park
Trentham, Stoke-on-Trent ST4 8AX
📞 **01782-657341**
Open all year ▲ ⏚ 🚐

Set in the 1000-acre Tretham Gardens, this park has woodland or more open pitches. The River Trent, lake and gardens are all acccessible from the park.

Size 35 acres, 250 touring pitches, 24 🍴, 92 WCs,
🚐 ✕ 📧 ⟁
➜ From M6 junction 15 onto A500, then take first slip road, signed A34 Stone and Stafford. Site 1 mile on right.

Redstone Caravan Park
The Rough, Stourport-on-Severn DY13 0LD
📞 **01299-823872 Fax 01299-828026**
Open 1 February- 31 December ⏚ 🚐
Size 12 acres, 36 touring pitches, 28 with electric hookup, 36 level pitches, 290 static caravans, 8 🍴, 24 WCs, 2 CWPs
£ car/caravan £8-£10, motorhome £8-£10
🚐 📧 ⊡ 🔋 ⚠ 🎪 🔲 Calor Gaz ⟁ ⻤
Last arrival time: 9:00
➜ A456 from Kidderminster, over bridge, second left into The Rough.

Dodwell Park
Evesham Road, Stratford-upon-Avon CV37 9ST
📞 **01789-204957 Fax 01926-336476**
Open all year ▲ ⏚ 🚐

Set in beautiful countryside two miles from Stratford-upon-Avon this is an ideal site for visiting the Cotswolds and Warwick Castle.

Size 17 acres, 50 touring pitches, 50 with electric hookup, 40 level pitches, 6 ↑, 7 WCs, 1 CWP
£ car/tent £7.50-£8.50, car/caravan £7.50-£8.50, motorhome £7.50-£8.50, motorbike/tent £6, children £0.70
CC   MasterCard Visa
🛒 🗗 📞 🗗 Calor Gaz & 🐾
Last arrival time: 9:30   →

← **Dodwell Park**

➜ From Stratford-upon-Avon take B439 to Bidford for 2 miles. Park lies on left (not racecourse site).

Elms Camp

Tiddlington, Stratford-upon-Avon CV37 7AG
☎ **01789-293356 Fax 01789-292312**
Open 1 April-31 October ⚊ 🚐 🚃
Size 12 acres, 35 touring pitches, 34 with electric hookup, 40 level pitches, 100 static caravans, 8 🚿, 3 WCs, 1 CWP
🔌 ✕¼ 🍴¼ 🔋 📺 ⚠ 🔲 Calor Gaz
➜ On B4086 from Stratford-upon-Avon.

Ulwell Cottage Caravan Park

Swanage
☎ **01929-422823 Fax 01929-422823**
Open 1 March-7 January ⚊ 🚐 🚃

Nestling under the beautiful 'Purbeck Hills', one mile from the beach. Ideal for families, walkers, golfers and all watersport enthusiasts. Open winter months.

Size 13 acres, 77 touring pitches, 40 with electric hookup, 40 level pitches, 140 static caravans, 24 🚿, 22 WCs, 3 CWPs
£ car/tent £10-£17, car/caravan £10-£17, motorhome £10-£17
Rental 🚐 Chalet. £120-£440
℀ MasterCard Visa
🔌 ✕ 🍴 🅾 🔋 🔲 📖 ⚠ 🔲 🔲 Calor Gaz 🐴
Last arrival time: 10:00
➜ Take A351 to Swanage and on seafront turn left. Follow this road towards Studland for 1½ miles and turn left just before telephone kiosk on left.

Camping & Caravanning Club Site

Kingsbury Water Park, Bodymoor Heath, Sutton Coldfield
☎ **01827-874101**
Open end March-start November ⚊ 🚐 🚃
Size 60 touring pitches, 18 with electric hookup, 4 🚿, 6 WCs, 1 CWP
£ car/tent £8.20-£10.40, car/caravan £8.20-£10.40, motorhome £8.20-£10.40, motorbike/tent £8.20, children £1.30
℀ MasterCard Visa
🅾 🔋 ♿ 🐴
Last arrival time: 11:00
➜ Off A4097 or A4091 take unclassified road and follow Water Park signs.

Drayton Manor Park

Fazeley, Tamworth B78 3TW
☎ **01827-287979 Fax 01827-288916**
Open Easter-end October ⚊ 🚐 🚃
Size 4 acres, 75 touring pitches, 37 level pitches, 12 🚿, 15 WCs, 2 CWPs
£ car/tent £9, car/caravan £11
℀ MasterCard Visa
✕ ✕¼ 🍴 🍴¼ 🔋 🔲 Gaz ♿ 🐴
➜ From M42 junction 9 or 10 take A5404 or A446 onto A4091.

Ashe Farm Camping & Caravan Site

Thornfalcon, Taunton TA3 5NW
☎ **01823-442567 Fax 01823-443372**
Open 1 April-31 October ⚊ 🚐 🚃

Peaceful, family run site with lovely views of the hills. Central for touring and within easy reach of the coast, hills and Somerset Levels.

Size 7 acres, 30 touring pitches, 30 with electric hookup, 30 level pitches, 3 static caravans, 5 ⋔, 10 WCs, 2 CWPs
£ car/tent £6, car/caravan £6-£7.50, motorhome £6-£7.50, motorbike/tent £6, children £1
Rental ⊟ £110-£140 week.
⊠ ✕¼ ⬤¼ ⬤ ⬤ ⬤ ⬤ ⬤ ⬤ ⬤ Calor Gaz ⬤ ⬤ WS
Last arrival time: 12:00
➜ Leave M5 at junction 25. Take A358 Chard road for 2½ miles. Along dual carriageway, turn right at Nags Head pub. Site ¼ mile on right.

Holly Bush Park
Culmhead, Taunton TA3 7EA
☎ **01823-421515** Fax **01823-421885**
🛆 ⊟ ⊟

A beautiful, quiet, family run site in an area of outstanding natural beauty. Numerous places of interest are within easy reach, including National Trust properties.

Size 2 acres, 40 touring pitches, 26 with electric hookup, 40 level pitches, 6 ⋔, 9 WCs, 1 CWP
£ car/tent £6-£7, car/caravan £6-£7, motorhome £6-£7, motorbike/tent £6
Rental 🛆 tent & equipment £10 daily.
⊠ ✕¼ ⬤¼ ⬤ ⬤ ⬤ Calor Gaz ⬤ ⬤ WS
Last arrival time: 10:00
➜ Take M5 junction 25 to Taunton. Turn left at the first traffic light. Follow signs for the race course. 3½ miles after Corfe, turn right at the crossroads. Site is 400 yards on left.

TAVISTOCK Devon   2C3

Harford Bridge Holiday Park
Peter Tavy, Tavistock PL19 9LS
☎ **01822-810349** Fax **01822-810028**   ➜

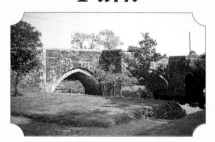

← Harford Bridge Holiday Park

Open mid March-mid October Å 🚐 🚎

Beautiful family run park in Dartmoor National Park offering glorious views. Level and sheltered with many trees and shrubs. Ideal for walking or touring.

Size 16 acres, 120 touring pitches, 40 with electric hookup, 120 level pitches, 16 static caravans, 6 🚿, 14 WCs, 2 CWPs
£ car/tent £6-£9, car/caravan £6-£9, motorhome £6-£9, motorbike/tent £6, children £0.80-£1.40
Rental 🚐 Chalet. £100-£285
🛒 🖥 📞 🖨 🍳 📠 GR 📷 📺 🔥 🏠 Calor Gaz 🦮 WS
Last arrival time: 9:00
➡ Off A386 Tavistock to Okehampton road. 2 miles N of Tavistock, take the Peter Tavy turn.

Higher Longford Farm
Moorshop, Tavistock PL19 9LQ
📞 **01822-613 360 Fax 01822-618 722**
Open all year Å 🚐 🚎
Size 6 acres, 52 touring pitches, 40 with electric hookup, 52 level pitches, 10 🚿, 14 WCs, 2 CWPs
£ car/tent £7.50-£8.50, car/caravan £7.50-£8.50, motorhome £7.50-£8.50, motorbike/tent £5.50, children £0.50-£0.75
Rental Chalet. Chalets £90-£160
🛒 ✕ 🍴 🖥 📞 🖨 🔥 🏠 🍳 Calor Gaz 🦮 WS
➡ Take B3357 Tavistock to Princetown. The road is 2½ miles from Tavistock on right before Park Hill.

Langstone Manor Camping & Caravan Park
Moortown, Tavistock PL19 9TZ
📞 **01822-613371**
Open 15 March-15 November Å 🚐 🚎
Size 5½ acres, 40 touring pitches, 14 with electric hookup, 40 level pitches, 25 static caravans, 6 🚿, 7 WCs, 1 CWP
£ car/tent £6-£7, car/caravan £6-£7, motorhome £6-£7, motorbike/tent £6, children £1
Rental 🚐 Chalet.
🛒 ✕ 📞 🖨 GR 📷 🔥 🏠 🍳 Calor Gaz ♿ 🦮
Last arrival time: 11:00
➡ Take B3357 from Tavistock to Princetown. After 2 miles, turn right at crossroads. Pass over cattle grid and turn left. Follow signs to site ½ mile on right.

Camping & Caravanning Club Site
Haughton, Telford TF6 6BU
📞 **01743-709334**
Open end March-start November Å 🚐 🚎
Size 18 acres, 160 touring pitches, 18 with electric hookup, 2 CWPs
£ car/tent £6.70-£8.30, car/caravan £6.70-£8.30, motorhome £6.70-£8.30, motorbike/tent £6.70, children £0.90
CC MasterCard Visa
📞 🔥 🏠 🦮
Last arrival time: 11:00
➡ Take A53 for 1½ miles passing Upper Astley, turn right and continue for about 1 mile.

Severn Gorge Caravan Park
Bridgnorth Road, Tweedale, Telford TF7 4JB
📞 **01952-684789 Fax 01952-684789**
Open all year Å 🚐 🚎

Set amongst woodland. This well organised site provides a perfect base for exploring Ironbridge and the rest of Shropshire. Open all year. Brochures available on request.

Size 10 acres, 79 touring pitches, 66 with electric hookup, 79 level pitches, 6 ☂, 11 WCs, 1 CWP
⚎ ⚎¼ ✗ 🔲 🔲 🔲 ⚠ 🔲 Calor Gaz ♿ ⋔ WS
Last arrival time: 11:45
➡ From M54 junction 4 follow signs for A442 Kidderminster, then take A442 and follow signs for Tweedale, past Cuckoo Oak pub. Site 300 yards on right.

Brooklands Farm Touring Caravan Park
Alderton, Tewkesbury
📞 **01242-620259**
Open 16 March-16 January ▲ ⊟ 🚐

Set around a small lake in 20 acres of farm land, the Cotswolds and surrounding area of natural beauty are on the doorstep.

Size 10 acres, 80 touring pitches, 70 with electric hookup, 80 level pitches, 8 ☂, 14 WCs, 3 CWPs
£ car/tent £6.50-£8, car/caravan £6.50-£8, motorhome £6.50-£8, motorbike/tent £6.50, children £1
⚎ ✗¼ ⚓¼ 🔲 🔲 🔲 🔲 GR 🔲 TV ⚠ 🔲 Calor ⋔
➡ From M5 junction 9, take the A46 Evesham road to Teddington roundabout. At roundabout take B4077 to Stow-on-the-Wold, site 3 miles on right.

Woodlands Caravan Park
Tenterden Road, Biddenden, Tenterden TN27 8BT
📞 **01580-291216**
Open 1 March-31 October ▲ ⊟ 🚐

In the heart of the beautiful Kent countryside, Woodlands offers a perfect base for visiting all tourist attractions. Located in a picturesque and tranquil location. The channel tunnel is only 35 minutes drive. Please call for our brochure.

Size 24 acres, 100 touring pitches, 36 with electric hookup, 100 level pitches, 13 static caravans, 8 ☂, 16 WCs, 1 CWP
£ car/tent £7.50-£9, car/caravan £7.50-£9, motorhome £7.50-£9, motorbike/tent £6, children £2-£2.80
⚎ ⚎¼ 🔲 🔲 🔲 🔲 ⚠ 🔲 ⊟ Calor Gaz ♿ ⋔ WS
➡ At 1¾ miles N of Tenterden on A28 turn left onto A262 for ¾ mile. Site entrance next to Woodlands Cafe and filling station.

Mill Marina Caravan Park
Midland Road, Thrapston NN14 4JR
📞 **01832-732850**
Open 1 April-31 October ▲ ⊟ 🚐
Size 10 acres, 45 touring pitches, 20 with electric hookup, 45 level pitches, 6 static caravans, 4 ☂, 5 WCs, 1 CWP
£ car/tent £6.75-£7.75, car/caravan £8.75-£9.75, motorhome £7.75-£8.75, motorbike/tent £6.75, children £1.50
Rental ⊟ £100-£150   ➡
🔲 🔲 🔲 🔲 ⊟ Calor Gaz ⋔
Last arrival time: 9:00

← Mill Marina Caravan Park

➜ Take exit 13 on the A14 and/or the Thrapston exit from the A605. Follow camping signs.

Brades Acre Caravan Site
Near Salisbury, Tilshead SP3 4RX
☎ 01980-620402
Å ⚏ ⚏
Size 1½ acres, 26 touring pitches, 21 with electric hookup, 26 level pitches, 2 🚿, 4 WCs, 1 CWP
£ car/tent £6-£7, car/caravan £6-£7, motorhome £6-£7, motorbike/tent £6, children £0.75
℃ Visa
🔋¼ ✕¼ ⚑¼ ▣ 🔌 🗐 🗙 Calor 🐕 WS
Last arrival time: 9:00
➜ 14 miles from Salisbury on A360 to Devizes.

Headland
Atlantic Road, Tintagel PL34 0DE
☎ 01840-770239 Fax 01840-770239
Open Easter-31 October Å ⚏ ⚏

A quiet, family run park in King Arthur's Tintagel. Overlooking cliffs, close to coast path, beaches, shops, pubs etc. Ideal for walking & touring.

Size 5 acres, 60 touring pitches, 18 with electric hookup, 20 level pitches, 30 static caravans, 7 🚿, 11 WCs, 3 CWPs

£ car/tent £6-£7.50, motorhome £5.50-£7, motorbike/tent £6, children £0.50-£1
Rental ⚏
🔋 ✕¼ ⚑¼ ▣ 🔌 🗙 Calor Gaz 🚻 🐕
Last arrival time: 9:00
➜ Signposted from B3263 through village to Headlands.

Minnows Camping & Caravan Park
Sampford Peverell, Tiverton EX16 7EN
☎ 01884-821770
Open March-January Å ⚏ ⚏
Size 41 touring pitches, 31 with electric hookup, 41 level pitches, 4 🚿, 6 WCs, 1 CWP
£ car/tent £7-£8, car/caravan £7-£8, motorhome £7-£8, motorbike/tent £7, children £1
🔋¼ ✕¼ ⚑¼ 🔌 🗐 🖉 🗙 Calor Gaz 🚻 🐕
Last arrival time: 8:00
➜ From M5 junction 27 onto A361 exit after 600 yards. Signed "Sampford Peverell", right at roundabout over bridge - site ahead

Widdicombe Farm Caravan Park
Marldon, Torquay TQ3 1ST
☎ 01803-558325 Fax 01803-558325
Open Easter-mid October Å ⚏ ⚏
Size 200 touring pitches, 170 with electric hookup, 170 level pitches, 3 static caravans, 18 🚿, 20 WCs, 3 CWPs
£ car/tent £6-£10, car/caravan £6-£10, motorhome £6-£10, motorbike/tent £6
Rental ⚏ £90-£250 weekly.
🔋 ✕ ⚑ ▣ 🔌 🗐 GR 🔍 🗙 Calor 🚻 🐕 WS
Last arrival time: 9:00
➜ On the A380 Torquay to Paignton/Brixham ring road.

Dolton Camping & Caravanning
Acorn Farmhouse, The Square, Dolton EX19 8QF
☎ 01805-804536
Open mid March-mid November Å ⚏ ⚏

Small quiet family run park with grassy pitches and lovely views of open countryside. Centrally located to places of interest; short walk to local shop and three village pubs.

Size 2½ acres, 25 touring pitches, 18 level pitches, 2 ⋔, 4 WCs, 1 CWP
£ car/tent £5-£7, car/caravan £5-£7, motorhome £5-£7, motorbike/tent £5, children £0.50
🍴¼ ✗¼ ☕¼ 🔌 Calor Gaz ☂
Last arrival time: 9:00
➡ Off B3220 S of Great Torrington turn onto B3217 to Dolton. Go into village, past Union pub, turn right into Fore Street. Site drive is off Square, left of Royal Oak pub.

Greenways Valley
Torrington EX38 7EW
📞 **01805-622153** Fax **01805-622320**
Open March-October Δ ⚡ 🚐
Size 8 acres, 8 touring pitches, 8 with electric hookup, 8 level pitches, 5 static caravans, 2 ⋔, 5 WCs, 1 CWP
£ car/tent £4-£8, car/caravan £4-£8, motorhome £4-£8, motorbike/tent £4, children £1-£3
Rental ⚡ Chalet. £90-£280 weekly.
🍴 ☐ 🔌 ☐ ☒ ☒ ⚠ ☒ Calor Gaz ☂
Last arrival time: 11:00
➡ B3227 towards South Moulton and turn right at Borough Road. Take third left onto Cadwell Lane. Site is ½ mile on the right.

Smytham Manor Holidays
Little Torrington, Torrington EX38 8PU
📞 **01805-622110**
Open March-October Δ ⚡ 🚐
Size 25 acres, 40 touring pitches, 20 with electric hookup, 20 level pitches, 45 static caravans, 4 ⋔, 9 WCs, 1 CWP

£ car/tent £6.50-£9, car/caravan £6.50-£9, motorhome £6.50-£9, motorbike/tent £5
CC MasterCard Visa
🍴 ✗ ☕ ☕¼ ☐ 🔌 ☐ ☒ ☒ ☒ ☒ ⚠ ☒ ⚡ Calor Gaz & ☂ WS
Last arrival time: 24 hrs
➡ 2 miles S of Great Torrington on A386. Entrance on left past Barns Cross garage.

Camping & Caravanning Club Site
Tretheake Manor, Veryan, Truro TR2 5PP
📞 **01872-501658**
Open late March-late September Δ ⚡ 🚐
Size 120 touring pitches,
£ car/tent £8.75-£11.55, car/caravan £8.75-£11.55, motorhome £8.75-£11.55, motorbike/tent £8.75, children £1.40
CC MasterCard Visa
☐ 🔌 ☂
Last arrival time: 11:00
➡ From A390 follow A3078 through Tregony. At filling station turn right towards Portloe, site is 2½ miles.

Carnon Downs Caravan & Camping Park
Carnon Downs, Truro TR3 6JJ
📞 **01872-862283**
Open 1 April-31 October Δ ⚡ 🚐
Size 14 acres, 150 touring pitches, 100 with electric hookup, 150 level pitches, 8 ⋔, 17 WCs, 2 CWPs
CC Visa
🍴 Calor Gaz WS
➡ On A39 2½ miles W of Truro. Left side of Truro to Falmouth road.

Cosawes Caravan Park
Truro, Perranarworthal TR3 7QS
📞 **01872-863724** Fax **01872-870268**
Δ ⚡ 🚐
Size 100 acres, 40 touring pitches, 24 with electric hookup, 100 static caravans, 4 ⋔, 6 WCs, 1 CWP
£ car/tent £6, car/caravan £7, motorhome £6.50, motorbike/tent £6
Rental ⚡ £60
🍴¼ ☐ 🔌 ☐ ☒ Calor Gaz & ☂ WS
➡ 6 miles W of Truro on A39.

Leverton Place Caravan & Camping Park

Green Bottom, Truro TR4 8QW
☎ 01872-560462 Fax 01872-560668
△ ⚙ 🚐

Explore Cornwall from this family run park. Excellent, modern, clean toilet block, heated in winter. Small enclosure separated by sheltering hedges. Heated swimming pool.

Size 10 acres, 107 touring pitches, 90 with electric hookup, 97 level pitches, 15 static caravans, 25 ⋔, 38 WCs, 2 CWPs
£ car/tent £7-£15.50, car/caravan £7-£15.50, motorhome £7-£15.50, motorbike/tent £7, children £1.10-£1.20
Rental ⚙ Chalet. £100-£370
℃ MasterCard Visa
⚡ ✗ 🍴 🗑 🔌 🔲 🎿 GR 🔍 ⚠ 🎣 🔌 Calor Gaz
👤 🦮 WS
Last arrival time: 10:00
➜ 3 miles W of Truro, from A30 take A390 to Truro. At first roundabout take the road to Chacewater, right at mini-roundabout. Leverton Place is on right.

Liskey Touring Park

Greenbottom, Truro TR4 8QN
☎ 01872-560274 Fax 01872-560274
Open 1 April-30 September △ ⚙ 🚐
Size 8 acres, 68 touring pitches, 46 with electric hookup, 44 level pitches, 8 ⋔, 9 WCs, 1 CWP
£ car/tent £5.40-£9, car/caravan £5.50-£9, motorhome £5.40-£9, motorbike/tent £5.40, children £1.20-£1.50
⚡ ✗¼ 🍴 🍴¼ 🗑 🔌 🔲 🔍 📺 ⚠ 🎣 Calor Gaz
🦮 WS
Last arrival time: 9:00

➜ From A30 Bodmin-Redruth road turn left onto A390 towards Truro. In 2 miles turn right at the roundabout and then immediately right. At mini-roundabout the site is on right in 600 yards.

Ringwell Holiday Park

Bissoe Road, Carnon Downs, Truro TR3 6LQ
☎ 01872-862194 Fax 01872-864343
Open April-October △ ⚙ 🚐

Ideally situated between the north and south coasts of the south west peninsula, a picturesque, relaxing valley park set in 12 acres with open country views. Swimming pool, bar and restaurant.

Size 12 acres, 35 touring pitches, 15 with electric hookup, 30 level pitches, 37 static caravans, 5 ⋔, 16 WCs, 1 CWP
£ car/tent £5-£10, car/caravan £5-£10, motorhome £5-£10, motorbike/tent £5
Rental ⚙ caravans £120-£430
℃ MasterCard Visa
⚡ ✗ 🍴 🗑 🔌 🔲 🔍 🔍 ⚠ 🎣 Calor Gaz 🦮 WS
Last arrival time: 9:30
➜ From Truro take A39 Falmouth road to roundabout in 2 miles. Follow signs to Calnon Downs, then turn right into Bissoe Road to site ¾ mile on right.

Summer Valley Touring Park

Shortlanesend, Truro TR4 9DW
☎ 01872-77878
Open 1 April-31 October △ ⚙ 🚐

An award-winning park, centrally located for Cornwall's beaches, gardens and historic houses. Ideal for visiting in the spring for the gardens, and in the autumn for quieter moments.

Size 3 acres, 60 touring pitches, 26 with electric hookup, 30 level pitches, 6 ☔, 9 WCs, 1 CWP
£ car/tent £5.50-£7.50, car/caravan £5.50-£7.50, motorhome £5.50-£7.50, motorbike/tent £5.50, children £0.75
🔋 ✗¼ ☂¼ ⊟ 🔧 ☐ ⚠ ☒ Calor Gaz ☂
Last arrival time: 9:00
➡ From A30 turn left onto B3284 Truro road and site is 1½ miles. Or take the B3284 from Truro and site is 2½ miles

TUXFORD Nottinghamshire   8B1

Greenacres Touring Park
Lincoln Road, Tuxford NG22 0JN
📞 **01777-870264 Fax 01777-872512**
Open 15 March-31 October ▲ ⬛ ⬛
Size 4 acres, 69 touring pitches, 50 with electric hookup, 60 level pitches, 19 static caravans, 4 ☔, 11 WCs, 1 CWP
£ car/tent £6.50, car/caravan £6.50, motorhome £6.50, motorbike/tent £6.50, children £0.50
Rental ⬛ caravans £75-£150
🔋 🔋¼ ✗¼ ☂¼ ⊟ 🔧 ☐ ⚠ ☒ Calor Gaz ☂ WS
➡ From A1 follow signs. Site is on A6075, 300 yards on left after Fountain pub.

Orchard Park Touring C & C Park
Marnham Road, Tuxford NG22 0PM
📞 **01777-870228**
Open March-October ▲ ⬛ ⬛

A quiet sheltered level site set in an old orchard, with excellent facilities. Ideal for the Sherwood Forest and Robin Hood country.

Size 8 acres, 65 touring pitches, 51 with electric hookup, 65 level pitches, 5 ☔, 7 WCs, 1 CWP
£ car/tent £6.50, car/caravan £6.50, motorhome £6.50, motorbike/tent £6.50, children £0.50
🔋 ⊟ 🔧 ⚠ ☒ Calor Gaz ☂ ☂ WS
Last arrival time: 10:00
➡ Turn off A1 onto A6075 (A57 Lincoln road), turn right after ¾ mile into Marnham Road, site on right after ¾ mile.

ULLSWATER Cumbria   10B2

Cove Caravan & Camping Park
Watermillock, Penrith CA11 0LS
📞 **01768-486549**
Open 1 March-31 October ▲ ⬛ ⬛
Size 5 acres, 50 touring pitches, 17 with electric hookup, 25 level pitches, 39 static caravans, 4 ☔, 8 WCs, 1 CWP
£ car/tent £6-£6.40, car/caravan £7.50-£8, motorhome £6-£6.40, motorbike/tent £6
Rental ⬛ £160-£220
🔋¼ ⊟ 🔧 ☐ ⚠ ☒ Calor Gaz ☂ ☂
Last arrival time: 21.30 - 12
➡ From M6 junction 40 take A66 to Keswick and at next roundabout take A592 to Ullswater. At the 'T' junction turn right. At Brackenrigs Hotel turn right and park is 1½ miles on left.

Hillcroft Park
Pooley Bridge, Ullswater CA10 2LT
📞 **01768-486363 Fax 01768-486010**
Open 10 March-31 October ▲ ⬛ ⬛
Size 21 acres, 25 touring pitches, 6 with electric hookup, 6 level pitches, 200 static caravans, 20 ☔, 36 WCs, 3 CWPs
£ car/tent £8-£11, car/caravan £11, motorhome £8-£11, motorbike/tent £8, children £1.50
🔋 ✗¼ ☂¼ ⊟ 🔧 ☐ ⚠ ☒ Calor Gaz ☂ ☂
➡ From M6 junction 40 take A66 towards Keswick, then A592 to Ullswater. At the head of the lake turn right, go through Pooley Bridge and bear right at church. Head straight through crossroads to site on left.

Park Foot Caravan & Camping Park

Howtown Road, Pooley Bridge, Ullswater CA10 2NA

☎ **01768-486309 Fax 01768-486041**

Open 15 March-31 October ⚊ 🚐 🚕

Size 20 acres, 110 touring pitches, 200 level pitches, 129 static caravans, 24 ☂, 50 WCs, 2 CWPs

£ car/tent £7-£10, car/caravan £12-£15, motorhome £7-£10, motorbike/tent £7, children £1

Rental Houses/log cabins - £40 night, £180-£480 week.

🔌 ✕ 🍽 ▣ 🔋 ▤ 🖳 🗝 🗔 GR ▣ TV ⟋ ⊠ 🔌 Calor Gaz 🚻 🐕

Last arrival time: 11:00

➤ From M6 junction 40 take A66 Keswick road. Take the A592 to Ullswater. At the 'T' junction turn left. At Pooley Bridge turn right and right again at crossroads. Site is 1 mile down the Howtown road on left.

Quiet Site

Watermillock, Ullswater CA11 0LS

☎ **01768-486337**

Open 1 March-14 November ⚊ 🚐 🚕

PARK FOOT
CARAVAN & CAMPING PARK

Size 6 acres, 60 touring pitches, 47 with electric hookup, 53 level pitches, 23 static caravans, 8 ☂, 15 WCs, 1 CWP

🔌 🔋 ▣ GR ▣ TV ⟋ ⊠ 🔌 Calor Gaz WS

Last arrival time: 9:00

➤ From M6 junction 40 take A66 to Keswick. After ¾ mile turn left onto A592 (signed Ullswater). After 4 miles turn right at T-junction. After 1½ miles turn right at Bracherring Hotel. Site is on right after 1½ miles

Waterfoot Caravan Park

Pooley Bridge, Ullswater CA11 0JF

☎ **01768-486302**

Open March-October 🚐 🚕

22 acres with level and sloping pitches. Sheltered quiet country park. Touring vans only. 5 mins walk to lake, good access to Lakeland Fells for walking.

Size 22 acres, 57 touring pitches, 57 with electric hookup, 30 level pitches, 123 static caravans, 6 ☂, 10 WCs, 1 CWP

£ car/caravan £11.50-£13

🔌 🍽 ▣ 🔋 ▣ ⟋ ⊠ Calor 🚻 🐕

➤ From junction 40 of M6 take A66 for 1 mile and then A592 to Ullswater. Park is on right 6 miles from M6.

Camping & Caravanning Club Site

Over Weir, Umberleigh EX37 9DU

☎ **01769-560009**

Open late March-early November ⚊ 🚐 🚕

Size 60 touring pitches, 34 with electric hookup, 6 ☂, 9 WCs, 1 CWP

£ car/tent £8.75-£11.55, car/caravan £8.75-
£11.55, motorhome £8.75-£11.55,
motorbike/tent £8.75, children £1.40
℀ MasterCard Visa
🔲 📞 ⬚ ⬚ ⬚ 🐾
Last arrival time: 11:00
➜ S from Barnstaple on A377. Turn right at
Umberleigh sign. Turn right again and
follow club sign.

WADEBRIDGE Cornwall   2B3

Dinham Farm Caravan & Camping Park

St Minver, Wadebridge PL27 6RH
📞 **01208-812878**
Open April-October 🏕 🚐 🚚

Lovely, secluded, family park overlooking the River Camel, surrounded by trees and shrubs, offering super pitch hookups and heated pool. Near Rock, Polzeath and Daymer Bay.

Size 2½ acres, 40 touring pitches, 15 with electric hookup, 20 level pitches, 20 static caravans, 4 🚿, 12 WCs, 1 CWP
£ car/tent £6, car/caravan £6, motorhome £5-£6, motorbike/tent £5, children £0.75-£1
Rental 🚐
🔲 📞 ⬚ ⬚ GR ⬚ TV ⬚ ⬚ Calor Gaz 🐾
➜ From Wadebridge travel on B3314 for 3 miles. Site on left.

Lanarth Hotel & Caravan Park

St Kew Highway, Bodmin, Wadebridge PL30 3EE
📞 **01208-841215**
Open end March-end October 🏕 🚐 🚚
Size 10 acres, 86 touring pitches, 9 with electric hookup, 40 level pitches, 4 🚿, 1 WCs, 1 CWP
✗ 🍴 📞 ⬚ ⬚ ⬚ ⬚ Calor WS
Last arrival time: any time

➜ On the A39 at St Kew Highway

Little Bodieve Holiday Park

Bodieve, Wadebridge PL27 6EG
📞 **01208-812323**
Open 1 April-31 October 🏕 🚐 🚚
Size 22 acres, 195 touring pitches, 60 with electric hookup, 195 level pitches, 76 static caravans, 24 🚿, 20 WCs, 5 CWPs
£ car/tent £6-£9, car/caravan £6-£9, motorhome £6-£9, motorbike/tent £6, children £1.50-£2.20
Rental 🚐 caravans £100-£390
℀ MasterCard Visa
🔅 ✗ 🍴 🔲 📞 ⬚ GR ⬚ ⬚ ⬚ Calor Gaz ♿ 🐾 WS
Last arrival time: 8:00
➜ 1 mile N of Wadebridge, just off A39. Take B3314 toward Rock and Port Isaac.

Southwinds Caravan & Camping Site

Polzeath, St Minver, Wadebridge PL27 6QU
📞 **01208-863267** Fax **01208-862080**
Open Easter-October 🏕 🚐 🚚
Size 6 acres, 50 touring pitches, 40 with electric hookup, 50 level pitches, 8 🚿, 14 WCs, 1 CWP   ➜

← Southwinds Caravan & Camping Site

CC MasterCard Visa
🌮 📞 🗄 ⚿ 🎇 Calor Gaz ♿
➡ 7 miles N of Wadebridge on the B3314.
Follow the signs to Polzeath.

St Minver Holiday Park
St Minver, Wadebridge PL27 6RR
📞 **01208-862305 Fax 01208-862265**
Open Easter-October ▲ ⊕
Size 44 acres, 120 touring pitches, 24 with
electric hookup, 123 static caravans, 15 🚿,
17 WCs
🐾 🌮 🗻 🎡 ♿
➡ A39 to Wadebridge, then B3314. Turn
right at mini roundabout heading for Port
Isaac. After 3 miles turn left to Rock and
park is 250 yards on right.

WAKEFIELD West Yorkshire   **11D4**

Nostell Priory Holiday Park
Nostell, Wakefield WF4 1QD
📞 **01924-863938 Fax 01924-862226**

Riverside Village
HOLIDAY PARK

*Why not come for a peaceful weekend or holiday at
our friendly family-run retreat. Alongside the River
Crouch in the countryside yet only 20 minutes from
Southend. We have a large playground, boule pitch
and special dog walks, with windsurfing, fishing,
marina and pub – all within 2 minutes. Try the ferry
to Burnham at the weekend or one of the special
evening boat trips. Enjoy the pleasant walks that
seem to end up at an 'Olde Worlde Inn'.
Or just relax in our peaceful and immaculate park.*

**WALLASEA ISLAND,
ROCHFORD, ESSEX SS4 2EY
Tel: (01702) 258297   Fax: (01702) 258555**

Open April-September ▲ ⊕ 🚐
Size 35 acres, 60 touring pitches, 60 with
electric hookup, 60 level pitches, 80 static
caravans, 8 🚿, 12 WCs, 1 CWP
£ car/tent £8-£9, car/caravan £8-£9,
motorhome £8-£9, children £0.50
🗄 📞 🗄 ⚿ 🎇 Calor Gaz 🔦 WS
Last arrival time: 9:00
➡ From A38 Wakefield to Doncaster road
turn left at Foulby.

WALLASEA ISLAND Essex   **5E2**

Riverside Village Holiday Park
Wallasea Island, Rochford SS4 2EY
📞 **01702-258297 Fax 01702-258555**
Open 1 March-31 October ▲ ⊕ 🚐

*A high quality, peaceful, family run park,
convenient for watersports and walking.
Ferry and boat trips can be arranged.*

Size 24 acres, 60 touring pitches, 36 with
electric hookup, 60 level pitches, 150 static
caravans, 4 🚿, 15 WCs, 2 CWPs
£ car/tent £2.50-£5, car/caravan £8-£9,
motorhome £8-£9, motorbike/tent £2.50
🐾¼ ✗¼ 🌮¼ 🗄 📞 🗄 ⚿ 🎇 Calor Gaz 🔦 WS
➡ A127 to Rochford, follow the caravan
signs through Hingdon to Wallasea, or A130
Battlesbridge past Hullbridge for Ashingdon
and Wallasea

WALLINGFORD Oxfordshire   **4B2**

Bridge Villa International Camping & Caravan Site
Crowmarsh Gifford, Wallingford OX10 8HB
📞 **01491-836860 Fax 01491-839103**
Open 1 March-31 October ▲ ⊕ 🚐   →

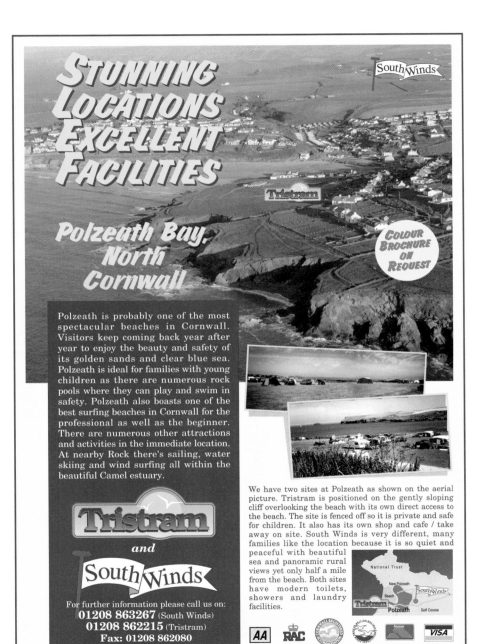

← Bridge Villa International

£ car/tent £6, car/caravan £6, motorhome £6, motorbike/tent £5, children £0.50
🏕 🏕¼ ✗¼ 🚽¼ 📞 🚰 Calor 🚻 ⛽ WS
➤ Site located off A4130.

Riverside Park
Crowmarsh, Hamble, Wallingford OX10 5EB
📞 01491-835232
Open 1 May-30 September 🛶 ⛺ 🚐
Size 1 acre, 25 touring pitches, 6 🚿, 6 WCs
🔲 Gaz
➤ A34 to Didcot, then follow the sign to Wallingford. Go over the main road bridge, then take the first left.

Camping & Caravanning Club Site
Theobalds Park, Bulls Cross Ride, Waltham Abbey
📞 01992-620604
Open late March-early November 🛶 ⛺ 🚐
Size 14 acres, 150 touring pitches, 12 with electric hookup, 4 🚿, 6 WCs, 1 CWP

£ car/tent £8.20-£10.40, car/caravan £8.20-£10.40, motorhome £8.20-£10.40, motorbike/tent £8.20, children £1.30
《 MasterCard Visa
⬛ 📞 GR 🅿 🔲 🚻 WS
Last arrival time: 11:00
➤ Leave M25 (jn 25), get in right hand lane, go under motorway, then right at traffic lights. Follow signs for Crews Hill, then Bulls Cross to site on right.

Birchwood Tourist Park
Bere Road, Coldharbour, Wareham BH20 7PA
📞 01929-554763
Open March-October 🛶 ⛺ 🚐

Large level, well drained pitches with direct access to forest trails on foot, bike or horseback. Situated in the centre of Wareham Forest.

Size 46 acres, 175 touring pitches, 82 with electric hookup, 175 level pitches, 14 ♠, 20 WCs, 2 CWPs
🏕 ➼ 🔟 🛢 🟥 🇬🇷 🔲 ⚠ 🗙 Calor Gaz ⟟ ⟟
Last arrival time: 10:00
➼ From A35 E of Bere Regis follow signs to Wareham. Second touring park on left.

Lookout Holiday Park
Stoborough, Wareham BH20 5AZ
📞 **01929-552546** Fax **01929-552546**
Open February-November ⚑ ⟟ ⟟

A quiet, family park, ideally situated for exploring the Purbecks. Touring pitches available on hardstandings or grass. Fully equipped caravans with colour TV for hire.

Size 15 acres, 150 touring pitches, 107 with electric hookup, 150 level pitches, 90 static caravans, 10 ♠, 17 WCs, 2 CWPs
£ car/tent £8.50-£10.50, car/caravan £8.50-£10.50, motorhome £8.50-£10.50, motorbike/tent £8.50
Rental ⟟ £90-£345
🏕 ➼ 🔟 🛢 🗙 🇬🇷 🔲 ⚠ 🗙 Calor Gaz WS
Last arrival time: 10:00
➼ From centre of Wareham proceed S to Swanage. Cross over River Frome, pass through village of Stoborough. Park on left of main road.

Manor Farm Caravan Park
East Stoke, Wareham BH20 6AW
📞 **01929-462870**
Open April-September ⚑ ⟟ ⟟
Size 2½ acres, 40 touring pitches, 30 with electric hookup, 40 level pitches, 4 ♠, 8 WCs, 1 CWP

£ car/tent £6.50-£8.50, car/caravan £6.50-£8.50, motorhome £6.50-£8.50, motorbike/tent £6.50
🏕 🔟 🛢 ⚠ 🗙 Calor Gaz ⟟
Last arrival time: 10:00

Wareham Forest Tourist Park
North Trigon, Wareham BH20 7NZ
📞 **01929-551393**
Open all year ⚑ ⟟ ⟟

Enjoy the peace and tranquillity of this site set in 42 acres of forest. An ideal base for exploring Dorset, with its sandy beaches and coves.

Size 42 acres, 175 with electric hookup, 25 ♠, 30 WCs, 1 CWP
🏕 🗙 ➼ 🔟 🔲 🇬🇷 ⚠ 🗙 Calor Gaz ⟟ ⟟ WS
➼ Off A35 between Wareham and Bere Regis.

WARRINGTON Cheshire 7E1

Hollybank Caravan Park
Warburton Bridge Road, Rixton, Warrington WA3 6HU
📞 **0161-775 2842**
Open all year ⚑ ⟟ ⟟
Size 9 acres, 75 touring pitches, 60 with electric hookup, 60 level pitches, 7 ♠, 10 WCs, 2 CWPs
£ car/tent £8.50-£10, car/caravan £9.50-£11, motorhome £9.50-£11, motorbike/tent £8.50, children £1
🏕 🏕¼ 🗙¼ ➼¼ 🔟 🛢 🇬🇷 🔲 ⚠ 🗙 Calor Gaz ⟟ ⟟ WS
Last arrival time: 9:00
➼ 2 miles E of M6 junction 21 on the A57 (Irlam). Turn right at lights into Warburton Bridge Road and site is on right.

Washington Caravan and Camping Park

London Road, Washington RH20 4AJ
☎ 01903-892869 Fax 01903-893252
Open all year 🛆 ⚏ ⛺
Size 4½ acres, 100 touring pitches, 20 with electric hookup, 4 ☕, 10 WCs, 1 CWP
£ car/tent £8.50, car/caravan £7.50, motorhome £7.50, motorbike/tent £8.50, children £3
℃ MasterCard Visa
🛒 🛒¼ ✕¼ 🖳 🛒 Calor Gaz ♿ 🐾
➜ N of Washington on A283. E of roundabout with A24, signposted South Downs Way. Site is below Chanctonbury Ring.

Doniford Bay Holiday Park

Watchet TA23 0TJ
☎ 01984-632423 Fax 01984-633649

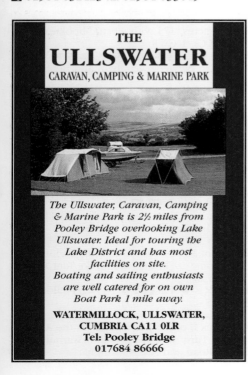

Open Easter-October 🛆 ⚏ ⛺
Size 55 acres, 120 touring pitches, 58 with electric hookup, 40 level pitches, 350 static caravans, 12 ☕, 23 WCs, 3 CWPs
℃ MasterCard Visa
🛒 🛒 🛒 🛒 🛒 🛒 🛒 🛒 ⚏ 🛒 🛒 Calor
Last arrival time: 10:00
➜ Leave M5 at junction 23 and follow Minehead signs on A39 until you get to West Quantoxhead. Fork right after St Audries garage. Site signposted on right in 1½ miles.

Warren Bay Caravan & Camping Park

Watchet TA23 0JR
☎ 01984-631460 Fax 01984-633999
🛆 ⚏ ⛺
Size 22 acres, 180 touring pitches, 30 with electric hookup, 15 level pitches, 155 static caravans, 12 ☕, 27 WCs, 2 CWPs
£ car/tent £3.50-£4, car/caravan £3.50-£6, motorhome £3.50-£4.50, motorbike/tent £3.50, children £1
Rental ⚏ £129-£205
℃ Visa
🛒 🛒 🛒 🛒 🛒 GR ⚏ 🛒 Calor Gaz ♿ WS
➜ From M5 junction 23 take A39 for 17 miles. Then B3191 at Watchet and follow sign for Blue Anchor.

Ullswater Caravan Camping Site

Watermillock, Ullswater CA11 0LR
☎ 01768-486666
Open 1 March-14 November 🛆 ⚏ ⛺

Situated in scenic countryside with its own lake access and ½ mile from Lake Ullswater. Ideal for touring the Lake District.

Size 14 acres, 40 touring pitches, 40 with electric hookup, 40 level pitches, 55 static caravans, 20 🚿, 35 WCs, 2 CWPs
£ car/tent £8, car/caravan £8, motorhome £6, motorbike/tent £8, children £1
Rental 🚐 Chalet. £150-£350
🛒 ♨ 🗄 🛒 🗑 GR TV 🅿 🎣 🔌 Calor Gaz ♿ ♞
Last arrival time: 9:00
➡ From M6 junction 40 take A592 to Ullswater, turn right at telephone kiosk, signposted Longthwaite and Watermillock church.

Gamlins Farm Caravan Site
Greenham, Wellington TA21 0LZ
📞 01823-672596 Fax 01823-672324
Open 28 March-September A 🚐 🏕

Pleasant, quiet site with excellent views. Children's play area. Coarse fishing available nearby. Swimming pool four miles.

Size 3 acres, 25 touring pitches, 25 with electric hookup, 25 level pitches, 4 🚿, 5 WCs, 1 CWP
£ car/tent £5-£7, car/caravan £6-£7, motorhome £6-£7, motorbike/tent £5, children £0.50
🛒 🗄 🛒 🗑 📮 ♞
Last arrival time: 8:00
➡ From Wellington SW on A38 for 5 miles. Turn right at sign for caravan park.

Mendip Heights Caravan & Camping Park
Priddy, Wells BA5 3BP
📞 01749-870241 Fax 01749-870241

Open 1 March-15 November A 🚐 🏕
Size 4¼ acres, 90 touring pitches, 10 with electric hookup, 40 level pitches, 1 static caravan, 4 🚿, 11 WCs, 1 CWP
£ car/tent £5.90-£6.40, car/caravan £5.90-£6.40, motorhome £5.90-£6.40, motorbike/tent £5.90, children £1.50
🛒 ✕¼ 🗄 🛒 🗑 🔍 🅿 🎣 Calor Gaz ♞ WS
Last arrival time: 11:30
➡ From Wells take A39 towards Bristol for 3 miles. Turn left at Green Ore traffic lights onto B3135 for 5 miles, then turn left at camp site sign.

Lower Lacon Caravan Park
Lerdene, Crabtree Lane, Wemsbrook Road, Wem SY4 5RP
📞 01939-232376 Fax 01939-233606
Open all year A 🚐 🏕
Size 48 acres, 270 touring pitches, 120 with electric hookup, 80 level pitches, 50 static caravans, 12 🚿, 25 WCs, 3 CWPs   ➡

← **Lower Lacon Caravan Park**

£ car/tent £9-£9.50, car/caravan £9-£9.50, motorhome £9-£9.50, motorbike/tent £5
CC MasterCard Visa
🐾 ✕ 🛒 🅿 🔌 🗑 🔲 GR TV ⚠ 🔲 🔌 Calor Gaz ♿ 🐕 WS
Last arrival time: 24 hrs
➔ From A49 take B506 to Wem. Go over level crossing onto B5065 Market Drayton road. Park is 1 mile on left.

WEST WITTERING West Sussex   4C4

Scotts Farm Camping Site
West Wittering PO20 8ED
📞 **01243-671720** Fax **01243-513669**
⚠ 🔌 🚐

Spacious family run site set in 30 acres of level grassland. Village and beach within easy walking distance, lovely country walks, play area, super pitches available.

Size 25 acres, 330 touring pitches, 130 with electric hookup, 330 level pitches, 29 🚿, 43 WCs, 3 CWPs
£ car/tent £8-£9, car/caravan £8-£9, motorhome £8-£9, motorbike/tent £8
🐾¼ ✕¼ 🛒¼ 🅿 🔌 🗑 ⚠ 🔲 Calor Gaz 🐕
Last arrival time: 11:30
➔ A286 from A27 to Chichester. After 4 miles turn left to East Wittering/Bracklesham Bay just past self service station on right. Carry on for 1 mile, turn right past Lively Lady pub. Go past East Wittering village and site on right.

WESTON-SUPER-MARE Somerset   3E1

Airport View Caravan Park
Moor Lane, Worle, Weston-super-Mare RS29 7LA
📞 **01934-622168** Fax **01934-628245**
Open 1 March-31 October ⚠ 🔌 🚐
Size 6½ acres, 200 touring pitches, 40 static caravans, 10 🚿, 15 WCs, 1 CWP
£ car/tent £5-£7.50, car/caravan £5-£7.50, motorhome £5-£7.50, children £0.50
Rental 🔌
CC MasterCard Visa
🐾 ✕ 🛒 🅿 🔌 GR ⚠ 🔲 🔌 ♿ 🐕 WS
Last arrival time: 9:00
➔ Opposite Airport (A371) turn into Moor Lane. Site 100 yards.

Country View Caravan & Touring Park
Sand Road, Sand Bay, Weston-super-Mare BS22 9UJ
📞 **01934-627595**
Open March-October ⚠ 🔌 🚐
Size 120 touring pitches, 82 with electric hookup, 120 level pitches, 65 static caravans, 8 🚿, 12 WCs, 1 CWP
£ car/tent £4-£12, car/caravan £6.50-£12, motorhome £6.50-£12, motorbike/tent £4
Rental 🔌 £90-£295
CC MasterCard Visa
🐾 ✕¼ 🛒¼ 🅿 🔌 🔲 GR ⚠ 🔲 🔌 Calor Gaz ♿ 🐕 WS
Last arrival time: 10:00
➔ From M5 (jn 21) follow signs to Weston-super-Mare, and then 100 yards bear left to Kewstoke/Sand Bay. Turn right at Homebase DIY store and go straight over three roundabouts. Turn right into Sand Road and site on right.

Dulhorn Farm Camping Site
Weston Road, Lympsham, Weston-super-Mare BS24 0JQ
📞 **01943-750298** Fax **01934-750913**
Open March-October ⚠ 🔌 🚐
Size 2 acres, 42 touring pitches, 28 with electric hookup, 42 level pitches, 3 static caravans, 2 🚿, 5 WCs, 1 CWP
£ car/tent £4.50-£6.50, car/caravan £4.50-£6.50, motorhome £4.50-£6.50, motorbike/tent £4.50
Rental 🔌 Chalet. £80-£218

✕¼ ▬¼ ⚠ ☒ Calor Gaz ⚲ WS
Last arrival time: 8:00
➜ From A38 take A370 to Weston-super-Mare. Site is ¼ mile on left.

Oak Farm Touring Park
Congresbury, Weston-super-Mare BS19 5EB
☎ 01934-833246
Open April-October ⚑ ⊕ ☒
Size 2 acres, 27 touring pitches, 20 with electric hookup, 4 ☔, 6 WCs
£ car/caravan £7.50-£10.50
▬¼ ✕¼ ▬¼ ☒ ☐ WS
Last arrival time: 11:00
➜ On A370, midway between Weston-super-Mare and Bristol, 4 miles from M5 junction 21.

Purn International Holiday Park
Bridgwater Road (A370), Bleadon, Weston-super-Mare BS24 0AN
☎ 01934-812342
Open 1 March-7 November ⚑ ⊕ ☒

Touring, camping, holiday homes, hire sales. Heated swimming pools. Free live entertainment plus dancing, bingo, children's club, licensed club and own Anchor Inn Pub.

Size 11 acres, 60 touring pitches, 40 with electric hookup, 60 level pitches, 110 static caravans, 6 ☔, 12 WCs, 2 CWPs
£ car/tent £5.50-£9.50, car/caravan £6.50-£9.50, motorhome £6-£9, motorbike/tent £5, children £0.75
Rental ⊕ caravans £115-£285
▬ ✕ ▬ ☒ ☒ ☐ ☒ ☒ ⚠ ☒ ⊟ Calor Gaz ⚲
WS
Last arrival time: 12:00

➜ From junction 21 take signs for Western & Hospital. Turn right at hospital roundabout onto A370. Site 1 mile on right after Anchor Inn pub.

West End Farm Caravan Park
Locking, Weston-super-Mare BS24 8RH
☎ 01934-822529
⚑ ⊕ ☒
Size 80 touring pitches, 80 with electric hookup, 20 static caravans, 4 ☔, 15 WCs, 1 CWP
£ car/tent £7-£8.40, car/caravan £7-£8.40, motorhome £7-£8.40, children £1.10-£1.30
CC MasterCard Visa
▬ ✕¼ ▬¼ ☐ ☒ ☒ ⚠ ☒ Calor ♿ ⚲ WS
Last arrival time: 10:00
➜ Leave M5 (jn 21) onto A370. Follow signs to International Helicopter Museum and take next turning on right after museum. Follow signs to site.

Weston Gateway Tourist Park
West Wick, Weston-super-Mare BS24 7TF
☎ 01934-510344
Open all year ⚑ ⊕ ☒   ➜

← Weston Gateway Tourist Park

Amenities on this level, grassy site include a club with bar, restaurant and TV lounge, and children's play area. Swimming pool three miles. Families and couples only.

Size 15 acres, 105 with electric hookup, 14 ℞, 59 WCs, 1 CWP
☎ ● ▯ ▢ ▥ △ ☒ ▯ Calor Gaz ♿ WS
Last arrival time: 11:30
➜ Leave M5 junction 21 to Weston-super-Mare. Branch left for West Wick. Park is on right after 500 yards.

Bagwell Farm Touring Park
Chickerell, Weymouth DT3 4EA
☎ 01305-782575
Open March-October ▲ ⛺ 🚐
Size 14 acres, 320 touring pitches, 174 with electric hookup, 320 level pitches, 12 ℞, 38 WCs, 1 CWP
☎ ✕¼ ● ▯ ▢ GR △ ☒ Calor Gaz ♿ WS
Last arrival time: 11:00
➜ 4 miles W of Weymouth on B3157, 500 yards past Victoria Inn.

East Fleet Farm Touring Park
Chickerell, Weymouth DT3 4DW
☎ 01305-785768
Open 15 March-15 January ▲ ⛺ 🚐

Family run park with modern amenities, in a peaceful and spacious setting on the edge of Fleet Water overlooking Chesil Beach and the sea.

Size 20 acres, 150 touring pitches, 80 with electric hookup, 150 level pitches, 17 ℞, 42 WCs, 2 CWPs
£ car/tent £4.50-£9, car/caravan £4.50-£9, motorhome £4.50-£9, motorbike/tent £4.50, children £0.25
☎ ☎¼ ▢ ▯ ▢ △ ☒ Calor Gaz ♿ ☇
➜ Off B3157, left at Chickerell TA camp.

Littlesea Holiday Park
Lynch Lane, Weymouth DT4 9DT
☎ 01305-774414 Fax 01305-760038
Open Easter-October ▲ ⛺
Size 210 touring pitches, 140 with electric hookup, 190 level pitches, 200 static caravans, 32 ℞, 30 WCs,
CC Visa

⚑ ⬤ 🔲 🔲 ⏚

➜ Head for Chicherall/Portland. At traffic lights go straight ahead into Benville Road, turn right and then left at next traffic lights into Lynch Lane. The park is at the end.

Osmington Mills
Weymouth DT3 6HB
📞 01305-832311 Fax 01305-835251

A family run holiday park where you can enjoy a friendly, relaxed atmosphere in the Dorset coastal countryside, or at nearby Weymouth, with all the facilities of a popular holiday resort.

Size 13 acres, 25 touring pitches, 225 level pitches, 62 static caravans, 18 🍴, 36 WCs, 1 CWP
⚑ ⬤ 🔲 ⏚ Calor Gaz WS
➜ 5 miles E of Weymouth, off A353 Weymouth to Wareham road, turn S at Osmington to Osmington Mills.

Pebble Bank Caravan Park
Camp Road, Wyke Regis, Weymouth DT4 9HF
📞 01305-774844 Fax 01305-774844
Open 1 April-early October ▲ ⏾ ⛺

Quiet family park in a picturesque situation close to Weymouth centre, with superb views.

Size 8 acres, 45 touring pitches, 40 with electric hookup, 40 level pitches, 95 static caravans, 5 🍴, 10 WCs, 1 CWP
£ car/tent £5-£9, car/caravan £6-£12, motorhome £5-£9, motorbike/tent £5, children £1
Rental ⏾ £125-£325
⚑¼ ✕¼ ⬤¼ 🔲 🔲 🔲 🔲 🔲 🔲 🔲 Calor Gaz 🐴
Last arrival time: 10:00
➜ From harbour roundabout at Weymouth continue up hill to mini roundabout opposite Rodwell pub. Turn right onto Wyke Road. Camp Road is 1 mile further on at the apex of sharp right hand bend at the bottom of hill.

Seaview Holiday Park
Preston, Weymouth DT3 6DZ
📞 01305-833037 Fax 01305-833169

Size 75 touring pitches, 7 🍴, 23 WCs
⚑ ⬤ 🔲 🔲 ⏚
➜ Take A353 from centre of Weymouth along seawall to Preston. Seaview is ½ mile beyond village up hill on right.

West Fleet Holiday Farm
Fleet, Weymouth DT3 4EF
📞 01305-782218 Fax 01305-775396
Open Easter-31 October ▲ ⏾ ⛺

Scenic sea and countryside views near the Fleet Nature Reserve. Closely mown grass, tree shelter and tarmac roads on site.

Size 20 acres, 250 touring pitches, 30 with electric hookup, 1 static caravan, 18 🍴, 28 WCs, 2 CWPs
£ car/tent £6.50-£11, motorhome £6.50-£11, motorbike/tent £6.50, children £1.50
Rental ⏾ Chalet.

➜

← West Fleet Holiday Farm

⚒ ✕ 🛞 🔲 🔲 🔲 🔲 🔲 ⚠ 🔲 🔲 Calor Gaz ⚡
Last arrival time: 9:30
➡ On coast W of Weymouth. Turn off the
B3157 Weymouth to Bridport road at
Chickerell mini-roundabout to Fleet. Park is
1 mile on right.

Weymouth Bay Holiday Park
Preston, Weymouth DT3 6BQ
📞 **01305-832271** Fax **01305-835101**
Open Easter-end October ▲
Size 75 touring pitches, 50 with electric
hookup, 75 level pitches, 65 static caravans,
8 🔲, 10 WCs,
⚒ ✕ 🔲 🔲 🔲 🔲 🔲 ⚓
➡ 3 miles from Weymouth sea front on
Preston Road.

Merebrook Caravan Park
Derby Road, Whatstandwell DE4 5HH
📞 **01773-852154**

Open all year ▲ 🔲 🔲
Size 11 acres, 50 touring pitches, 28 with
electric hookup, 50 level pitches, 116 static
caravans, 12 🔲, 24 WCs, 4 CWPs
£ car/tent £7, car/caravan £7, motorhome
£7-£8, motorbike/tent £1
Rental ▲ 🔲 Chalet.
🔲 🔲 Calor Gaz ♿ ⚡
Last arrival time: 11:00
➡ Entrance on A6 600 yards from river
bridge at Whatstandwell. 15 miles from
Derby and 5 miles from Matlock.

Hollins Farm
Glaisdale, Whitby YO21 2PZ
📞 **01947-897516**
Open Easter ▲
Size 1 acre, 2 🔲, 2 WCs,
£ car/tent £1.50, motorbike/tent £1.50
⚒¼ ✕¼ 🔲 ⚡

➜ From A171 take road to Glaisdale for 4 miles. In Glaisdale, opposite phone box, road leads up round church. Come up that road for 1½ miles, to site on left, 100 yards down a tarmac drive.

Middlewood Farm Holiday Park
Fylingthorpe, Robin Hood's Bay, Whitby YO22 4UF
📞 01947-880414 Fax 01947-880414
Open Easter-31 October Å 🚐 🚟
Size 6 acres, 20 touring pitches, 120 level pitches, 30 static caravans, 8 🚿, 18 WCs, 1 CWP
£ car/tent £6.50-£7.50, car/caravan £6.50-£7.50, motorhome £6.50-£7.50, motorbike/tent £6.50, children £0.50
Rental 🚐 statics £90-£295
🐕¼ ✗¼ 🚐¼ 🔟 📞 🗑 🔥 🏓 Calor Gaz 🐕
Last arrival time: 11:00
➜ 2½ miles S of Whitby on A171 turn E on B1447. After 1½ miles turn right to Fylingthorpe. At village crossroads continue straight ahead to park on Middlewood Lane.

Northcliffe Holiday Park
High Hawsker, Whitby YO22 4LL
📞 01947-880477 Fax 01947-880972
Open 15 March-31 October Å 🚐 🚟

A secluded family park situated on the beautiful, unspoilt Heritage Coast, between Whitby and Robin Hood's Bay, with panoramic sea views.

Size 26 acres, 30 touring pitches, 30 with electric hookup, 16 level pitches, 161 static caravans, 6 🚿, 10 WCs, 1 CWP
£ car/tent £4-£9.50, car/caravan £4-£9.50, motorhome £4-£9.50, motorbike/tent £4
Rental 🚐
℀ MasterCard Visa

🐕 🚐 🔟 📞 🇬🇧 🔥 🏓 Calor Gaz 🚹 🐕
Last arrival time: 9:00
➜ 3 miles S of Whitby on the A171 turn left onto B1447 (High Hawsker-Robin Hoods Bay). Through village and at top of hill turn left into a private lane for ½ mile.

Sandfield House Farm Caravan Park
Sandsend Road, Whitby YO21 35R
📞 01947-602660
Open March-October Å 🚐 🚟

Quiet, clean park set in beautiful undulating countryside in National Park. Quarter of a mile from long sandy beach. One mile to Whitby centre. Lovely walks and sea views.

Size 12 acres, 50 with electric hookup, 50 level pitches, 16 🚿, 22 WCs, 1 CWP
£ car/tent £6-£8, car/caravan £6-£8, motorhome £6-£8
🐕¼ ✗¼ 🚐¼ 🔟 📞 Calor Gaz 🐕
Last arrival time: 11:00
➜ 1 mile N of Whitby on A174 coast road to Sandsend, opposite golf course.

Whitby Holiday Park
Whitby YO22 4JX
📞 01947-602664 Fax 01947-850356
Å 🚐
Size 20 acres, 250 touring pitches, 30 with electric hookup, 100 level pitches, 50 static caravans, 13 🚿, 14 WCs
🐕 🚐 🍴
➜ Follow directions for Whitby Abbey, at the top of Green Lane turn right towards High Hawsker, second caravan park on left.

York House Caravan Park
High Hawkser, Whitby YO22 4LW
📞 **01947-880354 Fax 01256-896628**
Open 21 March-31 October ⛺ 🚐 🚃
Size 4 acres, 59 touring pitches, 59 with electric hookup, 20 level pitches, 41 static caravans, 8 🚿, 13 WCs, 1 CWP
£ car/tent £6.50-£7.50, car/caravan £6.50-£7.50, motorhome £6.50-£7.50, motorbike/tent £6.50, children £0.50
🛒 🛒¼ ✗¼ 🚰¼ 🔲 🔦 🗑 ⚠ 🎣 Calor Gaz 🐕 WS
Last arrival time: 10:00
➡ 3 miles S of Whitby on A171.

Hillcrest Camp Site
Southampton Road, Whiteparish SP5 2QW
📞 **01794-884471**
Open all year ⛺ 🚐 🚃
Size 2½ acres, 30 touring pitches, 12 with electric hookup, 15 level pitches, 3 🚿, 5 WCs, 1 CWP
£ car/tent £6.50, car/caravan £6.50, motorhome £6.50, motorbike/tent £6.50, children £1.50
🔲 🔦 🗑 Calor Gaz 🐕
Last arrival time: 10:00
➡ The entrance is off A36, Southampton to Salisbury road, 1¼ miles SE of the junction with A27. 8 miles from Salisbury, 13 miles from Southampton.

Seaview Caravan Park
St John's Road, Swalecliffe CT5 2RY
📞 **01227-373848 Fax 01227-740901**
Open Easter-31 October ⛺ 🚐 🚃
Size 100 acres, 46 touring pitches, 46 with electric hookup, 452 static caravans, 4 🚿, 8 WCs, 1 CWP
🛒 ✗ ✗¼ 🚰 🔦 🗑 GR ⚠ 🎣 🍴 Calor Gaz ♿
Last arrival time: 10:00
➡ Leave A299 at Chestfield roundabout, turning left under railway. Then at mini-roundabout turn right onto B2205 for ½ mile to park on left.

Camping & Caravanning Club Site
Sutton Hill, Woodlands, Wimborne Minster
📞 **01202-822763**
Open late March-early November ⛺ 🚐 🚃
Size 13 acres, 150 touring pitches, 72 with electric hookup, 8 🚿, 16 WCs, 1 CWP
£ car/tent £9.20-£12.05, car/caravan £9.20-£12.05, motorhome £9.20-£12.05, motorbike/tent £9.20, children £1.40
© MasterCard Visa
🔲 🔦 GR ⚠ 🎣 ♿ 🐕
Last arrival time: 11:00
➡ From Ringwood take B3081 through Verwood. Site is 1½ miles on right after Verwood.

Charris Camping & Caravan Park
Candy's Lane, Corfe Mullen, Wimborne Minster BH21 3EF
📞 **01202-885970**
Open 1 March-30 October ⛺ 🚐 🚃
Size 3 acres, 45 touring pitches, 45 with electric hookup, 22 level pitches, 4 🚿, 8 WCs, 1 CWP
£ car/tent £5-£6, car/caravan £5-£6, motorhome £5-£6, motorbike/tent £5, children £1
🛒 ✗¼ 🚰¼ 🔦 🗑 Calor Gaz 🐕 WS
Last arrival time: 11:00
➡ From Wimbourne take A31 to Dorchester. Turn left after Wimbourne Caravans, Little Chef and Esso Garage.

Merley Court Touring Park
Merley, Wimborne Minster BH21 3AA
📞 **01202-881488 Fax 01202-881484**
Open 1 March-7 January ⛺ 🚐 🚃
Size 15 acres, 160 touring pitches, 160 with electric hookup, 160 level pitches, 18 🚿, 36 WCs, 3 CWPs
£ car/tent £6-£11.30, car/caravan £6-£11.30, motorhome £6-£11.30, motorbike/tent £6, children £1.25-£1.65
🛒 ✗ 🚰 🔲 🔦 🗑 🔳 🔳 GR 🔳 ⚠ 🎣 🍴 Calor Gaz ♿ 🐕 WS
Last arrival time: 10:00
➡ Off A31 to S of junction with A349 and adjacent to Merley Bird Gardens junction. Follow signs to site.

Springfield Touring Park

Candy's Lane, Corfe Mullen, Wimborne
Minster BH21 3EF
☎ 01202-881719
Open mid March-October ▲ ⛺ 🚐

*Highly commended in Practical Caravan
1996 - 100 Best U.K. Parks. Set in Dorset
overlooking the Stour Valley and close to
Poole, Bournemouth, the New Forest.
Modern facilities, free showers, awnings.*

Size 3½ acres, 45 touring pitches, 45 with
electric hookup, 35 level pitches, 6 ﾛ, 8
WCs, 1 CWP
£ car/tent £5-£7, car/caravan £6-£7,
motorhome £6-£7, motorbike/tent £5,
children £1.25
🛒 ✕¼ ⛴¼ ▫ 🔌 🚽 ⚠ 🔥 Calor Gaz 🚿
Last arrival time: 10:00
➡ Turn off the A31 Wimbourne bypass at
Dorchester Western End roundabout
(signposted Corfe Mullen South). In ¼ mile,
turn right into Candys Lane. In ¼ mile
entrance on right past farm.

Wilksworth Farm Caravan Park

Cranborne Road, Wimborne Minster BH21
4HW
☎ 01202-885467
Open 1 March-30 October ▲ ⛺ 🚐

*Country park with excellent facilities in a
peaceful setting. Tennis courts, games room,
heated swimming pool and children's play
area are on site.*

Size 12 acres, 85 touring pitches, 70 with
electric hookup, 75 level pitches, 77 static
caravans, 10 ﾛ, 19 WCs, 1 CWP
£ car/tent £6-£10, car/caravan £6-£10,
motorhome £6-£10, motorbike/tent £6,
children £1
Rental 🚐
🛒 ✕ ✕¼ ▫ 🔌 🚽 🔲 🔍 GR 🔦 ⚠ 🔥 Calor Gaz
🚿 🐕 WS
Last arrival time: 9:30
➡ From A31 to Wimbourne town centre,
then B3048 N to Cranbourne. Park is on left.

WINCANTON Somerset 3F2

Wincanton Racecourse

Wincanton BA9 8BJ
☎ 01963-34276
Open end April-mid September ▲ ⛺ 🚐

➡

← **Wincanton Racecourse**

A peaceful rural site, 1 mile from Wincanton. Surrounded by numerous places to visit, i.e. the beautiful Stourhead Gardens. Golf course, pay and play.

Size 2 acres, 50 touring pitches, 18 with electric hookup, 50 level pitches, 4 ⋒, 7 WCs, 1 CWP
£ car/tent £6.50, car/caravan £5-£8, motorhome £5-£8, motorbike/tent £5, children £1
CC MasterCard Visa
⚡¼ ✗¼ ☞¼ 🔌 📺 Calor 🐾
Last arrival time: 8:00
➜ From A303 follow signs to Racecourse, then take B3081 Bruton Road.

WINDERMERE Cumbria   **10B2**

Fallbarrow Park
Rayrigg Road, Bowness, Windermere LA23 3DL
📞 **015394-44428**
Open 15 March-31 October 🚐 🚎

Beautiful lakeside park with state of the art touring pitches. Just 300 yards from the lakeland village of Bowness. National winner of 'campsite of the year', graded excellent.

Size 32 acres, 83 touring pitches, 83 with electric hookup, 83 level pitches, 248 static caravans, 9 ⋒, 14 WCs, 2 CWPs
£ car/caravan £10.60-£16.70, motorhome £10.60-£16.70
Rental 🚐 caravans £116-£477.
CC MasterCard Visa
⚡ ✗ ☞ 🔌 🔌 📶 📺 ⚠ 🔲 Calor 🐾
Last arrival time: 11:00
➜ One mile N of Windermere.

Limefitt Park
Patterdale Road, Windermere LA23 1PA
📞 **015394-32300**
Open March-October 🛖 🚐 🚎

Spectacular Lakeland valley location. Ten minutes drive from Lake Windermere. Tourers and family campers welcome. Friendly Lakeland pub with bar meals, plus full range of award winning facilities.

Size 132 acres, 165 touring pitches, 110 with electric hookup, 110 level pitches, 45 static caravans, 16 ⋒, 24 WCs, 2 CWPs
£ car/tent £9-£12, car/caravan £9-£12.50, motorhome £9-£12.50, children £1-£1.25
CC Visa
⚡ ✗ ☞ 🔌 📺 ⚠ 🔲 Calor Gaz
Last arrival time: 10:30
➜ At junction on A591 ½ mile N of Windermere, take the A592 to Ullswater and the park is on right.

Park Cliffe Camping & Caravan Estate

Birks Road, Tower Wood, Windermere LA23 3PG

☎ 015395-31344 Fax 015395-31971

Open March-October A ⊕ ⟺

Flat and gently sloping, grass and hardstanding, rural site with magnificent views over surrounding countryside. Highest tent pitches have commanding views over Lake Windermere and Langdale.

Size 25 acres, 45 touring pitches, 50 with electric hookup, 45 level pitches, 50 static caravans, 10 ☞, 15 WCs, 1 CWP
£ car/tent £8.80-£11.20, car/caravan £10-£11.20, motorhome £10-£11.20, motorbike/tent £8.80
Rental A
℃ MasterCard Visa
🛒 ✕ ⊕ 🗑 ☎ 🖥 ⚠ 🎏 ⛽ Calor Gaz 🐕 WS
Last arrival time: 10:00
➡ M6 junction 36 take A590 to Newby Bridge. Turn right onto A592, go 4 miles and turn right into Birks Road. The park is on third of a mile on right.

Bat and Ball

New Pound, Wisborough Green RH14 0EH

☎ 01403-700313

Open all year A ⊕ ⟺
Size 3 acres, 26 touring pitches, 26 level pitches, 2 ☞, 4 WCs, 1 CWP
£ car/tent £3.50, car/caravan £3.50, motorhome £3.50, motorbike/tent £3.50
✕ ⊕ ☎ 🖥 GR ⚠ 🎏 ⛽ Calor 🐕
➡ Off A272 on B2133 from S to N.

Witton Castle Caravan Site
Bishop Auckland, Witton-le-Wear DL14 0DE
☎ 01388-488230 Fax 01388-488008
Open 1 March-31 October **A 🚐 🚎**
Size 150 acres, 186 touring pitches, 50 with electric hookup, 100 level pitches, 298 static caravans, 9 🚿, 50 WCs, 1 CWP
£ car/tent £6.50-£14.25, car/caravan £6.50-£14.25, motorhome £6.50-£14.25, motorbike/tent £6.50, children £0.50
🏋 ✕ 🍴 🗑 📞 🔲 💱 GR TV 🎣 🎯 🔌 Calor Gaz
🐾 WS
➡ Signposted on E side of A68 between Toft Hill and Witton-le-Wear. 4 miles W of Bishop Auckland.

California Chalet & Touring Park
Nine Mile Ride, Finchampstead, Wokingham RG11 3NY
☎ 01734-733928

Open 1 March-30 October **A 🚐 🚎**

Pretty wooded family run park set alongside a lake with fishing available. Close to London, Windsor and Thorpe Park.

Size 5½ acres, 29 touring pitches, 24 with electric hookup, 29 level pitches, 3 🚿, 4 WCs, 1 CWP
£ car/tent £9-£10.75, car/caravan £9-£10.75, motorhome £9-£10.75, motorbike/tent £9, children £0.50
🏋 ✕¼ 🍴¼ 🗑 📞 🔲 💱 🎣 🎯 ♿ 🐾
Last arrival time: 10:00
➡ From M3 junction 3 onto A322 towards Bracknell, turn left onto B3430 towards Finchampstead. Site is on right in 6 miles.

Stanmore Hall Touring Park
Stourbridge Road, Bridgnorth WV15 6DT
☎ 01746-761 761
Open all year **A 🚐 🚎**

A 12½ acre touring park, with 131 electrically supplied pitches, surrounding a two acre lake and located near to Bridgnorth in Shropshire.

Size 12½ acres, 131 touring pitches, 131 with electric hookup, 131 level pitches, 13 ℞, 14 WCs, 4 CWPs
£ car/tent £9.80-£11, car/caravan £10.20-£11.80, motorhome £10.20-£11.80, motorbike/tent £8.60, children £1.30-£1.40
⚡ 🔲 🔌 🔲 Calor Gaz ♿ ✝
Last arrival time: 12:00
➜ From Bridgnorth take A458 to Stourbridge. Within two miles turn right into Stanmore Hall.

WOODBRIDGE Suffolk   9F4

Moon & Sixpence
Newbourn Road, Waldringfield, Woodbridge IP12 4PP
📞 01473-736650 Fax 01473-736270
Open 1 April-31 October ⛺ 🚐 🚍

Tranquil picturesque location with excellent faacilities. Sandy beach, lake, fishing in September and October. Neighbouring golf course, nearby rollerskating, ten pin bowling, indoor bowls, cinemas, water sports.

Size 85 acres, 90 touring pitches, 90 with electric hookup, 90 level pitches, 150 static caravans, 12 ℞, 24 WCs, 1 CWP
£ car/tent £10-£12, car/caravan £10-£12, motorhome £10-£12, motorbike/tent £10
CC MasterCard Visa
⚡ ✖ 🔲 🔲 🔌 🔲 🔲 🔲 🔲 🔲 🔲 🔲 🔲 Calor Gaz ✝
Last arrival time: 9:00
➜ Turn E off A12 Ipswich Eastern by-pass onto minor road signposted Newbourn and follow signs.

St Margaret's House Caravan Site
Shottisham, Woodbridge IP12 3HD
📞 01394-411247
Open 1 April-31 October ⛺ 🚐 🚍
Size 2½ acres, 30 touring pitches, 16 with electric hookup, 30 level pitches, 2 ℞, 4 WCs, 1 CWP
£ car/tent £5, car/caravan £5-£6.50, motorhome £5-£6.50, motorbike/tent £5, children £0.25
⚡¼ ✖¼ 🔲¼ 🔲 Calor Gaz ✝
Last arrival time: 11:00
➜ Turn right off A12 onto A1152 signposted Bawdsey/Orford. After 1½ miles fork right onto B1083 signposted Bawdsey. 4 miles to T junction, turn left into Shottisham, the site is on left, 100 yards past Sorrel Horse Pitt.

Tangham Campsite
Butley, Woodbridge IP12 3NF
📞 01394-450707
Open 1 April-10 January ⛺ 🚐
Size 7 acres, 90 touring pitches, 66 with electric hookup, 90 level pitches, 6 ℞, 12 WCs, 3 CWPs
£ car/tent £7-£8.50, car/caravan £7-£8.50, motorhome £7-£8.50, motorbike/tent £7, children £1-£2
⚡ 🔲 🔲 🔲 🔲 Calor Gaz ✝
Last arrival time: 9:00
➜ Take A1152 off A12 at Woodbridge and then left on B1084 to Orford. After 4 miles turn right into forest.

WOODHALL SPA Lincolnshire   8C2

Bainland Country Park
Horncastle Road, Woodhall Spa LN10 6UX
📞 01526-352903 Fax 01526-353730
Open all year ⛺ 🚐 🚍
Size 50 acres, 150 touring pitches, 150 with electric hookup, 150 level pitches, 10 static caravans, 13 ℞, 16 WCs, 53 CWPs
£ car/tent £8-£24, car/caravan £8-£24, motorhome £8-£24, motorbike/tent £8
Rental 🚐 Chalet. £160-£570
CC MasterCard Visa
⚡ ✖ 🔲 🔲 🔲 🔲 🔲 🔲 🔲 🔲 🔲 🔲 📺 🔲 🔲 🔲 Calor Gaz ♿ ✝ WS
Last arrival time: 9:00
➜ Situated on B1191 6 miles from Horncastle, on left just past Burmah petrol station. ½ mile from Woodhall Spa. ➜

Camping & Caravanning Club Site

Wellsyke Lane, Kirkby-on-Bain, Woodhall Spa

☎ 01526-352911

Open late March-early November Å ⚐ ⇄

Size 6 acres, 100 touring pitches, 36 with electric hookup, 6 ⋒, 9 WCs, 1 CWP

£ car/tent £8.75-£11.55, car/caravan £8.75-£11.55, motorhome £8.75-£11.55, motorbike/tent £8.75, children £1.40

ℂ MasterCard Visa

🔲 📞 ৬ ⟙

Last arrival time: 11:00

➡ Take A153 to Horncastle and then B1191 to Woodhall Spa. Turn left and go down Kirkby Lane for 1¾ miles to site.

Whitemead Caravan Park

East Burton Road, Wool BH20 6HG

☎ 01929-462241

Open March-October Å ⚐ ⇄

Size 5 acres, 95 touring pitches, 35 with electric hookup, 95 level pitches, 6 ⋒, 13 WCs, 1 CWP

£ car/tent £5.50-£8.50, car/caravan £5.50-£8.50, motorhome £5.50-£8.50, motorbike/tent £5.50

Rental Å ⚐ Chalet.

🛁 ✕¼ 🍽 🔲 ৬ ⚑ Calor Gaz ৬ ⟙ WS

Last arrival time: 11:00

➡ Off A352 Wareham to Weymouth & Dorchester road (East Burton Road).

Twitchen Park

Mortehoe, Woolacombe EX34 7ES

☎ 01271-870476 Fax 01271-870498

Open Easter-end October Å ⚐ ⇄

Popular family park, close to Woolacombe's glorious sandy beach and coastal walks. A licensed club is on site, with seasonal entertainment, free swimming lessons and more.

Size 45 acres, 51 touring pitches, 51 with electric hookup, 295 static caravans, 24 ⋒, 46 WCs, 2 CWPs

£ car/tent £6-£14, car/caravan £7.50-£18, motorhome £7.50-£18

Rental ⚐

ℂ MasterCard Visa

🛁 ✕ 🍽 🔲 📞 🗓 🏧 GR 🔲 ⚑ 🔲 ⊑ Calor Gaz

Last arrival time: 9:00

➡ From A361 10 miles N of Barnstaple take B3343 left for 1¾ miles to Woolacombe. Take right turn signed Mortehoe. Park entrance is 1½ miles on left.

Warcombe Farm Camping Park

Station Road, Mortehoe, Woolacombe EX34 7EJ

☎ 01271-870690 Fax 01271-871070

Open 15 March-31 October 🏕 ⛟ 🚐
Size 19 acres, 25 touring pitches, 22 with electric hookup, 140 level pitches, 6 ⛗, 12 WCs, 1 CWP
£ car/tent £5-£6, car/caravan £7.50-£9, motorhome £6.50-£8, motorbike/tent £5
🛒 ✕¼ 🍴¼ 🗑 🛁 🚿 ⚠ 🔲 Calor Gaz 🐕
➔ Turn left off A361 onto B3343. After 2 miles turn right onto road to Mortehoe. Site on right in less than 1 mile.

Woolacombe Bay Holiday Village
Sandy Lane, Woolacombe EX34 7AH
📞 01271-870221 **Fax** 01271-871042
Open Easter-October 🏕
Size 25 acres, 232 static caravans, 16 ⛗, 20 WCs, 1 CWP
£ car/tent £7.80-£17.60, motorbike/tent £7.80, children £1.95-£4.40
Rental ⛟ Chalet. caravans £110-£570
C MasterCard Visa
🛒 ✕ 🍴 🗑 🍹 🏧 🔲 GR 🍷 📺 ⚠ 🔲 ⊕ 🐕
Last arrival time: 12:00
➔ At Mullacott Cross on A361, W onto B3343 for 1¾ miles over bridge. Keep right for ½ mile and turn left on Sandy Lane. Site is ½ mile.

Riverside Holiday Park
Wooler NE71 6EE
📞 01668-281447 **Fax** 01668-282142
Open Easter-October 🏕 ⛟ 🚐
Size 80 acres, 55 touring pitches, 44 with electric hookup, 55 level pitches, 300 static caravans, 5 ⛗, 5 WCs, 1 CWP
C MasterCard Visa
🛒 🛒¼ ✕¼ 🍴 🛁 🍹 ⚠ 🔲 ⊕ Calor ♿
Last arrival time: 10:00
➔ On A697, 30 miles N of Morpeth and 16 miles S of Coldstragam.

Lenchford Meadow Caravan Park
Lenchford, Shrawley WR6 6TB
📞 01905-620246 **Fax** 01905-620246
Open 1 March-31 October 🏕 ⛟ 🚐

Size 8 acres, 20 touring pitches, 14 with electric hookup, 20 level pitches, 65 static caravans, 4 ⛗, 6 WCs, 1 CWP
£ car/tent £7, car/caravan £7, motorhome £7, motorbike/tent £7
🛒¼ ✕ ✕¼ 🍴¼ 🗑 🛁 🍹 GR ⚠ 🔲 ⊕ Calor ♿ 🐕
➔ On B4196 Holt Heath to Stourport.

Mill House Caravan & Camping Site
Hawford, Worcester WR3 7SE
📞 01905-451283 **Fax** 01905-754143
Open April-October 🏕 ⛟ 🚐
Size 8 acres, 150 touring pitches, 20 with electric hookup, 150 level pitches, 15 static caravans, 4 ⛗, 9 WCs, 3 CWPs
£ car/tent £5.50, car/caravan £5.50, motorhome £5.50, motorbike/tent £5.50
🛒 🍴 🛁 🍹 ⚠ 🔲 Calor Gaz ♿ 🐕 WS
➔ Site is 3 miles N of Worcester, on the E of A449.

Camping & Caravanning Club Site
The Walled Garden, Clumber Park, Worksop S80 3BA
📞 01909-482303
Open end March-start November 🏕 ⛟ 🚐
Size 2½ acres, 55 touring pitches, 16 with electric hookup, 2 ⛗, 6 WCs, 1 CWP
£ car/tent £8.15-£10.40, car/caravan £8.15-£10.40, motorhome £8.15-£10.40, motorbike/tent £8.15, children £1.30
C MasterCard Visa
🛁 🐕
Last arrival time: 11:00
➔ From A841 follow Clumber Park signs. After 2½ miles left at crossroads and follow signs for Estate Office. Right at office, site on left.

Greensprings Touring Park
Rockley Abbey, Worsbrough S75 3DS
📞 01226-288298 **Fax** 01226-288298
Open 1 April-31 October 🏕 ⛟ 🚐 ➔

← **Greensprings Touring Park**

Quiet secluded rural setting with pleasant walks. Ideal location for a relaxing break on journeys north and south and as a base for exploring Yorkshire and Derbyshire.

Size 4 acres, 60 touring pitches, 28 with electric hookup, 50 level pitches, 6 ℞, 9 WCs, 2 CWPs
£ car/tent £6, car/caravan £6, motorhome £6, motorbike/tent £6
Calor Gaz ⋔
Last arrival time: 9:00
➜ From M1 junction 36, take A61 towards Barnsley. Turn left after ¼ mile onto 'B' road signed Pilley. Follow road for ¾ mile. Site entrance is on left.

YARMOUTH, GREAT Norfolk   9F3

Bureside Holiday Park

Boundary Farm, Oby, Great Yarmouth NR29 3BW
📞 **01493-369233**
Open Whitsun-mid September Å ⊞ ⇶

Explore peaceful country lanes and river banks or go fishing in the carp and tench lake. Also river frontage, slipway, heated swimming and kiddies pools.

Size 12 acres, 170 touring pitches, 57 with electric hookup, 120 level pitches, 45 static caravans, 8 ℞, 26 WCs, 3 CWPs
£ car/tent £7, car/caravan £7, motorhome £7, motorbike/tent £7
🔌 ⊡ 🔧 ⊟ ⊠ ⊞ ⊠ GR ⊠ ⟁ ⊞ Calor Gaz ⋔
Last arrival time: 8:00
➜ From junction A47/A1064 W of Acle, take A1064 N to Billockby. Keep left on B1152 for 1½ miles, then left at crossroads along unclassified road (signed Oby) for 1 mile. Take second left, then go ¼ mile and turn right to site.

Burgh Castle Marina

Burgh Castle, Great Yarmouth NR31 9PZ
📞 **01493-780331**
Open 1 March-31 December Å ⊞ ⇶
Size 22 acres, 50 touring pitches, 27 with electric hookup, 50 level pitches, 150 static caravans, 2 CWPs
£ car/tent £7-£12, car/caravan £7-£12, motorhome £7-£12, motorbike/tent £7
🔌 ✕ 📮 ⊡ 🔧 ⊠ ⟁ ⊞ ⊟ Calor Gaz WS
➜ Approach from A143 and follow signs for Belton-Burgh Castle, then follow brown and white tourist signs.

Causeway Cottage Caravan Park

Bridge Road, Potter Heigham, Great Yarmouth NR29 5JB
📞 **01692-670238**
Open 17 March-12 October Å ⊞ ⇶
Size 1 acre, 5 touring pitches, 5 with electric hookup, 5 level pitches, 9 static caravans, 2 ℞, 4 WCs, 1 CWP
£ car/tent £6-£8, car/caravan £6-£8, motorhome £6-£8, motorbike/tent £6
Rental ⊞ caravans £60-£205
🔌¼ ✕¼ 📮¼ ⊡ ⊟ ⟁ ⊞ Calor Gaz
Last arrival time: 8:00
➜ A149 to Potter Heigham. Get to old bridge and river, site is 250 yards up road away from Great Yarmouth.

Grange Touring Park

Ormesby St Margaret, Great Yarmouth NR29 3QG
📞 **01493-730023**

Open 17 April-30 September **A ⊕ ⊞**
CC Visa
⅃ ✕ ⌷
➡ At junction of A149 and B1159, 3 miles N of Caister.

Liffens Holiday Park
Burgh Castle, Great Yarmouth NR31 9QB
☎ **01493-780357 Fax 01493-782383**
Open 1 April-30 October **A ⊕ ⊞**

A friendly family holiday park, set in lovely Broadland countryside but only ten minutes from Great Yarmouth.

Size 22 acres, 100 touring pitches, 100 with electric hookup, 150 level pitches, 130 static caravans, 16 ⋔, 28 WCs, 2 CWPs
£ car/tent £8-£11, car/caravan £8-£11, motorhome £8-£11, motorbike/tent £8
Rental ⊕ Chalet. £80-£350, 6 berth luxury caravans.
CC MasterCard Visa
⅃ ✕ ● ⌷ ⌷ ⌷ ⌷ ⌷ ⌷ GR ⌷ TV ⌷ ⌷ ⊟ Calor Gaz **⅏ ⚲** WS
Last arrival time: 11:00
➡ From Great Yarmouth take A12 over bridge and after two roundabouts watch for left turn to Burgh Castle. Follow two miles to T junction, turn right and follow signs to Liffens.

Willowcroft Camping and Caravan Park
Staithe Road, Repps-with-Bastwick, Great Yarmouth NR29 5JU
☎ **01692-670380**
Open all year **A ⊕ ⊞**

Size 2 acres, 40 touring pitches, 20 with electric hookup, 40 level pitches, 2 ⋔, 6 WCs, 1 CWP
£ car/tent £7, car/caravan £7, motorhome £7, motorbike/tent £7, children £0.75
⅃ ⅃¼ ⌷ Calor Gaz **⚲** WS
Last arrival time: 10:00
➡ Off main A149 Yarmouth to Potter Heigham Road, left into Church Road, past church and right into Staithe.

YORK North Yorkshire 11D3

Camping & Caravanning Club Site
Bracken Hill, Sheriff Hutton, York YO6 1QG
☎ **01347-878660**
Open end March-early November **A ⊕ ⊞**
Size 6 acres, 90 touring pitches, 42 with electric hookup, 6 ⋔, 9 WCs, 1 CWP
£ car/tent £8.75-£11.55, car/caravan £8.75-£11.55, motorhome £8.75-£11.55, motorbike/tent £8.75, children £1.40
CC MasterCard Visa
⌷ ⌷ ⌷ ⌷ ⅏ ⚲
Last arrival time: 11:00
➡ From York travel N on A64. Head towards village of West Lilling, turn left at T junction, site on left.

Cawood Holiday Park
Ryther Road, Cawood, York YO8 0TT
☎ **01757-268450 Fax 01757-268537**
Open 1 March-31 January **A ⊕ ⊞**

A country site ideal for York and the Dales, and one hour from coast. Fishing, lakeside bar with family entertainment. Disabled bungalows, five caravans and nine chalets for hire (own WCs). No single-sex groups. ➡

← **Cawood Holiday Park**

Size 8 acres, 60 touring pitches, 60 with electric hookup, 60 level pitches, 10 static caravans, 10 🍴, 12 WCs, 1 CWP
£ car/tent £8-£10, car/caravan £8-£10, motorhome £8-£10, motorbike/tent £8, children £1
Rental 🚐 Chalet. bungalow £195-£395, caravans £165-£365
CC MasterCard Visa
🏋 🌊 📷 🔧 🍳 🔲 🖼 🚲 GR 🅰 🖼 🔌 Calor Gaz ♿ 🍸
Last arrival time: 11:00
➡ From A1 or York, take B1222 to Cawood and turn right at traffic lights onto B1223 for 1 mile towards Tadcaster. Site is on left.

Moor End Farm
Acaster Malbis, York YO2 1UQ
📞 01904-706727
Open 17 April-31 October 🏕 🚐 🚍
Size ½ acre, 10 touring pitches, 10 with electric hookup, 10 level pitches, 5 static caravans, 2 🍴, 4 WCs, 1 CWP
£ car/tent £6, car/caravan £7, motorhome £6
Rental 🚐
🏋 ✗ 🌊 🅰 🖼 🍸
Last arrival time: 11:00
➡ Turn off A64 at Copmanthorpe and follow signs for Acaster Malbis. Park is signposted from Acaster crossroads.

Mount Pleasant Caravan Village
Acaster Malbis, York YO2 1UW
📞 01904-707078 Fax 01904-707078
Open 1 March-30 November 🏕 🚐 🚍

Rural park set in the countryside, yet only four miles from the centre of York. Level mown grass for tourers and tents. The camp has its own bus service to York throughout the day.

Size 18 acres, 60 touring pitches, 40 with electric hookup, 60 level pitches, 165 static caravans, 12 🍴, 45 WCs, 2 CWPs
£ car/tent £5.75, car/caravan £5.99, motorhome £5.99, motorbike/tent £5.75
Rental 🚐 caravan £33 per night
🏋 🔧 🅰 🖼 Calor Gaz
➡ Turn off A64, follow signs to Bishopthorpe, then for Acaster Airfield (disused). Follow signs for site.

Naburn Lock Caravan Site
Naburn, York YO1 4RU
📞 01904-728697 Fax 01904-728697
Open March-6 November 🏕 🚐 🚍

Small rural site, with nearby facilities for fishing and horse riding. Restaurant ½ mile, swimming pool four miles.

Size 4½ acres, 50 touring pitches, 30 with electric hookup, 50 level pitches, 8 🍴, 12 WCs, 2 CWPs
🏋 ✗¼ 🔧 Calor Gaz ♿
Last arrival time: 9:00
➡ 4 miles S of York. From A19 turn onto B1222. Site is 2½ miles on left.

Poplar Farm Caravan Park
Acaster Malbis, York YO2 1UH
📞 01904-706548
Open April-October 🏕 🚐 🚍
🏋 🎣
➡ S off A64 at Copmanthorpe. Site 2¼ miles.

Rawcliffe Manor Caravan Site
Manor Lane, Shipton Road, York YO3 6TZ
📞 01904-624422
Open all year 🏕 🚐 🚍

Well located near to York, with a daily bus service to the city from the site and next to a large shopping/leisure complex. Superb facilities for the disabled.

Size 5 acres, 120 touring pitches, 120 with electric hookup, 120 level pitches, 14 🚿, 24 WCs, 2 CWPs

£ car/tent £8.20-£11, car/caravan £7.50-£11, motorhome £7-£11, motorbike/tent £7.60, children £1-£1.20

CC MasterCard Visa

🗝¼ ✗ 🍴 🔲 🔋 🔲 🔲 🅶🆁 📺 ⬤ ⊠ 🔌 Calor Gaz ♿ 🐕

Last arrival time: 11:00

➡ ½ mile off A19 Thirsk road on York side of junction with A1237 (York Northern bypass).

Swallow Hall Caravan Park

Crockley Hill, York YO1 4SG

📞 **01904-448219** **Fax** 01904-448219

Open March-October ▲ 🚚 🚐

Size 4½ acres, 30 touring pitches, 22 with electric hookup, 4 🚿, 4 WCs, 1 CWP

£ car/tent £7-£10, car/caravan £7-£10, motorhome £7-£10

Rental Chalets & cottages £150-£200

📞 🔲 🅿🔲 ⬤ ⊠ Calor Gaz 🐕 WS

➡ From A64 take A19 S for Selby. After 2 miles turn left at Crockley Hill corner to Wheldrake. In 2 miles turn left at site sign.

Escape

At the RAC we can release you from
the worries of motoring

But did you know that we can also
give you invaluable peace of mind
when you go on holiday,

Or arrange your hotel bookings,

Or even organise your entire
holiday, all over the phone?

RAC Travel Insurance   0800 550 055

RAC Hotel Reservations   0345 056 042

RAC Holiday Reservations   0161 480 4810

Call us

RAC

SCOTLAND

Faichem Park, Invergarry

Lower Deeside Caravan Park

Maryculter, Aberdeen AB1 5FX
☎ 01224-733860 Fax 01224-732490
Open all year ⛺ 🚐 🚍

*An attractive country site only five miles
from Aberdeen. Ideal for touring the Royal
Deeside. Shop, games/tv room, laundry and
children play area. Luxury caravans and
pine lodges for hire.*

Size 14 acres, 40 touring pitches, 40 with
electric hookup, 40 level pitches, 35 static
caravans, 4 🚿, 5 WCs, 1 CWP
£ car/caravan £7-£11
Rental 🚐 Chalet.
CC MasterCard Visa
🦮 ✕¼ 🔌 🚻 GR 🅀 TV ⚠ 🎯 Calor Gaz
Last arrival time: 12:00
➡ From Aberdeen take B9077 (SW) for 5
miles from Bridge of Dee roundabout.
Adjacent to Old Mill Inn.

Aberfeldy Caravan Park

Dunkeld Road, Aberfeldy PH15 2AQ
☎ 01738-639911 Fax 01738-441690
⛺ 🚐 🚍
Size 5½ acres, 102 touring pitches, 132 with
electric hookup, 132 level pitches, 18 🚿, 36
WCs, 1 CWP
➡ 9 miles W of A9 (Ballinluig junction) on
A827 to Killin.

Trossachs Holiday Park

Gartmore, Aberfoyle FK8 3SA
☎ 01877-382614 Fax 01877-382732
Open 15 March-31 October A 🚐 🚍

A small exclusive enviromental caravan park, 1997 winner - Best park in Scotland. 45 landscaped touring pitches, tents welcome, Thistle award caravans and mountain bikes for hire.

Size 15 acres, 45 touring pitches, 45 with electric hookup, 45 level pitches, 60 static caravans, 4 🔥, 9 WCs, 1 CWP
£ car/tent £8-£10, car/caravan £8-£10, motorhome £8-£10, motorbike/tent £8
Rental 🚐 £125-£399
CC MasterCard Visa
🍴 ✗¼ 🚿¼ 🚽 📞 🚬 🅿 GR ⚠ 🏠 Calor Gaz 🐕 WS
Last arrival time: 9:00
➡ On E side of A81, 3 miles S of Aberfoyle.

Aboyne Loch Caravan Park

Aboyne AB34 5BR
☎ 013398-86244
Open 1 April-31 October A 🚐 🚍

Set in eight acres of woodland, surrounded by Loch Aboyne on three sides. Playground and swimming, fishing and boating on site. Three caravans and six chalets for hire.

Size 8 acres, 64 touring pitches, 60 static caravans, 16 🔥, 18 WCs, 1 CWP
🍴 🍴¼ ✗¼ 🚿¼ 📞 GR ⚠ 🏠 Calor Gaz 🚻 WS
Last arrival time: any time
➡ On N side of A93, ½ mile E of Aboyne. 29 miles W of Aberdeen.

Resipole Caravan Park

Acharacle PH36 4HX
☎ 01967-431235 Fax 01967-431777
Open 1 April-31 October A 🚐 🚍

Set amid the splendour of the West Highlands, a spacious graded touring park offering superb facilities, including an excellent restaurant and nine hole golf course.

Size 60 touring pitches, 20 with electric hookup, 20 level pitches, 6 🔥, 9 WCs, 1 CWP
£ car/tent £8.50-£9.50, car/caravan £8.50-£9.50, motorhome £8.50-£9.50, motorbike/tent £7.50, children £0.50-£1.50
Rental 🚐 Chalet. £120-£400
CC MasterCard Visa
✗ 🚿 📞 🚬 🅿 GR 🔍 🍴 Calor Gaz 🚻 🐕 WS
Last arrival time: 10:00
➡ Take Corran Ferry 8 miles S of Fort William on A82. Then A861 W. Park is 8 miles W of Strontifin on roadside.

Tullichewan Caravan Park

Old Luss Road, Loch Lomond, Balloch G83 8QP

☎ 01389-759475 Fax 01389-755563

⚐ ⊕ ⊞

Size 13 acres, 120 touring pitches, 90 with electric hookup, 120 level pitches, 35 static caravans, 10 ⏸, 30 WCs, 4 CWPs

£ car/tent £7.50-£11, car/caravan £7.50-£11, motorhome £7.50-£11, motorbike/tent £7.50, children £1

Rental ⊕ Chalet.

ℂℂ Visa

☒ ✗¼ ☞¼ ⊡ ☏ ⊟ 🕮 GR 🔍 📺 🚿 ☒ Calor Gaz 🚹 ⊼ WS

➡ N on A82 from Erskine Bridge, right at roundabout for Balloch on A811, first left.

Applecross Camp Site

via Loch Carron, Wester Ross, Applecross IV54 8ND

☎ 01520-744268 Fax 01520-744268

Open Easter-September

A flat, well drained site covering six acres providing a quiet family retreat and an ideal place to wind down, looking towards Raasay & Rona accross the Inner Sound. Licensed Flower Tunnel Restaurant and in-store bakery.

Size 6 acres, 60 touring pitches, 10 with electric hookup, 60 level pitches, 3 static caravans, 8 ⏸, 12 WCs, 1 CWP

ℂℂ Visa

☒ ✗ ☞ Calor Gaz

➤ From A896 turn left after Kishorn to Applecross - 11 miles. Caravans continue on A896 towards Shielding. After 7½ miles turn left to Applecross - 24 miles.

ARBROATH Angus 13E1

Red Lion Caravan Park
Dundee Road, Arbroath
☎ 01241-872038 Fax 01241-430324
Open March-October 🚐 🚍
Size 20 acres, 31 touring pitches, 31 with electric hookup, 31 level pitches, 239 static caravans, 6 🚿, 12 WCs, 1 CWP
£ car/caravan £8, motorhome £8
Rental 🚐
₵₵ MasterCard Visa
🛒 ✗ 🍺 🗑 🔌 ⚠ 🎣 Calor & 🐕
Last arrival time: 8:00
➤ Site on left of A92 on entering Arbroath.

ARISAIG Inverness-shire 14B4

Gorten Sands Caravan Site
Gorten Farm, Arisaig PH39 4NS
☎ 01687-450283
Open Easter-30 September 🏕 🚐 🚍

A peaceful, family run hill and coastal farm site in a historic scenic area with safe sandy beaches. The unspoilt location offers views to Skye and the isles.

Size 6 acres, 42 touring pitches, 20 with electric hookup, 42 level pitches, 3 static caravans, 6 🚿, 10 WCs, 1 CWP
£ car/tent £6.50-£8, car/caravan £8, motorhome £6.50-£7.50, motorbike/tent £6.50, children £0.75
Rental 🚐 £200-£300

🛒¼ ✗¼ 🍺¼ 🗑 🔌 🗑 Calor Gaz 🐕
Last arrival time: 11:00
➤ A830 Fort William to Mallaig road, turn left 2 miles W of Arisaig at signpost 'Back of Keppoch'. Continue ¾ mile to road end across cattle grid.

AVIEMORE Inverness-shire 15D3

High Range Touring Caravan Park
Grampian Road, Aviemore PH22 1PT
☎ 01479-810636 Fax 01479-811322
Open December-October 🏕 🚐 🚍

A small and select touring park situated in woodland grounds, 500 yards from the Aviemore centre. A launderette, playground, continental restaurant and bar, and motel and 'family' rooms are available.

Size 2 acres, 36 touring pitches, 36 with electric hookup, 36 level pitches, 4 🚿, 5 WCs, 1 CWP
£ car/tent £6-£8, car/caravan £6-£8, motorhome £6-£8, motorbike/tent £6
Rental Chalet.
₵₵ MasterCard Visa
🛒¼ ✗ 🗑 🔌 🗑 ⚠ 🎣 🍺 🐕
Last arrival time: 9:00
➤ From main A9 take B9152. Park is in complex at S end of Aviemore.

AYR Ayrshire 12C3

Middlemuir Holiday Park
Tarbolton, Mauchline, Ayr KA5 5NR
☎ 01292-541647 Fax 01292-541649
Open 1 March-31 October 🏕 🚐 🚍   ➤

← **Middlemuir Holiday Park**

Size 18 acres, 35 touring pitches, 18 with electric hookup, 64 static caravans, 4 📷, 8 WCs, 1 CWP
£ car/tent £5-£9, car/caravan £7-£13.50, motorhome £7-£13.50, motorbike/tent £5
Rental 🚐 £140-£300
🐾 ▣ 🔋 🗖 ɢʀ 🅰 ⊠ ⊩
➜ 5 miles E of Ayr on B743 Mauchline road.

BALMACARA Ross-shire   14B3

Reraig Caravan Site
Kyle of Lochalsh, Balmacara IV40 8DH
📞 **01599-566215**
Open 1 May-30 September ⚠ 🚐 🚏
Size 2 acres, 45 touring pitches, 28 with electric hookup, 40 level pitches, 4 📷, 9 WCs, 1 CWP
£ car/tent £6.50, car/caravan £6.50, motorhome £6.50
⊂⊂ MasterCard Visa
🐾¼ ✗¼ 🔋 ⊩
Last arrival time: 10:00

➜ Adjacent to Balmacara Hotel on A87, 1¾ miles W on junction with A890.

BANFF Banffshire   15F3

Wester Bonnyton Farm Site
Gamrie, Banff AB45 3EP
📞 **01261-832470**
Open March-October ⚠ 🚐 🚏
Size 3 acres, 30 touring pitches, 8 with electric hookup, 10 level pitches, 18 static caravans, 4 📷, 4 WCs, 1 CWP
£ car/tent £5-£6, car/caravan £6-£7, motorhome £6-£7, motorbike/tent £5
Rental 🚐 Chalet. caravans £150-£160
🐾 ▣ ɢʀ 🔲 🅰 ⊠ Calor ♿ ⊩ WS

BLAIR ATHOLL Perthshire   15D4

Blair Castle Caravan Park
Blair Atholl, Pitlochry PH18 5SR
📞 **01796-481263** ꜰᴀx **01796-481587**
Open 1 April-15 October ⚠ 🚐 🚏
Size 35 acres, 240 touring pitches, 120 with electric hookup, 107 static caravans, 28 📷, 97 WCs, 3 CWPs
⊂⊂ Visa
🐾 ♥ Calor Gaz ♿
➜ Turn off A9, 6 miles N of Pitlochry. Follow signs to Blair Atholl.

River Tilt Leisure Park
Bridge of Tilt, Blair Atholl PH18 5TE
📞 **01796-481467** ꜰᴀx **01796-481511**
Open March-November ⚠ 🚐 🚏

Situated on the banks of the River Tilt next to the golf course and overlooking the castle entrance. Panoramic views over the river.

Size 14 acres, 35 touring pitches, 35 with electric hookup, 35 level pitches, 45 static caravans, 4 🚿, 6 WCs, 1 CWP
£ car/tent £6-£8, car/caravan £11-£14, motorhome £10-£13, motorbike/tent £6
Rental 🚐 £250-£300, chalet £299-£475.
CC MasterCard Visa
🛒¼ ✗ 🍴 🍳 📞 🎱 🎰 🧺 📷 📠 /🔥 🎀 Calor Gaz
🐕 WS
Last arrival time: 11:00
➡ A9 N of Pitlochry onto B8079 signed Blair Atholl. On entering village turn left before hotel and follow sign.

Nether Craig Caravan Park
Alyth, Blairgowrie PH11 8HN
📞 **01575-560204 Fax 01575-560315**
Open mid March-end October 🏕 🚐 🚍

Enjoy the peace of rural Angus at this award winning, family run touring park, convenient for country pursuits and near much of historic interest.

Size 4 acres, 40 touring pitches, 40 with electric hookup, 40 level pitches, 5 🚿, 7 WCs, 1 CWP
£ car/tent £5, car/caravan £7-£9, motorhome £7-£9, motorbike/tent £5, children £0.85
🛒 🍳 📞 🍴 📷 /🔥 🎀 Calor Gaz ♿ 🐕 WS
Last arrival time: 9:00
➡ At roundabout S of Alyth join B954 signposted Glenisla. Follow caravan signs for 4½ miles. Do not go into Alyth.

Witches Craig Farm Camping & Caravanning Park
Blairlogie FK9 5PX
📞 **01786-474947**
Open 1 April-31 October 🏕 🚐 🚍
Size 5 acres, 60 touring pitches, 44 with electric hookup, 60 level pitches, 9 🚿, 11 WCs, 1 CWP
£ car/tent £9-£10, car/caravan £9-£10, motorhome £9-£10, motorbike/tent £9, children £0.50-£0.75
🍳 📞 🍴 /🔥 🎀 Calor Gaz ♿ 🐕 WS
Last arrival time: 9:00
➡ Leave Stirling, take St Andrews road, A91, 3 miles E of Stirling.

Boat of Garten Caravan & Camping Park
Boat of Garten PH24 3BN
📞 **01479-831652 Fax 01479-831652**   ➡
🏕 🚐 🚍

← Boat of Garten Caravan & Camping Park

Size 11 acres, 37 touring pitches, 24 with electric hookup, 37 level pitches, 50 static caravans, 8 ♠, 15 WCs, 1 CWP
£ car/tent £5-£8, car/caravan £6.50-£10.50, motorhome £6.50-£10.50, motorbike/tent £5
Rental ⊞ £159-£355
CC MasterCard Visa
🐕 ✗¼ 🍴¼ 🔲 🔌 🔲 Calor Gaz ♿ 🐾 WS
Last arrival time: 10:00
➦ From the A9 take A95 towards Grantown-on-Spey, then follow the signs for Boat of Garten. Park is situated in centre of village. Signposted.

Croft Na-Carn Caravan Park
Loch Garten, Boat of Garten
📞 **01309-672051 Fax 01309-672051**
Open all year 🏕 ⊞ 🚐

Located on the 'Road to the Ospreys' and surrounded by beautiful scenery; fishing, golf, a whisky trail and walking are just some of the attractions.

Size 4½ acres, 15 touring pitches, 10 with electric hookup, 15 level pitches, 10 static caravans, 2 ♠, 4 WCs, 1 CWP
£ car/tent £4.50-£6.50, car/caravan £5.50-£7.50, motorhome £5.50-£7.50, motorbike/tent £4.50, children £1

Rental ⊞ Chalet. £70-£350
🔲 🔌 Calor Gaz ♿ 🐾
Last arrival time: 8:30
➦ Leave A9 immediately N of Aviemore onto A95 heading for Grantown on Spey, turn right for Boat of Garten. Through village, cross River Spey at road junction of B970, turn left towards Nethybridge. In ½ mile turn right for Loch Garten, the park is 100 yards on the left. Alternatively follow RSPB roadsigns for osprey.

Corriefodly Holiday Park
Bridge of Cally PH10 7JG
📞 **01250-886236**
Open December-October 🏕 ⊞ 🚐

Situated in central Perthshire six miles north of Blairgowrie, the site is an ideal touring base. Open December-October, 17 acres, 55 tourers, apartments for hire.

Size 17 acres, 55 touring pitches, 55 with electric hookup, 35 level pitches, 57 static caravans, 4 🚿, 12 WCs, 1 CWP
£ car/tent £5-£7, car/caravan £7-£9, motorhome £7-£9, motorbike/tent £5
Rental Chalet.
🛒¼ ✕¼ 🅾 🔌 🍴 🔲 GR 🔴 🅰 🕁 🔌 Calor ♿ ☂
Last arrival time: 11:00
➡ A93 N from Blairgowrie for 6 miles. At junction of A93 and A924 fork onto A924. Site is 300 yards on left.

CALLANDER Perthshire   12C1

Keltie Bridge Caravan Park
Keltie Bridge, Callander FK17 8LQ
📞 **01877-330811 Fax 01877-330075**
Open 1 April-31 October ⚑ 🚐 🚗
Size 12 acres, 40 touring pitches, 30 with electric hookup, 40 level pitches, 40 static caravans, 5 🚿, 7 WCs, 1 CWP
£ car/tent £7-£8.50, car/caravan £7-£8.50, motorhome £7-£8.50, motorbike/tent £5.50
🅾 🔌 ♿ ☂ WS
➡ On A84 between Doune and Callander, near Heather centre.

CAMPBELTOWN Argyll   12B3

Camping & Caravanning Club Site
East Trodigal, Machrihanish, Campbeltown
📞 **01586-810366**
Open end March-end September ⚑ 🚐 🚗
Size 10 acres, 90 touring pitches, 39 with electric hookup, 4 🚿, 8 WCs, 1 CWP
£ car/tent £9.20-£12.05, car/caravan £9.20-£12.05, motorhome £9.20-£12.05, motorbike/tent £9.20, children £1.40
CC MasterCard Visa
🅾 🔌 🅰 🕁 ♿ ☂
Last arrival time: 11:00
➡ A82 from Glasgow to Tarbet. Then A83 to Campbletown. From town take B843 (to Machrihanish). Site is on N side of road, ½ mile before Machrihanish.

CANNICH Inverness-shire   14C3

Cannich Caravan Park
Cannich by Beauly
📞 **01456-415364 Fax 01456-415263**
Open February-December ⚑ 🚐 🚗

Size 8 acres, 50 touring pitches, 20 with electric hookup, 50 level pitches, 9 static caravans, 8 🚿, 10 WCs, 1 CWP
£ car/tent £5.50-£8.50, car/caravan £5.50-£8.50, motorhome £5.50-£8.50, motorbike/tent £3.50, children £0.50
Rental 🚐 £140-£190
🛒¼ ✕¼ ☕¼ 🅾 🔌 🍴 🔲 GR TV 🅰 🕁 Calor Gaz ♿ ☂ WS
Last arrival time: 11:00
➡ 100 yards off A831.

CARNOUSTIE Angus   13E1

Woodlands Caravan Park
Newton Road, Carnoustie DD7 6HR
📞 **01241-853246 Fax 01307-461889**
Open March-October ⚑ 🚐 🚗

In grounds of former Carnoustie House, a wooded site with a children's play area. Open from Easter to October.

Size 4½ acres, 108 touring pitches, 64 with electric hookup, 108 level pitches, 12 static caravans, 8 🚿, 12 WCs, 1 CWP
🛒¼ ✕¼ ☕¼ 🅾 🔌 🔳 🅰 🕁 Calor ♿ ☂
➡ A route to Woodlands is marked by caravan site signs from a point on the A90 seven miles N of Dundee.

CARRADALE Argyll   12B3

Carradale Bay Caravan Site
Kintyre, Carradale PA28 6QG
📞 **01583-431665**
Open Easter-30 September ⚑ 🚐 🚗
Size 12 acres, 56 touring pitches, 40 with electric hookup, 40 level pitches, 3 static caravans, 8 🚿, 16 WCs, 1 CWP   ➡

← Carradale Bay Caravan Site

£ car/tent £7-£11, car/caravan £7-£11, motorhome £7-£11, motorbike/tent £7, children £1.10-£1.20
Rental Chalet.
🅿¼ ✗¼ 🚐¼ ▣ 🅒 🗑 🖊 🖙 WS
Last arrival time: 10:00
➡ From Tarbert take A83 to Campbeltown, then B842 to Carradale. After 14 miles at T-junction, turn right onto B879 (signposted Carradale). After ½ mile turn right at Carwen Park sign and follow track to site.

CASTLE DOUGLAS Kirkcudbrightshire   12C4

Lochside Caravan Park
Castle Douglas DG7 1EZ
📞 **01556-502521**
Open Easter-October ▲ 🚐 🚟
Size 6 acres, 160 touring pitches, 97 with electric hookup, 161 level pitches, 16 🚿, 29 WCs, 3 CWPs
£ car/tent £6.75-£8.25, car/caravan £6.75-£8.25, motorhome £6.75-£8.25, motorbike/tent £6.75
🅿¼ ✗¼ 🚐¼ ▣ 🅒 🗑 🖼 🛆 🖂 🚻 🖊
➡ Off A75 in Castle Douglas by Carlingwark Loch.

COMRIE Fife   12C1

West Lodge Caravan Park
Comrie PH6 2LS
📞 **01764-670354**
Open 1 April-5 January ▲ 🚐 🚟
Size 3 acres, 20 touring pitches, 20 with electric hookup, 20 level pitches, 36 static caravans, 6 🚿, 10 WCs, 1 CWP
£ car/tent £6, car/caravan £8, motorhome £8, motorbike/tent £6, children £0.50
Rental 🚐 £19-£29 nightly. £99-£190 weekly.
🅿 ✗¼ 🚐¼ ▣ 🅒 🗑 Calor Gaz 🖊 WS
Last arrival time: 10:00
➡ On A85, 1 mile W of Comrie.

CONNEL Argyll   12B1

Camping & Caravanning Club Site
Barcaldine, Connel PA37 1SG
📞 **01631-720348**
Open end March-start November ▲ 🚐 🚟

Size 4 acres, 75 touring pitches, 38 with electric hookup, 4 level pitches, 6 🚿, 13 WCs, 2 CWPs
£ car/tent £8.75-£11.55, car/caravan £8.75-£11.55, motorhome £8.75-£11.55, motorbike/tent £8.75, children £1.40
CC MasterCard Visa
▣ 🅒 🄶🅁 🛆 🖂 🖊
Last arrival time: 11:00
➡ A828 Oban to Fort William road for 6 miles to N of Connel Bridge. Site is on right, just before Barcaldine village sign.

CONTIN Ross-shire   14C3

Riverside Chalets & Caravan Park
Strathteffer, Contin IV14 9ES
📞 **01997-421351**
Open all year ▲ 🚐 🚟
Size 2 acres, 15 touring pitches, 12 with electric hookup, 15 level pitches, 3 static caravans, 2 🚿, 5 WCs, 1 CWP
£ car/caravan £2.50
Rental Chalet.
🅿 ✗ 🚐 ▣ 🗑 Calor Gaz 🖊 WS
➡ On A835 between Inverness and Ullapool at Strathpeffer Junction.

CRAIGELLACHIE Banffshire   15E3

Aberlour Gardens Caravan Park
Aberlour-on-Spey, Craigellachie AB38 9LP
📞 **01340-871586**
Open April-October ▲ 🚐 🚟
Size 5 acres, 20 touring pitches, 18 with electric hookup, 14 level pitches, 26 static caravans, 5 🚿, 8 WCs, 1 CWP
£ car/tent £6-£6.50, car/caravan £7-£7.50, motorhome £7-£7.50, motorbike/tent £6
🅿 ▣ 🅒 🛆 🖂 Calor Gaz 🛆 🖊 WS
Last arrival time: 10:00
➡ Midway between Aberlour and Craigellachie off A95.

Camping & Caravanning Club Site
Speyside, Elchies, Craigellachie
📞 **01340-810414**
Open late March-early November ▲ 🚐 🚟

Size 75 touring pitches, 35 with electric hookup, 8 ⌂, 8 WCs, 1 CWP
£ car/tent £8.75-£11.55, car/caravan £8.75-£11.55, motorhome £8.75-£11.55, motorbike/tent £8.75, children £1.40
CC MasterCard Visa
▣ 📞 ⌂ ✕ ↜
Last arrival time: 11:00
➤ Situated on B9102, 2½ miles from junction with A941 Elgin to Craigellachie road.

CRAWFORD Lanarkshire   13D3

Crawford Caravan & Camp Site
Murray Place, Carlisle Road, Crawford ML12 6TW
📞 **01864-502258**
Open April-October ▲ 🚐 🚏
Size 2 acres, 25 touring pitches, 20 with electric hookup, 25 level pitches, 2 ⌂, 6 WCs, 1 CWP
£ car/tent £5, car/caravan £5, motorhome £5, motorbike/tent £3.50, children £0.50
▣¼ ✕¼ 🚐¼ ▣ 📞 ⌂ ✕ Calor ♿ ↜ WS
Last arrival time: 10:00
➤ Site in Crawford, off A74.

CREETOWN Wigtownshire   12C4

Castle Cary Holiday Park
Creetown DG8 7DQ
📞 **01671-820264 Fax 01671-820670**
Open all year ▲ 🚐 🚏

Set in superb parkland with hardwood woodlands, the site offers a range of facilities including indoor and outdoor heated pools, a country inn, shop, games, snooker and a solarium.

Size 12 acres, 50 touring pitches, 50 with electric hookup, 50 level pitches, 45 static caravans, 7 ⌂, 9 WCs, 1 CWP
£ car/tent £7.80-£10, car/caravan £7.80-£10, motorhome £7.80-£10, motorbike/tent £5, children £0.85
Rental 🚐 Chalet. £165-£315
CC Visa
▣ ✕ 🚐 ▣ 📞 ▤ 🍴 🎱 ⌂ 🖊 GR 🔍 TV ⌂ ✕ 🔌
Calor Gaz ♿ ↜ WS
Last arrival time: 12:00
➤ ½ mile S of Creetown village, on right directly off main A75.

Creetown Caravan Park
Silver Street, Creetown DG8 7HU
📞 **01671-820377 Fax 01671-820377**
Open 1 March-31 October ▲ 🚐 🚏
Size 3 acres, 20 touring pitches, 20 with electric hookup, 30 level pitches, 50 static caravans, 4 ⌂, 8 WCs, 1 CWP
£ car/tent £8-£10, car/caravan £8-£10, motorhome £8-£10, motorbike/tent £6
Rental 🚐 £95-£235
▣¼ ✕¼ 🚐¼ ▣ 📞 ⌂ ▤ GR ⌂ ✕ Calor ♿ ↜ WS
Last arrival time: 11:00
➤ Just off A75 in village of Creetown, turn down between Clock Tower and Ellangowan Hotel, sharp left on to Silver Street.
See advert on next page

Park of Brandedleys
Near Dumfries, Crocketford DG2 8RG
☎ 01556-690250 Fax 01556-690681
Open 1 March-31 October A ⊕ ⊐

Easily accessible landscaped park with fine views to the loch and hills. Top quality toilets with ensuite units, bath and baby/ hair care room.

Size 16 acres, 80 touring pitches, 80 with electric hookup, 50 level pitches, 28 static caravans, 13 ᛗ, 25 WCs, 2 CWPs
£ car/tent £8.50-£12.50, car/caravan £8.50-£12.50, motorhome £8.50-£12.50, motorbike/tent £8.50, children £2
Rental ⊕ Chalet. £125-£460
CC MasterCard Visa
🛒 🛒¼ ✕ ✕¼ ➥ ▣ ☎ ▧ ▨ ▩ ▦ ▩ GR ▩
⚠ ▦ ♿ Calor Gaz ⅙ ↟ WS
Last arrival time: 10:00
➠ Fork left off A75 Dumfries to Stranraer in Crocketford at park sign. Site on right in 160 yards.

Castle Point Caravan Park
Rockcliffe, Dalbeattie DG5 4QL
☎ 01556-630248
Open April-October A ⊕ ⊐

A small quiet coastal site near Rockcliffe Village in Galloway. The site and walks nearby have some of the best views along the Solway coast.

Size 3 acres, 29 touring pitches, 29 with electric hookup, 29 level pitches, 7 static caravans, 4 ᛗ, 10 WCs, 1 CWP
£ car/tent £7-£9, car/caravan £8.50-£9.50, motorhome £7-£9, motorbike/tent £7
Rental ⊕ £135-£230
Calor Gaz ⅙ ↟
Last arrival time: 9:30
➠ From Dalbeattie travel S along the A710 coastal road. After 5 miles turn right to Rockcliffe (1 mile). At brow of hill just after entering Rockcliffe turn left down signposted road to site.

Islecroft Caravan & Camping Site
Dalbeattie DG5 4HE
01556-502521 Fax 01556-502521
Open Easter-September ▲ ⛟ 🚐
Size 3½ acres, 74 touring pitches, 10 with electric hookup, 4 🚿, 10 WCs, 1 CWP
£ car/tent £5.25-£6.25, car/caravan £5.25-£6.25, motorhome £5.25-£6.25, motorbike/tent £5.25
🏪¼ ✕¼ 🍴¼ 🛒 🖳 ⚠ 🔀 🐕
➔ In Dalbeattie, off Mill Street and adjacant to Colliston Park.

DALKEITH Midlothian 13D2

Fordel Cravan & Camping Park
Lauder Road, Dalkeith EH22 2PH
0131-660 3921 Fax 0131-663 8891
Open March-October ▲ ⛟ 🚐
Size 4 acres, 45 touring pitches, 12 with electric hookup, 45 level pitches, 7 🚿, 6 WCs, 2 CWPs
£ car/tent £6.50-£7.50, car/caravan £8-£10.75, motorhome £8-£10.75, motorbike/tent £6.50
🏪 ✕ 🍴 🖳 🛒 ⚠ 🔀 ⊟ Calor Gaz ⛱ 🐕 WS
➔ 8 miles SE Edinburgh on main Edinburgh to Newcastle route, A68.

DINGWALL Ross-shire 15D3

Camping & Caravanning Club Site
Jubilee Park Road, Dingwall IV15 9QZ
01349-862236
Open end March-start November ▲ ⛟ 🚐
Size 6 acres, 90 touring pitches, 55 with electric hookup, 6 🚿, 13 WCs, 1 CWP
£ car/tent £9.20-£12.05, car/caravan £9.20-£12.05, motorhome £9.20-£12.05, motorbike/tent £9.20, children £1.40
℀ MasterCard Visa
🗑 🛒 ⛱ 🐕
Last arrival time: 11:00
➔ In Dingwall, coming from S, take by-pass and follow signs. First rignt down Hill Street, then right at junction, left over railway bridge, then first left. Site is signposted.

DRYMEN Stirlingshire 12C2

Camping & Caravanning Club Site
Milarrochy Bay, Balmaha, Drymen
01360-870236
Open end March-start November ▲ ⛟ 🚐
Size 7 acres, 140 touring pitches, 40 with electric hookup, 6 🚿, 11 WCs, 1 CWP
£ car/tent £9.20-£12.05, car/caravan £9.20-£12.05, motorhome £9.20-£12.05, children £1.40
℀ MasterCard Visa
🗑 🛒 ⚠ 🔀 ⛱ 🐕 WS
Last arrival time: 11:00
➔ From Dumbarton head N on A82, then follow A811 to Drymen. In Drymen, turn N for Balmaha on B837. Site on left after Balmaha.

DUNBAR East Lothian 13E2

Belhaven Bay Caravan Park
Spott Road, Dunbar EH42 1RS
01620-893348 Fax 01620-895623

Sheltered location on the beautiful East Lothian coastline. An ideal base to explore this scenic part of Scotland.

Camping & Caravanning Club Site
Barns Ness, Dunbar EH42 1QP
01368-863536
Open March ▲ ⛟ 🚐
Size 10 acres, 80 touring pitches, 42 with electric hookup, 80 level pitches, 4 🚿, 9 WCs, 1 CWP
£ car/tent £8.20-£10.40, car/caravan £8.20-£10.40, motorhome £8.20-£10.40, motorbike/tent £8.20, children £1.30
℀ MasterCard Visa

← Camping & Caravanning Club Site

🗐 📳 ⊁
Last arrival time: 11:00
➜ Look for signpost East Barns, 20 miles N
of Berwick-on-Tweed on A1. Turn at
junction signposted to site.

Inver Guest House
Inver, Dunbeath KW6 6EH
📳 01593-731252
Open April-October 🅰 🚐 🚏

*Flat, grassy, sheltered site, near to the sea on
the rocky coastline. A good access point for
bird watchers, archeologists and Niel M.
Gunn enthusiasts. Forty miles south of John
O' Groats.*

Size 15 touring pitches, 15 level pitches, 2
🖾, 4 WCs, 1 CWP
£ car/tent £2-£2.50, car/caravan £2-£2.50,
motorhome £2-£2.50, motorbike/tent £2,
children £1
🅾¼ ✗¼ ⬤¼ 📳 🗐 ⅙ ⊁
➜ Follow the A9 N. Bypass Dunbeth village,
over the bridge for ½ mile. The site is
directly behind Inver Guest House on left.

Stratheck International Caravan Park
Loch Eck, Dunoon PA23 8SG
📳 01369-840472 Fax 01369-840472
Open March-December 🅰 🚐 🚏

Size 13 acres, 70 touring pitches, 45 with
electric hookup, 70 level pitches, 80 static
caravans, 8 🖾, 18 WCs, 1 CWP
£ car/tent £6.50-£8.50, car/caravan £5-£7,
motorhome £6.50-£8.50, motorbike/tent
£6.50, children £5-£7
Rental 🚐 £140-£290
🅾 🗐 📳 🗐 🖾 🆁 ⚠ 🖾 Calor Gaz ⅙ ⊁ WS
Last arrival time: 8:00
➜ 7 miles N of Dunoon on A815. 500 yards
past Younger Botanic Gardens

Sango Sands Camping & Caravan Site
Sangomore, Durness IV27 4PP
📳 01971-511262 Fax 01971-511205
Open 1 April-15 October 🅰 🚐 🚏
Size 8½ acres, 82 touring pitches, 20 with
electric hookup, 60 level pitches, 12 🖾, 18
WCs, 2 CWPs
£ car/tent £6.60, car/caravan £6.60,
motorhome £6.60, motorbike/tent £6.60
🅾 🅾¼ ✗ ⬤ 🗐 📳 🗐 Calor Gaz ⊁
Last arrival time: 6:00
➜ On A838 in centre of Durness village,
overlooking Sango Bay.

Mortonhall Caravan Park
36 Mortonhall Gate, Frogston Road East,
Edinburgh EH16 6TJ
📳 0131-664 1533 Fax 0131-6645387
Open 27 March-31 October 🅰 🚐 🚏

*Country estate just 15 minutes from the city
centre. Excellent amenities, restaurant and
bar, games room, TV room, laundry,
modern toilet and shower block.*

Size 200 acres, 250 touring pitches, 50 with electric hookup, 18 static caravans, 2 CWPs
CC Visa
🛁 ✕ 🚐 🗊 ♿
➡ From N or S, leave city bypass at Lothianburn or Straiton junctions and follow signs for Mortonhall Caravan Park. From city centre, take main road S from either E or W end of Princes Street.

Size 14 acres, 37 touring pitches, 37 with electric hookup, 37 level pitches, 60 static caravans, 8 🏠, 20 WCs, 2 CWPs
Rental 🚐
🛁 🛁¼ ✕ ✕¼ 🚐¼ 🗓 📞 🗑 🗺 📁 🖾 ⚠ 🖾
Calor Gaz 🐕
➡ From Elgin 5 miles on coast road between Lossiemouth and Burghead.

Red Craig Hotel & Caravan Park
Burghead, Elgin IV30 2XX
📞 **01343-835663 Fax 01343-835663**
Open 1 April-31 October 🏕 🚐 🚃

A family run hotel and caravan park with every facility on site. Excellent food and carryouts. Weekend entertainment. Panoramic views. Well positioned for the castle and whisky trails.

Size 4 acres, 38 touring pitches, 10 with electric hookup, 10 level pitches, 8 static caravans, 4 🏠, 6 WCs, 1 CWP
£ car/tent £6-£7, car/caravan £8-£9, motorhome £8-£9, motorbike/tent £6
CC MasterCard Visa
🛁¼ ✕ 🚐 🗓 📞 🗑 🗺 ⚠ 🖾 🍴 Calor ♿ 🐕 WS
Last arrival time: 10:30
➡ From A96 turn right 2 miles outside Elgin onto B9013. Entering Burghead turn right onto B9040.

Station Caravan Park
Hopeman, Elgin IV30 2RU
📞 **01343-830880**
Open April-October 🏕 🚐 🚃

Angecroft Caravan Park
Ettrick TD7 5HY
📞 **01750-62251 Fax 01721-730627**
🏕 🚐 🚃

Overlooking water and surrounded by woodland, Angecroft is the ideal place to get away and enjoy the peace and quiet of the Scottish Borders.

Size 5 acres, 10 touring pitches, 10 with electric hookup, 10 level pitches, 30 static caravans, 4 🏠, 8 WCs, 1 CWP
£ car/tent £5-£7, car/caravan £7-£8.70, motorhome £7-£8.70, motorbike/tent £5
Rental 🚐 Chalet. £90-£215
🛁 ✕¼ 🗓 📞 🗑 🖾 🖾 Calor Gaz ♿ 🐕 WS
➡ From A74/M74 enter Lockerbie and take B723 through Borland to Eskdalemuir. Turn left onto B709 and park is on left 11 miles N of Eskdalemuir. From A7 at Langholm take B709 to park (23 miles). From A7 at Hawick take B711. Park is 4 miles W of Tushielaw on B709.

EYEMOUTH Berwickshire   13F2

Scoutscroft Holiday Centre
St Abbs Road, Coldingham, Eyemouth
☎ 018907-71338 Fax 018907-71338
Open 1 March-31 October Å 🚐 🚙
Size 14 acres, 60 touring pitches, 40 with
electric hookup, 60 level pitches, 120 static
caravans, 12 🚿, 40 WCs, 2 CWPs
£ car/tent £5.50-£7.50, car/caravan £7-£9,
motorhome £7-£9, motorbike/tent £5.50
Rental 🚐 Chalet. caravans £130-£270
CC MasterCard Visa
🛁¼ ✗ 🍺 🔲 🔃 📻 🔳 GR TV ⚠ 🔲 🔌 Calor Gaz
🔥 ♿ WS
Last arrival time: 12:00
➡ Off A1.

FOCHABERS Morayshire   15E3

Burnside Caravan Site
The Nurseries, Fochabers IV32 7ES
☎ 01343-820362
Open 1 April-30 October Å 🚐 🚙

SCOUTSCROFT
HOLIDAY CENTRE

*This family run Park Graded Excellent (5 ticks) by the
Scottish Tourist Board is situated in the picturesque village
of Coldingham in the Scottish Borders, 12 miles north of
Berwick-upon-Tweed.
The Centre has a new Touring and Camping Park with
gravelled super pitches, electric and non electric hook ups,
ample space for tents and a children's adventure play area.
Situated in a well lit family atmosphere are Scoutscroft
Thistle Awarded Holiday Homes for hire. Live entertainment
for kids and adults plus the New Priory Restaurant makes
Scoutscroft Holiday Centre and ideal family holiday.*

**COLDINGHAM, BERWICKSHIRE, SCOTLAND TD14 5NB
Tel: (018907) 71338 Fax: (018907) 71746**

Size 11 acres, 110 touring pitches, 40 with
electric hookup, 110 level pitches, 8 🚿, 24
WCs, 2 CWPs
£ car/tent £7, car/caravan £7, motorhome £7
🛁¼ ✗¼ 🍺¼ 🔲 🔃 🔳 GR ⚠ 🔲
➡ From junction on A96 and A98 travel S on
A96 for ½ mile. Site on right.

FORFAR Angus   13E1

Drumshademuir Caravan Park
Roundyhill, Forfar DD8 1QT
☎ 01575-573284
Open mid March-end October Å 🚐 🚙
Size 7½ acres, 80 touring pitches, 46 with
electric hookup, 80 level pitches, 30 static
caravans, 8 🚿, 12 WCs, 2 CWPs
£ car/tent £5.50-£6, car/caravan £8-£9,
motorhome £8-£9, motorbike/tent £5
Rental Chalet.
🛁 ✗ 🍺 🔲 🔃 🔲 ⚠ 🔲 🔌 Calor Gaz 🔥 ♿ WS
Last arrival time: 9:00
➡ Take A928 from A94 at Glamis for
Kirriemuir, 3 miles N of Glamis Castle on
Kirriemuir road.

Lochside Caravan Site
Forfar Country Park, Forfar DD8 1BT
☎ 01307-64201
Open April-mid October Å 🚐 🚙
*On the east shore of Forfar Loch, next to
Lochside Leisure Centre, within Forfar
Country Park. No gas available. Swimming
pool ½ mile. Open from April to mid
October.*

Size 4 acres, 72 touring pitches, 72 with
electric hookup, 72 level pitches, 8 🚿, 13
WCs, 2 CWPs
🛁¼ ✗¼ 🍺¼ 🔲 🔃 🔲 ⚠ 🔲 ♿
➡ Leave A929/A94 at first signpost to Forfar.
Centrally situated in town of Forfar.

FORRES Morayshire   15E3

Riverview Caravan Park
Mundole Court, Forres IV36 0SZ
☎ 01309-673932
Open 1 April-31 October Å 🚐 🚙

A 4 tick Scottish Tourist Board Rating site with a function hall, shop, launderette, salmon and trout fishing and riverside walks. Situated within the local whisky and castle trail.

Size 34 acres, 60 touring pitches, 40 with electric hookup, 60 level pitches, 50 static caravans, 8 🚿, 6 WCs, 1 CWP
£ car/tent £8, car/caravan £9, motorhome £9, motorbike/tent £8
Rental 🚐
🛒 ✗¼ 🕁¼ 🛢 📞 🗖 GR TV ⚠ ✗ 🔌 Calor ♿ ⚡ WS
➡ From Inverness onto A96 through Nairn, Brodie onto Findhorn Bridge situated just before Forres. Turn right to Mundole, ½ mile then turn right into park. From Aberdeen A96, Elgin then Forres bypass. 1 mile out of Forres, before going over bridge turn sharp right, to Mundole ½ mile then turn right into park.

FORT WILLIAM Inverness-shire 14C4

Glen Nevis Caravan & Camping Park
Glen Nevis, Fort William PH33 6SX
📞 **01397-702191 Fax 01397-703904**
Open 15 March-31 October 🏕 🚐 🚚
Size 30 acres, 380 touring pitches, 180 with electric hookup, 280 level pitches, 34 🚿, 73 WCs, 3 CWPs
£ car/tent £7.10-£9.50, car/caravan £7.40-£9.80, motorhome £7.10-£9.50, motorbike/tent £6.50, children £0.90-£1.25
CC MasterCard Visa
🛒 ✗ 🕁 🛢 📞 🗖 ⚠ ✗ 🔌 Calor Gaz ♿ ⚡
Last arrival time: 11:00
➡ A82 to mini roundabout at N outskirts of Fort William. Exit for Glen Nevis Park. Site is 2½ miles on right.

Linnhe Caravan & Chalet Park
Corpach, Fort William PH33 7NL
📞 **01397-772376 Fax 01397-772007**
Open 15 December-31 October 🏕 🚐 🚚

Beautifully landscaped with magnificent views over Loch Eil. Enjoy a host of outdoor activities or simply relax in well tended surroundings. Graded "Excellent". Private beach. ➡

← **Linnhe Caravan & Chalet Park**

Size 13½ acres, 67 touring pitches, 54 with electric hookup, 67 level pitches, 75 static caravans, 8 ⋒, 15 WCs, 1 CWP
£ car/tent £6.50-£8, car/caravan £8-£10, motorhome £8-£10, motorbike/tent £6.50
Rental ⇋ £145-£375, chalets £275-£495.
ℂℂ MasterCard Visa
🛒 ▣ ☎ ▣ 🖩 ⚠ ⊠ Calor Gaz ⊁ WS
Last arrival time: 11:00
➡ On A830, 1½ miles W of Corpach village, signposted, 5 miles from Fort William.

Lochy Caravan & Camping Park
Camaghael, Fort William PH33 7NF
☎ **01397-703446 Fax 01397-706172**
Open March-October ▲ ⇋ 🚐
Size 10 acres, 80 touring pitches, 30 with electric hookup, 50 level pitches, 18 static caravans, 10 ⋒, 12 WCs, 1 CWP
£ car/tent £7.60-£9.80, car/caravan £8-£10.60, motorhome £7.60-£9.80, motorbike/tent £6
Rental ⇋ Chalet. £180-£460
ℂℂ MasterCard Visa

LOCHY
CARAVAN PARK

Small family owned and operated park offering excellent views of Ben Nevis and surrounding mountains.

Ideal touring centre for Western Highlands. The park is only two miles from the town centre.

CAMAGHAEL, FORT WILLIAM, HIGHLAND PH33 7NF
Tel: 01397 703446 Fax: 01397 706172

🛒 ▣ ☎ ▣ Calor Gaz ⊁
Last arrival time: 10:00
➡ 2 miles N of Fort William on A82 turn W on A830 for 500 yards and take first turn on right past Lochaber High School.

Camping & Caravanning Club Site
Well Road, Rosemarkie, Fortrose
☎ **01380-621117**
Open end March-end September ▲ ⇋ 🚐
Size 4 acres, 4 ⋒, 16 WCs, 2 CWPs
£ car/tent £8.75-£11.55, car/caravan £8.75-£11.55, motorhome £8.75-£11.55, motorbike/tent £8.75, children £1.40
ℂℂ MasterCard Visa
▣ ♿ ⊁
Last arrival time: 11:00
➡ Follow A9 over Kessock Bridge, turn right at Tore roundabout on A832 signposted Fortrose and Cromarty. In Fortrose turn right.

Gruinard Bay Caravan Park
Laide, Achnasheen IV22 2ND
☎ **01445-731225 Fax 01445-731225**
Open 1 April-31 October ▲ ⇋ 🚐

Level, grassy site adjacent to a sandy beach. Quiet and restful with superb views over Gruinard Bay to the islands and mountains.

Size 34 touring pitches, 18 with electric hookup, 18 level pitches, 14 static caravans, 4 ⋒, 9 WCs, 1 CWP
£ car/tent £7, car/caravan £7, motorhome £7, motorbike/tent £7

Rental 🚐 £120-£205
℃ MasterCard Visa
🔋 🔋¼ ✕¼ 🛁¼ ⊟ 🔌 ⊟ ⚠ 🎏 Calor Gaz 🐕
Last arrival time: 10:00
➜ From A835(T) Inverness to Ullapool road, at Brawmore junction (near Corrieshalloch Falls), turn left onto A832 signposted to Gairloch/Ayltbea/Inverewe Gardens. Park is on right.

Sands Holiday Centre
Gairloch IV21 2DL
🔌 01445-712152 Fax 01445-712518
Open 1 April-15 October 🏕 🚐 🚏

Positioned beside a sandy beach with views westward. Ideally located for walking, fishing, watersports and touring.

Size 50 acres, 300 touring pitches, 60 with electric hookup, 20 static caravans, 22 🚿, 54 WCs, 1 CWP
£ car/tent £7-£9, car/caravan £7-£12, motorhome £7-£9, motorbike/tent £6.50
Rental 🚐
℃ MasterCard Visa
🔋 ⊟ 🔌 ⊟ ⚠ 🎏 Calor Gaz 🐕
Last arrival time: 10:00
➜ Follow A382 to Gairloch. At Gairloch take B8021 to Melvaig, 4 miles along this road will bring you to park.

GARVE Ross-shire 15D3

Badrallach Bothy Campsite
Croft No 9, Dundonnell, Garve IV23 2QP
🔌 01854-633281
🏕 🚐 🚏
Size 1 acre, 15 touring pitches, 15 level pitches, 2 🚿, 5 WCs,

£ car/tent £5.88, car/caravan £5.88, motorhome £5.88, motorbike/tent £5.88, children £1.18
Rental Chalet.
🔌 ⊟ 🅖🆁 ♿ 🐕
➜ Off A832 take single track road 1 mile E of Dundonnel Hotel. 7 miles to Lochshore campsite.

GATEHOUSE OF FLEET Kirkcudbrightshire 12C4

Auchenlarie Holiday Farm
Near Castle Douglas, Gatehouse of Fleet DG7 2EX
🔌 01557-840251
🏕 🚐 🚏

Situated on the Galloway coast, this family owned holiday park, is geared to the needs of families and is an ideal touring base for holidaying in the Dumfries and Galloway area.

Size 20 acres, 287 touring pitches, 35 with electric hookup, 163 static caravans, 10 🚿, 30 WCs, 2 CWPs
🔋 🛁 🍴 Calor ♿
➜ 4 miles W of Gatehouse.

GLASGOW 12C2

Craigendmuir Park
3 Campsie View, Stepps, Glasgow G33 6AF
🔌 0141-779 4159 Fax 0141-779 4057
Open all year 🏕 🚐 🚏
Size 2½ acres, 20 touring pitches, 12 with electric hookup, 20 static caravans, 10 🚿, 10 WCs, 2 CWPs
£ car/tent £6, car/caravan £6, motorhome £6, motorbike/tent £6

➜

← Craigendmuir Park

Rental 🚐 Chalet. from £150
CC MasterCard Visa
⚡ ✕ 🚿 🔋 🚽 Calor ♿ 🐕
➔ From junction 11 on M8 follow A80 to Cumberland/Stirling. From N on A80 to Stepps.

Strathclyde Country Park
366 Hamilton Road, Motherwell ML1 3ED
📞 **01698-266155 Fax 01698-252925**
Open April-October ▲ 🚐 🚎

One of Scotlands leading centres for outdoor recreation, with a wide range of activities including, land and water sports, sandy beaches, play areas and a programme of special events.

Size 14 acres, 250 touring pitches, 100 with electric hookup, 100 level pitches,
£ car/tent £6.45, car/caravan £7.50, motorhome £7.50, motorbike/tent £6.45
⚡ ✕¼ 🚐¼ 🚿 🔋 🎏/⚠ 🎯 Calor ♿ 🐕 WS
➔ From M74 junction 5 take A725 (Belshill). Park signed off roundabout, also off motorway.

Invercoe Caravans
Invercoe, Glencoe PA39 4HP
📞 **01855-811210 Fax 01855-811210**
Open 1 April-31 October ▲ 🚐 🚎
Size 5 acres, 60 touring pitches, 40 with electric hookup, 55 level pitches, 5 static caravans, 9 🚿, 14 WCs, 3 CWPs
£ car/tent £8-£9, car/caravan £9-£10, motorhome £9-£10, motorbike/tent £8, children £0.50
Rental 🚐 £170-£265
⚡ ✕¼ 🚐¼ 🚿 🔋 🚽 ⚠ 🎯 Calor Gaz ♿ 🐕
Last arrival time: 11:00
➔ From Glasgow follow A82 to Glencoe. At Glencoe Hotel turn right onto B863 for ¼ mile.

Cock Inn Caravan Park
Auchenmalg, Glenluce DG8 0JT
📞 **01581-500227**
Open 1 March-31 October ▲ 🚐 🚎
Size 6 acres, 30 touring pitches, 20 with electric hookup, 15 level pitches, 60 static caravans, 6 🚿, 15 WCs, 3 CWPs
£ car/tent £6.50-£10.50, car/caravan £6.50-£10.50, motorhome £6.50-£10.50, motorbike/tent £6
Rental 🚐 Chalet.
⚡ 🚐 🚿 🔋 🚽 🔲🅶🆁 ⚠ 🎯 🚰 Calor Gaz ♿ 🐕 WS
Last arrival time: 11:00
➔ From A75 Glenluce bypass turn onto A747 Glenluce to Fort William road for 5 miles.

Glenluce Caravan and Camping
Glenluce DG8 0QR
☎ **01581-300412**
Open mid March-mid October ▲ 🚐 🚎

Peaceful, secluded, family run sun trap park. Close to the village, beach, golfing, bowling, pony trekking, fishing and superb walks.

Size 5 acres, 18 touring pitches, 12 with electric hookup, 18 level pitches, 30 static caravans, 4 🚿, 7 WCs, 1 CWP
£ car/tent £6.50-£7.50, car/caravan £7.50-£8.50, motorhome £7.50-£8.50, motorbike/tent £6.50
Rental 🚐 £96-£288
⚡¼ ✕¼ 🚰¼ 🗑 🔌 🛢 🛆 🏞 Calor Gaz 🐕 WS
Last arrival time: 11:00
➡ Exit A75 to Glenluce village. Park entrance is opposite Inglenook restaurant in centre of village.

Whitecairn Farm Caravan Park
Glenluce DG8 0NZ
☎ **01581-300267** Fax **01581-300267**
Open March-October ▲ 🚐 🚎

Situated north of Glenluce village with panoramic views over Luce Bay and surrounding countryside. Ideal base for

golfing, fishing, ponytrekking and walking holidays. Large area for all touring units with super hook-ups.

Size 3 acres, 10 touring pitches, 10 with electric hookup, 10 level pitches, 40 static caravans, 4 🚿, 4 WCs, 4 CWPs
£ car/tent £7-£8
Rental 🚐 £270-£125
⚡ 🗑 🔌 🛢 Calor Gaz 🚿 🐕 WS
➡ 1½ miles N of Glenluce off A75. Follow signs to Motor Museum and park is in 1 mile.

GREENLAW Berwickshire 13E2

Greenlaw Caravan Park
Bank Street, Greenlaw TD10 6XX
☎ **01361-810341** Fax **01361-810715**
Open 1 March-30 November ▲ 🚐 🚎
Size 7 acres, 3 touring pitches, 3 with electric hookup, 65 level pitches, 55 static caravans, 8 🚿, 8 WCs, 1 CWP
£ car/tent £8.50, car/caravan £8.50, motorhome £8.50, motorbike/tent £8.50, children £8.50
⚡¼ ✕¼ 🚰¼ 🔌 🛢 Calor Gaz 🐕 WS
➡ In Greenlaw Village turn N on A6105. Site is situated on left close to nature reserve.

GRETNA Dumfriesshire 13D4

Braids Caravan Park
Annan Road, Gretna DG16 5DQ
☎ **01461-337409** Fax **01461-337409**
Open all year ▲ 🚐 🚎

Family run full facility park in an ideal touring centre. Touring advice. Open all year. Rallies welcome. Nicely placed away from motorway. B&B in owners bungalow.

➡

← Braids Caravan Park

Size 4 acres, 84 touring pitches, 58 with electric hookup, 50 level pitches, 5 static caravans, 8 ⋔, 10 WCs, 3 CWPs
£ car/tent £6-£7, car/caravan £6.75-£7.75, motorhome £6.75-£7.75, motorbike/tent £6
⚊ ✕¼ 🛢 🔌 🚿 ⬣ 🏕 Calor Gaz ♿ ⚲ WS
Last arrival time: 12:00
➜ A74 N, A75, second left into Gretna.

The Monks' Muir Caravan Park
Haddington EH41 3SB
📞 **01620-860340** Fax **01620-860340**
Open all tear ⚊ 🚐 🚏
Size 7 acres, 72 touring pitches, 50 with electric hookup, 21 static caravans, 8 ⋔, 16 WCs, 2 CWPs
➜ Access directly from A1, 3 miles E of Haddington.

Bonchester Bridge Caravan Park
Bonchester Bridge, Hawick
📞 **01450-860676**
Open 1 April-31 October ⚊ 🚐 🚏
Size 2 acres, 20 touring pitches, 20 with electric hookup, 20 level pitches, 1 static caravans, 4 ⋔, 10 WCs, 1 CWP
£ car/tent £5-£6.50, car/caravan £6-£7, motorhome £5-£6.50, motorbike/tent £5, children £1.50-£3
Rental 🚐 static £110
⚊ ⚊¼ ✕ ✕¼ 🛢 🔌 🚿 🍴 Calor Gaz ♿ ⚲
Last arrival time: 9:00
➜ Off A68 and A7.

Inchmartine Caravan Park & Nurseries
Inchture
📞 **01821-670212** Fax **01821-670266**
Open end March-end October ⚊ 🚐 🚏

Size 4 acres, 45 touring pitches, 36 with electric hookup, 36 level pitches, 3 🛁, 10 WCs,
£ car/tent £7.50, car/caravan £7.50, motorhome £7.50, motorbike/tent £7.50
🛒¼ ✗¼ 🍴¼ Calor Gaz 🐕 WS
Last arrival time: 8:00
➡ Site signed from A85 Perth/Dundee road, 1½ miles from Perth.

INVERARAY Argyll   12B1

Argyll Caravan & Camping Park
Inveraray PA32 8XT
📞 **01499-302285 Fax 01499-302421**
Open 1 April-31 October 🏕 🚐 🚏
Size 8 acres, 60 touring pitches, 40 with electric hookup, 60 level pitches, 200 static caravans, 16 🛁, 80 WCs, 2 CWPs
£ car/tent £6.20-£7.80, car/caravan £7.80-£9.30, motorhome £7.80-£9.30, motorbike/tent £6.20
🛒 ✗ 🍴 🗄 📞 🖨 ▶ 🔍 ✂ GR 🔎 ⚠ 🎯 🍴 Calor Gaz ♿ 🐕
➡ 2 miles SW of Inveraray on A83.

INVERGARRY Inverness-shire   14C4

Faichem Park
Ardgarry Farm, Faichem, Invergarry PH35 4HG
📞 **01809-501226**
Open April-October 🏕 🚐 🚏

A quiet, family run park, spotlessly clean and well maintained. Set amidst mountains and pines. A perfect location for touring the Western Highlands. B.G.H.P. graded excellent. Award for excellence in sanitation facilities and attractive environment.

Size 2 acres, 30 touring pitches, 14 with electric hookup, 11 level pitches, 2 🛁, 6 WCs, 1 CWP
£ car/tent £6-£6.50, car/caravan £6-£6.50, motorhome £6-£6.50, motorbike/tent £6, children £0.25
Rental 🚐 Chalet. £80-£405
🗄 📞 🗄 Calor Gaz 🐕
Last arrival time: 10:00
➡ From A82 at Invergarry take the A87. Continue for 1 mile and turn right at Faichem signpost. Bear left up hill and entrance is first on right.

Faichemard Farm Camping & Caravanning Park
Faichem, Invergarry PH35 4HG
📞 **01809-501314**
Open April-October 🏕 🚐 🚏

A unique ten acre site, 40 pitches each with its own picnic table and magnificent view.

Size 10 acres, 30 touring pitches, 14 with electric hookup, 25 level pitches, 4 🛁, 8 WCs, 1 CWP
£ car/tent £5, car/caravan £5, motorhome £5, motorbike/tent £5
🗄 📞 🗄 ♿ 🐕
➡ I mile W of Invergarry, turn right and go past Ardgarry Farm and Faichem Park campsite. Turn right at sign for A & D Grant.

INVERNESS Inverness-shire   15D3

Auchnahillin Caravan Park
Daviot East, Inverness IV1 2XQ
📞 **01463-772286 Fax 01463-772286**
Open Easter-mid October 🏕 🚐 🚏   ➡

← Auchnahillin Caravan Park

*Highly Commended park with excellent
amenities. Set amid splendid Highland
scenery and nestling in a peaceful valley
with views of the surrounding forests and
mountains, Auchnahillin is the ideal base
for touring or enjoying the multitude of
activities in this lovely area.*

Size 12 acres, 65 touring pitches, 35 with
electric hookup, 65 level pitches, 22 static
caravans, 6 ♦, 18 WCs, 1 CWP
£ car/tent £5.50-£7.50, car/caravan £7.50-£9,
motorhome £7.50-£9, motorbike/tent £4.50,
children £0.50
Rental ⛊ Chalet. £90-275
⛊ ✗ ♥ ▣ ◖ ⬚ 🖾 ◲ ⚠ ✸ ⬛ Calor Gaz ⬙
🐾 WS
Last arrival time: 10:00
➜ B9154 loop 5 miles S of Inverness off A9.
North end signed Daviod East, south signed
for Moy.

Bunchrew Caravan Park
Bunchrew, Inverness IV3 6TD
☎ **01463-237802 fax 01463-225803**
Open April-December 🛆 ⛊ 🚐

*Situated on the shore of the Beauly Firth
with wonderful views of the water and hills.
A perfect base for touring the Highlands.*

Size 15 acres, 100 touring pitches, 50 with
electric hookup, 100 level pitches, 14 static
caravans, 8 ♦, 18 WCs, 1 CWP

£ car/tent £7.50-£8, car/caravan £7.50-£8,
motorhome £7.50-£8, motorbike/tent £6,
children £1
Rental ⛊ £140-£225
⛊ ✗¼ ▣ ◖ ⚠ ⬛ Calor Gaz WS
➜ Leave Inverness on A862, site is 3 miles
W of town.

Coulmore Bay Site
North Kessock, Inverness
☎ **01463-731322**
Open April-September 🛆 ⛊ 🚐
Size 3 acres, 30 touring pitches, 8 with
electric hookup, 1 static caravan, 4 ♦, 4
WCs
⛊ ✗ ▣ Calor
➜ 3 miles W of North Kessock.

Scaniport Camping & Caravanning Park
Scaniport, Inverness IV1 2DL
☎ **01463-751351**
Open Easter-September 🛆 ⛊ 🚐
Size 2 acres, 30 touring pitches, 30 level
pitches, 2 ♦, 6 WCs, 1 CWP
£ car/tent £4.50, car/caravan £5.50-£6.50,
motorhome £5.50-£6.50, motorbike/tent
£4.50, children £0.75
◖ ▣ Calor Gaz ⬙ 🐾
➜ From Inverness take the B862 towards
Dores, 5 miles on site is opposite telephone
box at Scaniport.

Cunninghamhead Estate Caravan Park
Irvine, Kilmarnock KA3 2PE
☎ **01294-850238**
Open 1 April-30 September 🛆 ⛊ 🚐
Size 10 acres, 60 touring pitches, 18 with
electric hookup, 60 level pitches, 50 static
caravans, 4 ♦, 14 WCs, 1 CWP

£ car/tent £6.50-£8, car/caravan £6.50-£8, motorhome £6.50-£8, motorbike/tent £6
Rental 🚐 £110-£210
🗑 📞 🖬 🎮 🖨 GR 🅰 🎯 ⏁ Gaz 🐾 WS
Last arrival time: 10:00
➔ From S take A78 to Irvine by-pass. From Newhouse interchange take A736 Glasgow Road (long drive) through Oldhall roundabout and Newmoor roundabout until you reach Stanecastle roundabout. Turn right onto B769 Stewarton Road. The park is 2½ miles on left.

JEDBURGH Roxburghshire 13E3

Camping & Caravanning Club Site
Elliot Park, Jedburgh TD8 6EF`
📞 **01835-863393**
Open end March-start September 🅰 🚐 🚏
Size 3 acres, 60 touring pitches, 25 with electric hookup, 9 🚿, 7 WCs, 1 CWP
£ car/tent £8.20-£10.40, car/caravan £8.20-£10.40, motorhome £8.20-£10.40, motorbike/tent £8.20, children £1.30
CC MasterCard Visa
🗑 📞 🐾
Last arrival time: 11:00
➔ From S on A68 keep to main road. First turn after bridges. Site is on northern outskirts of Jedburgh.

JOHN O'GROATS Caithness 15E1

John O'Groats Caravan Site
John O'Groats KW1 4YS
📞 **01955-611329**
Open April-October 🅰 🚐 🚏

On the sea front overlooking Pentland Firth and the Orkney islands. Day trips available. Magnificent cliff scenery. 1½ miles from hotel. Snack bar, restaurant, harbour, museum, craft shops 200 yards. Wild life cruises. Seal colony three miles.

Size 4 acres, 90 touring pitches, 28 with electric hookup, 70 level pitches, 8 🚿, 10 WCs, 2 CWPs
£ car/tent £6.50-£7.50, car/caravan £6.50-£7.50, motorhome £6.50-£7.50, motorbike/tent £5
🛒¼ ✕¼ 🍺¼ 🗑 📞 🖬 Calor Gaz ♿ 🐾
Last arrival time: 10:00
➔ Entrance on right at N end of A9 on seafront beside last house in Scotland.

KELSO Roxburghshire 13E3

Springwood Caravan Park
Springwood Estate, Kelso TD5 8LS
📞 **01573-224596 Fax 01573-224033**
Open April-October 🚐 🚏

Situated in wooded parkland adjacent to River Teviot, only one mile from market town of Kelso. Riverside walks adjacent to park, short grass and clean facilities.

Size 30 acres, 41 touring pitches, 41 with electric hookup, 15 level pitches, 245 static caravans, 8 🚿, 30 WCs, 1 CWP
£ car/caravan £8-£9, motorhome £8-£9, children £0.50
CC MasterCard Visa
🗑 📞 GR 🔍 🅰 🎯 Calor ♿ 🐾
Last arrival time: 10:00
➔ A699 from Kelso to Selkirk. Site in 1 mile.
See advert on next page

Kenmore Caravan & Camping Park

Kenmore, Aberfeldy PH15 2HN
☎ 01887-830226 Fax 01887-830211
Open mid March-mid October Å ⊕ ⇔

A well located site by the River and Loch Tay in magnificent Highland Perthshire. First class facilities available, including bar, restaurant and golf course.

Size 14 acres, 160 touring pitches, 140 with electric hookup, 60 level pitches, 60 static caravans, 14 ⋒, 45 WCs, 4 CWPs
£ car/tent £7-£8, car/caravan £8-£9, motorhome £8-£9, motorbike/tent £6, children £0.50
CC MasterCard Visa
⚡ ✕ 🍴 🗑 📞 🚰 ▶ ✂ 🧺 📺 ⋒ 🏠 ⊕ Calor Gaz ♿ 🐕 WS
Last arrival time: 10:00
➡ W off A9 at Ballinluig to Aberfeldy on A827. Take A827 W 7 miles to Kenmore. Through village and on right.

Arduaine Caravan & Camping Park

Kilmelford PA34 4XA
☎ 01852-200331 Fax 01852-200337
Open March-October Å ⊕ ⇔

Grassy site beside the sea with spectacular views of off-shore island. Ideal for water-based activities or just watching seals and otters in the bay.

Size 5 acres, 40 touring pitches, 14 with electric hookup, 6 level pitches, 2 ⋒, 5 WCs, 1 CWP
➡ Signposted by offical signs advanced to A816 between roads and sea.

Pettycur Bay Caravan Park

Kinghorn Road, Kinghorn KY3 9YE
☎ 01592-890321 Fax 01592-891420
Open 1 March-31 October Å ⊕ ⇔

Terraced site overlooking the Firth of Forth. 40 caravans with own WCs for hire - two nights minimum. Open from the 1 March to the 31 October.

Size 42 acres, 50 touring pitches, 45 with electric hookup, 34 level pitches, 450 static caravans, 12 🅟, 20 WCs, 3 CWPs
£ car/tent £8-£11, car/caravan £8-£11, motorhome £8-£11, motorbike/tent £8
Rental Å 🚐 £90-£350
℃ MasterCard Visa
🔋 ✕ 🌐 📶 🔌 🔲 📺 🔌 Calor 🐶 WS
➡ On N side of A92, ¾ mile W of Kinghorn.

KINLOCH RANNOCH Perthshire   15D4

Kilvrecht Camping & Caravan Site
Tay District Forestry Commission, Inver Park, Dunkeld PH8 0JR
📞 **01350-727284** Fax **01350-728635**
Open 26 March-25 October Å 🚐 🚌

Looking for a campsite with a restaurant, disco and uninterrupted views of static caravans? Don't come to Kilvrecht. It's trees, streams, walks, peace and quiet.

Size 3 hectares, 60 touring pitches, 60 level pitches, 4 WCs, 1 CWP
£ car/tent £5, car/caravan £5, motorhome £5, motorbike/tent £3
🏍 🚻 🐶
➡ From Kinloch Rannoch take the South Loch Rannogh road for 3½ miles to the site which is set in Birch Woods, ¾ mile from southern shore of Loch Rannogh.

KINTORE Aberdeenshire   15F3

Hillhead Caravan Park
Kintore AB51 0YX
📞 **01467-632809** Fax **01467-633173**
Open 29 March-31 October Å 🚐 🚌
Size 1½ acres, 24 touring pitches, 18 with electric hookup, 24 level pitches, 5 static caravans, 4 🅟, 6 WCs, 1 CWP
£ car/tent £5.75-£7.30, car/caravan £5.75-£7.30, motorhome £5.75-£7.30, motorbike/tent £5.75
Rental 🚐 Chalet. £100-£245
℃ MasterCard Visa
🔋 🔌 🌐 🏍 🚻 Calor Gaz ♿ 🐶 WS
Last arrival time: 10:00
➡ From Aberdeen go to centre of Kintore. Turn left signposted Ratch Hill, in ½ mile turn left signposted Blairs, in ½ mile caravan park is on left.

KIRKCUDBRIGHT Kirkcudbrightshire   12C4

Silvercraigs Caravan & Camping Site
Kirkcudbright DG6 4BT
📞 **01557-330123**
Open Easter-October Å 🚐 🚌
Size 5 acres, 50 touring pitches, 49 with electric hookup, 40 level pitches, 4 🅟, 8 WCs, 1 CWP
£ car/tent £6.25-£7.75, car/caravan £6.25-£7.75, motorhome £6.25-£7.75, motorbike/tent £6.25
🔋¼ ✕¼ 🌐¼ 🔌 🔲 🔌 🏍 🚻 🐶
Last arrival time: 12:00
➡ In Kirkcudbright off Silvercraigs Road, overlooking town.

Dunroamin Caravan Park
Main Street, Lairg IV27 4AR
📞 01549-402447 Fax 01549-402447
Open 1 April-31 October ▲ ⛺ 🚐

Situated in the village of Lairg on the south side of the A839, 300 yards from the village centre. Holiday caravans for rent. Tents caravans and motorhomes all welcome.

Size 4 acres, 50 touring pitches, 16 with electric hookup, 50 level pitches, 10 static caravans, 2 🚿, 5 WCs, 1 CWP
£ car/tent £4.50-£6.50, car/caravan £5.50-£7.50, motorhome £5.50-£7.50, motorbike/tent £4.50, children £0.50
CC MasterCard Visa
🚿¼ ✕ 🛒 🔯 📞 🔯 🔌 Calor Gaz 🐕
Last arrival time: 11:00
➡ S side of A839, 300 yards from Lairg village centre and Loch Shin. Immediately adjacent to Crofters restaurant.

Woodend Caravan & Camping Park
Achnairn, Lairg IV27 4DN
📞 01549-402248
Open 1 April-30 September ▲ ⛺ 🚐

Quiet craft site with beautiful views of Loch Shin, woodlands and hills. Ideal touring centre for all of northwest Sutherland, with many forest walks.

Size 4 acres, 55 touring pitches, 22 with electric hookup, 5 static caravans, 4 🚿, 9 WCs, 1 CWP
£ car/tent £5.50, car/caravan £5.50-£6.50, motorhome £5.50-£6.50, motorbike/tent £5.50
Rental 🚐 £130 weekly, £18 nightly.
🚿 🔯 📞 🔯 🔯 🔯 Calor Gaz 🐕
Last arrival time: 11:00
➡ From Lairg take A836 for 3 miles. Then take A838 and follow site signs.

Clyde Valley Caravan Park
Kirkfieldbank, Lanark ML11 9JW
📞 01555-663951
Open 1 April-31 October ▲ ⛺ 🚐

Set in the orchards of the Clyde Valley, with two fishing rivers running by, and a children's play area. Restaurant and shop adjacent.

Size 10 acres, 50 touring pitches
🔯
➡ ½ mile W of Lanark on A73 turn left A72, at ½ mile on, turn right just before River Clyde bridge.

Crossburn Caravan Park
Douglas, Lanark ML11 0QA
📞 01555-851029
Open all year ▲ ⛺ 🚐

Size 4 acres, 50 touring pitches, 50 with electric hookup, 50 level pitches, 6 🚿, 14 WCs, 1 CWP

£ car/tent £5.50, car/caravan £6.50, motorhome £6.50, motorbike/tent £5.50

℅ MasterCard Visa

🛒¼ ✗¼ 🛒 🅿 🔾 Calor 🐕

➧ 2 miles W of M74 on Edinburgh to Ayr road, then A70 to village of Douglas.

LAUDER Berwickshire 13E2

Thirlestane Castle Caravan & Camping Park

Lauder TD2 6RU

📞 **01578-722254 Fax 01578-718749**

Open 1 April-1 October 🛆 🚐 🚏

Size 4 acres, 50 touring pitches, 12 with electric hookup, 30 level pitches, 8 🚿, 10 WCs, 1 CWP

£ car/tent £6, car/caravan £6, motorhome £6, motorbike/tent £5

📞 🖻 ♿ 🐕 WS

➧ Signed off A68 and A697, ½ mile S of Lauder.

LAURENCEKIRK Kincardineshire 15F4

Dovecot Caravan Park

Northwaterbridge, Laurencekirk AB30 1QL

📞 **01674-840630**

Open 1 April-31 October 🛆 🚐 🚏

Size 6 acres, 25 touring pitches, 25 with electric hookup, 25 level pitches, 40 static caravans, 6 🚿, 9 WCs, 1 CWP

£ car/tent £6.75-£7.75, car/caravan £6.75-£7.75, motorhome £6.75-£7.75, motorbike/tent £5.50

Rental 🚐

🛒 🖻 📞 🖻 🅿 🔾 Calor ♿ 🐕 WS

Last arrival time: 8:00

➧ Turn off A90 at signpost for RAF base. Edzell is 500 yards on left.

LEVEN Fife 13E1

Woodland Gardens Caravan & Camping Site

Lundin Links, Leven KY8 5QG

📞 **01333-360319**

➧

← **Woodland Gardens**

Open March-October △ ⊕ ⇝
Size 1 acre, 20 touring pitches, 20 with electric hookup, 20 level pitches, 5 static caravans, 2 ⋒, 7 WCs, 1 CWP
£ car/tent £6.60, car/caravan £6.60, motorhome £6.60, motorbike/tent £6.60, children £1
Rental ⊕
⚡ ⊡ 📞 ⊟ GR TV ⚠ ⊠ Calor Gaz ⊀ WS
Last arrival time: 10:00
➡ Turn N off A915 at E end of Lundin Links. Site is signposted on A915 and is ½ mile from main road.

LOCKERBIE Dumfriesshire   13D4

Halleaths Touring Camping & Caravan Park
Lochmaben, Lockerbie DG11 1NA
📞 **01387-810630**
Open mid March-16 November △ ⊕ ⇝
Size 8 acres, 70 touring pitches, 60 with electric hookup, 70 level pitches, 9 static caravans, 8 ⋒, 12 WCs, 1 CWP

HODDOM CASTLE
Caravan Park

A pleasant, spacious park in partially wooded parkland making an ideal base to explore Southwest Scotland and the Borders.

SHOP • LOUNGE BAR • RESTAURANT
GAMES ROOM • CHILDREN'S PLAYGROUND
CRAZY GOLF • 9 HOLE GOLF COURSE

Fishing available on the River Annan.

RAC
APPROVED

**AA Four Pennant
CC Approved**

**LOCKERBIE, DUMFRIES DG11 1AS
Tel: 01576-300251**

£ car/tent £5, car/caravan £7, motorhome £7, motorbike/tent £5, children £0.50
Rental ⊕ £7/person/night + £2 g/e
⚡ ⚡¼ ⊡ 📞 ⊟ ⚠ ⊠ Calor Gaz �& ⊀ WS
➡ From M74 Lockerbie take A709 following signs to Lochmaben and Dumfries. Site on right 3 miles W of Lockerbie

Hoddom Castle Caravan Park
Hoddom, Lockerbie DG11 1AS
📞 **01576-300251** **Fax** **01576-300757**
Open Easter-October △ ⊕ ⇝
Size 24 acres, 140 touring pitches, 140 with electric hookup, 170 level pitches, 30 static caravans, 15 ⋒, 60 WCs, 1 CWP
£ car/tent £6.50-£10.50, car/caravan £6.50-£10.50, motorhome £6.50-£10.50, motorbike/tent £5.50
⚡ ✕ ⬤ ⊡ 📞 ⊟ P⊠ ↗ GR ◨ ⚠ ⊠ ⊕ Calor Gaz �& ⊀ WS
➡ Turn off A74 at Ecclefechan. Turn left at roundabout towards village. At church turn right onto B725 to Dalton. Entrance is 2½ miles on right.

LONGNIDDRY Lothian   13E2

Seton Sands Holiday Park
Longniddry EM32 0QF
📞 **01875-811425**
Open March-October ⊕ ⇝

A family holiday park with beautiful beaches nearby and only 12 miles from the capital of Scotland - Edinburgh, the parks boasts a new indoor pool, kids club and a wide range of leisure facilities, restaurants and bars, excellent cabaret entertainment. A 'British Holidays Park'.

Size 60 touring pitches, 32 with electric hookup, 620 static caravans, 6 🛁, 11 WCs, 1 CWP

CC MasterCard Visa

🛒 💧 🗑 📞 🔲 🔳 🔲 🔲 ⚠ 🗙 🔌 Calor 🐕

➜ From Trament roundabout turn on B6371 for Cockenzie and then right on B1348. Site is 1 mile on right.

LUSS Dunbartonshire   12C2

Camping & Caravanning Club Site

Luss, Loch Lomond, Nr Glasgow

📞 **01436-860658**

Open end March-start November 🔺 ⛺ 🚐

Size 10 acres, 90 touring pitches, 16 with electric hookup, 7 🛁, 12 WCs, 1 CWP

£ car/tent £9.20-£12.05, car/caravan £9.20-£12.05, motorhome £9.20-£12.05, motorbike/tent £9.20, children £1.40

CC MasterCard Visa

📞 ⚠ 🗙 🐕

Last arrival time: 11:00

➜ Site is on lochside ¼ mile N of Luss on A82 Glasgow to Fort William road. It lies between road and Loch Lomond.

MAYBOLE Ayrshire   12C3

Camping & Caravanning Club Site

Culzean Castle, Maybole KA19 8JX

📞 **01655-760627**

Open end March-start November 🔺 ⛺ 🚐

Size 6 acres, 90 touring pitches, 60 with electric hookup, 4 🛁, 9 WCs, 1 CWP

£ car/tent £8.75-£11.55, car/caravan £8.75-£11.55, motorhome £8.75-£11.55, motorbike/tent £8.75, children £1.40

CC MasterCard Visa

🗑 📞 ⚠ 🗙 ♿ 🐕

Last arrival time: 11:00

➜ Entrance to Culzean Castle and site S from Ayr on A719, signposted.

MOFFAT Dumfriesshire   13D3

Camping & Caravanning Club Site

Hammerland's Farm, Moffat DG10 9QL

📞 **01683-20436**

Open end March-start November 🔺 ⛺ 🚐

Size 12 acres, 200 touring pitches, 70 with electric hookup, 8 🛁, 20 WCs, 1 CWP

£ car/tent £9.20-£12.05, car/caravan £9.20-£12.05, motorhome £9.20-£12.05, motorbike/tent £9.20, children £1.40

CC MasterCard Visa

Last arrival time: 11:00 ➜ Take A708 NE from Moffat. Site approach is on right before Caspers Inn. Turn left at cadet hut, then left over bridge, follow signs.

MONTROSE Angus   15F4

South Links Caravan Park

Traill Drive, Montrose DD10 8SW

📞 **01674-672044**

Open 22 March ⛺ 🚐

Size 160 touring pitches, 47 with electric hookup, 160 level pitches, 14 🛁, 32 WCs, 3 CWPs

🛒 🛒¼ 🗙¼ 💧¼ 📞 ⚠ 🗙 ♿

Last arrival time: 12:00

➜ From North: enter town, pass first set of traffic lights, second left, follow road to beach, pass beach cafe, 200 yards on left. From South: enter town, take first right after bridge, pass docks (where road goes left), straight through junction, first right after Academy School, over lock bridge, and site is 100 yards on right.

MUIR OF ORD Ross-shire   15D3

Druimorrin Caravan & Camping Park

Orrin Bridge, Urray, Muir Of Ord IV6 7UL

📞 **01997-433252**

Open Easter-end September 🔺 ⛺ 🚐

Size 5½ acres, 60 touring pitches, 24 with electric hookup, 60 level pitches, 4 🛁, 13 WCs, 1 CWP

£ car/tent £5-£7, car/caravan £6-£7, motorhome £5.50-£6.50, motorbike/tent £4.50

🛒 🗑 📞 🗑 Calor Gaz 🐕 WS

Last arrival time: 12:00

➜ From Inverness take A9 N to Tore roundabout. A832 signposted Muir of Ord, pass through village and continue W on A832 for 2½ miles, site is on right.

MUSSELBURGH Midlothian   13D2

Drum Mohr Caravan Park
Levenhall, Musselburgh EH21 8JS
☎ 01316-656867 Fax 01316-536859
Open 1 March-31 October ▲ 🚐 🚛

Family run and set in beautiful surroundings with easy access to Edinburgh. Situated between the B1361 and B1348.

Size 10 acres, 120 touring pitches, 100 with electric hookup, 120 level pitches, 12 🚿, 20 WCs, 2 CWPs
£ car/tent £8-£9, car/caravan £8-£9, motorhome £8-£9, motorbike/tent £8, children £1
🔋 🖥 📞 🛗 🖽 Calor Gaz & 🐕
Last arrival time: 10:00
➜ Situated between B1361 and B1348, midway between Musselburgh and Prestonpans, above the mining museum.

NAIRN Nairnshire   15D3

Spindrift Caravan Park
Little Kildrummie, Nairn IV12 5QU
☎ 01667-453992
Open 1 April-31 October ▲ 🚐 🚛

Small, secluded family run park, overlooking the River Nairn. Winner of the AA's Environmental Award 1996 and an ideal base from which to explore the Highlands.

Size 3 acres, 40 touring pitches, 28 with electric hookup, 40 level pitches, 4 🚿, 8 WCs, 2 CWPs
£ car/tent £5.50-£7.50, car/caravan £5.50-£7.50, motorhome £5.50-£7.50, motorbike/tent £5.50
🔋¼ ✗¼ 🚐¼ 🖥 📞 🖽 Calor Gaz & 🐕
Last arrival time: 10:00
➜ From Nairn take B9090 Cawdor road S for 1½ miles. Turn right at sharp left hand bend onto unclassified road (Little Kidrummie). The entrance is 400 yards on your left.

NEWTON STEWART Wigtownshire   12C4

Cock Inn Caravan Park
Auchenmalg, Glenluce, Newton Stewart DG8 0JH
☎ 01581-500227
Open 1 March-31 October ▲ 🚐 🚛

Quiet family park overlooking Luce Bay offering a full range of facilities including a shop, sauna, sunbed, laundry room, free showers and holiday caravans. Ideal for fishing, golf and hillwalking. Tourers welcome.

Size 7 acres, 30 touring pitches, 20 with electric hookup, 13 level pitches, 60 static caravans, 5 🚿, 12 WCs, 3 CWPs
£ car/tent £6-£7.50, car/caravan £6.50-£11, motorhome £6.50-£11, motorbike/tent £6, children £0.50
Rental 🚐 Chalet. £130-£135
🔋 ✗ 🖥 📞 🖽 🎱 🛗 🖽 Calor Gaz & 🐕 WS
Last arrival time: 10:30

➜ From A75 Newton Stewart/Stranraer road take A747 to Port William for 5 miles to Auchenmalg.

Three Lochs Caravan Park
Balminnoch, Kirkcowan, Newton Stewart DG8 OEP
📞 **01671-830304** Fax **01671-830335**
🛆 ⊿ 🚐
Size 22 acres, 45 touring pitches, 29 with electric hookup, 75 level pitches, 100 static caravans, 8 🚿, 16 WCs, 1 CWP
£ car/tent £8-£9, car/caravan £8-£9, motorhome £8-£9, motorbike/tent £8
Rental ⊿ £115-£245 weekly, £28 nightly.
🏋 ➤ 📞 🗇 🔄 🔀 🔳 GR 🔍 ⚠ 🔳 Calor Gaz 🔥 WS
Last arrival time: 9:00
➜ 7 miles W of Newton Stewart on A75 heading towards Stranraer turn right at crossroads signed Dirnow/Three Lochs. Then follow signs for holiday park.

NORTH BERWICK East Lothian   13E2

Tantallon Caravan Park
Dunbar Road, North Berwick EH39 5NJ
📞 **01620-893348** Fax **01620-895623**

Easy access to the beach and Glen golf course. Reception, games room, showers, toilets and laundry.

OBAN Argyll   12B1

Crunachy Caravan & Camping Site
Bridge of Awe, Taynuilt PA35 1HT
📞 **01866-822612**
Open March-November 🛆 ⊿ 🚐

Situated alongside the River Awe amongst the best scenery in Scotland, with a magnificent view of Ben Cruachan.

Size 9 acres, 80 touring pitches, 42 with electric hookup, 80 level pitches, 6 static caravans, 8 🚿, 20 WCs, 1 CWP
£ car/tent £7.50, car/caravan £7.50, motorhome £7.50, motorbike/tent £5
Rental ⊿ Chalet. chalet £150-£275, caravan £110-£180
CC MasterCard Visa
🏋 ✕ ➤ 🗇 📞 🗇 GR ⚠ 🔳 Calor Gaz 🔥 WS
Last arrival time: 10:00
➜ Alongside main Tyndrum to Oban road (A85), 2 miles E of village of Taywilt and 14 miles E of Oban.

Ganavan Sands Touring Caravan Park
Ganavan, Oban PA34 5TU
📞 **01631-562179**
Open April-October 🛆 ⊿ 🚐

Set in tranquil surroundings with a sandy beach and spectacular views, an ideal location for touring the West Coast and islands. Bar and well equipped dive centre on site. ➜

← **Ganavan Sands Touring Caravan Park**

Size 76 touring pitches, 68 with electric hookup, 62 level pitches, 6 🐟, 10 WCs, 1 CWP
£ car/tent £7-£8, car/caravan £7-£8, motorhome £7-£8, motorbike/tent £7
🔌 🍴 ▣ 🛒 🅰 🅇 ⊟ ♿
➜ From town centre follow Esplanade coast road keeping sea immediately adjacent on left for 2 miles.

Oban Caravan & Camping Park
Gallachmore Farm, Oban
📞 **01631-562425** fax **01631-566624**
Open Easter-October 🛖 🚐 🚍
Size 15 acres, 150 touring pitches, 73 with electric hookup, 15 static caravans, 8 🐟, 16 WCs, 1 CWP
£ car/tent £6-£7, car/caravan £6-£7, motorhome £6-£7, motorbike/tent £6
Rental 🚐 Chalet. £160-£300
🔌 ▣ 🛒 ⊟ 📺 ᴳᴿ 📺 🅰 🅇 Calor Gaz 🐕
Last arrival time: 11:00
➜ From Oban town centre follow signs to Gallanach, sea on right 2½ miles from town, site beside sea.

Oldshoremore
by Lairg, Oldshoremore
📞 **0197182-281**
Open April-September 🛖 🚐 🚍

A one acre site, part grass, part hard standing. Ten minutes walk from a mile long golden sandy beach. Ideal for hill climbing, fishing, beautiful scenery.

Size 1 acre, 13 touring pitches, 3 with electric hookup, 13 level pitches, 2 static caravans, 1 🐟, 4 WCs, 1 CWP
£ car/tent £6-£6.50, car/caravan £6.20-£6.75, motorhome £6.20-£6.75, motorbike/tent £5.80, children £0.50-£0.75
Rental 🚐 £60-£150
▣ ⊟ 🐕
➜ Take A838 to Rhiconich, there join B801 in Kinlochbervie 4 miles. Then take unclassified road to Oldshoremore - 2 miles.

Mount Pleasant
Westray KW17 2DH
📞 **01857-677229**
🛖 🚐 🚍
Size 0.125 acre, 2 touring pitches, 2 with electric hookup, 2 level pitches, 4 static caravans, 3 🐟, 3 WCs,
£ car/tent £4, car/caravan £6, motorhome £6, motorbike/tent £3
Rental 🚐 £10-£12 per night
🔌¼ ✕¼ 🍴¼ ▣ 🛒 ⊟ Calor Gaz 🐕
Last arrival time: 10:00

Pickaquoy Caravan & Camp Site
Pickaquoy Road, Kirkwall KW15 1RR
📞 **01856-873535** fax **01856-876327**
Open May-September 🛖 🚐 🚍
Size 30 touring pitches, 6 with electric hookup, 1 CWP
£ car/tent £3.25-£4.35, car/caravan £4.85-£7.70, motorhome £4.85-£7.70, motorbike/tent £3.25
🔌¼ ✕¼ 🍴¼ ▣ 🛒
➜ Just off main A965 road from Stromness to Kirkwall, 150 yards SW of foot of hill coming down into Kirkwall.

Point of Ness Caravan & Camping Site
Ness Road, Stromness KW16 3DN
📞 **01856-873535** fax **01856-876327**
Open May-September 🛖 🚐 🚍
30 touring pitches, 6 with electric hookup, 1 CWP
£ car/tent £3.25-£4.35, car/caravan £4.85-£7.70, motorhome £4.85-£7.70, motorbike/tent £3.25
🔌¼ ✕¼ 🍴¼ ▣ 🛒 ♿ 🐕
➜ One mile W of the Pierhead.

PEEBLES Peeblesshire 13D2

Crossburn Caravan Park
Edinburgh Road, Peebles EH45 8ED
01721 20501
Open April-October
Size 40 touring pitches

Rosetta Caravan Park
Rosetta Road, Peebles EH45 8PG
01721-720770
Open 1 April-31 October

A beautiful, family owned, wooded park, graded 5 ticks excellent. The 1990 Calor Award Winner 'Best Park in Scotland'; finalist in 1993. Licensed bar, adjacent golf course, fishing arranged.

Size 24 acres, 130 touring pitches, 130 with electric hookup, 130 level pitches, 28 static caravans, 12, 27 WCs, 3 CWPs
£ car/tent £6-£6.50, car/caravan £8.25-£8.75, motorhome £8.25-£8.75, motorbike/tent £6
Rental £130-£160
¼ ¼ Calor Gaz
→ Signposted on main roads into Peebles.

PENPONT Dumfriesshire 13D3

Penpont (Floors) Caravan Park
Thornhill, Penpont DG3 4BH
01848-330470
Open April-October
Size 1½ acres, 20 touring pitches, 8 with electric hookup, 10 level pitches, 1 static caravans, 6, 7 WCs, 1 CWP
£ car/tent £6.50-£7.25, car/caravan £6.50, motorhome £6.50, motorbike/tent £6.50
Rental
¼ Calor Gaz WS
Last arrival time: 11:00
→ On S side of A702, ½ mile E of Penpont.

PERTH Perthshire 13D1

Camping & Caravanning Club Site
Scone Palace Caravan Park, Old Scone, Perth PH2 6BB
01738-552323
Open end March-early November
Size 12 acres, 150 touring pitches, 76 with electric hookup, 8, 28 WCs, 1 CWP
£ car/tent £9.20-£12.05, car/caravan £9.20-£12.05, motorhome £9.20-£12.05, motorbike/tent £9.20, children £1.40
CC MasterCard Visa
Last arrival time: 11:00
→ Site lies 2 miles N of Perth, adjacent to the racecourse. Signposted.

Cleeve Caravan Park
Glasgow Road, Perth PH2 0PH
01738-639521 Fax 01738-441690
Open 27 March-27 October

Quiet, well screened, wooded site with a high standard of facilities and a good reputation. Children's play area. Easy access to the centre of Perth. Off-season discount for OAPs.

Size 5 acres, 100 touring pitches, 80 with electric hookup, 80 level pitches, 11, 20 WCs, 4 CWPs
£ car/tent £6.80, car/caravan £7.45-£8.70, motorbike/tent £5.80, children £0.75
CC MasterCard Visa
¼ Calor Gaz
→

← Cleeve Caravan Park

Last arrival time: 8:00
➡ ½ mile E of A9/M90, on W side of Perth (A93).

Faskally Home Farm Caravan Site
Pitlochry PH16 5LA
☎ 01796-472007
Open 15 March-31 October ▲ ⛺ 🚐
Level grassy site. Children's play area. Fishing on Loch Faskally and rivers Tummel and Garry. Forty caravans for hire (own WCs). Open from the 15 March to 31 October.

Size 23 acres, 250 touring pitches, 20 with electric hookup, 60 static caravans, 18 🚿, 78 WCs
🛒 ✕ 🖨 📶 ♿
➡ 2 miles N of Pitlochry on A924 (A9).

Milton Of Fonab Caravan Site
Pitlochry PH16 5NA
☎ 01796-472882 Fax 01796-474363
Open Easter-October ▲ ⛺ 🚐

A quiet family run site on the banks of the River Tummel. Spectacular scenery. Mountain bike hire and free trout fishing. Static caravans for hire.

Size 15 acres, 154 touring pitches, 130 with electric hookup, 130 level pitches, 36 static caravans, 9 🚿, 4 WCs, 1 CWP
£ car/tent £8.50-£9, car/caravan £8.50-£9, motorhome £8.50-£9, children £0.50
Rental ⛺ from £39 nightly, from £210 weekly.
🛒 🛒¼ ✕¼ 🛒¼ 🖨 📶 🖨 📶 Calor Gaz ♿ 🐕 WS
Last arrival time: 9:30
➡ ½ mile S of Pitlochry opposite Bells Distillery.

Camping & Caravanning Club Site
Inverewe Gardens, Poolewe, Achnasheen
☎ 01445-781249
Open end March-start November ▲ ⛺ 🚐
Size 3 acres, 60 touring pitches, 18 with electric hookup, 8 🚿, 10 WCs, 1 CWP
£ car/tent £8.75-£11.55, car/caravan £8.75-£11.55, motorhome £8.72-£11.55, motorbike/tent £8.75, children £1.40
℃ MasterCard Visa
🖨 🛒 ♿ 🐕
Last arrival time: 11:00
➡ Site is on A832, just N of Poolewe.

Castle Bay Caravan Park
Portpatrick DG9 9AA
☎ 01776-810462
Open March-October ▲ ⛺ 🚐
Size 22½ acres, 26 touring pitches, 26 with electric hookup, 20 level pitches, 96 static caravans, 2 🚿, 5 WCs, 1 CWP
£ car/tent £5, car/caravan £7, motorhome £7, motorbike/tent £5
Rental ⛺ £140-£195
🛒 ✕¼ 🛒¼ 🖨 🛒 🖨 📶 GR 🅿 🎣 Calor Gaz ♿ 🐕 WS
Last arrival time: 11:30
➡ Into Portpatrick on A77, left opposite Old Mill Restaurant. Continue for ¾ mile, under railway bridge, site on right.

Galloway Point Holiday Park
Portpatrick, Stranraer DG9 9AA
☎ 01776-810561 Fax 01776-810561
Open Easter-mid October ▲ ⛺ 🚐
Size 18 acres, 40 touring pitches, 40 with electric hookup, 15 level pitches, 60 static caravans, 7 🚿, 20 WCs, 1 CWP
£ car/tent £6-£10, car/caravan £9-£10, motorhome £8-£10, motorbike/tent £6
Rental ⛺ £175-£275
🛒¼ ✕ 🛒 🖨 🛒 🖨 🅿 🎣 🍴 Calor Gaz 🐕 WS
Last arrival time: 9:00
➡ A75 from Dumfries, A77 from Glasgow, first left opposite Old Mill, park is on right opposite Barn Inn.

Sunnymeade Caravan Park
Portpatrick, Stranraer DG9 8LN
☎ 01776-810293

Open mid March-end October **Å 🚐 🚏**
Size 8 acres, 15 touring pitches, 14 with electric hookup, 60 static caravans, 4 🏠, 9 WCs, 1 CWP
£ car/tent £7-£9, car/caravan £7-£9, motorhome £7-£9, motorbike/tent £7
Rental 🚐 from £110
🛒¼ **✗**¼ **🛁**¼ 🔲 🔳 🔲 🔲 Calor 🐕 WS
➡ Take A75 to Portpatrick and turn left on entering town. Site is ¾ mile on left.

ROY BRIDGE Inverness-shire   14C4

Inveroy Caravan Park
Inveroy, Roy Bridge PH31 4AQ
📞 **01397-712275**
Open March-October 🚐 🚏
Size 6 touring pitches
➡ Off A86, 2 miles from Spean Bridge, 1 mile from Roy Bridge

SANDHEAD Wigtownshire   12B4

Sandhead Caravan Park
Sandhead DG9 9JN
📞 **01776-830296**
Open April-October **Å 🚐 🚏**
Size 10 acres, 30 touring pitches, 20 with electric hookup, 30 level pitches, 80 static caravans, 5 🏠, 15 WCs, 2 CWPs
£ car/tent £7-£8, car/caravan £7-£8, motorhome £6.50-£7.50, motorbike/tent £5
Rental 🚐 £200-£220
🛒 🔲 🔳 🔳 Calor Gaz 🐕
➡ From A75 turn S on A716 towards Drummore, site on left approaching Sandhead village.

Sands Of Luce Caravan Park
Sandhead, Stranraer DG9 9JR
📞 **01776-830456 Fax 01776-830456**
Open 1 April-31 October **Å 🚐 🚏**

Peaceful, friendly park extending onto beautiful sandy beach and large dune area.

Touring pitches beside the beach. New toilet blocks provide excellent facilities. A warm welcome awaits all our visitors.

Size 12 acres, 26 touring pitches, 26 with electric hookup, 15 level pitches, 34 static caravans, 8 🏠, 16 WCs, 1 CWP
£ car/tent £6.50-£8, car/caravan £6.50-£8, motorhome £6-£7.50, motorbike/tent £5.70, children £0.40
Rental 🚐 £125-£260
🛒 🔲 🔳 🔳 🔳 🔲 🔺 🔳 Calor 🚶 🐕 WS
Last arrival time: 10:00
➡ From Stranraer follow A77 to turn off to Portpatrick. Keep on A716 signposted to Dummore (do not turn right to Portpatrick). Entrance to caravan park is 1 mile past village of Stoneykirk at A716/ B7084 junction.

SELKIRK Selkirkshire   13E3

Victoria Park Caravan Site
Victoria Park, Buccleugh Road, Selkirk TD7 5DN
📞 **01750-20987 Fax 01896-757003**
Open 1 April-31 October **Å 🚐 🚏**   ➡

INVERROY
CARAVAN & CAMPING

Inveroy Caravan Park is close by Roy Bridge in the beautiful Braes of Lochaber. Just two acres, with a total of twelve static caravans and usually a few tents and touring caravans, Inveroy is a small friendly site set amidst the most magnificent scenery in Scotland. The views across the glen to the Grey Corries mountains are spectacular. Glen Spean is probably the most central point in Scotland for Highland, history, walking, climbing, skiing, wildlife and just sheer wilderness and beauty.

TOURERS & TENTS – £5 per unit with 2 adults
ELECTRIC HOOKUP – £1 extra

ROY BRIDGE IN GLEN SPEAN,
FORT WILLIAM PH31 4AR
Tel: 01397-712275

← **Victoria Park Caravan Site**

Pleasant location in open parkland. Convenient for Selkirk town centre. Touring centre for Ettrick, Yarrow and Walter Scott country. Open from the 1st of April to the 31st of October. Closed from the 7th to 15th of June.

Size 3 acres, 60 touring pitches, 22 with electric hookup, 60 level pitches, 6, 11 WCs, 1 CWP
¼ ¼ ¼ Calor
Last arrival time: 9:00
→ A7 N follow signs from Selkirk market place. A7 S turn at town entrance signposted A72 Peebles then A708 Moffat.

SKELMORLIE Ayrshire 12B2

Mains Camping & Caravan Park

Skelmorlie PA17 5EU
01475-520794 Fax 01475-520794
Open March-October
Size 4 acres, 20 touring pitches, 20 with electric hookup, 20 level pitches, 70 static caravans, 13, 23 WCs, 1 CWP
£ car/tent £5-£6, car/caravan £7-£9, motorhome £6, motorbike/tent £5
Rental Chalet. £175-£340
Calor Gaz WS
Last arrival time: 12:00
→ Signposted off A78, 4 miles N of Largs.

SPEAN BRIDGE Inverness-shire 14C4

Stornaba Caravan Site

Spean Bridge PH34 4DX
01397-712259
Open April-October
Size 4 acres, 20 touring pitches, 4 with electric hookup, 18 level pitches, 4, 6 WCs, 1 CWP
£ car/tent £6-£7, car/caravan £6-£7, motorhome £6-£7, motorbike/tent £6, children £0.50-£1
WS
Last arrival time: 10:00
→ 2½ miles N of Spean Bridge on A82, gateway signposted.

ST ANDREWS Fife 13E1

Cairnsmill Caravan Site

St Andrews KY16 8NN
01334-73604
Open April-October
Ideal touring base with easy access to a range of beaches and golf courses. Games room, coffee bar, heated swimming pool. Open from April to October.

Size 20 acres, 80 touring pitches, 185 static caravans, 10, 23 WCs, 2 CWPs
Rental
Calor Gaz WS
Last arrival time: 10:00
→ 1 mile S of St Andrews on A915.

ST CYRUS Kincardineshire 15F4

East Bowstrips Caravan Park

St Cyrus, Montrose DD10 0DE
01674-850328 Fax 01674-850328
Open 1 April-31 October

Quiet family park by the coast with excellent facilities, and a particular welcome for disabled visitors. Only one mile from the glorious sandy St Cyrus beach and nature reserve.

Size 4 acres, 30 touring pitches, 27 with electric hookup, 25 level pitches, 18 static caravans, 4, 7 WCs, 1 CWP

£ car/tent £5.50-£6.50, car/caravan £6.50-£7.50, motorhome £6.50-£7.50, motorbike/tent £5.50
Rental 🚐 £80-£199
🛊 🛊¼ ✗¼ 🍴¼ 🗑 📞 🚻 ⚠ 🎠 Calor 🚻 🐕
Last arrival time: 10:00
➔ Travelling N on A92 coast road enter village of St Cyrus. Pass hotel on left, then first left, second right (signposted).

Loch Earn Caravan Park
South Shore Road, St Fillans
📞 **01764-685270 Fax 01764-685270**
Open end March-end October ▲ 🚐 🚙
Size 2 acres, 40 touring pitches, 30 with electric hookup, 30 level pitches, 200 static caravans, 8 🚿, 19 WCs,
£ car/tent £8, car/caravan £8, motorhome £8
🛊 ✗ 🍴 🗑 📞 🚻 📋 GR ⚠ 🎠 🔌 Calor 🐕
Last arrival time: 8:00
➔ Travelling W on A85 from Crieff turn left onto South Loch Earn Road, just before St Fillans. Continue to site in 1 mile at lochside.

Auchenbowie Caravan Site
Aucenbowie, Stirling FK7 8HE
📞 **01324-82211 Fax 01324-822950**
Open April-October 🚐 🚙

A peaceful site in rural surroundings, centrally located and ideal for touring. A wide range of activities are available locally.

Size 3½ acres, 60 touring pitches, 40 with electric hookup, 60 level pitches, 7 static caravans, 6 🚿, 12 WCs, 2 CWPs
₢ MasterCard Visa
📞 ⚠ 🎠 🚻 WS

➔ Leave M9/M80 at junction 9 and head S on A872 for ½ mile, turn right for further ½ mile.

Cairnryan Caravan & Chalet Park
Stranraer DG9 8QX
📞 **01581-200231 Fax 01581-200207**
Open 1 March-31 October

Overlooks Loch Ryan and the ferry terminal. Six caravans and ten chalets for hire (own WCs). ➔

← **Cairnryan Caravan & Chalet Park**

Size 7½ acres, 10 touring pitches, 5 with electric hookup, 10 level pitches, 82 static caravans, 6 🚿, 8 WCs, 1 CWP
🔌¼ ✗¼ 🚻 🔧 🏧 GR 🏪 🏥 🔌 Calor ♿
Last arrival time: 11:00
➜ 5 miles N of Stranraer on A77 in village of Cairnryan directly opposite ferry terminal for Ireland.

TAIN Ross-shire   15D2

Meikle Ferry Caravan Park
Meikle Ferry, Tain IV19 1JX
📞 **01862-892292**
Open 15 January-15 December ▲ 🚐 🚛
Size 3½ acres, 30 touring pitches, 15 with electric hookup, 30 level pitches, 15 static caravans, 4 🚿, 8 WCs, 1 CWP
£ car/tent £4.50, car/caravan £6, motorhome £6, motorbike/tent £4.50, children £0.50
Rental 🚐 £90-£210
🔌 ✗¼ 🚻 🚻 🔧 🏪 🏥 🐕 WS
Last arrival time: 11:00
➜ 2 miles N of Tain on A9, straight on at roundabout for new Dornoch bridge. Park access is 300 yards on right.

LOCH LOMOND
— Holiday Park —

A peaceful 13 acre park set in an idyllic location on the banks of Loch Lomond. Just 40 miles from Glasgow and an ideal base for touring the Highlands. All fully serviced touring pitches have superb views across the Loch. Award winning holiday homes are also available for hire.

**INVERUGLAS,
DUNBARTONSHIRE G83 7DW
Tel/Fax: 01301 704224**

TARBERT, LOCH FYNE Argyll   12B2

Point Sands Caravan Park
Tayinloan, Tarbert PA29 6XG
📞 **01583-441263 Fax 01583-441216**
Open 1 April-31 October ▲ 🚐 🚛
Size 69 static caravans, 7 🚿, 17 WCs, 2 CWPs
£ car/tent £6-£8, car/caravan £8-£9.50, motorhome £7-£9.50, motorbike/tent £5
Rental 🚐 £125-£295
₵ Visa
🔌 🔌¼ 🚻 🚻 🔧 🏪 🏥 Calor Gaz ♿ 🐕 WS
➜ From Tarbert travel S on A83 for 17 miles, then right to site (in ½ mile).

TARBET Dunbartonshire   12C1

Loch Lomond Holiday Park
Inveruglas, Tarbet G83 7DW
📞 **01301-704224 Fax 01301-704206**
Open Mar-Oct, Dec-Jan 🚐 🚛
Size 13 acres, 18 touring pitches, 18 with electric hookup, 18 level pitches, 72 static caravans, 5 🚿, 7 WCs, 2 CWPs
£ car/caravan £6.50-£12, motorhome £6.50-£12
Rental 🚐 Chalet. caravans £125-£285, chalets £190-£575
₵ MasterCard Visa
🔌 ✗¼ 🚻 🚻 🏧 📺 🏪 🏥 Calor Gaz ♿ 🐕
Last arrival time: 11:45
➜ 3 miles N of Tarbet on A82.

WHITHORN Wigtownshire   12C4

Burrowhead Holiday Village
Whithorn, Isle of Whithorn Village, Newton Stewart DG8 8OA
📞 **019885-252**
Open 1 March-31 October
Large coastal park on a headland. Calor gas only. Two caravans and ten chalets for hire (own WCs). Open from the March to the 31 October.

Size 100 acres, 40 touring pitches, 12 with electric hookup, 40 level pitches, 180 static caravans, 6 🚿, 12 WCs, 2 CWPs
🔌 ✗ 🍽 🚻 GR
Last arrival time: flexible
➜ A746, A750, just before Isle of Whithorn village right. 2 miles to Burrow Head.

WALES

Tyddyn Llwyn Caravan Park & Camp Site, Porthmadog

ABERAERON Cardiganshire   6B3

Aeron Coast Caravan
North Road, Aberaeron SA46 0JF
📞 01545-570349
Open Easter-end October ▲ 🚐 🚙
Size 22 acres, 50 touring pitches, 50 with
electric hookup, 50 level pitches, 150 static
caravans, 8 🐾, 36 WCs, 2 CWPs
£ car/tent £5.50-£8.50, car/caravan £6-£9,
motorhome £5.50-£8.50, children £0.50
⚱¼ ✗¼ 🍺 🍺¼ 🆗 🍴 🔲 🔳 GR 🔲 TV 🔺 🔲
🍺 Calor Gaz 🐕
Last arrival time: 8:00
➜ Main coastal road A487 on northern edge
of Aberaeron. Filling Station at entrance.

ABERGAVENNY Monmouthshire   7D4

Pyscodlyn Farm
Abergavenny NP7 7ER
📞 01873-853271 **Fax** 01873-853271
Open 1 April-31 October ▲ 🚐 🚙
Size 4½ acres, 60 touring pitches, 40 with
electric hookup, 60 level pitches, 4 🐾, 6
WCs, 1 CWP
£ car/tent £5-£6, car/caravan £6-£7,
motorhome £5-£7, motorbike/tent £5,
children £0.75-£1
Rental 🚐
🍺 🍺 🍴 🔲 Calor Gaz 🚻 🐕
Last arrival time: flexible
➜ 2 miles from Abergavenny on A40 (to
Brecon). 1½ miles from Nevill Hall Hospital,
50 yards past telephone box on left.

ABERGELE Conwy   6C1

Henlleys Farm
Abergele
📞 01745-351208
Open 15 April-15 October ▲ 🚐 🚙

*A family run park overlooking open
farmland, and near to the attractions of the
town and Rhyl. Ideally located for touring
North Wales.*

Size 11 acres, 280 touring pitches, 280 with
electric hookup, 280 level pitches, 19 🐾, 50
WCs, 1 CWP
£ car/tent £7.50-£9, car/caravan £8-£11
⚱¼ 🍺 🍺 🍴 🔺 🔲 Calor Gaz 🚻 🐕
➜ A55 turn off at Towyn, follow signs to
crossroads and village. Turn off just past
church.

Pen Isaf Caravan Park
Llangernyw, Abergele LL22 8RN
📞 01745-860276 **Fax** 01745-860220
Open March-October
Size 20 static caravans,
Rental 🚐
🍺 🍺 GR 🔲 Calor 🐕

ABERPORTH Cardiganshire   6B3

Llety Caravan Park
Tresaith, Aberporth, Cardigan SA43 2ED
📞 01239-810354
Open 1 March- 31 October ▲ 🚐 🚙

*This family run park is only five minutes
walk from the beach, shop, restaurant and
local inn. An ideal location with panoramic
views of Cardigan Bay.*

Size 12 acres, 20 touring pitches, 20 with
electric hookup, 20 level pitches, 80 static
caravans, 5 🐾, 18 WCs, 1 CWP
£ car/tent £6-£7.50, car/caravan £6-£7.50,
motorhome £6-£7.50, motorbike/tent £6
⚱¼ ✗¼ 🍺¼ 🍺 🍺 🍴 Calor Gaz 🐕 WS
Last arrival time: 6:00

➜ Turn off A487 towards Aberporth along B4333. Take coastal road towards Tresaith where park is situated ½ mile on left.

ABERSOCH Caernarfonshire 6B2

Bryn Cethin Bach Caravan Park
Lon Garmon, Abersoch LL53 7UL
☎ **01758-712719**
Open March-October 🚐 🚙
Size 22 acres, 15 touring pitches, 15 with electric hookup, 14 level pitches, 53 static caravans, 6 🚿, 7 WCs, 1 CWP
£ car/caravan £9-£11, motorhome £9-£11
✗¼ 🚻¼ 🔲 📞 🔟 🔳 Calor ☂
Last arrival time: 6:00
➜ A499 to Abersoch. At Land & Sea Garage fork right - Bryn Cethin Bach ½ mile up hill on right.

Sea View Camping & Caravan Park
Sarn Bach, Abersoch LL53 7ET
☎ **01758-712052 Fax 01758-713243**
Open April-October 🛆 🚐 🚙

Family site with magnificent views overlooking Abersoch harbour. Short walk down to quiet beach. Hook ups. Open April to October.

Size 4 acres, 60 touring pitches, 20 with electric hookup, 40 level pitches, 6 🚿, 10 WCs, 1 CWP
£ car/tent £6-£7.50, car/caravan £7.50-£9, motorhome £7.50-£9, motorbike/tent £6
🔲 📞 🔟 ☂ WS
➜ 1 mile from Abersoch towards Sarn Bach. Turn left at crossroads in Sarn Bach. Site is 250 yards on right.

Tyn-Y-Mur Touring & Camping Site
Lon Garmon, Abersoch LL53 7UL
☎ **01758-713223**
Open 1 March-31 October 🛆 🚐 🚙
Size 5½ acres, 40 touring pitches, 27 with electric hookup, 40 level pitches, 16 🚿, 16 WCs, 1 CWP
£ car/tent £8, car/caravan £10, motorhome £8, motorbike/tent £8
🚻¼ 🚰¼ 🔲 📞 🔟 🔺 🔳 Calor Gaz ♿ ☂
Last arrival time: 11:00
➜ Turn sharp right at the Land & Sea Garage on approach to Abersoch. Site is then ½ mile on left.

ABERYSTWYTH Cardiganshire 6B3

Aberystwyth Holiday Village
Penparcau Road, Aberystwyth SY23 1BP
☎ **01970-624211 Fax 01970-611536**
Open 1 March-31 October 🛆 🚐 🚙
Size 152 touring pitches, 100 with electric hookup, 152 static caravans, 30 🚿, 30 WCs, 3 CWPs
Rental 🚐 Chalet.

← **Aberystwyth Holiday Village**

℃ MasterCard Visa
🅱 🅱¼ ✕ ✕¼ 🖱 🖱¼ 🔲 📞 🔲 🔲 📶 🔲 🔲 🔲 GR
🔲 📺 🔲 🔲 Calor ✚ WS
➡ Take A487 out of Aberystwyth S for 1½ mile.

Glan-Y-Mor Leisure Park
Clarach Bay, Aberystwyth SY23 3DT
📞 **01970-828900 Fax 01970-828890**
Open 1 March-1 November

PENGARREG
CARAVAN PARK

Beach front location, surrounded by wooded hillsides. Indoor leisure centre with jacuzzi, sauna, sunbeds, steam room and fitness gym, plus bowling alley. Children's play areas and organised activities. Easy access to Aberystwyth and Mid Wales resorts and attractions.

Size 12 acres, 100 touring pitches, 40 with electric hookup, 75 level pitches, 160 static caravans, 14 🚿, 14 WCs, 2 CWPs
£ car/caravan £6-£10
℃ MasterCard Visa
🅱 ✕ 🍺 📞 🔲 GR 🔲 🔲 🔲 🔲 Calor Gaz ♿ WS
Last arrival time: 12:00
➡ Leave A487 at Bow Street where Claracia Bay is signposted. Follow signs for North Beach for 2 miles. Site entrance is at beach front.

Midfield Caravan Park
Southgate, Aberystwyth SY23 4DX
📞 **01970-612542**
Open April-October ⛺ 🚐 🚍
Size 6 acres, 75 touring pitches, 28 with electric hookup, 40 level pitches, 57 static caravans, 14 🚿, 12 WCs, 1 CWP
£ car/tent £7.70-£8.30, car/caravan £7.70-£8.30
🅱¼ ✕¼ 🍺¼ 📞 🔲 🔲 🔲 Calor Gaz ♿ ✚
Last arrival time: 10:00
➡ 1½ miles SE of Aberystwyth on A4120 and 200 yards from junction with A4817.

Pengarreg Caravan Park
Llanrhystyd, Aberystwyth SY23 5JD
📞 **01974-202247**
Open 1 March-31 October ⛺ 🚐 🚍
Size 75 touring pitches, 20 with electric hookup, 75 level pitches, 10 🚿, 20 WCs, 1 CWP
£ car/tent £4.50-£6.50, car/caravan £4.50-£6.50, motorhome £4.50-£6.50, motorbike/tent £4.50
🅱 ✕ 🍺 🔲 🔲 🔲 GR 🔲 🔲 Calor Gaz ♿ ✚ WS
➡ At S end of Llanrhystyd on A487, turn W opposite Lloyd Motor garage. Site signposted.

Woodlands Caravan Park

Llanon, Aberystwyth SY23 5LX

📞 **01974-202342**

Open March-October 🛆 🚐 🚛

Size 10 acres, 40 touring pitches, 16 with electric hookup, 40 level pitches, 39 static caravans, 6 🚿, 14 WCs, 1 CWP

£ car/tent £7, car/caravan £7, motorhome £7, motorbike/tent £5.50, children £0.25

🔋 ✗¼ 🚰¼ 🗑 🔌 🚽 Calor Gaz 🐕

Last arrival time: 10:00

➜ A487 Aberystwyth to Cardigan coast road. Through village of Llanon if approaching from N. Turn right at sign towards sea.

BALA Caernarfonshire   6C2

Camping & Caravanning Club Site

Crynierth Caravan Park, Cefn-Ddwysarn, Bala LL23 7LN

📞 **01678-530324**

Open end March-end October 🛆 🚐 🚛

Size 50 touring pitches, 48 with electric hookup, 6 🚿, 14 WCs, 1 CWP

£ car/tent £8.75-£11.55, car/caravan £8.75-£11.55, motorhome £8.75-£11.55, motorbike/tent £8.75, children £1.30

℃ MasterCard Visa

🗑 🔌 🚿 🚽 ♿ 🐕 🖘

Last arrival time: 11:00

➜ 3 miles to E of Bala, ½ mile from A494 between Bala and Corwen. Leave A5 at Druid.

Pen-Y-Garth Caravan & Camping Park

Rhos-y-Gwaliau, Bala LL23 7ES

📞 **01678-520485**

Open 1 March-31 October 🛆 🚐 🚛

Generous pitches, acres of space and a quiet, peaceful atmosphere in beautiful suroundings. The toilet block is modern with free hot water, laundry and washing-up rooms.

Size 20 acres, 35 touring pitches, 35 with electric hookup, 40 level pitches, 50 static caravans, 10 🚿, 12 WCs, 1 CWP

£ car/tent £5-£8, car/caravan £6-£8, motorhome £6-£8, motorbike/tent £5, children £1.50

Rental 🚐 £120-£250 weekly, £25-£35 nightly.

🔋 ✗ 🚰 🗑 🔌 🚽 🆖 🔍 ⚠ 🚿 Calor Gaz ♿ 🐕

Last arrival time: 10:30

➜ Take B4391 Bala to Llangynog road. 1½ mile from Bala fork right at signpost to Lake Vyrnwy and Rhos-y-Gwalian. Site entrance in 600 yards.

Penybont Touring & Camping Park

Llangynog Road, Bala LL23 7PH

📞 **01678-520549** Fax **01678-520006**

Open 1 April-31 October 🛆 🚐 🚛

A small, picturesque, privately owned touring and tenting park, with new free facilities, including water related and other sporting activities. The site is located 100 yards from Lake Bala and is the nearest park to Bala town just three quarters of a mile away.

Size 5 acres, 35 touring pitches, 35 with electric hookup, 30 level pitches, 9 🚿, 11 WCs, 1 CWP

£ car/tent £6.35-£7.55, car/caravan £7.45-£8.75, motorhome £7.55-£8.25, motorbike/tent £6.35

℃ MasterCard Visa

🔋 🔋¼ ✗¼ 🚰 🚰¼ 🗑 🔌 🚽 Calor ♿ 🐕 WS

Last arrival time: 12:00

➜ From main Bala road (A494), turn onto B4391. Site ¾ mile on right.

See advert on next page

PEN Y BONT
The Lovely Little Park

RAC
APPOINTED

TOURING & CAMPING PARK
Llangynog Road, Bala, Gwynedd LL23 7PH
Tel: 01678-520549 Fax: 01678-520006

THIS SMALL FAMILY RUN, PEACEFUL, PICTURESQUE, LANDSCAPED TOURING AND CAMPING PARK IN UNSPOILT SURROUNDINGS 100 YARDS FROM BALA LAKE IS PROUD TO LIST THE FOLLOWING

TOP 10 *FOR YOUR ENJOYMENT . . . . . .*

(1) FREE, NEW Hot Showers of **CONTINENTAL** Standard

(2) NEAREST Park to Bala Town (a gentle 10 minute walk)

(3) FREE, NEW Spacious Private **VANITY** Cubicles with Individual Lights, Mirrors and Shaving Points.

(4) FREE, NEW Disabled Room and **FREE, NEW** Baby Room

(5) CLOSEST Park to Bala Sailing Club & Small Gauge Railway

(6) NEW Laundry with Washer, Dryer, Iron and Deep Sink

(7) CALOR GAS and Provisions in Well Stocked **SHOP**

(8) DOGS Welcome on our Park and Country Lane Dog Walk Area

(9) NEW All Electric **FLAT HARD STANDING** Pitches

(10) MODERN UNDERCOVER Dishwashing & Food Prep Area

For Brochure or Advance Bookings, please phone **01678 520549**
or Fax us on **01678 520006**

BANGOR Caernarfonshire 6B1

Treborth Hall Farm Camping & Caravan
Trebroth Road, Bangor LL57 2RX
☎ 01248-364399 Fax 01248-364333
▲ ⊕ ⊞

Beautiful setting located between the Britannia Bridge and the Menai Suspension Bridge. Close to the Menai Straights. Touring site contained in old walled orchard.

Size 25 touring pitches, 25 with electric hookup, 100 level pitches, 8 ↟, 10 WCs, 1 CWP

▢ ⚠ ⊞ ㅎ ↟ WS
➜ Turn off A55 dual carriageway just before crossing Britannia Bridge onto Angelsey. Turn onto A487 for Bangor, ¾ mile on left towards Bangor. Entrance to site signposted.

BARGOED Caerphilly 3D1

Parc Cwm Darran Caravan & Camping Site
Cwn Lwydrew Farm, Bargoed CF8 9AB
☎ 01443-875557 Fax 01443-836944
Open 1 March-30 October ▲ ⊕ ⊞

Park Cwm Darran is a peaceful country park, tucked away from it all in the Darran Valley. An ideal base for exploring South Wales, including the Brecon Beacons and Cardiff. £2 discount with this listing.

Size 2 acres, 30 touring pitches, 20 with electric hookup, 20 level pitches, 4 ↟, 5 WCs, 1 CWP
£ car/tent £3.50-£4.50, car/caravan £4.50-£5.50, motorhome £4.50-£5.50, motorbike/tent £4.50
⚁¼ ✕ ➤ ▢ ⊟ ⊡ ⚠ ⊞ ㅎ ↟ WS
➜ Follow A469 through Bargoed, turn left under viaduct. Turn left on next sharp bend and follow road through Deri. It is 1 mile to other side of Deri. From other direction: A469 from Buke, turn right to Pontlottyn and follow sign to Fochriw. Park is 1 mile past Fochriw.

BARMOUTH Caernarfonshire 6C2

Benar Beach Camping & Touring Site
Tal-y-Bont, Barmouth LL43 2AR
☎ 01341-247571 Fax 01341-247571
Open March-October ▲ ⊕ ⊞

Close to a wide, safe, sandy beach with miles of picturesque dunes. Extra facilities available in high season. Swimming pool one mile. Golf, tennis, sea fishing, canoeing, boating, horse riding within five miles. Open from March to October.

Size 9 acres, 155 touring pitches, 22 with electric hookup, 155 level pitches, 7 ↟, 8 WCs, 1 CWP
£ car/tent £4-£6, car/caravan £5-£10, motorhome £5-£10, motorbike/tent £3
⚁¼ ✕¼ ➤¼ ▢ ⊟ ↟ WS
Last arrival time: flexible
➜ 5 miles N of Barmouth, after Tal-y-Bont village, turn left by Llanddwywe church. Site is 100 yards from beach.

Hendre Mynach Touring Caravan & Camping Park
Llanaber Road, Barmouth LL42 1YR
☎ 01341-280262
Open 1 March-31 October ▲ ⊕ ⊞ ➜

← Hendre Mynach

Only 100 yards from a safe sandy beach, 15 minutes walk to the town centre, many mountain walks, courtesy bus to the local pub, games room, children's room

Size 10 acres, 60 touring pitches, 60 with electric hookup, 60 level pitches,
£ car/tent £6–£8, car/caravan £7–£11, motorhome £6–£10, motorbike/tent £6, children £1–£11
🛉 ✗ 🖤 🖸 🔋 🗗 ⚠ ⛱ Calor Gaz ♿ 🐕
Last arrival time: 10:30

➡ ½ mile N of Barmouth on A496. Barmouth Harlech Road on the seaward side.

BARRY Vale of Glamorgan	3D1

Fontygary Leisure Park
Rhoose, Barry CF62 3ZT
📞 01446-711074 **Fax** 01446-710613
Open 1 March–6 January 🚐 🚐

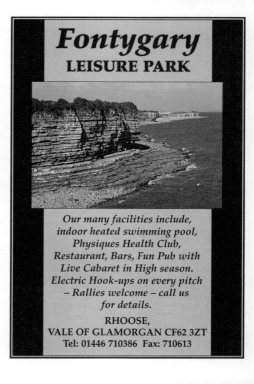

A gently sloping grassed site, with family facilities, overlooking the Bristol Channel. Ideal base to tour South Wales.

Size 30 acres, 26 touring pitches, 26 with electric hookup, 430 static caravans, 6 ⛌, 8 WCs, 2 CWPs
£ car/caravan £12-£20, motorhome £12-£20
Rental ⊟
((Visa
⧗ ✕ ✕¼ ☛ ⊟ ⌧ ⊟ 🗓🗓🗓 GR ⊟ ⚠ ⊠ ⊟
Calor ⅋ ⊢
➜ Leave M4 junction 33 and follow signs for Cardiff Wales Airport. At airport follow Dragon directional signs to park.

Vale Touring Caravan Park
Port Road (West), Barry
☎ **01446-719311**
Open 1 April-1 October ⊟ ⊟
Size 3 acres, 40 touring pitches, 15 with electric hookup, 40 level pitches, 4 ⛌, 6 WCs, 1 CWP
£ car/caravan £6-£7, motorhome £6-£7, children £1-£1.50
⧗¼ ✕¼ ☛ ⊟ ⚠ ⊠ Calor ⅋ ⊢

➜ Follow A4226 Barry to St Athan. The park is on left 1½ miles out of Barry.

Kingsbridge Caravan Park
Llanfaes, Beaumaris LL58 8LR
☎ **01248-490636**
Open March-October ⋏ ⊟ ⊟
Size 13 acres, 148 touring pitches, 25 with electric hookup, 40 level pitches, 29 static caravans, 6 ⛌, 13 WCs, 2 CWPs
£ car/tent £5-£6, car/caravan £7.50-£9.50, motorhome £5-£6, motorbike/tent £5, children £1.25-£1.50
Rental ⊟ caravans £100-£250
⧗ ⧗¼ ☛ ⊟ ⚠ ⊠ Calor Gaz ⊢
➜ Through Beaumaris, past Castle for 1½ miles, turn left, park is 400 yards on right.

Beddgelert Forest Campsite
Beddgelert LL55 4UU
☎ **01766-86288**   →

At the heart of Snowdonia National Park

BEDDGELERT FOREST CAMPSITE

OPEN ALL YEAR ROUND
20 acres, 105 electrical hookup pitches, 60 all-weather pitches and 100 grass pitches.

Three shower and toilet blocks located through the site.

Beddgelert Campsite is set among woodlands situated within the picturesque Snowdonia National Park. Close to the castles of North Wales, the area is ideal for wayfaring, hill walking, climbing...

ADVANCE BOOKINGS WELCOME
Forest Enterprise, Beddgelert, Gwynedd LL55 4UU
Telephone: 01766 890288

← **Beddgelert Forest Campsite**

Open all year **⋏ ⇔ ⇕**
Size 25 acres, 280 touring pitches, 15 with
electric hookup, 280 level pitches, 11 ⋒, 32
WCs, 2 CWPs
⦿ ⅋
➡ 1 mile NW of Beddgelert on A4085.

BENLLECH BAY Anglesey   6B1

Plas Uchaf Caravan & Camping Park
Benllech Bay, Benllech LL74 8NU
☎ 01407-763012
Open March-October **⋏ ⇔ ⇕**
Size 9 acres, 88 touring pitches, 75 with
electric hookup, 75 level pitches, 25 static
caravans, 6 ⋒, 16 WCs, 2 CWPs
£ car/tent £6-£7, car/caravan £6-£7,
motorhome £6-£7, motorbike/tent £6
⦿¼ **✗**¼ **⇔**¼ **⊟ ⚠ ⊞** Calor **🛉** WS
Last arrival time: 10:00
➡ From A5025 take B5108. Site is signposted
and is ½ mile from Benllech.

BETWS-Y-COED Conwy   6C1

Cwmlanerch Caravan Park
Betws-y-Coed LL24 0BG
☎ 01690-710363
Open March-31 October **⇔ ⇕**

*Family run site. Restaurants, shops, golf one
mile.*

Size 3 acres, 16 touring pitches, 16 with
electric hookup, 16 level pitches, 32 static
caravans, 4 ⋒, 10 WCs, 2 CWPs
£ car/caravan £7, motorhome £6.50-£8
Rental ⇔ caravans £100-£190
☎ ⊟ Calor **⦿ 🛉**
➡ One mile N of Betws-y-Coed on B5106,
Betws-y-Coed to Conwy road. Signposted
on entrance on right.

BODORGAN Anglesey   6B1

Pen-y-Bont Touring Site
Malltraeth, Bodorgan LL62 5BA
☎ 01407-840209
Open April **⋏ ⇔ ⇕**
Size 4 acres, 25 touring pitches, 20 with
electric hookup, 25 level pitches, 1 static
caravans, 4 ⋒, 6 WCs, 1 CWP
£ car/tent £4-£6, car/caravan £6-£8.50,
motorhome £6, motorbike/tent £4
Rental ⇔
⦿¼ **✗**¼ **⇔**¼ **⊟ ⊟ ⚠ ⊞** Calor Gaz **⦿ 🛉** WS
Last arrival time: 11:00
➡ On approaching Anglesey over Brittania
Bridge on A5, take left road, A4080 to
Brynsigncyn. Follow A4080 to Newborough
through forestry, before village of Malltraeth
site is on left.

BORTH Cardiganshire   6C3

Brynowen Holiday Village
Borth SY24 5LS
☎ 01970-87366 Fax 01970-871125
Open Easter-end October

Size 30 acres, 104 level pitches, 105 static
caravans
⟪ MasterCard Visa
⦿ ⦿ ✗¼ **☒ 🛉**
➡ Take B4353 off A487 between
Aberystwyth and Machynlleth. Entrance on
left, just after the southern end of Borth
seafront.

Cambrian Coast Caravan Park
Ynyslas, Borth SY24 5JU
☎ 01970-871233 Fax 01970-871856
Open March-November **⋏ ⇔ ⇕**

An 'Excellence' graded park close to a sandy 'Blue Flag' beach. The site offers a club with family entertainment, and children's activities, go-karts and bouncy castle. Concessionary use of Glan-y-Mor Park pool.

Size 12 acres, 75 touring pitches, 48 with electric hookup, 75 level pitches, 144 static caravans, 9 🚿, 9 WCs, 1 CWP
£ car/tent £6.50-£10, car/caravan £6.50-£10
CC MasterCard Visa
🅿 ✕ 🛒 🔌 🚻 🔲 🅰 🎣 🍴 Calor Gaz ♿ WS
Last arrival time: 12:00
➡ From A487 N of Aberystwyth to Borth. Park entrance is on seafront road, 1 mile N of Borth village.

Glanlerry Caravan Park
Borth
📞 **01970-871413**
Open Easter-October Å 🚐 🚏

A small family-owned site, well sheltered with level pitches. The site is within easy walking distance of Borth, with its 3 miles of unspoilt sand.

Size 7 acres, 40 with electric hookup, 40 level pitches, 6 🚿, 11 WCs, 1 CWP
£ car/tent £6.50-£6.75, car/caravan £6.75-£9, motorhome £6.50-£8
🔲 📞 🚻 🅰 🎣 Calor Gaz WS
➡ 5 miles NE of Aberystwyth (A487), turn N on B4353. Site 2 miles.

Mill House Caravan & Camping Park
Dol-y-Bont, Borth SY24 5LX
📞 **01970-871481**
Open Easter-mid October Å 🚐 🚏   →

← **Mill House**

Select sheltered site beside a trout stream, with modern amenities. One mile from the seaside village of Borth, with sandy beaches, safe bathing and rock pools.

Size 8 acres, 16 touring pitches, 16 with electric hookup, 16 level pitches, 15 static caravans, 2 ⓡ, 5 WCs, 1 CWP
£ car/tent £8, car/caravan £8, motorhome £8
▣ Calor Gaz ⼘ WS
Last arrival time: 8:00

Brynich is a family run park near the foothills of the Brecon Beacons. Situated on the A470, 200 metres from the junction with the A40, 1½ km EAST of Brecon. The site extends to 15 acres (6½ hectares) and consists of two well screened and sheltered fields which are closely mown to give a lawn effect. Over the years we have been operating, friendly service and cleanliness have been our major priority.

Brecon, Powys LD3 7SH, Wales
Tel/Fax: 01874 623325

➡ From Borth to Aberyswyth B4353, 1 mile from Borth fork left by railway bridge and white railings into Doly-Bont village and follow signs.
See advert on previous page

Ty Mawr Caravan & Camping Park
Ynyslas, Borth SY24 5LB
☎ 01745-832079 Fax 01745-827454
Open March-October ⋀ ⼦
🅿 ♿
➡ W off A487 at Tre'r-ddol onto B4353. Site in 3 miles.

BRECON Powys	7D4

Brynich Caravan Park
Brecon LD3 7SH
☎ 01874-623325 Fax 01874-623325
Open 1 April-6 October ⋀ ⼦ ⼦

With panoramic views and a friendly atmosphere to greet you, this quiet, immaculate site offers a wide range of facilities, including free hot water and disabled and baby rooms. Cleanliness is a priority.

Size 15 acres, 130 touring pitches, 78 with electric hookup, 120 level pitches, 18 ⓡ, 24 WCs, 3 CWPs
£ car/tent £6.50-£7.50, car/caravan £7-£8, motorhome £7-£8, motorbike/tent £6.50, children £1
🔋 ▣ ☎ ⎘ ⚠ 🗙 Calor Gaz ♿ ⼘ WS
➡ 1 mile E of Brecon on A470 (Builth Wells), 200 yards from roundabout with A40 (Abergavenny).

Llynfi Holiday Park

Llangorse Lake, Llangorse, Brecon LD3 7TR
📞 **01874-658283** Fax **01874-658575**
Open April-October ⚠ 🚐 🚏
Size 17 acres, 60 touring pitches, 40 with electric hookup, 60 level pitches, 100 static caravans, 8 🚿, 12 WCs, 2 CWPs
£ car/tent £7-£9, car/caravan £7-£9, motorhome £7-£9, motorbike/tent £7, children £1.50-£2
⛟¼ ✗¼ 🔲 📞 🔲 🔲 GR 🔲 TV 🔲 🔲 🔲 Calor Gaz WS
Last arrival time: 11:00
➤ Follow A40 via Bwlch to Llangorse Lake via B4560. From A438 via Talgarth on B4560.

Anchorage Caravan Park

near Brecon, Bronllys LD3 0LD
📞 **01874-711246**
Open all year ⚠ 🚐 🚏

A park with high standards and panoramic views of the Brecon National Park. Ideally situated for touring and walking in south and mid-Wales.

Size 13 acres, 60 touring pitches, 40 with electric hookup, 25 level pitches, 8 🚿, 20 WCs, 1 CWP
£ car/tent £6, car/caravan £6, motorhome £6, motorbike/tent £6
⛟ ⛟¼ ✗¼ 🍺¼ 🔲 📞 🔲 TV 🔲 🔲 Calor Gaz 🔲 🔲 WS
Last arrival time: 11:00
➤ 8 miles NE of Brecon on A438 on W side of Bronllys village.

Riverside International Caravan & Camping Site

Talgarth, Near Brecon, Bronllys LD3 0HL
📞 **01874-711320**

Open Easter-October ⚠ 🚐 🚏

Well maintained, clean and friendly family run site, situated in the heart of Wales with panoramic views of the Black Mountains. Warm welcome assured.

Size 10 acres, 84 touring pitches, 78 with electric hookup, 84 level pitches, 12 🚿, 32 WCs, 2 CWPs
£ car/tent £8-£9, car/caravan £8-£9, motorhome £8-£9, motorbike/tent £8, children £1-£1.20
⛟¼ ✗ 🍺 🔲 📞 🔲 🔲 🔲 🔲 🔲 GR 🔲 TV 🔲 🔲 🔲 Calor Gaz ♿ WS →

← Riverside International

➜ Situated on A479 between Bronllys and Talgarth, directly opposite Bronllys Castle.

BRYNSIENCYN Anglesey	6B1

Fron Caravan & Camping Site

Brynsiencyn, Llanfairpwllgwyngyll LL61 6TX
☎ **01248-430310**
Open Easter-end September ▲ ⊕ ⊐
Size 5 acres, 70 touring pitches, 35 with electric hookup, 60 level pitches, 8 ♣, 9 WCs, 1 CWP
£ car/tent £4.50-£7.50, car/caravan £7.50, motorhome £7-£7.50, motorbike/tent £7
⚡ ⊡ ⊟ ⊞ ⊡ GR ◙ ⚠ ✕ Calor Gaz ⅃ ✝
Last arrival time: 11:00
➜ Leave Brittania Bridge at first sliproad signed A4080 Llanfairpwllgwynn, after 400 yards turn left again signed Brynsiencyn. Site is ½ mile on right after village.

BRYNTEG Anglesey	6B1

Ad Astra Caravan Park

Brynteg LL78 7JH
☎ **01248-853283**
Open 1 March-31 October ▲ ⊕ ⊐
Size 3½ acres, 12 touring pitches, 12 with electric hookup, 12 level pitches, 38 static caravans, 4 ♣, 8 WCs, 1 CWP
£ car/tent £6, car/caravan £7.50-£9, motorhome £7.50-£9, motorbike/tent £6
Rental ⊕ £150-£220
⚡¼ ✕ ✕¼ ⊡ ⚡ ⊟ Calor ⅃ ✝ WS
➜ 2 miles W of Benllech off B5108 (Brynteg), on B5110 (Llangfeni) road.

BUILTH WELLS Powys	6C3

Forest Fields Caravan & Camping Park

Hundred House, Builth Wells LD1 5RT
☎ **01982-570406** Fax **01982-570220**
Open Easter-October ▲ ⊕ ⊐

A beautiful, tranquil, family run site with no clubhouse or statics. Immaculately maintained facilities. Hill and farm walks direct from the site. Graded 4 ticks. Award for environmental excellence. 'A rare gem of a site'.

Size 7 acres, 60 touring pitches, 40 with electric hookup, 40 level pitches, 6 ♣, 8 WCs, 1 CWP
£ car/tent £5-£6, car/caravan £7, motorhome £6, motorbike/tent £3
⊡ ⚡ ⊟ ⊡ Calor Gaz ✝ WS
➜ 4 miles E of Builth Wells on A481.

Llewelyn Leisure Park

Cilmery, Builth Wells LD2 3NU
☎ **01982-552838** Fax **01982-552838**
Open Easter-31 October ▲ ⊕ ⊐

Customer comments - 'treated like royalty', 'friendly and relaxed atmosphere', 'comfortable and clean', 'peaceful with wonderful views'. Nearby fishing, golf, and theatre. Adjacent inn with meals. Bus and train services 200 yards.

Size 2.16 acres, 25 touring pitches, 18 with electric hookup, 10 level pitches, 30 static caravans, 2 ♣, 3 WCs, 2 CWPs

£ car/tent £6-£8, car/caravan £6-£9, motorhome £6-£9, motorbike/tent £4
Rental 🛖 Chalet. £49-£299.
€ MasterCard Visa
🛱 ✕¼ 🖃 🖳 🖂 🅰 🆁 🅶🆁 🆀 📺 Calor Gaz & 🦮 WS
Last arrival time: 10:30
➡ 2 miles W of Builth Wells on south side of A483 in Cilmery Village, adjacent to Prince Llewelyn inn/restaurant.

CAERNARFON Caernarfonshire   6B1

Bryn Gloch Caravan & Camping Park
Betws Garmon, Caernarfon LL54 7YY
📞 **01286-650216 Fax 01286-650216**
Open all year 🏕 🛖 🚐
Size 12 acres, 150 touring pitches, 110 with electric hookup, 100 level pitches, 15 static caravans, 14 🚿, 20 WCs, 3 CWPs
£ car/tent £6.50-£8, car/caravan £6.50-£8, motorhome £6.50-£8, motorbike/tent £6.50, children £1.50
Rental 🛖 £100-£260
🛱 ✕ 🍺 🖳 🅶🆁 📺 🍴 Calor Gaz &
➡ On A4085 Caernarfon to Beddgelert road, 7 miles from Beddgelert on left, 5 miles from Caernarfon on right. Site entrance on main road.

Brynteg Holiday Park
Llantug, Caernarfon LL55 4RF
📞 **01286-871374**
Open 1 March-14 January 🏕 🛖 🚐

Brynteg Holiday Park is truly unique. Set in wooded grounds overlooking Snowdonia. Superb countryside with a leisure complex, heated pool and much more.

Size 38 acres, 150 touring pitches, 286 static caravans, 10 🚿, 35 WCs

🛱 ✕ 🖃
➡ A4086 into village of Llanrug. Turn by Glyn Twrog pub, signs to site.

Dinlle Caravan Park
Dinas Dinlle, Caernarfon LL54 5TW
📞 **01492-623355 Fax 01492-623921**
Open 1 March-31 October

With extremely good and well maintained facilities and touring pitches, particularly well spaced out on large areas of open grassland, this is an ideal site for discerning tourers.

← **Dinlle Caravan Park**

Size 22 acres, 250 touring pitches, 150 with electric hookup, 250 level pitches, 138 static caravans, 25 🚿, 50 WCs, 2 CWPs
CC MasterCard Visa
🛒 ➡ 📞 🔲 GR ⚠ 🏠 🔌 Calor Gaz ♿ WS
Last arrival time: 10:00
➡ A499 out of Caernarfon towards Pwhelli (4 miles), right for Dinas Dinlle & Caernarfon airport. Park on right.

Glan Gwna Holiday Park
Caeathro, Caernarfon LL55 2SG
📞 **01286-673456 Fax 01286-673456**
Open Easter-September 🏕 ⛟ 🚐
Size 200 acres, 100 touring pitches, 80 with electric hookup, 120 static caravans, 7 🚿, 15 WCs, 1 CWP
£ car/tent £7-£12, car/caravan £7-£12, motorhome £7-£12, motorbike/tent £5
Rental ⛟ Chalet.
🛒 ✕ ➡ 📞 🔲 🔳 🔲 📂 📺 ⚠ 🏠 🔌 Calor 🐕
Last arrival time: 11:00
➡ 1½ miles S of Caernarfon, off A4085.

CAERNARFON

Mr & Mrs W.C. & M.J. Evans
TYN RHOS FARM CARAVAN SITE
Saron, Llanwnda, Caernarfon,
Gwynedd LL54 5UH

Clean, quiet select family site for tourers on 2½ acre level grass land with panoramic views in outstanding beauty, 3 miles south of Caernarfon 2½ m beach. Easy reach of Snowdonia, Anglesey and the Lleyn Peninsula. All electric hookups, toilets, showers on site.

OPEN MARCH-OCTOBER MODERATE CHARGES
For full details ring: **01286 830362**
Site Recommended
Turn off A487 (Caernarfon-Portmadoc Road) after crossing bridge ½ mile at signpost Llanfaglan Saron. In 3m at right bend continue through gate to site.

Riverside Camping
Caer Glyddyn, Pontrug, Caernarfon LL54
📞 **01286-678781 Fax 01286-67723**
Open Easter-October 🏕 ⛟ 🚐
Size 6 acres, 60 touring pitches, 8 with electric hookup, 60 level pitches, 4 🚿, 8 WCs, 1 CWP
£ car/tent £4-£6, car/caravan £6.50-£9, motorhome £6-£8.50, motorbike/tent £4
🛒¼ ✕¼ ➡¼ 🔲 🔳 ⚠ 🏠 Gaz 🐕
➡ 2 miles E of Caernarfon on Llanberis road A4086.

Tyn Rhos Farm Caravan Site
Saron, Llanwnda, Caernarfon LL54 5UH
📞 **01286-830362**
Open March-October ⛟ 🚐
Size 2¼ acres, 20 touring pitches, 20 with electric hookup, 20 level pitches, 2 🚿, 4 WCs, 1 CWP
♿
➡ Turn off A407 Caernafon to Porthmadog road after crossing bridge at signpost to Saron. Site is after 3 miles on right.

Tyn-yr-Onnen Camping & Caravan Site
Waunfawr, Caernarfon LL55 4AX
📞 **01286-650281 Fax 01286-650281**
Open April-October 🏕 ⛟ 🚐

Welcome to a traditional upland farm, secluded and off the beaten track. Freedom to roam our beautiful hills, interesting walks, friendly animals. Immaculate facilties, free showers, toddlers bathroom, games and TV lounge. SAE for brochure.

Size 4 acres, 30 touring pitches, 30 with electric hookup, 20 level pitches, 3 static caravans, 6 🚿, 6 WCs, 1 CWP
£ car/tent £6-£7, car/caravan £7-£8, motorhome £6-£7, motorbike/tent £5, children £1

➡

GLAN GWNA
HOLIDAY PARK

Welcomes you to Snowdonia

Glan Gwna is an enchanting holiday village hidden amongst the woods and meadows of an old country estate. Within easy reach of historic castles, golden beaches, lakes, and breath-taking mountain walks.

Glan Gwna has many amenities including excellent Coarse and Game fishing on four lakes and the river Seiont, horse-riding on site, tennis court, heated (outdoor) swimming pool, clubhouse with live entertainment, and poolside bar with meals and takeaway.

SHOP • HAIRDRESSING SALON • LAUNDERETTE • GAMES ARCADE • COACH EXCURSIONS.

Excellent touring facilities for caravans, tents and motor homes, full time warden on site – dogs welcome.
Super pitches available.

BOOKING ESSENTIAL
BANK HOLIDAYS AND
SUMMER MONTHS.

Directions to site:
1½ miles from
Caernarfon on A4085.

For brochure and bookings phone or fax
CAEATHRO, NR. CAERNARFON, GWYNEDD, NORTH WALES LL55 2SG
Tel/Fax: Caernarfon (01286) 673456

← Tyn-yr-Onnen Camping & Caravan Site

Rental 🚐 Chalet.
℃ Visa
🐕 🚿¼ ✗¼ 🚰¼ 🔲 🔋 🗑 🅿 📠 GR 🔍 TV ⚠ 🗒
Calor Gaz 🚻 🐎 WS
Last arrival time: 10:00
➡ 4 miles from Caernarfon on A4085 turn left at Maurfawr Post Office. Site is signposted from there.

CARDIFF Cardiff   **3D1**

Pontcanna Caravan Site
Pontcanna Fields, Cardiff CF1 9JL 🚐 🚛
📞 **01222-398362**
Open all year
Size 20 acres, 43 touring pitches, 43 with electric hookup, 43 level pitches, 8 🚿, 10 WCs, 1 CWP
🚻
➡ W of Cardiff city centre. Entrance on E side of A4119 Cathedral Road, via Sophia Close.

CARDIGAN Cardiganshire   **6B4**

Bron Gwyn Mawr Farm Camping & Caravan Park
Penparc, Near Cardigan SA43 1SA
📞 **01239-613644 Fax 01239-613644**
Open March-October ⛺ 🚐 🚛

Small, select park, peacefully secluded in unspoilt countryside near the beautiful sandy beaches of Mwnt and Aberporth, and the quaint old market town of Cardigan. Ideal for walking, fishing, sight-seeing or relaxing.

Size 5 acres, 19 touring pitches, 6 with electric hookup, 19 level pitches, 3 static caravans, 1 🚿, 4 WCs, 1 CWP
£ car/tent £5-£6, car/caravan £5-£6, motorhome £5-£6, motorbike/tent £5
Rental 🚐 Chalet. £100-£275
🐕¼ ✗¼ 🔲 🔋 🗑 GR 🔍 ⚠ 🗒 🐎
Last arrival time: 12:00
➡ From Cardigan take A487 towards Aberystwyth for 2½ miles. Turn left at crossroads in Penparc village signed Ferwig & Mwnt. Carry on over crossroads. Entrance is on right about ½ mile from main road.

Camping Blaenwaun
Mwnt Cardigan, Ceredigion, Cardigan SA43 1QF
📞 **01239-612165**
Open April-October ⛺ 🚐 🚛
Size 10 acres, 50 touring pitches, 5 with electric hookup, 40 level pitches, 34 static caravans, 2 🚿, 3 WCs,
£ car/tent £6-£7, car/caravan £6-£7, motorhome £6-£7, motorbike/tent £6
Rental 🚐
🐕 🔲 🔋 🗑 🚰 Calor Gaz 🐎

CARMARTHEN Carmarthenshire   **6B4**

Pendine Sands Holiday Park
Carmarthen SA33 4NZ
📞 **01345-508508**
Open March-October 🚐 🚛

A family run park adjacent to the famous Pendine beach, boasting a heated indoor pool and kids clubs in the wide range of leisure facilities. Restaurant and bar, excellent cabaret entertainment. A 'British Holidays Park'.

Size 30 touring pitches, 10 with electric hookup, 550 static caravans, 6 ↑, 16 WCs, 2 CWPs

ℂℂ MasterCard Visa

🔋 🚐 🔲 🔳 🔳 🔳 🔳 🔳 🔳 Gaz 🐾

Last arrival time: 9:00

➡ Take A40 trunk road from Carmarthen to St Clears. Pendine/Pentywyn is signposted to left along A4066, 8 miles from junction with A40. Pass through village of Laugharne and park reception is 5 miles further on right.

COLWYN BAY Conwy	6C1

Bron-y-Wendon Caravan Park

Wern Road, Llanddulas, Colwyn Bay LL22 8HG

📞 **01492-512903**

Open 21 March-30 October 🚐 🚍

A new caravan park offering excellent modern facilities and sea views, easily reached from the A55.

Size 8 acres, 130 touring pitches, 125 with electric hookup, 100 level pitches, 13 ↑, 31 WCs, 2 CWPs

£ car/caravan £8-£9, motorhome £8-£9, children £0.50

Rental 🅰 🚐 Chalet.

ℂℂ Visa

🔋¼ ✕¼ 🚐¼ 🔲 🔳 GR 🔳 TV Calor & 🐾

➡ Turn off A55 at Llanddulas onto A547 and follow signs to park.

CONWY Conwy	6C1

Conwy Touring Park

Bwlch Mawr, Conwy LL32 8UX

📞 **01492-592856 Fax 01492-580024**

Open Easter-October 🅰 🚐 🚍

Set in spectacular scenery, the perfect location for touring Snowdonia and coastal resorts. Pitches from £4.85 per night. Special offers available.

Size 70 acres, 319 touring pitches, 270 with electric hookup, 300 level pitches, 50 ↑, 72 WCs, 7 CWPs

£ car/tent £4-£9.95, car/caravan £4.85-£9.95, motorhome £4.85-£9.95, motorbike/tent £4

ℂℂ MasterCard Visa

🔋 ✕ 🚐¼ 🔲 🔳 GR 🔳 🔳 Calor Gaz & 🐾

Last arrival time: 7:30

Conwy Touring Park is only one and a quarter miles from Ancient Conwy with its mediaeval castle, centuries old buildings and complete town walls. Conwy is one of the most picturesque and historic towns of Great Britain, its location and harbour make it ideal for sailing and water sports. Regular sea angling trips operate from the Quay and the Conwy River is famous for its trout and salmon.

BWLCH MAWR, CONWY, GWYNEDD LL32 8UX
Tel: 01492 592856 Fax: 01492 580024

← Conwy Touring Park

➜ Follow A55 to Conwy. Turn left at mini roundabout in front of Conwy Castle. Follow B5106 for 1½ miles. Look for sign on left.

Tyn Terfyn Caravan Park
Tal-y-Bont, Conwy LL32 8YX
☎ 01492-660525
Open 14 March-31 October ▲ 🚐 🚛
Size 2 acres, 15 touring pitches, 12 with electric hookup, 15 level pitches, 2 🚿, 3 WCs, 1 CWP
£ car/tent £23, car/caravan £24.50, motorhome £24.50
🛒¼ ✗¼ 🍺¼ 🗑 Calor Gaz 🐕
Last arrival time: 10:00
➜ 5 miles S of Conwy on B5106. First house on left after road sign 'Tal y Bont'.

CORWEN Denbighshire   7D2

Hendwr Caravan Park
Llandrillo, Corwen LL21 0SN
☎ 01490-440210
Open 1 April-31 October ▲ 🚐 🚛

A delightful, select level park with easy access, situated on a family farm beside a stream and offering clean, modern facilities.

Size 10 acres, 40 touring pitches, 40 with electric hookup, 40 level pitches, 80 static caravans, 8 🚿, 10 WCs, 2 CWPs
£ car/tent £4-£6, car/caravan £6, motorhome £6, children £1
🛒 🗑 ☎ 🗑 🎱 Calor Gaz 🐕 WS
Last arrival time: 10:30
➜ From Corwen take A5 turning onto B4401 for 4 miles. At sign for Hendwr turn right down a wooded driveway for ¼ mile. Site is on right.

CRICCIETH Caernarfonshire   6B2

Camping & Caravanning Club Site
Tyddyn Sianel, Llanystumdwy, Criccieth
☎ 01766-522855
Open end March-start November ▲ 🚐 🚛
Size 4 acres, 70 touring pitches, 46 with electric hookup
£ car/tent £9.20-£12.05, car/caravan £9.20-£12.05, motorhome £9.20-£12.05, motorbike/tent £9.20, children £1.40
CC MasterCard Visa
🗑 🛒 ♿ 🐕
Last arrival time: 11:00
➜ The site is signposted from Criccieth on A497 between Pwllheli and Porthmadog.

Llwyn Bugeilydd Farm
Criccieth LL52 0PN
☎ 01766-522235
Open March-31 October ▲ 🚐 🚛

Quiet family site with good views of Cardigan Bay and Snowdonia. This is the nearest site to Criccieth - one mile on the B4411 - and within easy walking distance of the beach and shops.

Size 6 acres, 20 touring pitches, 20 with electric hookup, 20 level pitches, 2 🚿, 6 WCs, 1 CWP
£ car/tent £4.50-£6.50, car/caravan £6-£7.50, motorhome £6-£7.50, motorbike/tent £4.50
🛒 🗑 ⚠ 🎱 Calor Gaz 🐕
➜ From A55 take A487 through Caernarvon, then just after Bryncir turn right onto B4411. Site 3½ miles on left. From Porthmadog along A497, turn right in Criccieth onto B4411, site 1 mile on right.

CRICKHOWELL Powys   7D4

Riverside Caravan & Camping Park
New Road, Crickhowell NP8 1AY
☎ 01873-810397 Fax 01873-811989
Open 1 March-31 October ▲ 🚐 🚛
Size 3½ acres, 25 touring pitches, 25 with electric hookup, 25 level pitches, 20 static caravans, 14 🚿, 16 WCs, 1 CWP
£ car/tent £5-£7, car/caravan £5.50-£10.50, motorhome £4.50-£8.50, motorbike/tent £4.50

�море¼ ✕¼ 🚐¼ 📞 ⬛ Calor Gaz & ⽊
Last arrival time: 11:00
➡ Between A40 and A4077 in Crickhowell.

➡ Take A487 out of Fishguard towards Cardigan, turning on your left. Signpost on right, about 3 miles.

Station House Caravan Park

Bodfari, Denbigh LL16 4DA
📞 **01745-710372**
Open 1 April-31 October ▲ 🚐 🚙

Size 1½ acres, 26 touring pitches, 18 with electric hookup, 20 level pitches, 2 🚿, 4 WCs, 1 CWP
£ car/caravan £5.25-£5.75, children £0.50-£0.75
⽊¼ ✕¼ 🚐¼ ⬛ 🔍 ⬛ 🔲 Calor ⽊
Last arrival time: 9:00
➡ From A541 turn N on B5429 to Tremeirchion. Park is on left after 50 yards.

Fishguard Bay Caravan Park

Dinas Cross, Fishguard SA42 0YD
📞 **01348-811415 Fax 01348-811425**
Open 1 March-10 January ▲ 🚐 🚙

Beautiful views and walks available from this secluded park on Pembrokeshire's Heritage Coast. Modern caravans equipped to a high standard.

Size 6 acres, 20 touring pitches, 20 with electric hookup, 20 level pitches, 50 static caravans, 4 🚿, 10 WCs, 1 CWP
Rental 🚐
 Ⓒ MasterCard Visa
⽊ ⬛ 📞 ⬛ 🔲 📺 🔲 🔲 Calor Gaz ⽊ WS

Hasguard Cross Caravan Park

Hasguard Cross, Little Haven, Haverfordwest SA62 3SL
📞 **01437-781443 Fax 01437-781443**
Open all year 🚐 🚙

A level, grassland park, tastefully screened with trees and views overlooking St Brides Bay and the Milford Haven. The licensed bar serves good food and beer.

Size 3¼ acres, 25 touring pitches, 25 with electric hookup, 25 level pitches, 35 static caravans, 6 🚿, 10 WCs, 1 CWP
£ car/caravan £5.50-£7.50, motorhome £5.50-£7.50
Rental 🚐 £85-£265
 Ⓒ Visa
✕ 🚐 ⬛ 📞 ⬛ 🔲 🔲 Calor & ⽊ WS
Last arrival time: 11:00
➡ In Haverfordwest follow Dale signs through town. At the Bellevue Inn bear left on B4327 Dale road. After 7 miles turn right at cross roads signed Little Haven. Turn into park 200 yards on right.

Nine Wells Camping & Caravan Park

Nine Wells, Solva, Haverfordwest SA62 6UH
📞 **01437-721809**
Open Easter-October ▲ 🚐 🚙
Size 4 acres, 50 touring pitches, 4 with electric hookup, 15 static caravans, 3 🚿, 7 WCs, 1 CWP
£ car/tent £4-£7, car/caravan £5-£7
⽊¼ ✕¼ 🚐¼ ⽊ WS

← Nine Wells Camping & Caravan Park

→ From Haverfordwest take A457 signposted St Davids and go through Solva. About ¼ mile out of Solva is Nine Wells. Turn left at Nine Wells and go 150 yards into site.

Redlands Touring Caravan Park
Little Haven, Haverfordwest SA62 3UU
☎ 01437-781301 Fax 01437-781093
Open Easter-end October Å 🚐 🚏
Size 5 acres, 64 touring pitches, 53 with electric hookup, 64 level pitches, 4 🚿, 12 WCs, 1 CWP
£ car/tent £6-£7, car/caravan £6-£7, motorhome £6-£7
✗¼ 🚐¼ 🔲 📞 🔲 🐕 🛒
→ 6½ miles S of Haverfordwest take B4327 Dale road. Site on right. Do not approach via Broad Haven.

Scamford Caravan Park
Keeston, Camrose, Haverfordwest SA62 6HN
☎ 01437-710304 Fax 01437-710304
Open March-mid October 🚐 🚏

Our peaceful country park is situated halfway between Haverfordwest and Newgale Sands, near the Pembrokeshire Coast Path, the island seabird sanctuaries and many lovely beaches.

Size 3½ acres, 5 touring pitches, 5 with electric hookup, 5 level pitches, 25 static caravans, 2 🚿, 4 WCs, 1 CWP
£ car/caravan £5-£7, motorhome £5-£7
Rental 🚐 Chalet. £90-£315
🔲 📞 🛗 🔲 Calor 🛒
Last arrival time: 8:00
→ From Haverfordwest take A487. In 4 miles turn right to Keeston. Follow signs for Scamford Caravan Park.

South Cockett Caravan & Camping Park
Broadway, Little Haven, Haverfordwest SA62 3TU
☎ 01437-781296 Fax 01437-781296
Open Easter-October Å 🚐 🚏
Size 6 acres, 10 touring pitches, 60 with electric hookup, 6 🚿, 12 WCs, 2 CWPs
£ car/tent £4.50-£5.50, car/caravan £5-£6.75, motorhome £4.50-£6.25, motorbike/tent £4
🔲 📞 🔲 Calor Gaz 🐕 WS
→ From Haverfordwest take B4341 signed Broad Haven for 4¼ miles, then left signposted Milford Haven to site after 300 yards.

KILGETTY Dyfed　　　　6B4

Woodland Vale Caravan Park
Ludchurch, Narberth, Kilgetty SA67 8JE
☎ 01834-831319
Open Easter-30 September 🚐 🚏
Size 11 acres, 30 touring pitches, 30 with electric hookup, 30 level pitches, 80 static caravans, 4 🚿, 8 WCs, 1 CWP
£ car/caravan £6, motorhome £6
Rental 🚐
🛥 🔲 📞 🔲 🔲 🚴 🏔 🎫 🍺
→ From St Clears take A477 signposted Tenby and Pembroke. After 9½ miles turn left for Ludchurch; X mile turn right for Ludchurch and Narberth, then 1X miles to Ludchurch village. Woodland Vale is on left as you pass through village.

LAMPETER Cardiganshire　　　　6B4

Moorlands Caravan Park
Llangybi, Lampeter SA48 8NN
☎ 01570-493543
Open March-October Å 🚐 🚏

Set in a sheltered valley one mile from the village. Ideal touring base for Devil's Bridge, Tregaron Marsh and Llyn Brianne Dam. Golf and fishing are available nearby.

Size 5 acres, 10 touring pitches, 6 with electric hookup, 10 level pitches, 49 static caravans, 2 ⋔, 5 WCs, 1 CWP
£ car/tent £6-£7, car/caravan £6-£7, motorhome £6-£7, motorbike/tent £6
⚥ ✕ 🍴 🗎 🔌 🖸 🗊 ⚠ 🎯 ⏻ Calor Gaz ♿ ♞ WS
Last arrival time: 6:00
➡ From Lampeter take A485 towards Tregaron. After 4 miles go through Llangybi village. After school and village shop a sign indicates site is 1½ miles up a lane.

Ants Hill Caravan & Camping Park
Laugharne SA33 4QN
📞 **01994-427293 Fax 01994-427293**
Open Easter-31 October

Situated in Dylan Thomas country and ideal for inland and coastal touring. Near the famous Pendine sands.

Size 9 acres, 60 touring pitches, 30 with electric hookup, 60 level pitches, 60 static caravans, 8 ⋔, 20 WCs, 1 CWP
⚥ ⚥¼ ✕¼ 🍴 🍴¼ 🔌 🖸 🗊 GR ⚠ 🎯 ⏻ Calor WS
Last arrival time: 10:30
➡ M4 to Carmarthen, A40 towards St Clears. A4066 for Laugharne. Take first left turning before signpost of Laugharne.

Refail Caravan & Camping Site
Refail, Llanbedrog LL53 7NP
📞 **01258-740511**
Open Easter-October ▲ 🚐 🚂
Size 2 acres, 33 touring pitches, 27 with electric hookup, 27 level pitches, 6 ⋔, 6 WCs, 1 CWP
£ car/tent £6.50-£8, car/caravan £6.50-£8, motorhome £6.50-£8, motorbike/tent £6.50
⚥¼ ✕¼ 🍴¼ 🖸 🔌 🖸 Calor Gaz ♞ WS
➡ Take A499 from Pwllheli. Turn right in Llanbedrog onto B4413 (signposted Llanbedrog Village & Aberdaron). Park is 200 yards on right.

Ty Newydd Caravan Park & Country Club
Llanbedrgoch LL76 8TZ
📞 **01248-450677 Fax 01248-450711**
Open March-October ▲ 🚐 🚂

Family run park on edge of small village in open country. Excellent toilet facilities, health & fitness centre, swimming pools and a licensed bar. Tourers and campers are made to feel very welcome.

Size 9 acres, 40 touring pitches, 40 with electric hookup, 40 level pitches, 61 static caravans, 4 ⋔, 8 WCs, 1 CWP
£ car/tent £5-£16, car/caravan £5-£16, motorhome £5-£16, motorbike/tent £5
Rental 🚐 £180-£300
⚥ ✕ 🍴 🖸 🔌 🖸 🗊 🗊 🎯 📺 GR ⚠ 🎯 ⏻ Calor Gaz ♿ ♞ WS
Last arrival time: 12:00
➡ Take A5025 from Pentraeth. After ½ mile turn left at layby. Site is 1 mile on right.

LLANDOVERY Carmarthenshire   6C4

Camping & Caravanning Club Site
Rhandirmwyn, Llandovery
☎ 01550-760257
Open end March-early November Å 🚐 🚍
Size 11 acres, 90 touring pitches, 47 with electric hookup, 6 🚿, 9 WCs, 1 CWP
£ car/tent £9.20-£12.05, car/caravan £9.20-£12.05, motorhome £9.20-£12.05, motorbike/tent £9.20, children £1.40
CC MasterCard Visa
🔲 📞 ⚠ 🔀 ♿ 🐾
Last arrival time: 11:00
➡ From A483 in Llandovery take road signed Rhandirmwyn for 7 miles. Turn left at Post Office in Rhandirmwyn. Site is signposted.

Erwlon Caravan & Camping Park
Llandovery SA20 0RD
☎ 01550-20332
Open all year Å 🚐 🚍

Family run park beautifully located alongside a babbling brook at the foothills of the Brecon Beacons. The site provides the ideal base for a touring holiday.

Size 8 acres, 40 touring pitches, 15 with electric hookup, 40 level pitches, 4 static caravans, 6 🚿, 14 WCs, 2 CWPs
🚿¼ ✗¼ 🚰¼ 🔲 ⚠ 🔀 Calor ♿ WS
➡ Beside A40 between Brecon and Llandovery, ½ mile from Llandovery.

LLANDRINDOD WELLS Powys   6C3

Disserth Caravan Park
Disserth, Howey, Llandrindod Wells LD1 6NL
☎ 01597-860277 Fax 01597-860277

Open March-October Å 🚐 🚍
Size 3 acres, 47 touring pitches, 40 with electric hookup, 47 level pitches, 19 static caravans, 6 🚿, 8 WCs, 1 CWP
£ car/tent £6.25-£7.50, car/caravan £6.25-£7.50, motorhome £6.25-£7.50, motorbike/tent £6.25, children £0.90
Rental 🚐 £95-£275
🚿 ✗ 🔲 📞 🔀 ♿ Calor Gaz 🐾 WS
Last arrival time: 10:30
➡ Just 1 mile off A483 (Llandrindod Wells-Builth Wells road), follow signs for Disserth. Park alongside 13th century church and River Ithon.

Park Motel Caravan & Camping Park
Rhayader Road, Crossgates, Llandrindod Wells LD1 6RF
☎ 01597-851201 Fax 01597-851201
Open 1 March-31 October Å 🚐 🚍

Situated in three acres, amidst beautiful mid Wales countryside near the famous Elan Valley and centrally situated for touring.

Size 3 acres, 15 touring pitches, 5 with electric hookup, 15 level pitches, 15 static caravans, 2 🚿, 4 WCs, 1 CWP
£ car/tent £6-£6.75, car/caravan £6-£6.75, motorhome £6-£6.75, motorbike/tent £6, children £1
Rental 🚐 Chalet.
🚿 ✗ 🚰 📞 🔲 🔳 GR ⚠ 🔀 ♿ Calor Gaz 🐾 WS
Last arrival time: 10:00
➡ Situated on A44, ½ mile W of Crossgates (Rhayader) roundabout towards Rhayader, 3 miles N of Llandrindod Wells (A483).

LLANDYSUL Carmarthenshire 6B4

Camping & Caravanning Club Site
Llwynhelyg, Cross Inn, Llandysul SA44 6LW
☎ 01545-560029
Open end March-start November ▲ 🚐 🚍

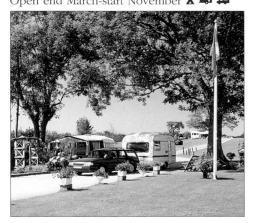

Set in an area of great variety - pony trekking, beaches and coastal walks all in easy reach. Just 10 minutes walk from Cross Inn Village.

Size 13½ acres, 90 touring pitches, 43 with electric hookup, 4 🚿, 10 WCs, 1 CWP
£ car/tent £8.75-£11.55, car/caravan £8.75-£11.55, motorhome £8.75-£11.55, motorbike/tent £8.75, children £1.40
CC MasterCard Visa
🛢 ✕ 🍴 🍶 🔧 ⚠ ⊞ ♿ ⚓
Last arrival time: 11:00
➡ From A486 towards New Quay, turn left after public house (Penrhiw Galed Arms). Site is one mile on right.

Rhydygalfe Caravan Park
Pontwelli, Llandysul SA44 5AP
☎ 01559-362738
Open all year ▲ 🚐 🚍
Size 3 acres, 70 touring pitches, 18 with electric hookup, 70 level pitches, 2 static caravans, 2 🚿, 4 WCs, 1 CWP
£ car/tent £4-£6, car/caravan £6, motorhome £6, motorbike/tent £4
Rental 🚐
🛢¼ ✕¼ 🍴¼ 🔧 🍶 ⚙ ⚠ ⊞ Calor ⚓ WS
➡ On right hand side of A486 (New Quay-Llandysul). ¼ mile S of Llandysul.

LLANGADOG Carmarthenshire 6C4

Abermarlais Caravan Park
Llangadog SA19 9NG
☎ 01550-777868
Open 15 March-1 November ▲ 🚐 🚍
Size 16 acres, 88 touring pitches, 43 with electric hookup, 80 level pitches, 8 🚿, 14 WCs, 1 CWP
£ car/tent £7, car/caravan £7, motorhome £7, motorbike/tent £6.50
🛢 🔧 🍶 ⚠ ⊞ Calor Gaz ⚓ WS
Last arrival time: 11:00
➡ W of A40, ¾ mile N of junction with A4069 and 1¼ miles SW of junction with A482.

LLANRWST Conwy 6C1

Bodnant Caravan Park
Nebo Road, Llanrwst LL26 0SD
☎ 01492-640248
Open 1 March-31 October ▲ 🚐 🚍

A small quiet landscaped site for touring caravans and tents, and a winner of "Wales in Bloom" for 23 years. Centrally situated, near Llanrwst, for exploring the mountains and beaches of North Wales.

Size 4 acres, 60 touring pitches, 47 with electric hookup, 6 🚿, 9 WCs, 1 CWP
£ car/tent £6-£7.50, car/caravan £6-£7.50, motorhome £6-£7.50, motorbike/tent £6, children £0.50
Rental Chalet.
🛢¼ ✕¼ 🍴¼ 🔧 ⚠ ⊞ Calor Gaz ♿ ⚓
Last arrival time: 9:30
➡ S of Llanrwst turn off A470 opposite Birmingham garage onto B5427, signposted Nebo. Site is 30 yards past sign.

Plas Meirion Caravan Park
Gower Road, Llanrwst LL27 0RZ
☎ 01492-640247 Fax 01492-640247
Open April-October ⚏ 🚐
Size 2 acres, 5 touring pitches, 5 with
electric hookup, 5 level pitches, 30 static
caravans, 2 🚿, 5 WCs, 1 CWP
£ car/caravan £6.50-£10.25, motorhome
£6.50-£10.25
Rental ⚏
🛁¼ ✕¼ 🍴¼ 🖨 ☎ WS
Last arrival time: 10:30
➡ From Llanrwst leave on B5106, crossing
River Conwy to Trefriw. Site 300 yards on
right.

Tyddyn Isaf Camping & Caravan Site
Dulas, Lligwy Bay LL70 9PQ
☎ 01248-410203 Fax 01248-410667
Open March-October ⚑ ⚏ 🚐
Size 16 acres, 80 touring pitches, 50 static
caravans, 8 🚿, 14 WCs, 1 CWP
£ car/tent £5-£9, car/caravan £10-£11.50,
motorhome £8-£10, motorbike/tent £5,
children £0.80

TUDOR GLEN
CARAVAN PARK

*A family run site,
ideal for touring the area,
with superb beaches, walks, castles
– all within easy reach.*

OPEN MARCH – OCTOBER

**JAMESTON, MANORBIER,
DYFED SA70 7SS**
Tel: 01834 871417 Fax: 01834 871832

Rental ⚏ £100-£270
🛁 ✕ 🍴 🖨 ☎ 🖨 📺 🏔 🖼 ⚏ Calor Gaz 🐕 WS
Last arrival time: 10:00
➡ Travel over Brittannia Bridge onto Isle of
Anglesey and take A5025 to Moelfre. Left at
roundabout onto A5025 for 2 miles. At
phonebox/craft shop at Brynrefail turn right
and site is ½ mile on right.

Tudor Glen Caravan Park
Jameston, Manorbier SA70 7SS
☎ 01834-871417 Fax 01834-871832
Open March-October ⚑ ⚏ 🚐
Size 6 acres, 30 touring pitches, 30 with
electric hookup, 30 level pitches, 20 static
caravans, 7 🚿, 14 WCs, 1 CWP
£ car/tent £4-£7, car/caravan £5-£8,
motorhome £5-£8, motorbike/tent £4,
children £1
Rental ⚏
🛁 ✕¼ 🍴¼ 🖨 ☎ 🖨 GR 🏔 🖼 Calor WS
Last arrival time: 8:00
➡ Off Tenby to Pembroke road (A4239).
Entrance is as you enter village of Jameston
on right side from Tenby direction.

Grawen Farm Camping & Caravan Site
Cwm Taff, Cefn Coed, Merthyr Tydfil CF48
2HS
☎ 01685-723740
Open April-October ⚑ ⚏ 🚐
Size 4 acres, 50 touring pitches, 8 with
electric hookup, 30 level pitches, 3 🚿, 7
WCs, 1 CWP
£ car/tent £5-£6, car/caravan £6-£7,
motorhome £5-£6, motorbike/tent £5,
children £0.50
℃ MasterCard Visa
🛁 🖨 ☎ 🖨 Calor 🐕 WS
Last arrival time: 12:00
➡ Site on A470, ½ mile from village of
Cefen Coed y-Cymmer.

Bank Farm Caravan Park
Middletown SY21 8EJ
☎ 01938-570526

Open March-October **⋀ ⚐ ⚏**
Size 30 touring pitches, 24 with electric hookup, 20 level pitches, 38 static caravans, 3 ☗, 6 WCs, 2 CWPs
£ car/tent £5, car/caravan £6.50, motorhome £5, motorbike/tent £5
Rental ⚐ caravans £85-£140
⚑¼ ✗¼ ☗¼ ▣ ▤ ▦ GR ⚠ ✗ Calor ♿ ✝ WS
Last arrival time: 10:00
➡ On A458, 12 miles from Shrewsbury, 5 miles from Welshpool, on the roadside near village of Middletown.

MYNACHLOGDDU Pembrokeshire   6B4

Trefach Caravan Park
Clynderwen, Crymmych SA66 7RU
📞 **01994-419225** Fax **01994-419225**
Open March-October **⋀ ⚐ ⚏**

Ideally situated to explore the Pembrokeshire countryside and beaches, or to relax by our heated pool, Trefach has all modern facilities for a successful holiday.

Size 18 acres, 20 touring pitches, 10 with electric hookup, 6 level pitches, 45 static caravans, 4 ☗, 13 WCs, 2 CWPs
£ car/tent £6-£10, car/caravan £6-£10, motorhome £6-£10, motorbike/tent £6
Rental ⚐
⚑ ✗ ☍ ▣ ▤ ▦ ✗ GR ▦ ▥ ⚠ ✗ ⊟ Calor Gaz ♿ ✝ WS
Last arrival time: 12:00
➡ 1½ miles off Cardigan-Tenby road (A478).

NARBERTH Pembrokeshire   6B4

Allensbank Holiday Park
Narberth SA67 8RF
📞 **01834-860243** Fax **01834-861622**

Open Easter-October **⚐ ⚏ ⋀**
Size 5 acres, 10 touring pitches, 10 with electric hookup, 19 static caravans, 4 ☗, 4 WCs, 1 CWP
£ car/tent £6-£12, car/caravan £6-£12, motorhome £6-£12, motorbike/tent £6, children £0.25
Rental ⚐ Chalet. £100-£350
▣ ▤ ▥ ▦ ▦ GR ▦ ⚠ ✗ ⊟ ✝
Last arrival time: 10:30
➡ 1 mile S of Narberth on A478 towards Tenby.

Noble Court Caravan Park
Redstone Road, Narberth SA67 7ES
📞 **01834-861191** Fax **01834-861484**
Open March-November **⋀ ⚐ ⚏**
Size 8 acres, 92 touring pitches, 92 with electric hookup, 50 level pitches, 60 static caravans, 12 ☗, 15 WCs, 2 CWPs
£ car/tent £8-£13.50, car/caravan £8-£13.50, motorhome £8-£13.50, motorbike/tent £8
℃ MasterCard Visa
⚑¼ ✗ ☍ ▣ ▤ ▥ ▦ GR ▥ ⚠ ✗ ⊟ Calor ♿ ✝ WS
➡ ½ mile off A40 trunk road on B4313, within ½ mile of Narbeth.

Cei Bach Country Club
New Quay SA45 9SL
☎ 01545-580237
Open Easter-end September Å ⊕ ⊐

Award winning site set in Cei Bach Bay. All modern facilities including bar, take-away, games room, ball and play park, launderette and shop (100 yards). New Quay 1½ miles.

Size 60 touring pitches, 50 with electric hookup, 1 static caravan, 6 ♔, 12 WCs, 1 CWP
£ car/tent £6-£12, car/caravan £6-£12, motorhome £6-£12, motorbike/tent £6
℃ MasterCard Visa
🚻¼ ✗¼ ➡ 🗑 🔌 🚿 GR 🅰 🎯 🔌 Calor Gaz 🐾
Last arrival time: 10:00
➡ From Aberystwyth S on A487 for 25 miles, then right onto B4342 signed New Quay. Turn right at Cambrian Hotel and follow signs.

Afon Teifi Caravan & Camping Park
Pentre Cagal, Newcastle Emlyn SA38 9HT
☎ 01559-370532
Open all year Å ⊕ ⊐
Size 23 acres, 110 touring pitches, 95 with electric hookup, 110 level pitches, 9 ♔, 16 WCs, 1 CWP
£ car/tent £6-£7, car/caravan £6-£7, motorhome £6-£7, motorbike/tent £5
🚻¼ ✗¼ ➡¼ 🗑 🔌 🚿 🔌 GR 🔍 🅰 🎯 Calor Gaz
🐾 WS

➡ On A484 Carmarthen to Cardigan road, 2 miles E of Newcastle Emlyn. From M4 take A484.

Cenarth Falls Holiday Park
Cenarth, Newcastle Emlyn SA38 9JS.
☎ 01239-710345 ⓕ 01239-710345
Open March-November Å ⊕ ⊐

A friendly, family run park offering luxury caravan accommodation and touring/camping facilities of the highest standard. An ideal base for exploring West Wales.

Size 12 acres, 30 touring pitches, 20 with electric hookup, 30 level pitches, 89 static caravans, 4 ♔, 7 WCs, 1 CWP
£ car/tent £7.75-£12.75, car/caravan £7.75-£12.75, motorhome £7.75-£12.75, motorbike/tent £7.75
℃ MasterCard Visa
🚻 ✗ ➡ 🗑 🔌 🚿 🔌 GR 📺 🅰 🎯 🔌 Calor Gaz
♿ 🐾
Last arrival time: 10:00
➡ Turn right at signs, ¼ mile after crossing Cenarth Bridge on A484.

Moelfryn Caravan & Camping Park
Ty Cefn, Pant-y-Bwlch, Newcastle Emlyn SA38 9JE
☎ 01559-371231 ⓕ 01559-371231
Open 28 February-10 January Å ⊕ ⊐
Size 2.5 acres, 25 touring pitches, 25 level pitches, 4 ♔, 5 WCs, 1 CWP
£ car/tent £4.50-£5.50, car/caravan £5.50-£6.50, motorhome £5.50-£6.50, motorbike/tent £4.50, children £0.25
Rental Å ⊕
🐾
Last arrival time: 10:00

Moelfryn
CARAVAN & CAMPING PARK

Panoramic views and a tranquil rural setting. 15 minutes drive from safe sandy beaches at Tresaith and Llangranog. The site is 25 level grass pitches for all types of touring units, with magnificent views across the Teifi Valley. Free hot showers.

TY CEFN, PANT-Y-BWLCH, NEWCASTLE EMLYN, DYFED SA38 9JE Tel/Fax: 01559 371231

NEWPORT Pembrokeshire   6A4

Llwyngwair Manor Holiday Park
Newport SA42 0LX
☎ **01239-820498**
Open April-October Å 🚐 🚐

Set in 55 acres of beautiful parkland bounded by the River Nevern, renowned for fishing, in Pembrokeshire National Park. One mile from the Coastal Path.

Size 36 acres, 80 touring pitches, 54 with electric hookup, 80 level pitches, 100 static caravans, 6 🕮, 10 WCs, 1 CWP

£ car/tent £8-£10, car/caravan £8-£11, motorhome £8-£11, motorbike/tent £8
Rental 🚐 Chalet. caravans £80-£220, chalet £120-£250
CC MasterCard Visa
🐾 ✕ 🛒 ▫ 🔋 🗂 🗄 🗜 🗃 🖊 GR 🔍 TV 🅰 🎯 🔌
Calor 🦽 🐕 WS
Last arrival time: 10:00
➜ On main A487 coast road, 1 mile E of Newport.

Morawelon Camping & Caravan Site
Parrog, Newport SA42 0RW
☎ **01239-820565**
Open March-end October Å 🚐 🚐

Gently sloping, well sheltered site with scenic views over Newport Bay and the Presen Hills. Direct access to Parrog Beach. Ideal location for windsurfing, boating etc. Close to town, shops and restaurants.

Size 5 acres, 90 touring pitches, 5 with electric hookup, 4 🕮, 6 WCs, 1 CWP
£ car/tent £6.35-£8.17, car/caravan £8.50
🐾 ✕¼ 🛒 Calor Gaz 🐕
➜ From Fishguard to Newport A487, turn left down road signed Parog/Parog Beach. ½ mile to last house by Quay Wall.

NEWTOWN Powys   7D3

Llwyn Celyn Holiday Park
Adfa, Newtown SY16 3DG
☎ **01938-810720**
Open 1 April-31 October Å 🚐 🚐   ➜

← Llwyn Celyn Holiday Park

Llwyn Celyn offers peace and quiet with excellent views from a well drained, elevated, flat grass area. Take-away meal service, many local attractions and excellent walking.

Size 10 acres, 16 touring pitches, 11 with electric hookup, 6 level pitches, 55 static caravans, 3 showers, 4 WCs, 1 CWP
£ car/tent £5-£8, car/caravan £8, motorhome £8, motorbike/tent £5
¼ WS
➜ Off B4390 leading from A483. Follow signs, W of New Mills.

Tynycwm Camping Site

Aberhafesp, Newtown SY16 3JF
01686-688651
Open May-October
Size 3 acres, 50 touring pitches, 50 level pitches, 8 static caravans, 2 showers, 3 WCs, 1 CWP
£ car/tent £5, car/caravan £5
➜ Follow A489 to Caersws, turn right onto B4569 to Aberhafesp. At first crossroads go straight over B4568 ignoring sign for Aberhafesp. At next crossroads turn left at Bwlch-y-Garreg signpost. Farm and site 1 mile on right.

PENTRAETH Anglesey 6B1

Rhos Caravan Park

Pentraeth LL75 8DZ
01248-450214 Fax 01248-852777
Open 1 May-30 September

Size 5 acres, 176 with electric hookup, 60 level pitches, 176 static caravans, 8 showers, 9 WCs, 1 CWP
¼ ¼ Calor Gaz
Last arrival time: 9:00
➜ 1½ miles N from Pentraeth (A5025), turn right signed Red Wharf Bay.

PORT EYNON Swansea 2C1

Carreglwyd Camping & Caravan Park

Port Eynon, Swansea SA3 1NN
01792-390795 Fax 01792-390796
Open March-December

Beautifully situated alongside the sandy bay of Port Eynon, and an ideal base for exploring the magnificent Gower peninsula. Particularly suitable for families with young children.

Size 20 acres, 180 touring pitches, 16 with electric hookup, 100 level pitches, 16 showers, 24 WCs, 1 CWP
£ car/tent £7.50, car/caravan £12, motorhome £7.50, motorbike/tent £7.50, children £0.50
¼ ¼ Calor Gaz
Last arrival time: 10:00
➜ Follow A4118 from Swansea to village of Port-Eynon (16 miles). Drive through car park to site entrance.

Newpark Holiday Park

Port Eynon SA3 1NL
01792-390292 Fax 01792-391245
Open April-October

Striking scenic views overlooking the Bristol Channel. Camping on level plateaux, luxury bungalows for six with superb views.

Size 14 acres, 112 touring pitches, 80 with electric hookup, 80 level pitches, 47 static caravans, 20 WCs, 2 CWPs
£ car/caravan £8-£15
Rental Chalet. chalet £60-£300
⚒ ✕¼ 🚿¼ 🅾 📞 ⌂ 🔲 Calor Gaz ♿ 🐕 WS
➡ From Swansea take A4118 for 14 miles. Down hill into Port Eynon. Large splayed entrance into site on left.

PORTHCAWL Brigend   **3D1**

Happy Valley Caravan Park
Wigfach, Porthcawl CF32 0NG
📞 **01656-782144 Fax 01656-782146**
Open 1 April-30 September 🏕 🚐 🚍
Size 100 touring pitches, 30 with electric hookup, 50 level pitches, 8 🚿, 16 WCs, 1 CWP
£ car/tent £5.50-£6.50, car/caravan £5.50-£6.50, motorhome £5.50-£6.50, motorbike/tent £5.50
Rental 🚐
💳 MasterCard Visa
⚒ ✕ 🚿 🅾 📞 GR 🔲 ⌂ 🔲 🍴 Calor Gaz ♿ 🐕 WS
➡ From A48 take A4106 Bridgend/Porthcawl road. 1 mile to Wigfach turning. Immediately on right.
See advert on next page

PORTHMADOG Caernarfonshire   **6B2**

Black Rock Touring & Camping Park
Morfa Bychan, Porthmadog LL53 9LD
📞 **01766-513919**
Open March-October 🏕 🚐 🚍

An ideal family park situated behind the dunes of Black Rock beach. The site offers high class facilities including showers and toilets.

Size 9 acres, 150 touring pitches, 40 with electric hookup, 150 level pitches, 18 🚿, 16 WCs, 1 CWP
£ car/tent £8-£9, car/caravan £10-£11, motorhome £10-£11, motorbike/tent £8
🛒¼ ✗¼ 🍴¼ 🔲 🔌 🚽 ⚠ 🎯 Calor Gaz 🐕
Last arrival time: 10.30

➜ Cross tollgate at Porthmadog, turn left at Woolworths in the High Street, and follow Morfa Bychan road to end. At beach entrance bear right to park.

Greenacres Holiday Park
Blackrock Sands, Morfa Bychan, Porthmadog LL49 9YB
📞 01442-248668 Fax 01442-232459
Open March-October 🚐 🚙

A family holiday park with direct access to a lovely sandy beach, indoor pool, kids clubs, great live entertainment, bars and hot food. A 'British Holidays Park'.

Size 80 acres, 71 touring pitches, 61 with electric hookup, 71 level pitches, 180 static caravans, 10 🚿, 8 WCs, 1 CWP
£ car/caravan £6.50-£17, motorhome £6.50-£17, children £1.50
Rental 🚐
CC MasterCard Visa
🛒 ✗ 🍴 🔲 🔌 🚽 🔍 🎯 GR 🔍 ⚠ 🎯 🔌 Calor 🐕
Last arrival time: 11:00
➜ After arriving at toll bridge at Porthmadog, go along High Street and turn between Post Office and Woolworths towards Black Rock Sands, Greenacres is on road, the other side of small village of Morfa Bychan.

Tyddyn Llwyn Caravan Park & Camp Site
Morfa Bychan Road, Porthmadog LL49 9UR
📞 01766-512205 Fax 01766-512205
Open Easter-31 October ⛺ 🚐 🚙

Situated within twenty minutes walk of town and close to beach, golf club and water sports.

Size 12 acres, 200 touring pitches, 50 with electric hookup, 20 level pitches, 50 static caravans, 12 ⬔, 24 WCs, 3 CWPs
£ car/tent £6-£10, car/caravan £6-£10, motorhome £6-£10, motorbike/tent £6
Rental ⛺ Chalet. £139-£285
⬔ ✕ ⬗¼ ▣ ⬔ ◨ ⊞ ⬔ ⬔ ⬔ ⊡ ⬔ ⊞ ⬔ Calor Gaz ⬔
Last arrival time: 11:00
➜ From Porthmadog High Street turn by Woolworths towards Morfa Bychan. After passing sign to Borth-y-Gest only, signs for site on roadside at bottom of hill. Drive for park on right immediately opposite signs.

PRESTATYN Denbighshire　　　　6C1

Nant Mill Touring Caravan Park
Nant Mill Farm, Prestatyn LL199L4
☎ 01745-852360
Open 1 April-15 October ⛺ ⛺
Size 5 acres, 150 touring pitches, 97 with electric hookup, 150 level pitches, 4 ⬔, 15 WCs, 1 CWP
⬔¼ ✕¼ ⬗¼ ⬔ ▣ ⬔ ⊞ Calor Gaz ⬔
Last arrival time: 10:30
➜ ½ miles E of Prestatyn on A548 coast road. Site is close to junction with A547.

Presthaven Sands Holiday Park
Shore Road, Gronant, Prestatyn LL19 9TT
☎ 01745-856471 Fax 01745-886646
Open Easter-October ⛺ ⛺

Size 12 acres, 100 touring pitches, 64 with electric hookup, 97 level pitches, 1180 static caravans, 8 ⬔, 20 WCs,
Rental ⛺ Chalet.
⬔ ✕ ⬔ ⊡ ⬔ ⬔
➜ 1 mile on A548 from Prestatyn.

RHAYADER Powys　　　　6C3

Wyeside Caravan Park
Rhayader
☎ 01597-810183
Open 1 February-end November ⬔ ⛺ ⛺

Nestling peacefully on bank of the River Wye, yet just 400 yards from Rhayader town centre and 3 miles from Elan Valley Reservoir complex. Entrance to site 400 yards from Rhayader on A487 Aberystwyth road.

Size 40 touring pitches, 17 with electric hookup, 39 static caravans, 12 ⬔, 22 WCs, 2 CWPs
£ car/tent £4.80-£6, car/caravan £6.40-£8, motorhome £6.40-£8, motorbike/tent £4.80, children £1
▣ ⬔ ⊞ Calor ⬔ ⬔
Last arrival time: 11:00
➜ Off A44, Aberystwyth to Rhayder road.

RHOSSILI West Glamorgan　　　　2C1

Pitton Cross Caravan Park
Swansea SA3 1PH
☎ 01792-390593
Open 1 April-31 October ⬔ ⛺ ⛺

Personally supervised by its owners, this is a level site with several small paddocks overlooking the sea and close to surfing beaches. An ideal base for walking, bird watching and hang-gliding.

Size 6 acres, 100 touring pitches, 50 with electric hookup, 100 level pitches, 8 ⋔, 12 WCs, 2 CWPs
£ car/tent £7-£7.50, car/caravan £8-£9.50, motorhome £7.25-£8.75, motorbike/tent £7
CC MasterCard Visa
🛢 🖫 🔌 🗔 ⚠ 🖾 Calor Gaz ⅄ 🛉 WS
Last arrival time: 9:00
➡ From A4118 turn right at Scurlage (from Swansea 16miles) onto B4247 signposted Rhossilli. Park is 2 miles on left.

RHUALLT Flintshire   7D1

Penisar Myndd Caravan Park
Caerwys Road, Rhuallt
☎ 01745-582227
Open Easter-31 October 🚐 🚛
Size 2 acres, 26 with electric hookup, 30 level pitches,
£ car/caravan £6, motorhome £6
🔌 ⚠ 🖾 Calor Gaz 🛉
➡ From Chester A55, take first turning right (crossing central reservation) 1 mile past the Sundawn Nurseries and Tea Pot Cafe.

SAUNDERSFOOT Pembrokeshire   6B4

Mill House Caravan Park
Pleasant Valley, Stepaside, Narbeth SA67 8LN
☎ 01834-812069
Open Easter-September 🛆 🚐 🚛

Size 2 acres, 6 touring pitches, 6 with electric hookup, 4 level pitches, 15 static caravans, 2 ⋔, 5 WCs, 2 CWPs
£ car/tent £3-£6, car/caravan £6-£9, motorhome £4-£7, motorbike/tent £3
Rental ⋔ 🚐 £59-£269
🛢¼ ✗¼ ◖¼ 🖫 🔌 🗔 ⚠ 🖾 Calor ⅄ 🛉 WS
Last arrival time: 12:00
➡ From A40 take A477 just past St Clears. After 10 miles leave trunk road at first turning off roundabout for Stepside. After ½ mile turn left and site is on left.

Moreton Farm Leisure Park
Moreton, Saundersfoot SA69 9EA
☎ 01834-812016 Fax 01834-811890
Open March-December 🛆 🚐 🚛

Set in secluded valley 15 - 20 minutes walk from Saundersfoot. Heated toilet/shower block, access for disabled, covered dish washing and laundry facilities. Lodges and cottages available. Open March to December.

Size 60 touring pitches, 14 with electric hookup, 6 ⋔, 6 WCs, 2 CWPs
£ car/tent £5-£6, car/caravan £8-£11.50, motorhome £7-£10.50, motorbike/tent £5
Rental Chalet. £170-£350
🛢 ✗¼ 🖫 🔌 🗔 🗔 ⚠ 🖾 Calor
➡ From St Clears on A477 left onto A478 for Tenby, site on left 1½ miles opposite chapel, 400 yards under railway bridge to site. Signposted at entrance.

ST DAVID'S Pembrokeshire   6A4

Caerfai Bay Caravan & Tent Park
Caerfai Bay, St David's SA62 6QT
☎ 01437-720274 Fax 01437-720274
Open 1 April-31 October 🛆 🚐 🚛

A quiet family run park, uniquely situated within the Pembrokeshire Coast National Park and just 200 yards of the sandy Caerfai Bay bathing beach. The site offers unsurpassed panoramic sea views of coastal scenery and St Davids with its magnificent cathedral is only ¾ mile away.

Size 10 acres, 85 touring pitches, 46 with electric hookup, 40 level pitches, 32 static caravans, 7 ℟, 17 WCs, 2 CWPs
£ car/tent £4.25-£5, car/caravan £6-£8.50, motorhome £4.25-£5, motorbike/tent £4.25, children £1
Rental ⊕ £100-£300
⚲¼ ✗¼ ⛟¼ ▣ ☎ ▤ Calor Gaz ★
Last arrival time: 8:00
➡ Turn off A487 near Marine Life Centre and follow signs to Caerfai Bay. Entrance to park is at end of road on right.

Camping & Caravanning Club Site
Dwr Cwmdig, St David's SA62 6DW
☎ **01348-831376**
Open end March-end September ▲ ⊕ ⏏
Size 4 acres, 40 touring pitches, 24 with electric hookup, 4 ℟, 7 WCs, 1 CWP
£ car/tent £8.20-£10.40, car/caravan £8.20-£10.40, motorhome £8.20-£10.40, motorbike/tent £8.20, children £1.30
℀ MasterCard Visa
▣ ☎ ★
Last arrival time: 11:00
➡ 4 miles N of St Davids, off the coast road (A487) signposted to Fishguard.

Hendre Eynon Camping
St David's SA62 6DB
☎ **01437-720474**
Open April-September ▲ ⊕ ⏏

Large, level, grassy site on working farm adjacent to nature reserve inside National Park, and within easy reach of the coastal walk. Riding stables, Swimming pool three miles. Open from April to September.

Size 7 acres, 50 touring pitches, 46 with electric hookup, 8 ℟, 13 WCs, 1 CWP
£ car/tent £4-£8.50, car/caravan £4-£8.50, motorhome £4-£8, motorbike/tent £4
▣ ☎ ▤ Calor ⅙ ★ WS
Last arrival time: 6:00
➡ From St Davids N on A487 for ½ mile, left on B4583 for ¼ mile. Keep right for 1½ miles to site on right.

Rhos-Y-Cribed
St David's SA62 6RR
☎ **01437-720336**
Open all year ▲ ⊕ ⏏
Size 6 acres, 5 touring pitches, 2 ℟, 4 WCs, 1 CWP
£ car/tent £3.50, car/caravan £5.50, motorhome £4, motorbike/tent £3
⅙ ★
Last arrival time: 10:30
➡ Follow Porthclais road from St David's via Porthclais Harbour. Site signed.

Tretio Caravan & Camping Park
St David's SA62 6DE
☎ **01437-781359 Fax 01437-781600**
Open Easter-end October ▲ ⊕ ⏏
Size 5 acres, 40 touring pitches, 25 with electric hookup, 40 level pitches, 16 static caravans, 4 ℟, 8 WCs, 1 CWP
£ car/tent £4.25-£6.75, car/caravan £4.75-£7.25, motorhome £4.25-£6.75, motorbike/tent £4.25
Rental ⊕ 6 berth holiday homes £105-£230
⚲ ☎ ▤ ▣⚠ ✕ Calor Gaz ⅙ ★ WS

← Tretio Caravan & Camping Park

➜ On leaving St David's keep left at RFC and carry on for 3 miles until sign. Park on right.

SWANSEA Swansea   2C1

Riverside Caravan Park
Ynysforgan Farm, Morriston, Swansea SA6 6QL
📞 **01792-775587**
Open all year ▲ 🚐 🚚

Flat, level, grassy site with hardstandings, alongside the River Tawe. Ideal base for touring all of Gower, the Mumbles, Swansea, and the attractions of the Vale of Neath.

Size 7 acres, 120 touring pitches, 100 with electric hookup, 120 level pitches, 13 🏠, 15 WCs, 1 CWP
℀ MasterCard Visa
🔌 ▣ 🔋 🔲 🔳 🔲 🔲 GR ⌂ 🔲 🔲 Calor Gaz ♿ 🐕 WS
Last arrival time: 10:00
➜ Direct access to park from roundabout at junction 45 off M4. Park completely secluded from motorway.

TALSARNAU Caernarfonshire   6C2

Barcdy Caravan & Camping Park
Cae Bran, Talsarnau LL47 6YG
📞 **01766-770736**
Open Easter-31 October ▲ 🚐 🚚

A quiet, friendly family park in beautiful natural surroundings, with facilities of a high standard. Ideally situated for touring this spectacular part of Wales.

Size 40 acres, 68 touring pitches, 44 with electric hookup, 44 level pitches, 30 static caravans, 10 🏠, 14 WCs, 2 CWPs
£ car/tent £6.50-£8, car/caravan £6.50-£8, motorhome £6.50-£8, motorbike/tent £6.50, children £0.75-£1
Rental 🚐 Chalet. £160-£240
🔋 ▣ 🔋 🔲 Calor Gaz
➜ Travelling S via Trawsfyndd take left turning at Maentwrog onto A496. Site is 4 miles along on left.

Buttyland Touring Caravan & Tent Park

Manorbier, Tenby SA70 7SN
☎ **01834-871278**
Open Easter-October ⚑ ⇔ ⇔

A quiet ten acre family site, with children's play area, new shower and toilet facilities, hair drying facilities and launderette washroom. Riding stables on adjoining farm. Manorbier Bay one mile. Rallies welcome.

Size 10 acres, 30 touring pitches, 30 with electric hookup, 30 level pitches, 6 ₲, 16 WCs, 2 CWPs
£ car/tent £3-£5, car/caravan £3.40-£5.50, motorhome £3.40-£5.50, motorbike/tent £3
☇ ⬤ ⚠ ☒ ⊢
➡ Site is signed from main road 400 yards on right, first entrance past school.

Cross Park Holiday Centre

Dept RAC, Broadmoor, Kilgetty, Tenby SA68 0RS
☎ **01834-813205** Fax **01834-814300**
Open 22 March-31 October ⚑ ⇔ ⇔

Delightful family holiday park in eleven acres of landscaped gardens and lawns, surrounded by mature trees, colourful flowers and shrubs. Family clubhouse with nightly entertainment.

Size 11 acres, 51 touring pitches, 51 with electric hookup, 25 level pitches, 85 static caravans, 8 ₲, 18 WCs, 2 CWPs
£ car/tent £6-£14, car/caravan £6-£14, motorhome £6-£14, motorbike/tent £6
Rental ⇔ £79-£419
⊂⊂ MasterCard Visa
☇ ✗ ⬤ ▣ ☇ ⬚ ▣ ⊞ ⊺⊽ ⚠ ☒ ⊣ Calor ⊢
Last arrival time: 9:00
➡ Travel on A477 for 1½ miles W of Kilgetty, turn right at crossroads (B4586). Site on left.

Kiln Park Holiday Park

Marsh Road, Tenby SA70 7RB
☎ **01834-844121** Fax **01834-845159**
Open March-October ⇔ ⇔   →

← **Kiln Park Holiday Park**

A family holiday park set amidst the beauty of the Pembrokeshire Coast National Park. Indoor/outdoor heated pools, kids clubs, tennis and bowling included in the wide range of leisure facilities, restaurants and bars, excellent cabaret entertainment. A 'British Holidays Park'.

Size 95 acres, 60 touring pitches, 40 with electric hookup, 490 level pitches, 620 static caravans, 20 ₨, 47 WCs, 1 CWP

RUMBLEWAY
Caravan & Tent Park

Luxury caravans to let, also caravans for sale – sites available.

Touring caravan and tent park hook-ups. Heated swimming and paddling pools – bar – restaurant – take-away – shop – children's amusement room – adventure fort. Family run. No pets.

NEW HEDGES, TENBY, PEMBROKESHIRE SA70 8TR
Tel/Fax: Tenby (01834) 845155

CC MasterCard Visa

Ⅎ Ⅎ¼ ✗ ✗¼ ☕ ☕¼ ▨ ☎ ▯ ▦ ▣ ▨ GR
⚠ ▦ ⏚ Calor Gaz ♿ ♞
Last arrival time: 10:00
➜ Approaching Tenby, arrive at Kilgetty roundabout and follow A478 to Tenby for 6 miles. Follow signs to Penally. The park is ½ mile on left.

Rowston Holiday Park
New Hedges, Tenby SA70 8TL
☎ **01834-842178 Fax 01834-842178**
Open 15 March-15 November ▲ ⛺ ☷
Size 20 acres, 110 touring pitches, 110 with electric hookup, 126 static caravans, 12 ₨, 18 WCs, 2 CWPs
£ car/tent £8-£13, car/caravan £8-£13, motorhome £8-£13, motorbike/tent £4
Rental ⛺ Chalet. £110-£420
Ⅎ ✗¼ ☕¼ ▨ ☎ ▯ ⚠ ▦ Calor Gaz ♿ ♞
Last arrival time: 9:00
➜ 1½ miles N of Tenby on A478.

Rumbleway Caravan & Tent Park
New Hedges, Tenby SA70 8TR
☎ **01834-843719**
Open March-November ▲ ⛺ ☷

Children's play area with swings, slide, see-saw, roundabout, sandpit and large model elephant. Amusement room next door to clubhouse also caters for children. Five caravans and one chalet available for hire (own WC's).

Size 23 acres, 40 touring pitches, 40 with electric hookup, 30 level pitches, 130 static caravans, 4 ₨, 2 WCs, 1 CWP

£ car/tent £6-£8, car/caravan £8-£12, motorhome £6-£10, motorbike/tent £6
Rental 🚐 £100-£350
🦽 ✕ 🛒 ⊡ 📞 ⊟ ⊡ GR ⚠ ✗ 🔌 Calor Gaz ♿ WS
Last arrival time: 9:00
➡ Take A477 from Carmarthen to Begelly roundabout, left on A478 to New Hedges roundabout. Site is 500 yards on right.

Stone Pitt Camping Site
Begelly, Kilgetty SA68 OXE
📞 **01834-811086**
Open March-October ⛺ 🚐 🚙

This peaceful friendly site is set in a rural village near Tenby, ideal for exploring Pembrokeshire, which has everything for an enjoyable holiday.

22 touring pitches, 22 with electric hookup, 15 level pitches, 5 🚿, 7 WCs, 1 CWP
£ car/tent £6-£7, car/caravan £6-£7, motorhome £6-£7, motorbike/tent £6, children £1
🛒 📞 ⊟ ⚠ ✗ Calor Gaz ♿ WS
Last arrival time: 9:30

Trefalun Park
Devonshire Drive, Florence, Tenby SA70 8RH
📞 **01646-651514 Fax 01646-651746**
Open March-October ⛺ 🚐 🚙
Size 11 acres, 60 touring pitches, 40 with electric hookup, 60 level pitches, 10 static caravans, 6 🚿, 9 WCs, 1 CWP
£ car/tent £5-£8, car/caravan £6-£10, motorhome £6-£10, motorbike/tent £5, children £0.50

Rental 🚐 £100-£330
CC MasterCard Visa
🛒 ⚠ ✗ Calor Gaz ♿
Last arrival time: 8:00
➡ A477 Kilgetty to Sageston, turn left onto B4318. After 2 miles turn left opposite wildlife park, Trefalun second entrance on left.

Well Park
New Hedges, Tenby SA70 8TL
📞 **01834-842179**
Open 1 March-31 October ⛺ 🚐 🚙
Size 7 acres, 80 touring pitches, 50 with electric hookup, 80 level pitches, 42 static caravans, 10 🚿, 20 WCs, 1 CWP
£ car/tent £4.50-£9, car/caravan £5-£10, motorhome £5-£10
Rental 🚐 Chalet.
🦽 ✕¼ 🛒¼ ⊡ 📞 ⊟ GR ⚐ TV ⚠ ✗ Calor Gaz ♿
Last arrival time: 10:30
➡ 1 mile before Tenby, on right side of A478.

Whitewell Caravan Park
Near Lydstep Beach, Tenby SA70 7RY
☎ 01834-842200
Open Easter-September 🚐 🚎

Small country site, half a mile from Lystep beach. Free hot water showers, and electric hookups available.

Size 10 acres, 20 touring pitches, 25 with electric hookup, 40 level pitches, 50 static caravans, 6 🚿, 25 WCs, 1 CWP
🛒 ⊟ GR ⚠ 🔧 🔌 ⚓
➡ Take A4139 W of Tenby past Penall village to Lydstep beach.

Wood Park Caravans
New Hedges, Tenby SA70 8TL
☎ 01834-843414
🛆 🚐 🚎

Size 10 acres, 60 touring pitches, 30 with electric hookup, 10 level pitches, 90 static caravans, 6 🚿, 14 WCs, 1 CWP
£ car/tent £4-£8, car/caravan £5-£10, motorhome £5-£10, motorbike/tent £4
Rental 🚐 £100-£330
🛒 ✕¼ ⊟ 🔋 ⊟ GR ⚠ 🔧 🔌 Calor Gaz ♿
Last arrival time: 10:00
➡ At roundabout 2 miles N of Tenby follow A478 towards Tenby. Take second right and right again.

TYWYN Caernarfonshire   6B2

Woodlands Holiday Park
Bryncrug, Tywyn LL36 9UH
☎ 01654-710471
Open Easter-end September 🚐 🚎

Within the Snowdonia National Park and now offering the latest hookup services including electric, water, TV and sewage disposal. On site country club.

Size 25 acres, 20 touring pitches, 20 with electric hookup, 20 level pitches, 122 static caravans, 2 🚿, 4 WCs, 1 CWP
£ car/caravan £6-£7.50
Rental 🚐 Chalet.
🛒 ⊟ 🔋 🔲 GR 🔲 📺 ⚠ 🔧 🔌 Calor 🐕
➡ At Bryncrug, 18 miles S of Dolgellau and 2 miles N of Tywyn, turn E on B4405 for 1 mile to site on left.

WREXHAM Wrexham   **7D1**

Camping & Caravanning Club Site
c/o the Racecourse, Bangor-Is-Y-Coed,
Wrexham LL13 ODA
☎ **01978-781009**
Open April-October Å ⊟ ⊞
Size 6 acres, 100 touring pitches, 30 with
electric hookup, 6 ⋔, 10 WCs, 1 CWP
£ car/tent £8.20-£10.40, car/caravan £8.20-
£10.40, motorhome £8.20-£10.40,
motorbike/tent £8.20, children £1.30
CC MasterCard Visa
🛒 ⊟ ⑂ ⋔
Last arrival time: 11:00

James Caravan Park
Ruabon, Wrexham LL14 6DW
☎ **01978-820148 Fax 01978-820148**
Open all year Å ⊟ ⊞
Size 8 acres, 40 touring pitches, 60 with
electric hookup, 25 level pitches, 6 ⋔, 6
WCs, 1 CWP
£ car/tent £6.50-£7.50, car/caravan £6.50-
£7.50, motorhome £6.40-£7.50
🛒¼ ✗¼ ⛺¼ ☎ Calor Gaz ⑂ ⋔
Last arrival time: 10:30
➜ Situated on A539 Llangollen-Whitchurch
road on W side of junction with A483 at
Ruabon.

Plassey Touring Caravan & Leisure Park
Eyton, Wrexham LL13 0SP
☎ **01978-780277 Fax 01978-780019**
Open March-November Å ⊟ ⊞

Size 9 acres, 120 touring pitches, 80 with
electric hookup, 120 level pitches, 1 static
caravans, 10 ⋔, 20 WCs, 8 CWPs
£ car/tent £7-£9, car/caravan £7-£9,
motorhome £7-£9, motorbike/tent £7
CC MasterCard Visa
🛒 ✗ ⛺ ⊟ ☎ ⊟ ⊠ ▦ ⏃ ▣ ⌐ ▣ ⑃ ⎗ ⊟
Calor Gaz ⑂ ⋔ WS
➜ Take A483 S of Wrexham. Follow brown
and cream signs to Plassey at exit to B5426.
Site 2½ miles on left.

*Set in beautiful countryside with level, grassy
pitches and many amenities on site. Ideal for
walking, fishing, golfing and touring North
Wales.*

Escape

At the RAC we can release you from
the worries of motoring

But did you know that we can also
give you invaluable peace of mind
when you go on holiday,

Or arrange your hotel bookings,

Or even organise your entire
holiday, all over the phone?

RAC Travel Insurance   0800 550 055

RAC Hotel Reservations   0345 056 042

RAC Holiday Reservations   0161 480 4810

Call us

RAC

Full details on request

NORTHERN IRELAND

REPUBLIC *of* IRELAND

Eagle Point Caravan & Camping Site, Bantry

Banbridge Touring Caravan & Camping Park

200 Newry Road, Banbridge BT32

☎ 018206-23322 Fax 018206-23114

Å ⚐ 🚐

Size 2 acres, 16 touring pitches, 8 with electric hookup, 8 level pitches, 2 🕿, 6 WCs, 1 CWP

£ car/tent £4, car/caravan £8, motorhome £8, motorbike/tent £4

CC MasterCard Visa

🖾¼ ✗ 🍴¼ 🕿 ⚠ 🖾 ♿

Last arrival time: 7:00

➔ Adjacent to Banbridge Gateway tourist information centre, on the main Belfast to Dublin trunk route (A1).

Maghery Caravan Park

Maghery

☎ 01762-322205

Open April-September Å ⚐ 🚐

Situated on the southern shore of Lough Neagh, in the heart of Northern Ireland, the tranquil park offers wonderful views of Coney Island and Lough Neagh.

Size 30 acres, 20 touring pitches, 9 with electric hookup

✗ ⚠ 🖾

➔ From M1 (junction 12) take B196 to Maghery and follow signs.

CASTLEROCK Co. Londonderry   17E1

Downhill National Trust Campsite
Castlerock
📞 01265-848728
Open all year 🏕
➜ On A2, 1 mile W of Castlerock

CUSHENDUN Co. Antrim   17F1

Cushendun National Trust Campsite
Cushendun
📞 012667-61254
Open end March–start October 🏕 🚐
Size 15 touring pitches

MONEYMORE Co. Londonderry   17E2

Springhill National Trust Caravan Park
Moneymore
📞 016487-48210
Open all year 🚐
Size 40 touring pitches

NEWTOWNABBEY Co. Antrim   17F2

Jordanstown Loughshore Park
Shore Road, Newtownabbey BT37 0ST
📞 01232-868751 Fax 01232-365407
Open all year 🏕 🚐 🚲
Size ½ acre, 6 touring pitches, 6 with electric hookup, 6 level pitches, 2 🚿, 2 WCs, 1 CWP
£ car/tent £6.50, car/caravan £6.50, motorhome £6.50, motorbike/tent £6.50
🏕¼ ✗¼ 🅿¼ 🔌 🏧 🎣 ♿ 🐕
Last arrival time: 3:00
➜ 5 miles N of Belfast on Shore Road, A2 (Belfast to Carrickfergus road). Signposted on right between Whiteabbey village and University of Ulster.

STRANGFORD Co. Down   17F3

Castle Ward National Trust Campsite
Strangford
📞 01396-881680
Open 17 March–31 October 🏕 🚐
Size 45 touring pitches

Keel Sandybanks Caravan & Camping Park
Keel, Achill Island
☎ 094-32054
Open 24 May-6 September 🅰 ⛺ 🚐
Size 14 acres, 40 touring pitches, 40 with electric hookup, 40 level pitches, 17 static caravans, 7 ℝ, 15 WCs, 1 CWP
£ car/tent £4.50-£6, car/caravan £6-£7.50, motorhome £6-£7.50, motorbike/tent £4.50
Rental ⛺ Chalet. £170-£250
🛁¼ ✗¼ ♿¼ 🔲 🔋 🗑 🔳 📺 ⚠ 🔲 ♿ 🔭
Last arrival time: 10:30
➜ Castlebar to Newport to Mulranny to Achill Sound then R319 from Achill Sound. At western end of Sandybanks beside Keel Village and immediately adjacent to Keel Beach. Visable from road.

Hodson Bay Caravan and Camping Park
Hodson Bay, Kiltoom, Athlone
☎ 0902-92448
Open 9 May-15 September 🅰 ⛺ 🚐
Size 2 acres, 34 touring pitches, 20 with electric hookup, 30 level pitches, 6 ℝ, 9 WCs, 1 CWP
£ car/tent £7.50, car/caravan £8, motorhome £8, motorbike/tent £7, children £1
🛁¼ ✗¼ ♿¼ 🔲 🔋 🔳 📺 ⚠ 🔲 Calor Gaz 🔭
Last arrival time: 10:30
➜ From N6 take N61 for 2½ miles. Turn right and follow signs.

Belleek Caravan & Camping Park
Ballina
☎ 096-71533
Open 1 March-31 October 🅰 ⛺ 🚐
Size 10 acres, 32 touring pitches, 32 with electric hookup, 36 level pitches, 6 static caravans, 8 ℝ, 10 WCs, 1 CWP
£ car/tent £7, car/caravan £7, motorhome £7, motorbike/tent £7, children £1
🛁 ✗ 🔲 🔋 🗑 🔳 🔲 ♿ 📺 Calor Gaz 🔭

Last arrival time: 24 hrs
➜ 3 km from Ballina. Just 300 meters off the R314 to Killala.

Parklands Holiday Park
Listowel Road, Ballybunion
☎ 068-27275 **Fax** 068-27942
Open Easter-30 September 🅰 ⛺ 🚐
Size 6 acres, 20 touring pitches, 20 with electric hookup, 19 level pitches, 68 static caravans, 5 ℝ, 13 WCs
£ car/tent £7.50-£8, car/caravan £10.50-£11.50, motorhome £10.50-£11.50, motorbike/tent £7
Rental ⛺ £100-£320
🛁¼ ✗¼ ♿¼ 🔲 🔋 🗑 🔳 🔲 ♿ 📺 ⚠ 🔲 Calor 🔭
Last arrival time: 10:00
➜ Located on main Listowel-Ballybunion road. Signposted. Direct access via Tarbert and Listowel.

Sonas Caravan & Camping Park
Ring Strand, Ballymacoda
☎ 024-98132
Open April-October 🅰 ⛺ 🚐

'Sonas', the Irish word for peace, describes our family run park. Set in an unspoilt rural birdwatching seaside area, where a warm welcome awaits you.

Size 10 acres, 30 touring pitches, 10 with electric hookup, 20 level pitches, 30 static caravans, 5 ⋔, 5 WCs, 1 CWP
£ car/tent £7, car/caravan £8, motorhome £7.50, motorbike/tent £6, children £0.50
🐾 🗑 🗜 🗄 🗮 🗟 TV ⚠ 🗷 Calor Gaz ♿ 🛈
➔ From Rosslare take N25 to Youghal, turn left for Ballymacoda 2 miles past Youghal. Park is 4km from Ballymacoda village. From Cork, N25 to Castlemarytr, turn right to Ladybridge, and turn left to Ballymacoda.

BANTRY Co. Cork   18B4

Eagle Point Caravan & Camping Site
Ballylickey, Bantry
☎ 027-50630
Open 26 April-30 September ▲ 🚐 🚛

Located on a peninsula with direct access to safe pebble beaches suitable for all forms of water activities. Top standard amenities and central for touring.

Size 20 acres, 200 touring pitches, 150 with electric hookup, 200 level pitches, 18 ⋔, 33 WCs, 2 CWPs
£ car/tent £9-£9.50, car/caravan £9-£9.50, motorhome £9-£9.50, motorbike/tent £4
🐾¼ ✗¼ ⚓¼ 🗑 🗜 🗄 🗮 🗟 TV ⚠ 🗷 ♿
Last arrival time: 10:00
➔ Site is 4 miles N of Bantry on N71.

BENNETTSBRIDGE Co. Kilkenny   19E2

Nore Valley Park
Bennettsbridge
☎ 056-27229 Fax 056-63955
Open 1 March-31 October ▲ 🚐 🚛

Situated on a working and visitor farm overlooking the scenic River Nore valley. Home baked bread, scones and pies available. Irish breakfast June - August inclusive.

Size 2 acres, 70 touring pitches, 40 with electric hookup, 40 level pitches, 5 ⋔, 10 WCs, 2 CWPs
£ car/tent £6-£9, car/caravan £9-£10, motorhome £8-£9, motorbike/tent £5, children £0.50
🐾 ✗ ⚓ 🗑 🗜 🗄 TV ⚠ 🗷 Calor Gaz ♿ 🛈 WS
Last arrival time: 10:00
➔ From Kilkenny take T20 (R700) to Bennettsbridge. Just before bridge turn right at sign to park.

CAHERDANIEL Co. Kerry   18A4

Wave Crest Caravan & Camping Park
Caherdaniel
☎ 066-75188 Fax 066-75188
Open March-October ▲ 🚐 🚛
Size 4½ acres, 45 touring pitches, 45 with electric hookup, 30 level pitches, 4 static caravans, 10 ⋔, 11 WCs, 1 CWP
£ car/tent £8.50, car/caravan £8.50-£10.50, motorhome £8.50, motorbike/tent £7, children £0.50
🐾 ✗¼ 🗑 🗜 🗄 GR 🗮 TV ⚠ 🗷 Calor Gaz ♿ WS
Last arrival time: 11:00
➔ From Kenmare take N70 SW for 30 miles. Site is on left just before Caherdaniel village.

Carrick-on-Suir C & C Park

Ballyrichard, Kilkenny Road, Carrick-on-suir
☎ 051-640461 **Fax** 051-640204
A ⊞ ⊞

The ideal centre for the south east. A modern site with beautiful views of the hills and mountains. A five minute walk to the town centre, with entertainment most evenings.

Size 2½ acres, 30 touring pitches, 23 with electric hookup, 6 static caravans, 2 🚿, 5 WCs, 1 CWP
£ car/tent £6, car/caravan £7.50, motorhome £7.50, motorbike/tent £3, children £0.50
Rental ⊞ Chalet.
🛁 ⊡ 🔌 ⊡ Calor Gaz 🐾 WS
Last arrival time: 11:00
➡ From Rosslare to Carrick. Through traffic lights, second turn right, under railway bridge sharp right, 200m on left to reception - Lonergans shop. Or: From Conmel to Carrick. First left after fire station, straight through next junction via Mart, 200m on the left to reception.

Carra Caravan & Camping Park

Castlebar, Belcarra
☎ 094-32054
Open 8 June-7 September A ⊞ ⊞
Size 1 acre, 20 touring pitches, 8 with electric hookup, 20 level pitches, 2 🚿, 4 WCs, 1 CWP
£ car/tent £4-£5, car/caravan £5, motorhome £5, motorbike/tent £4
Rental ⊞ £125-£180 weekly.

🛁¼ ✗¼ 🍴¼ ⊡ 🔌 ⊡ Calor ♿ 🐾 WS
Last arrival time: 9:00
➡ 8 km S of Castlebarr, close to village centre.

Parsons Green Caravan & Camping Park

Clogheen
☎ 052-65290 **Fax** 052-65290
Open all year A ⊞ ⊞

Small, family run park with excellent on-site facilities. Centrally situated for touring the whole south of Ireland.

Size 20 touring pitches, 20 with electric hookup, 20 level pitches, 6 🚿, 9 WCs, 1 CWP
£ car/tent £5-£7, car/caravan £8, motorhome £8, motorbike/tent £5
Rental Chalet.
🛁¼ ✗ 🍴 ⊡ 🔌 ⊡ 🔍 🎣 ⊡ GR 🔍 ⊡ 📺 🎿 🎯 ♿ 🐾
➡ Nearest town Clogheen: take R668 from Cahir and Lismore or take R665 from Clonmel and Mitchels Town.

Desert House Caravan & Camping Park

Ring Road, Clonakilty
☎ 023-33331 **Fax** 023-33048
Open Easter/May-October A ⊞ ⊞

Set on a dairy farm with sandy beaches, golf, riding, and bicycles for hire nearby. The historic town of Clonakilty has pubs, restaurants, ballad sessions and a model village. Bird watching is possible on the estuary.

Size 5 acres, 36 touring pitches, 14 level pitches, 5 🚿, 6 WCs, 1 CWP
£ car/tent £6, car/caravan £7, motorhome £8, motorbike/tent £6
CC MasterCard Visa
🔲 🔌 📺 ⚠ 🐕
Last arrival time: 11:30
➜ 1 mile SE of Clonakilty, off N71 Cork-Bandon-Clonakilty road, on road to Ring village.

CLONMEL Co. Tipperary 19D3

Power's The Pot Caravan Park
Harney's Cross, Clonmel
📞 052-23085 **Fax** 052-23893
Open May-end September 🅰 🚐 🚚

Peaceful, family run touring park, situated nine kilometres south east of Clonmer. Ideal centre for hill walking, traditional music and dance. Wine bar with excellent cuisine.

Size 4 acres, 35 touring pitches, 35 with electric hookup, 35 level pitches, 3 🚿, 7 WCs, 1 CWP
£ car/tent £6-£7, car/caravan £6-£7, motorhome £6-£7, motorbike/tent £6, children £0.50-£1
Rental 🅰 🚐 Chalet.
🔲 ✖ 🔌 📺 ⚠ 🔲 Gaz 🐕
➜ Exit N24 Clonmel. From the E turn left at first traffic light, cross river and straight on (via golf club). From W through town and follow signs for Golf Club.

CONG Co. Mayo 16B4

Cong Caravan & Camping Park
Lisloughrey, Quay Road, Cong
📞 092-46089 **Fax** 092-46448
🅰 🚐 🚚
Size 2½ acres, 40 touring pitches, 30 with electric hookup, 25 level pitches, 7 🚿, 7 WCs, 1 CWP
£ car/tent £7.50, car/caravan £7.50, motorhome £7.50, motorbike/tent £7.50, children £1
Rental Chalet. £250 ➜

← Cong Caravan & Camping Park

🛠 🛠¼ 🚐 ⊡ 🔌 🗄 GR ⊞ TV ⋀ ☒ Calor Gaz 🐾
Last arrival time: 10:00

DONARD Co. Wicklow   **19F1**

Moat Farm
Donard
📞 045-404727 Fax 045-404727
Open all year ⛺ � �

*Select family run park. Secluded rural setting
yet only a one minute walk from the village.
Fully serviced. Ideal for relaxing or a base
for touring, hill walking, mountain
climbing. One hour from Dublin, 1½ hrs
from Rosslare.*

Size 3 acres, 20 touring pitches, 20 with
electric hookup, 20 level pitches, 7 �🚿, 7
WCs, 1 CWP
£ car/tent £10, car/caravan £10, motorhome
£10, motorbike/tent £7, children £0.50
🛠 ✕¼ 🚐 ⊡ 🔌 🗄 TV ⋀ ☒ Gaz ♿ 🐾 WS
Last arrival time: 12:00
➡ From Dun Laoghaire follow signs marked
N4 and N7 then onto N81. 15 kms S of
Blessington turn left at The Old Toll House
pub. Park 2 kms from here.

DUBLIN Co. Dublin   **19F1**

Camac Valley Tourist Caravan &
Camping
Naas Road, Clondalkin, Dublin 22
📞 01-464 0644 Fax 01-464 0643
⛺ 🚐 🚐

Size 15 acres, 163 touring pitches, 163 level
pitches, 12 🚿, 20 WCs, 2 CWPs
£ car/tent £7-£8, car/caravan £7-£8,
motorhome £6-£7, motorbike/tent £6
🛠 ⊡ 🔌 🗄 TV ⋀ ☒ Calor Gaz ♿ 🐾
➡ From Cork or Limerick on N7 pass by
turns for Rathcoole and Saggart, then 5 km
further on go under Citywest bridge. The
park is 2 km further on N7 clearly
signposted on left. From Dublin take N7.
When you reach Newlands Cross signposts
clearly indicate route to take. Go to Citywest
Business Park on N7 and cross bridge
following signs for Camac Valley. Coming
from either direction on M50 motorway (jn
9) take N7 S to Cork. Once on N7 follow
signs as above.

DUGORT Co. Mayo   **16A3**

Seal Caves Caravan Park
The Strand, Achill Island, Dugort
📞 098-43262
Open 1 April-30 September ⛺ 🚐 🚐

*Set in sheltered and scenic area beside safe
bathing beach. Place of interest near by,
deserted village colony settlement.*   ➡

CAMAC VALLEY
Tourist Caravan and Camping Park

Camac Valley is located just 35 minutes drive from central Dublin, convenient to all access roads and ferryports. Excellent facilities coupled with pleasant parkland surroundings make Camac Valley the ideal choice for families and backpackers alike. The No. 69 bus passes the campsite gate making access to Dublin simple and safe. Restaurants, shops, cinemas and similar services are all within easy reach.

Camac Valley is set in the grounds of Corkagh Park with its acres of woodland walks, joggers' trails, and kiddies' playground. Detailed maps and tourist information on Dublin available from Reception. Strict 24-hour security on-site.

Camac Valley is open for the complete year and can cater for groups or rallies at certain times. Dogs are not permitted during July and August, though there is a good kennels about 500 metres from the Park.

Open: all year.

No. of pitches: 163
Tents: 50 Caravans/Dormobiles: 113

Area: 15 acres.

We are located on the N7 road near Clondalkin. Please follow the signs to the park. For brochure fax/phone us.

NAAS ROAD, CLONDALKIN, DUBLIN 22
Tel: 4640644 from UK: 00353-1-4640644
Fax: 4640643 from UK: 00353-1-4640643

← Seal Caves Caravan Park

Size 1½ acres, 30 touring pitches, 30 with electric hookup, 30 level pitches, 10 🅿, 16 WCs, 2 CWPs
🅶 Gaz
➜ R319 from Achill Sound to Bunacurry junction, turn right, onto valley crossroads, turn left, drive 3 miles to park.

Casey's Caravan Park
Clonea, Dungarvan
📞 0044-58-41919 Fax 0044-58-41919
Open 2 May-7 September 🅰 🚐 🚎

Family run park adjacent to beaches and a hotel with a leisure centre. Many scenic drives are nearby.

Size 20 acres, 118 touring pitches, 83 with electric hookup, 284 level pitches, 166 static caravans, 18 🅿, 36 WCs, 2 CWPs
£ car/tent £9.50-£10, car/caravan £9.50-£10, motorhome £9.50-£10, motorbike/tent £7.50
🅿¼ ✕¼ ☕¼ 🔋 🔌 🍴 GR 🔍 TV 🅰 🎣 Calor Gaz
♿ 🐕 WS
Last arrival time: 10:00
➜ 2½ miles off N25. ½ mile off R675.

Campail Theach An Aragail
Gallarus Dingle
📞 066-55143
Open 1 May-25 September 🅰 🚐 🚎
Size 2 acres, 36 touring pitches, 12 with electric hookup, 36 level pitches, 6 🅿, 9 WCs, 1 CWP
🅿 ✕ ☕ 🔋 🔌 🍴 🅰 🎣 Calor
Last arrival time: 9:00
➜ 5 miles W of Dingle. Follow Gallarus Oratory signs.

Barna House Caravan Park
Barna Road, Barna, Galway & Salthill
📞 091-592469
Open Easter-13 September 🅰 🚐 🚎
Size 5½ acres, 96 touring pitches, 50 with electric hookup, 30 level pitches, 12 static caravans, 6 🅿, 14 WCs, 1 CWP
£ car/tent £7-£8.50, car/caravan £7-£8.50, motorhome £7-£8.50, motorbike/tent £6
Rental 🚐
🅿 🔌 🔋 🍴 TV Calor Gaz 🐕
Last arrival time: 10:00
➜ 3 miles W of Galway on R336/R337. Follow bypass using Spittal signs. Park on left.

Meadow Camping Park
Glandore
📞 028-33280
Open 15 March-30 September 🅰 🚐 🚎

Size 1.5 acres, 9 touring pitches, 4 with electric hookup, 10 level pitches, 3 ⛺, 6 WCs, 1 CWP
£ car/tent £7-£8, car/caravan £8-£9, motorhome £7-£8, motorbike/tent £6, children £1

🖫 🔌 🖫

Last arrival time: 12:00
➜ On N71 at Rosscarbery R597 to Glandore. Site is on R597, 1 mile E from Glandore towards Rosscarbery.

GLENGARRIFF Co. Cork   18B4

O'Shea's Camping Site
Inchantaggart, Glengarriff
📞 027-63140
Open March-October 🅰 🚐
Size 4 acres, 15 touring pitches, 15 with electric hookup, 4 ⛺, 5 WCs, 1 CWP
£ car/tent £7, car/caravan £7

🛒¼ ✗¼ 🛍¼ 🔌 🖫 🐕 🚻

Last arrival time: 12:00
➜ 2 km W of Glengarriff on Castletown Bay road.

KILKENNY Co. Kilkenny   19E2

Tree Grove Caravan & Camping Park
Danville House, Kilkenny
📞 056-21512
🅰 🚐 🚑

Ideal site for touring Kilkenny and the South East. Excellent hygiene standards. Personally supervised. Camping equipment on site. Route planning and advice given for tourers by owners.

KILLARNEY Co. Kerry   18B3

Flesk Camping & Caravan Park
Muckross Road, Killarney
📞 064-31704
Open Easter-October 🅰 🚐 🚑
Size 7 acres, 75 touring pitches, 21 with electric hookup, 30 level pitches, 5 static caravans, 10 ⛺, 16 WCs, 1 CWP
℃ Visa
🛒 Calor Gaz &
➜ On N71 to Kenmare, 1½ km S of Killarney town centre. Follow signs for Killarney National Park and Lakes.

White Villa Farm Caravan & Camping Site
Cork Road, Killarney
📞 064-32456
Open Easter-31 October 🅰 🚐 🚑
Size 4 acres, 23 touring pitches, 22 with electric hookup, 24 level pitches, 1 static caravans, 5 ⛺, 6 WCs, 2 CWPs
£ car/tent £6.50-£7.50, car/caravan £6.50-£7.50, motorhome £6.50-£7.50, motorbike/tent £6.50, children £0.50
Rental 🚐 Chalet. from £120 for two people.

🖫 🔌 🖫 🗔 📺 ⚠ 🖾 & 🚻

Last arrival time: 9:00
➜ 3 km E of Killarney on N22 Cork road. Park entrance is 300 yards E of N72 Mallow junction. Follow signposts.

KILLORGLIN Co. Kerry   18B3

West's Holiday Park
Killarney Road, Killorglin
📞 066-61240 **Fax** 066-61833
Open Easter-end October 🅰 🚐 🚑   ➜

Size 2½ acres, 30 touring pitches, 12 with electric hookup, 30 level pitches, 4 ⛺, 6 WCs, 1 CWP
£ car/tent £7, car/caravan £8, motorhome £8, motorbike/tent £6
Rental 🅰 Chalet. chalets £150, tents £12.

🛒¼ 🛍¼ 🖫 🔌 🖫 GR 📺 ⚠ 🖾 Calor Gaz & 🚻 WS

← **West's Holiday Park**

Family run site, where relaxing comes as naturally as the surrounding beauty. Wonderful central location. Luxury, mobile homes for hire. Ferry inclusive prices available.

Size 5 acres, 20 touring pitches, 12 with electric hookup, 20 level pitches, 60 static caravans, 4 🅿, 5 WCs,
Rental ⛟ From £99
CC Visa
🔲 🅻 🔳 🔲 🔲 GR 🔲 TV ⚠ 🔲 Calor Gaz & 🐕 WS
➜ On Ring of Kerry. At Killorglin bridge take Killarney road R562. Park is 1½ km from town on right.

KILMUCKRIDGE Co. Wexford   **19F2**

Morriscastle Strand Caravan Park
Kilmuckridge
📞 **01-453 5355 Fax 01-454 5916**
Open 4 May-29 September 🛆 ⛟ 🚐

This site nestles at the end of a country road overlooking the longest stretch of sandy beach in Ireland. Ideal for families with small children. Village within two miles.

Size 16 acres, 100 touring pitches, 60 with electric hookup, 105 level pitches, 145 static caravans, 11 🅿, 10 WCs, 2 CWPs
£ car/tent £8-£10, car/caravan £8-£10, motorhome £7-£9, motorbike/tent £4.50
🔲 🔲 🔲 🅻 🔲 🔲 GR 🔲 Calor Gaz & 🐕
Last arrival time: 11:00
➜ From Wexford take R742 to Kilmuckridge and follow signposts. Site is at very end of public road.

KINSALE Co. Cork   **18C4**

Garrettstown House Holiday Park
Kinsale
📞 **021-778156 Fax 021-778156**
Open May-September 🛆 ⛟ 🚐
Size 20 acres, 80 touring pitches, 50 with electric hookup, 80 level pitches, 90 static caravans, 10 🅿, 16 WCs, 1 CWP
£ car/tent £7-£8, car/caravan £8-£9, motorhome £8-£9, motorbike/tent £7, children £0.50
Rental ⛟ 2 bed £130-£290, 3 bed £150-£330
CC MasterCard Visa
🔲 ✕¼ 🔲 🔲 🅻 🔲 🔲 🔲 GR 🔲 TV ⚠ 🔲 Calor Gaz & 🐕 WS
Last arrival time: 11:00
➜ From Cork take R600 through Kinsale for 6 miles. Go through Ballinspittle village, past school and football pitch on main road to beach.

LAHINCH Co. Clare   **18B1**

Lahinch Camping & Caravan Park
Lahinch
📞 **065-81424 Fax 065-81194**
Open 1 May-30 September 🛆 ⛟ 🚐

Located just south of Lahinch Village, with a sandy beach. Ideal for visits to the Cliffs of ➜

GARRETTSTOWN HOUSE

HOLIDAY PARK

Garrettstown House is a Holiday Park apart, set on the grounds of the historic 18th C. Garrettstown Estate. A beautiful and tranquil setting with numerous top class facilities for families in high season. Blue Flag beach 1km. Picturesque rural countryside. Historical Old Head of Kinsale 2.5 miles, Kinsale town 6 miles. Clonakilty 20 mins.

Convenient day trips – Blarney, Fota, Cobh, Cork City. Outdoor Activity Centre interests for teenagers nearby. Cork Airport and Ringaskiddy Ferryport within 25 miles.

AA 4 Pennants. Recommended by: ADAC, ACSI, ANWB

Telephone: 021-778156
Fax: 021-778156

← Lahinch Camping & Caravan Park

Moher, the Burren and the Aran Islands or for lovely scenic walks.

Size 7 acres, 62 touring pitches, 36 with electric hookup, 62 level pitches, 30 static caravans, 11 ℞, 24 WCs, 2 CWPs
£ car/tent £8-£9, car/caravan £9-£10, motorhome £8-£9, motorbike/tent £6, children £1
🛒¼ ✗¼ 🍴¼ ▤ 📞 ⊟ GR 🔍 TV ⚠ 🎣 Calor 🐕 WS
Last arrival time: 12:00
➜ 200 yards S of village coast road.

Creveen Lodge
Healy Pass, Lauragh Village
📞 **064-83131**
Open Easter-31October ⛺ 🚐 🚍

This small family run park, set in the heart of the beautiful scenery of south Kerry, provides a high standard of personal supervision, and is fully serviced with excellent amenities.

Size 4 acres, 20 touring pitches, 7 with electric hookup, 15 level pitches, 2 ℞, 5 WCs, 1 CWP
£ car/tent £7, car/caravan £7, motorhome £7, motorbike/tent £7, children £0.50
Rental Chalet.
✗ ▤ 📞 ⊟ TV ⚠ 🎣 Gaz 🐕 WS
Last arrival time: 12:00
➜ From Kenmare turn right at sound bridge onto R571. Follow signs at Lauragh for site. Site is on Healy Pass road (R574).

Chawke Caravans
Dublin Road, Castletroy, Limerick
📞 **061-330033/330824 Fax 061 330421**
Luxury Touring Caravans for hire at reasonable rates.
Extensive Caravan Accessory Shop with a large range of spares and accessories for all leading makes.

Burkes Caravan & Camping Park
Shanagarry, Middleton
📞 **021-646796**
Open 1 May-1 October ⛺ 🚐 🚍

Size 4 acres, 10 touring pitches, 8 with electric hookup, 8 level pitches, 39 static caravans, 2 ℞, 4 WCs,
£ car/tent £7-£8, car/caravan £7-£8, motorhome £7-£8, motorbike/tent £7
Rental 🚐 mobile homes £130-£250
🛒 ✗¼ 🍴¼ ▤ GR Calor 🐕
Last arrival time: 10:30
➜ Turn off N25 at Castlemartyr for Ladysbridge, Garryvoe. At Garryvoe hotel turn right for Shanagarry/Ballycotton, 1 mile from Garryvoe.

Lough Ennel Caravan & Camping
Tudenham, Mullingar
📞 **044-48101 Fax 044-48101**
Open 1 April-end September ⛺ 🚐 🚍

On the shore of Lough Ennel. Children's play area. Windsurfing equipment and tuition. Some gas available. Caravans for hire.

Size 50 touring pitches, 50 with electric hookup, 50 static caravans, 8 ↑↑, 20 WCs, 1 CWP
£ car/tent £8, car/caravan £8, motorhome £8, motorbike/tent £8
⬛ ✗ 🍵 ⬛ 🔋 TV ⛰ 🔲 Calor 🐕 WS
Last arrival time: 11:00
➡ N52 from Mullingar to Kilbeggan for 5 miles, right at Lough Ennel-Tudenham to site.

O'BRIENS BRIDGE Co. Clare   18C2

Shannon Cottage Caravan Park
O'Briens Bridge
📞 061-377118 **Fax** 061 377966
Open all year ⬛ ⬛
Size 2 acres, 21 touring pitches, 21 with electric hookup, 21 level pitches, 4 ↑↑, 5 WCs, 1 CWP
CC MasterCard Visa
⬛ ⬛¼ ✗ 🍵 🔋 □ 🔲 GR 🔲 ⛰ 🔲
Last arrival time: 10:00
➡ From N7 Bird Hill take R466 to O'Brien's Bridge. Turn right after crossing bridge to site 50 meters along cul-de-sac. N7 Daly's Cross, signposted to O'Brien's Bridge.

OMEATH Co. Louth   17E3

Tain Holiday Village
Ballyvoonan, Omeath
📞 042-75385 **Fax** 042-75417
Open 14 March-1 November ⚊ ⬛ ⬛

Size 10 acres, 90 touring pitches, 87 with electric hookup, 90 level pitches, 9 static caravans, 16 ↑↑, 16 WCs,
£ car/tent £14.50-£16.50, car/caravan £16.50-£18.50, motorhome £16.50-£18.50, motorbike/tent £14.50, children £3-£3.50
Rental ⬛
CC MasterCard
⬛ ✗ 🍵 ⬛ 🔋 🔲 🔲 🔲 🔲 GR 🔲 TV ⛰ 🔲 Calor 🔲 🐕
Last arrival time: 9:30
➡ 10km from Newry, just off main Belfast to Dublin road, on coastal road from Newry to Dundalk. Go through Omeath village 1 mile. Camp site is on left as you drive towards Carlingford village.

RATHANGAN Co. Kildare   19E1

Carasli Holiday Centre
Rathangan
📞 045-524331
Open Easter-31 October ⚊ ⬛ ⬛
Size 2 acres, 15 touring pitches, 15 with electric hookup, 15 level pitches, 3 static caravans, 2 ↑↑, 4 WCs, 1 CWP   ➡

← **Carasli Holiday Centre**

£ car/tent £7, car/caravan £7, motorhome £7, motorbike/tent £6, children £0.50
🛁 🛁¼ ✕ ✕¼ 🚰 🚰¼ 🔌 🗑 🔋 Calor Gaz 🐕
Last arrival time: 10:00
➡ Dublin motorway N7 to Kildare Town, Rathangan 6 miles from Kildare Town. Follow signs.

REDCROSS Co. Wicklow   19F2

Johnson's Caravan & Camping Park
Ballintin, Redcross
📞 0404-48133
Open 14 March-28 September 🏕 🚐 🚙
Size 8 acres, 18 touring pitches, 18 with electric hookup, 18 level pitches, 43 static caravans, 6 🚿, 11 WCs, 1 CWP
£ car/tent £7-£8, car/caravan £7-£8, motorhome £7-£8, motorbike/tent £5, children £1
Rental 🚐 £140-£245
🛁 🚰 🔌 🗑 🔋 🔲 📶 TV 🚼 🔋 Calor Gaz WS
Last arrival time: 8:30
➡ From Dublin follow N11 and travel S via Ashford, turn right in Rathnew and then left onto Wexford/Wicklow road (under railway bridge). Drive for 11 km and turn right at Lil Doyles pub. Park is 1 mile on right.

ROSBEG Co. Donegal   16C2

Tramore Beach Caravan Park
Rosbeg
📞 075-51491 Fax 075-51492
Open Easter-September
Size 20 touring pitches
➡ From Donegal take N56, then R261.

ROSCREA Co. Tipperary   19D

Streamstown Caravan & Camping Park
Roscrea
📞 0505-21519 Fax 0505-21519
Open 9 May-30 September 🏕 🚐 🚙
Size 3 acres, 30 touring pitches, 10 with electric hookup, 2 static caravans, 1 🚿, 5 WCs, 1 CWP

£ car/caravan £8-£9
Rental 🚐 £20-£25
🛁¼ 🚰 🔌 🗑 GR 🔲 TV 🚼 🚼
➡ 1½ miles W of Roscrea on L34 (R491), near St Joseph's Abbey.

ROSSES POINT Co. Sligo   16C3

Greenlands Caravan & Camping Park
Rosses Point
📞 087-414009
Open May-September 🏕 🚐 🚙
Size 4 acres, 78 touring pitches, 78 with electric hookup, 78 level pitches, 12 static caravans, 8 🚿, 15 WCs, 1 CWP
£ car/tent £7.50-£8.50, car/caravan £7.50-£8.50, motorhome £7.50-£8.50, motorbike/tent £7.50
Rental 🚐 £100-£280
🛁¼ ✕¼ 🚰¼ 🚰 🔌 🗑 P GR TV Calor Gaz ♿ 🐕
Last arrival time: 10:00
➡ From Sligo city, 8 km W to Rosses Point. Site is beside golf club.

ROSSLARE Co. Wexford   19F3

Burrow Caravan & Camping Park
Rosslare
📞 053-32190
Open 15 March-10 November 🏕 🚐 🚙
Size 14 acres, 100 touring pitches, 100 with electric hookup, 100 level pitches, 150 static caravans, 6 🚿, 10 WCs, 1 CWP
CC MasterCard Visa
🛁 ✕¼ 🚰 🔌 🗑 🔲 🚼 GR 🔲 TV 🚼 🚼 Calor Gaz ♿
Last arrival time: 10:00
➡ N25 W from Rosslare Harbour to Kilrane, then turn N onto R736. Site ¾ mile N of Rosslare village.

Rosslare Holiday Park
Rosslare
📞 053-32427 Fax 053-32427
Open 1 May-1 October 🏕 🚐 🚙

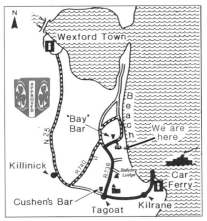

Site conveniently positioned close to Rosslare Ferry Terminal. A children's play area and tennis court are on site. Close to the beach and restaurant.

Size 6½ acres, 50 touring pitches, 50 with electric hookup, 6 🚿, 7 WCs, 1 CWP
£ car/tent £7-£8, car/caravan £7-£8, motorhome £7-£8, motorbike/tent £6.50, children £0.50
🔒 🔒¼ ✗¼ 🔲 🔲 🔲 🔲 🔲 🔲 Gaz ♿ 🐕
Last arrival time: 11:00
➡ From N25 turn onto R376 at Tagoat (Cushen's Bar). Take third junction right. After 3 km site entrance is opposite Bay Bar.

ROUNDWOOD Co. Wicklow 19F1

Roundwood Camping & Caravanning Park
Roundwood
📞 **01-281 8163**
Open April-September 🛖 🚐 🚙
Size 7 acres, 30 touring pitches, 30 with electric hookup, 55 level pitches, 6 🚿, 10 WCs, 1 CWP
£ car/tent £9-£10, car/caravan £9-£10, motorhome £9-£10, motorbike/tent £8, children £1
🔒 ✗¼ 🔲¼ 🔲 🔲 🔲 🔲 🔲 🔲 Calor Gaz 🐕 WS
Last arrival time: 11:00
➡ From Dublin & Dun Laothaire take N11. Turn right at Kilmacanogue, follow signs for Glendalough. From Rosslare take N11, turn left at Ashford village.

SHANKILL Co. Dublin 19F1

Shankill Caravan & Camping Park
Sherrington Park., Shankill
📞 **01-280011**
Open all year 🛖 🚐 🚙

Caravan park and camp site with lovely view of the Dublin mountains. Nearest caravan park to Stenaline and HSS fast ferry. 8 km from Dun Laoghaire car ferry terminal. 16 km south of Dublin city centre. 3 km from Bray and the sea.

Size 7 acres, 70 with electric hookup, 50 level pitches, 15 🚿, 20 WCs, 2 CWPs
£ car/tent £7-£8, car/caravan £7-£8, motorhome £7-£8, motorbike/tent £7, children £0.50
Rental 🚐 Mobile homes £180 high season pw
🔒 ✗¼ 🔲¼ 🔲 🔲 🔲 Gaz ♿ 🐕
➡ East of N11 Dublin/Wicklow road. Direct bus from Dublin city centre and Dun Laoghaire car ferry terminal. Fast electric train service (DART) from Shankill station serving Dublin, Dun Laoghaire and Bray.

STRANDHILL Co. Sligo 16C3

Strandhill Caravan & Camping
Strandhill
📞 **087-414009**
Open mid May-mid September 🛖 🚐 🚙
Size 15 acres, 48 touring pitches, 32 with electric hookup, 48 level pitches, 15 static caravans, 8 🚿, 12 WCs, 1 CWP
£ car/tent £7.50-£9, car/caravan £7.50-£9, motorhome £7.50-£9, motorbike/tent £7.50
🔒¼ ✗¼ 🔲¼ 🔲 🔲 🔲 🔲 🔲 🐕
Last arrival time: 10:00

← Strandhill Caravan & Camping

➜ From village of Strandhill, just off airport road. Right opposite surf club.

TRAMORE Co. Waterford   19E3

Fitzmaurice's Caravan Park
Riverstown, Tremore
📞 051-81968
Open 1 April-30 September ▲ 🚐 🚏
Size 5½ acres, 4 🚿, 23 WCs, 1 CWP
£ car/tent £9, car/caravan £9, motorhome £9, motorbike/tent £9
Rental 🚐
🐕 🖃 📞 🎱 🛒 🖥 🚾 ⚓
➜ 7 miles from Waterford city on the main Waterford to Tramore road. Site situated in Tramore 500 yards from beach.

WATERVILLE Co. Kerry   18A3

Waterville Caravan & Camping Park
Waterville
📞 066-74191 **Fax** 066-74538
Open 17 April-21 September ▲ 🚐 🚏
Size 5 acres, 58 touring pitches, 58 with electric hookup, 58 level pitches, 23 static caravans, 12 🚿, 15 WCs, 2 CWPs
£ car/tent £8.50-£9, car/caravan £9-£9.50, motorhome £9-£9.50, motorbike/tent £7.50, children £0.50
Rental 🚐 £137-£352
CC MasterCard Visa
🐕 ✕¼ 🛒 🖃 📞 🖥 🚾 🎱 🛒 📺 ⛰ 🎯 Gaz ♿ ⚓
Last arrival time: 10:00
➜ ½ N of Waterville, just off N70 'Ring of Kerry' road.

WEXFORD Co. Wexford   19F3

Carne Beach Caravan & Camping Park
Wexford
📞 053-31131
Open May-September ▲ 🚐 🚏

Beach site with swimming, angling and riding available. Close to Rosslare ferry.

Size 30 acres, 50 touring pitches, 50 with electric hookup, 50 level pitches, 300 static caravans, 16 🚿, 30 WCs, 2 CWPs
🐕 ✕ 🛒 📞 🖥 🚾 🎱 🛒 🛒 📺 ⛰ 🎯 🔌 Calor Gaz WS
Last arrival time: 11:00
➜ From Rosslare Harbour take N25 W to Kilrane, then due S to coast.

THE COUNTRY CODE

❧ Enjoy the countryside and respect its life and work

❧ Guard against all risk of fire

❧ Keep your dogs under close control

❧ Keep to the public paths across farmland

❧ Use gates and stiles to cross fences, hedges and walls

❧ Leave livestock, crops and machinery alone

❧ Take your litter home

❧ Help to keep all water clean

❧ Protect wildlife, plants and trees

❧ Take special care on country roads

❧ Make no unnecessary noise

Grandstand Campsite, Douglas

Glen Dhoo Camping Site

Hillberry, Onchan, Douglas IM4 5BJ
☏ 01624-621254 Fax 01624-621254
Open April-October ⚑ 🚐 🚲
Size 9 acres, 50 touring pitches, 8 with
electric hookup, 12 level pitches, 11 🚿, 12
WCs, 1 CWP
£ car/tent £8, motorhome £8, motorbike/tent
£7.80, children £1.70
Rental Chalet.
🔌 🚽 ☏ 🚻 Calor Gaz 🐕
 Last arrival time: 11:00
➡ 100 yds before Hillberry Corner on A18
and TT course. Entrance on left travelling
from Douglas. 2½ miles from car ferry.

Grandstand Campsite

Nobles Park, Douglas IM2 1JJ
☏ 01624-621132 Fax 01624-662792
Open mid June-mid August ⚑ 🚐 🚲

*Situated next to Nobles Park, an ideal base
for touring the island, or enjoying the park
amenities and visiting Douglas.*

Size 2 acres, 30 touring pitches, 20 with
electric hookup, 8 🚿, 16 WCs, 1 CWP
£ car/tent £5, car/caravan £5, motorhome
£5, motorbike/tent £5
🔌¼ ✕¼ 🚽 ☏ ▶🛒 ⚠ 🎣 & 🐕
➡ From ferry terminal travel along
promenade to first set of traffic lights, turn
left, then right at next traffic lights. The
campsite is behind the TT Grandstand, a
further 500 yards on right.

Peel Camping Park

Derby Road, Peel
☏ 01624-842341 Fax 01624-844010
Open mid May-late September ⚑ 🚐 🚲

*Situated on the edge of the town in a rural
setting, just three miles from the TT course. A
level site with facilities for the disabled.*

Size 4 acres, 100 touring pitches, 12 with
electric hookup, 100 level pitches, 8 🚿, 10
WCs, 1 CWP
£ car/tent £7, motorhome £9, motorbike/tent
£7, children £1.75
🔌¼ ✕¼ ▶¼ 🚽 ☏ 📺 &
➡ A1 from Douglas and turn right at first
crossroads entering Peel. Follow signs to
site on A20 on edge of town, adjacent to
primary school.

GUERNSEY 2A2

Fauxquets Valley Farm
Castel, St Peter Port
☎ 01481-55460 Fax 01481-51797
Open Easter-14 September ▲ 🚐
Size 3½ acres, 90 touring pitches, 80 with electric hookup, 90 level pitches, 14 ⋔, 17 WCs, 1 CWP
£ car/tent £8-£9.40, motorhome £8-£9.40, motorbike/tent £8
Rental ▲ £196 for up to 6 people.
℃ MasterCard Visa
🛢 ✗ 🗪 🖻 🔧 🗄 🔲 🆖 🔍 📺 🏧 ✖   Calor Gaz
🐕
➡ Turn right off main St Andrews road at sign for German underground hospital. Take fourth lane on left.

La Bailloterie Camping
Vale GY3 5HA
☎ 01481-43636 Fax 01481-43225
Open 15 May-15 September ▲
Size 8 acres, 120 touring pitches, 4 with electric hookup, 120 level pitches, 12 ⋔, 12 WCs, 1 CWP
£ car/tent £6-£7.50, motorbike/tent £6, children £1.50-£1.95
Rental ▲ £50-£195
🛢 🛢¼ ✗¼ 🗪 🗪¼ 🖻 🔧 🗄 🆖 📺 🏧 ✖
Calor Gaz 🐕

➡ Leave St Peter Port to the N. Bear left at Half Way Plantation following signs for Pembroke and L'Ancrosse. At the second set of traffic lights turn right, then take first left. Follow signpost.

Le Vaugrat Campsite
Route de Vaugrat, St Sampsons GY2 4TA
☎ 01481-57468 Fax 01481-51841
Open 1 May-16 September
Size 5 acres, 150 touring pitches, 120 level pitches, 8 ⋔, 12 WCs, 1 CWP
🛢 ✗ 🗪 Calor Gaz

JERSEY 2A2

Beuvelande Camp Site
Beuvelande, St Martins JE3 6EZ
☎ 01534-853575 Fax 01534-857788
Open May-mid September ▲ 🚐
Size 6 acres, 60 touring pitches, 20 with electric hookup, 60 level pitches, 30 ⋔, 20 WCs, 1 CWP
£ car/tent £8-£10, motorbike/tent £8, children £3
Rental ▲
℃ Visa
🛢 🛢¼ ✗ ✗¼ 🖻 🔧 🗄 🆖 🔍 📺 🏧 ✖
Calor Gaz ♿ 🐕
➡ A6 from St Helier to St Martin's church, then follow signs.

The Caravan Towing Code

Reproduced by kind permission of the National Caravan Council.

SCOPE OF THE CODE

The Code applies to all trailer caravans of maximum laden weight not exceeding 2,030kg (4,475 lbs), overall width not exceeding 2.3m (approx 7'6") and overall length not exceeding 7m (approx 23'), excluding the drawbar and coupling. This is legally the maximum size of trailer that can be towed by a motor car.

Objectives

✔ To provide simple, easily understood advice on the safe matching of towing vehicles to caravans;

✔ To make recommendations on the selection of the ratio of caravan weight to towing vehicle weight so that safe towing may be achieved under the varying conditions which may be met on the road;

✔ To give advice on the engine size and power required for satisfactory towing both for the ability to restart on a gradient and to maintain a reasonable speed relative to the traffic flow on various types of road;

✔ To set out the factors the caravan user needs to take into account before towing a caravan.

DEFINITIONS OF TERMS USED

The caravan
EX WORKS WEIGHT
The maximum weight of the caravan as stated by the caravan manufacturer, as new with standard fixtures and fittings. (Note: because of the differences in the weight of materials supplied for the construction of caravans, variations of + or -5% of the manufacturer's stated ex works weight can be expected.)

ACTUAL LADEN WEIGHT
The total weight of the caravan and its contents when being towed.

MAXIMUM LADEN WEIGHT
The maximum weight for which the caravan is designed for normal use when being towed on a road, laden.

NOSEWEIGHT
That part of the weight of the caravan supported by the rear of the towing vehicle.

The towing vehicle
KERB WEIGHT
The weight of the towing vehicle as defined by the vehicle manufacturer.
This is normally:

✔ with a full tank of fuel;

✔ with an adequate supply of other liquids incidental to the vehicle's propulsion;

✔ without driver or passengers;

✔ without any load except loose tools and equipment with which the vehicle is normally provided;

✔ without any towing bracket.

The Caravan/Towing Vehicle Combination
Caravan/Towing vehicle weight ratio
The actual laden weight of the caravan expressed as a percentage of the kerb weight of the towing vehicle, ie:

$$\frac{\text{actual laden weight of caravan}}{\text{kerb weight of towing vehicle}} \times 100 = \_\_\%$$

How to estimate the actual laden weight:
The basic items required for two people to go caravanning will weigh a minimum of 100kg in total. These will include food, crockery, cutlery, cooking utensils, clothing, bedding, gas bottles and water carrier. The weight of any additional items required (eg battery, awning, portable toilet, spare wheel, TV, etc) must be added to the basic total.

A further 25kg for each additional person should be allowed for basic items.

Having established the total weight of items to be carried by the caravan this must be added to the ex works weight to obtain the estimated actual laden weight.

If in doubt this can be done on a public weighbridge.

The address of the nearest public weigh bridge in a locality may be obtained from the area Trading Standards Department (Weights and Measures).

The Department's telephone number will be found under: County Council; Metropolitan Council, London Borough Council or Regional Council (for Scotland).

Note: Weighbridges have varying weight tolerance levels.

FACTORS WHICH MUST BE CONSIDERED FOR SAFE TOWING

Driver's towing experience

Experience of towing is not essential for taking up caravanning but drivers without experience should take greater care when manoeuvring. Speed should be built up gradually in order to get used to the handling and braking characteristics.

For those who would like training, there are courses available and details may be obtained from the specialist clubs. Further experience should be gained before tackling the more difficult elements of towing (higher weight ratios, mountain passes, difficult terrain, etc).

Caravan/towing vehicle weight ratio

This ratio has a major influence on stability. It is recommended that:

a) the actual laden weight of the caravan should always be kept as low as possible. The lower it is when the caravan is being towed on a road, the safer the caravan/towing vehicle combination will be.

b) as a general rule, the actual laden weight of a caravan should not exceed the kerb weight of the towing vehicle, particularly if the latter is a conventional car (saloon, coupé, hatchback, estate, convertible, etc).

c) the greater the actual laden weight of the caravan is in relation to the kerb weight of the towing vehicle, the more careful and experienced the driver needs to be.

d) care must always be taken not to exceed the towing vehicle's loading and towing limits.

The law requires that caravans and their towing vehicle and the loads that they carry must all be in such a condition that no danger or nuisance of any kind is caused.

Power to weight ratio of towing vehicle to caravan

The performace of the towing vehicle has an important bearing on its suitability for towing and, therefore, on the selection of the caravan to match the towing vehicle.

There are many factors involved, which are often contradictory, such as brake horsepower, gearing, torque characteristics, turbo-charging and fuel injection.

No hard and fast rules can be stated but, as a general guide, conventional petrol engines with a capacity up to approximately 1500cc should be adequate for towing a caravan weighing around 85% of the kerb weight of the towing vehicle. Above 1500cc such engines should manage a caravan weighing up to 100% of the kerb weight of the towing vehicle and still give adequate performace but it should be noted that the towing vehicle manfacturer's limit is, in some cases, less than the kerb weight.

While the towing vehicle may manage 100%, attention is again drawn to the recommendation under the previous heading. 'Caravan/towing vehicle weight ratio', that weight ratio of 85% is an ideal starting point.

Diesel engines of whatever size have a lower performance for a given cubic capacity compared to petrol engines.

When climbing, a 10% loss of power with a petrol engine and slightly less with a diesel engine should be expected for every 1,000 metres gain in height. A good reserve of power is, therefore, very necessary for towing up gradients at altitude. Vehicles with automatic transmission may need additional cooling for the gearbox when towing. The advice of the manufacturer should be sought.

WHEELS

Caravan wheelnuts should be tightened to the setting stated by the caravan manufacturer (user instructions) and should be checked with the use of a torque wrench regularly. If a spare wheel and tyre is carried it must be suitable for use on that caravan.

Types of tyre fitted

The tyres specified by the caravan manufacturer should be satisfactory for towing in the United Kingdom of speeds up to 62mph (100kph) at the maximum laden weight of the caravan. In certain countries overseas, it is legal to tow at higher speeds. If it is intended to visit such countries and tow up to the higher speed limits then it is important that the suitability of the tyres is first checked with a caravan dealer.

Tyre pressures

Caravan and towing vehicle tyres must be at the pressures recommended for towing or heavy loading. Towing stability may otherwise be affected. The pressures should be given in the towing vehicle and caravan handbooks.

DISTRIBUTION OF WEIGHT IN THE CARAVAN AND CAR

Equipment and effects should be loaded in the caravan so that any heavy items are low down near the floor and mainly over or in from the axle(s). The remainder should be distributed to give a suitable noseweight at the towing coupling.

Incorrect caravan loading will result in poor towing stability. Overloading of the ,towing vehicle's rear suspension will also result in poor towing stability.

The weight should be distributed so that each caravan wheel carries approximately the same load.

Noseweight

It is recommended that the noseweight should be varied to find the optimum for towing, dependent upon the actual laden weight of the caravan. Experience has shown that the noseweight should be approximately 7% of the actual laden weight (i.e. between 50 and 90kg).

Measurement of Noseweight

The noseweight may be measured using a proprietary brand of noseweight indicator. Such equipment is obtainable from caravan dealers.

Another simple method is to use bathroom scales under the coupling head with a piece of wood fitted between the coupling head and the scales, of such length that the caravan floor is horizontal with the jockey wheel raised.

STABILISERS

A stabiliser should never be used to try to improve a caravan/towing vehicle combination which has poor stability, because instability will reappear at a higher speed. However, a good stabiliser can make an acceptable caravan/towing vehicle combination more stable and safer to handle.

TOWING VEHICLE'S REAR SUSPENSION

It is important that the towing vehicle's rear suspension is not deflected excessively by the noseweight on the tow ball. If it is, the steering and stability will be affected. The greater the towing vehicle's rail overhang (the distance between rear axle and towing ball) the greater the effect the noseweight will have on the towing vehicle's suspension.

After trying out the caravan it may be found that stiffening of the rear suspension is necessary, but note that this may give the towing vehicle a firmer ride when not towing. There are a number of suspension aids available and advice should be sought on which to use and how to fit them. It is important to ensure that the caravan is towed either level or slightly nose down.

Servicing

A caravan is a road vehicle and, therefore, requires regular servicing, with particular attention to the braking system, wheels and tyres, and road lighting. These items are fully covered in the standard servicing schedule of the Caravan Service Centre Scheme run by the NCC. There are over 150 RAC inspected workshops in the Scheme, which is operated in conjunction with both RAC and the Caravan Club.

MIRRORS

The driver of the towing vehicle must have an adequate view to the rear. If there is no rear view through the caravan windows it is essential that additional exterior towing mirrors are fitted to provide a view along both sides of the caravan.

Any rear view mirror must not project more than 200mm beyond:
a) the width of the caravan when being towed.
b) the width of the towing vehicle when driven solo.
Note: Any rear view mirror fitted shall be 'e' marked and cover the field of view as stipulated by type approval requirements.

ROADLIGHTING

Make sure:
a) All cable connections are of correct length to avoid disconnection or trailing of the cable on the ground.
b) All road lights and indicators are working correctly before setting off.

Conventional connection of 12N and 12S seven pin sockets

Power for the caravan's roadlights and electrical equipment is transferred from the towcar by means of a pair of seven pin plugs (on the caravan) and sockets (on the car). Though these look similar at first glance they are not interchangeable because they have different arrangements of pins and contact tubes.

The roadlight plug/socket is known as type 12N (normal) and is usually coloured black. The second plug/socket is known as 12S (supplementary) and is conventionally coloured grey.

An arrangement whereby the car's rear foglights are extinguished when the caravan roadlights are connected (to prevent glare from light reflected off the caravan's front wall) is permissable. All other lights on the rear of the car must work when the caravan is being towed

Connections for the caravan battery charging and refrigerator circuits should be controlled by relays. These ensure that the caravan battery is never recharged at the expense of the car battery; and that power is transmitted to the fridge only when the car engine is running to avoid the risk of flattening the car battery.

BRAKES

For caravans exceeding a maximum weight of 1500kg the braking device must be such that the caravan is stopped automatically if the coupling breaks.

For caravans below 1500kg a breakaway cable is required. If there is not an automatic stopping device always ensure that the breakaway cable, when fitted, is secured to the towing vehicle.

VEHICLE CARAVAN CONNECTION

Always ensure that the towing hitch is correctly locked to the ball prior to setting off.

SPEED LIMITS AND MOTORWAY DRIVING
Reduce speed
a) In high or cross winds
b) Downhill
c) In poor visibility

HIGH SIDED VEHICLES
Extra care should be taken when passing or being passed by high sided vehicles. As much space as possible should be given between vehicles to avoid air buffeting.

Remember, courtesy and safety.

General Advice

ROADSIDE CAMPING

Camping or siting a caravan on verges or lay-bys is not allowed. However, permission to camp on land near by can often be obtained from the farmer or landowner.
If an outbreak of foot and mouth or swine vesicular disease occurs, campers must be very careful to follow all necessary precautions.

LONDON

If you are visiting London with a caravan on tow, try to avoid travelling across the centre of London, particularly during the rush hours Monday to Friday 0800-1000 and 1600-1800 hours, and if you are unfamiliar with the route.
Parking of car/caravan outfits at meter bays is not permitted. It is best to leave a caravan at the site and visit central London solo, or by public transport. If it is essential to park an outfit in London, find a suitable car park. Underground and multi-storey carparks often have a height limit which will not permit access for caravans or motor caravans.
As well as the sites listed under London,

the following sites are within reasonable distance; Brands Hatch – Thriftwood Camping Site, Hoddesdon – Dobb's Weir Caravan Park, Windsor – The Willows Riverside Park.

MOTORWAY SERVICE AREAS

Caravans are permitted to park at motorway service areas for the purpose of utilizing the facilities. Parking for the purpose of cooking meals etc., is not usually permitted, and at some service areas it is forbidden to lower the corner legs of a caravan for any reason. Charges for overnight stops are available on application to the individual service areas.

TRAVEL INFORMATION

For information on current UK traffic conditions and roadworks call the RAC 'Motorist's hot line' on 0891- 500 242. Calls are charged at 49p per minute 8am-6pm Monday to Friday, and 39p per minute at all other times.
To contact the RAC Camping and Caravanning Guide, please telephone 0181-686 0088, or write to: RAC Motoring Services, PO Box 100, Bartlett Street, South Croydon, CR2 6XW.

Useful Addresses

British Holiday & Home Parks Association
Chichester House, 6 Pullman Court, Great Western Road, Gloucester GL1 3ND
Tel: 01452-526911/411574

The Camping and Caravanning Club
Greenfields House, Westwood Way, Coventry, West Midlands CV4 8JH
Tel: 01203-694995

The Caravan Club
East Grinstead House, East Grinstead, West Sussex RH19 1UA
Tel: 01342-326944

The Motor Caravanners' Club
22 Evelyn Close, Twickenham, Middlesex TW2 7BN   Tel: 0181-893 3883

National Caravan Council Limited
Catherine House, Victoria Road, Aldershot, Hampshire GU11 1SS   Tel: 01252-318251
(comprehensive list of members includes manufacturers, dealers, parks and traders)

Society of Motor Manufacturers & Traders Ltd,
Motor Caravan Section
Forbes House, Balkin Street, London SW1X 7DS
Tel: 0171-235 7000
(listing of members available)

BRITISH TOURIST AUTHORITY

Tourist Information Centres are located in cities and towns throughout Great Britain with information on places of interest for tourists. These Information Centres are indicated by distinctive 'i' signs placed in their vicinity. The addresses of the National and Regional Tourist Boards are as follows.

English Tourist Board
Head Office: Thames Tower, Black's Road, Hammersmith, London W6 9EL
(written enquiries only)

Scottish Tourist Board
Head Office: 23 Ravelston Terrace, Edinburgh
EH4 3EU
Tel: 0131-332 2433
(written and telephone enquiries only)

Wales Tourist Board
Head Office: Brunel House, 2 Fitzalan Road,
Cardiff CF2 1UY
Tel: 01222-499909

Northern Ireland Tourist Board
Head Office: St Anne's Court, North Street,
Belfast BT1 1ND
Tel: 01232-231221

LONDON OFFICE: 11 Berkeley Street, London
W1X 5AD
Tel: 0171-493 0601

Irish Tourist Board (Bord Failte)
Head Office: Baggot St. Bridge, Dublin 2
Tel (00 3531) 2844768

LONDON OFFICE: 150 New Bond Street, London
W1Y 0AQ
Tel: 0171-493 3201

Channel Islands
STATES OF GUERNSEY TOURIST COMMITTEE
PO Box 23, White Rock, St Peter Port,
Guernsey
Tel: 01481-723552

STATES OF JERSEY TOURISM COMMITTEE
Liberation Square, St Helier, Jersey
Tel: 01534-78000

NATIONAL PARKS

The most beautiful, spectacular and dramatic
expanses of country in England and Wales
have been given the status of National Parks
under the National Parks and Access to the
Countryside Act, 1949, in recognition of their
national importance. Ten National Parks were
established during the 1950s: Brecon Beacons,
Exmoor, Dartmoor, Lake District,
Northumberland, North York Moors, Peak
District, Pembrokeshire Coast, Snowdonia and
the Yorkshire Dales. In addition, the Norfolk
and Suffolk Broads (The Broads), were
established in 1989. Although not a National
Park by name, it has equal status to the Parks.
The New Forest is also considered by many to
be of comparable quality to a National Park
and legislation that will provide it with similar
protection is currently being drafted.

The essence of each of these areas is in
the striking quality and remoteness of much of
their scenery, the harmony between activity
and nature that they display and the
opportunities they offer for suitable forms of
recreation. National Parks are 'national' in the
vital sense that they are of special value to the
whole nation. But designation of an area as a
National Park does not affect the ownership of
the land. It does not remove from local
communities the right to live their own lives,
nor does it give the public any right of access.

The 1949 Act also created Areas of
Outstanding Natural Beauty. The landscape in
these areas is no less beautiful but the
opportunities for extensive outdoor recreation
are lacking. The following 39 Areas of
Outstanding Natural Beauty have been
designated:

Anglesey; Arnside and Silverdale;
Blackdown Hills; Cannock Chase; Chichester
Harbour; Chilterns; Clwydian Range; Cornwall;
Cotswolds; Cranborne Chase & West Wiltshire
Downs; Dedham Vale; Dorset; East Devon;
East Hampshire; Forest of Bowland; Gower
Peninsula; High Weald; Howardian Hills; Isles
of Scilly; Isle of Wight; Kent Downs;
Lincolnshire Wolds; Lleyn; Malvern Hills;
Mendip Hills; Norfolk Coast; North Devon;
North Pennines; Northumberland Coast; North
Wessex Downs; Quantock Hills; Shropshire
Hills; South Devon; South Hampshire Coast;
Suffolk Coast and Heaths; Surrey Hills; Sussex
Hills; Sussex Downs; Solway Coast, Wye
Valley.

Although there are no National Parks or
Areas of outstanding Natural Beauty in
Scotland, there are 40 National Scenic Areas
(NSAs), designated in 1980 under the 1972
Town and Country Planning (Scotland) Act,
which are given a measure of protection
through special development control
procedures. Protection of the NSAs is the duty
of Scottish Natural Heritage (formed from the
merger of the Countryside Commission for
Scotland and the Nature Conservancy Council
for Scotland in 1992).

Countryside Commission
John Dower House, Crescent Place,
Cheltenham, Gloucestershire GL50 3RA
Tel: 01242-521381

The Countryside Council for Wales
Plas Penrhos, Fford Penrhos, Bangor,
Gwynedd, LL57 2LQ
Tel: 01248-370444

FOREST PARKS

The Forestry Commission
231 Corstorphine Road, Edinburgh, EH12 7AT
Tel: 0131-334 3303

The Forestry Commission is one of Britain's largest providers of tourist and recreation facilities, attracting over 50 million day-visitors every year and encouraging the public to enjoy the publicly-owned forests in its care through its freedom to roam policy. It also provides for many activities including walking, picnics, mountain biking, orienteering, skiing, field sports, water sports and nature study.

THE NATIONAL TRUST

The National Trust is an independent charity responsible for the preservation of many historic houses, industrial monuments, formal and romantic gardens, nature reserves, open countryside and hundred of miles of Britain's coastline.

Details of the various National Trust activities can be obtained from:

The National Trust
36 Queen Anne's Gate, London SW1H 9AS
Tel: 0171-222 9251

The National Trust, North Wales Office
Trinity Square, Llandudno, Gwynedd LL30 2DE
Tel: 01492-860123

The National Trust, South Wales Office
The King's Head, Bridge Street, Llandeilo, Dyfed SA19 6BB
Tel: 01558-822800

The National Trust, Northern Ireland
Rowallane House, Saintfield, Ballynahinch, Co. Down BT24 7LH
Tel: 01238-510721

The National Trust for Scotland
5 Charlotte Square, Edinburgh, EH2 4DU
Tel: 0131-226 5922

ENGLISH HERITAGE

Over 350 ancient monuments, buildings and other sites are looked after by English Heritage (formerly known as the Historic Buildings and Monuments Commission). Further details can be obtained from:

English Heritage
Fortress House, 23 Savile Row, London W1X 1AB   Tel: 0171-973 3000

UK TOWING BRACKET SUPPLIERS

Towing brackets should be made to British Standard BSAU 114b or the 28th July 1993 equivalent international standard ISO 3853.

Anchor Towbars Ltd
Orchard House, Appleby Hill, Austrey, Atherstone, Warwicks CV9 3ER
Tel: 01827-830039

Bumper to Bumper Ltd
38 Melford Court, Hardwick Grange, Woolston, Warrington, Cheshire WA1 4SD
Tel: 01925-815661

B. Dixon-Bate Ltd
Unit 45, First Avenue, Deeside Industrial Park, Deeside, Clwyd CH5 2LG
Tel: 01244-288925

Exhaust Ejector Co
11 Wade House Road, Shelf, Halifax, West Yorkshire HX3 7PE
Tel: 01274-679524/5/6

PCT Leisure Ltd
Holbrook Industrial Estate, New Street, Halfway, Sheffield S19 5GH
Tel: 0114-2510210

Peter J. Lea Co Ltd
Shaw Road South, off Shaw Heath, Stockport, Cheshire SK3 8JG
Tel: 0161-480 2377

Speedograph Ltd
Rolleston Drive, Arnold, Nottingham NG5 7JR
Tel: 0115-9264235

Tanfield Ltd
Blatchford Road, Horsham, West Sussex RH13 5QR
Tel: 01403-269100

Towsure Products Ltd
151-183 Holme Lane, Sheffield S6 4JR
Tel: 0114-2340542

Watling Engineers Ltd
88 Parkstreet Village, St. Albans, Hertfordshire AL2 2LR
Tel: 01727-873661

Witter Towbars Ltd
18 Canal Side, Chester CH1 3LL
Tel: 01244-341166

KEY TO MAPS

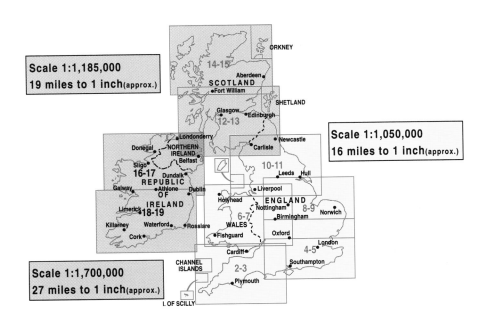

Scale 1:1,185,000
19 miles to 1 inch (approx.)

ORKNEY

14-15
Aberdeen
SCOTLAND
Fort William

SHETLAND

Glasgow
Edinburgh
12-13

Scale 1:1,050,000
16 miles to 1 inch (approx.)

Londonderry
Donegal
NORTHERN
IRELAND
Belfast

Newcastle
Carlisle

10-11

Leeds Hull

Sligo
Dundalk
16-17
REPUBLIC
Galway
Athlone Dublin
OF
IRELAND
18-19
Limerick
Killarney Waterford Rosslare
Cork

Liverpool
Holyhead
ENGLAND
Nottingham
6-7
Birmingham
WALES
Oxford
Fishguard
Cardiff
2-3

8-9
Norwich

London
4-5
Southampton

CHANNEL
ISLANDS

Plymouth

Scale 1:1,700,000
27 miles to 1 inch (approx.)

I. OF SCILLY

LEGEND

Symbol	Description	Symbol	Description
M5 / S	**Motorway** / Service Station	EXMOOR	**National Park**
2 / 5	Restricted Junction / Junction	■ PLYMOUTH	**Towns with Camping and Caravanning Location**
A381	**Primary Route Dual Carriageway**	■ SWINDON	
A385	**Primary Route**	◉ Ashford	
A697 / A38	**'A' Road (Dual Carriageway)**	• Sandown	
B3165	**'B' Road**		**Urban Area**
	Ferry Route	··············	**National Boundary**
		··············	**County Boundary**

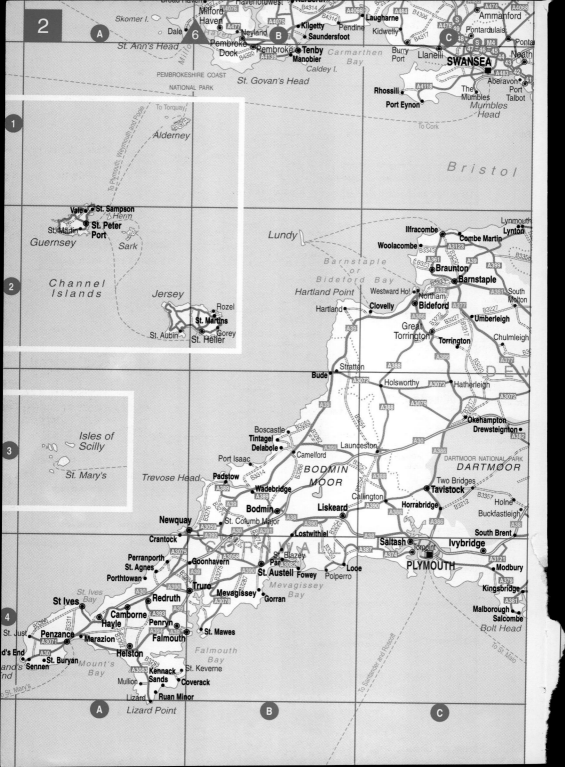

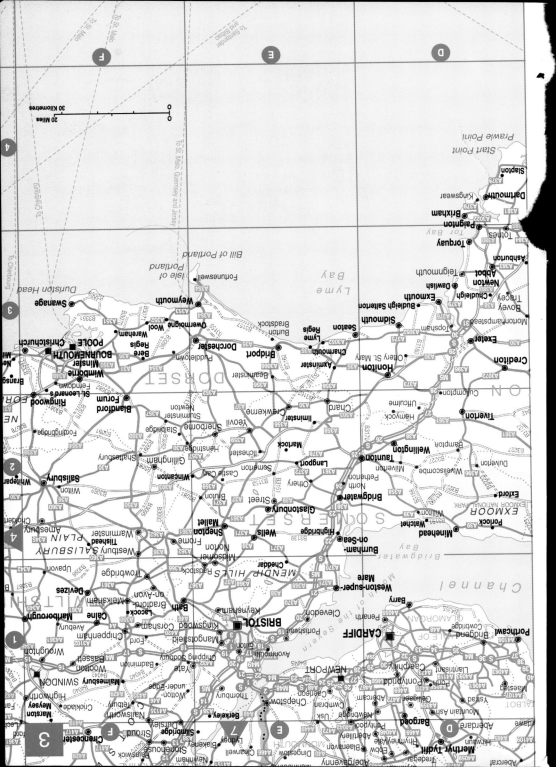

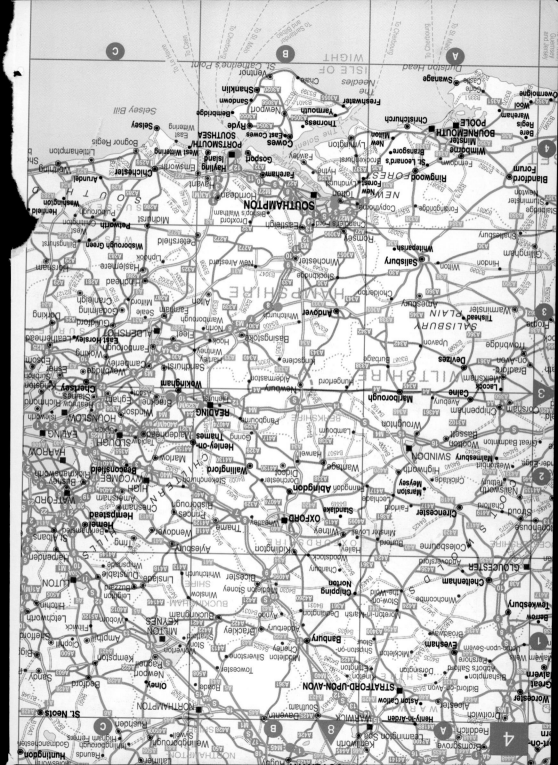

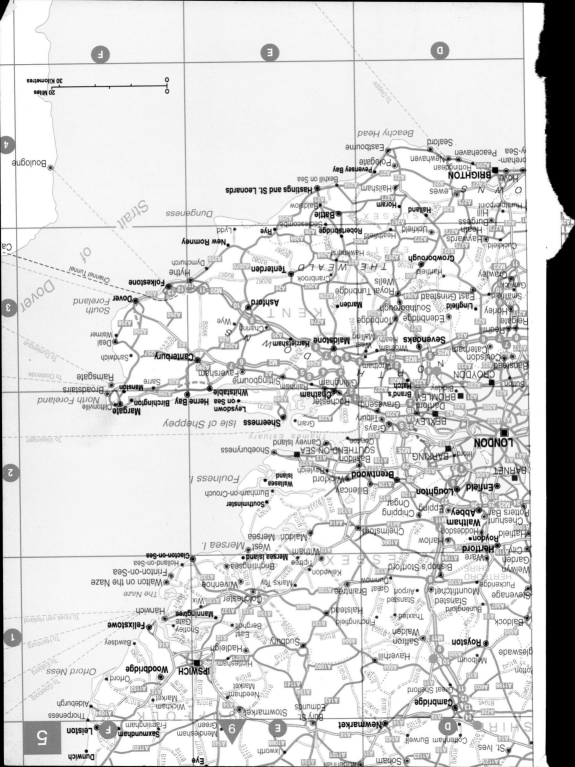

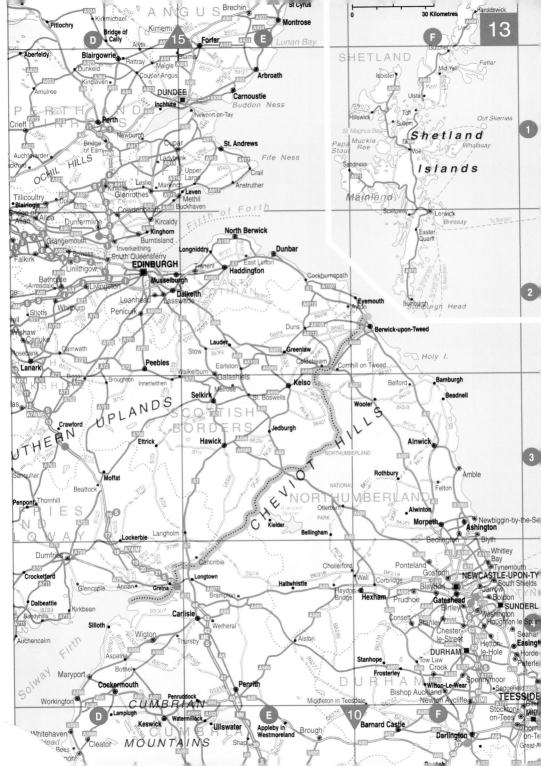

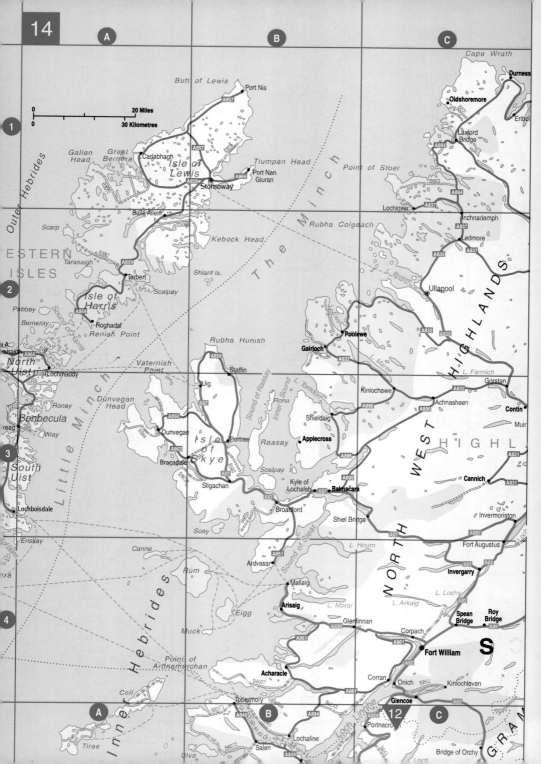